Theories of the Policy Process

Theoretical Lenses on Public Policy

Series Editor, Paul A. Sabatier

Theories of the Policy Process

edited by

Paul A. Sabatier
University of California, Davis

Westview Press
A Member of the Perseus Books Group
1999

Theoretical Lenses on Public Policy

Copyright © 1999 by Westview Press, A Member of the Perseus Books Group

Published in 1999 in the United States of America by Westview Press, 5500 Central Avenue, Boulder,
Colorado 80301-2877, and in the United Kingdom by Westview Press, 12 Hid's Copse Road, Cumnor
Hill, Oxford OX2 9JJ

Find us on the World Wide Web at www.westviewpress.com

Library of Congress Cataloging-in-Publication Data
Theories of the policy process / edited by Paul A. Sabatier.
    p.   cm. — (Theoretical lenses on public policy)
  Includes bibliographical references and index.
  ISBN 0-8133-9985-8 (hc.) — ISBN 0-8133-9986-6 (pbk.)
  1. Policy sciences.   2. Political planning.   I. Sabatier, Paul A.
II. Series.
H97.T46   1999
321'.6—dc21   99-27844
                                                                              CIP

The paper used in this publication meets the requirements of the American National Standard for
Permanence of Paper for Printed Library Materials Z39.48-1984.

10   9   8   7   6   5   4   3   2   1

Contents

Theories of the Policy Process

PART I

Introduction

The Need for Better Theories

PAUL A. SABATIER

The process of public policymaking includes the manner in which problems get conceptualized and brought to government for solution; governmental institutions formulate alternatives and select policy solutions; and those solutions get implemented, evaluated, and revised.

SIMPLIFYING A COMPLEX WORLD

For a variety of reasons, the policy process involves an extremely complex set of interacting elements over time:

1. There are normally hundreds of actors from interest groups and from governmental agencies and legislatures at different levels of government, researchers, and journalists involved in one or more aspects of the process. Each of these actors (either individual or corporate) has potentially different values/interests, perceptions of the situation, and policy preferences.
2. This process usually involves time spans of a decade or more, as that is the minimum duration of most policy cycles, from emergence of a problem through sufficient experience with implementation to render a reasonably fair evaluation of program impact (Kirst and Jung, 1982; Sabatier and Jenkins-Smith, 1993). In fact, a number of recent studies suggest that time periods of twenty to forty years may be required to obtain a reasonable understanding of the impact of a variety of socioeconomic conditions and the accumulation of scientific knowledge about a problem (Derthick and Quirk, 1985; Baumgartner and Jones, 1993; Eisner, 1993).
3. In any given policy domain, such as air pollution control or health policy, there are normally dozens of different programs involving multiple

3

levels of government that are operating, or being proposed for operation, in any given locale, such as the state of California or the city of Los
Angeles. Since these programs deal with interrelated subjects and involve many of the same actors, many scholars would argue that the appropriate unit of analysis should be the policy subsystem or domain,
rather than a specific governmental program (Hjern and Porter, 1981;
Ostrom, 1983; Sabatier, 1986; Rhodes, 1988; Jordan, 1990).

4.   Policy debates among actors in the course of legislative hearings, litiga-
     tion, and proposed administrative regulations typically involve very
     technical disputes over the severity of a problem, its causes, and the
     probable impacts of alternative policy solutions. Understanding the
     policy process requires attention to the role that such debates play in
     the overall process.

5.   A final complicating factor in the policy process is that most disputes
     involve deeply held values/interests, large amounts of money, and, at
     some point, authoritative coercion. Given these stakes, policy disputes
     seldom resemble polite academic debates. Instead, most actors face
     enormous temptations to present evidence selectively, to misrepresent
     the position of their opponents, to coerce and discredit opponents, and
     generally to distort the situation to their advantage (Riker, 1986; Moe,
     1990a,b; Schlager, 1995).

In short, understanding the policy process requires a knowledge of the goals
and perceptions of hundreds of actors throughout the country involving possibly
very technical scientific and legal issues over periods of a decade or more when
most of those actors are actively seeking to propagate their specific "spin" on
events.

Given the staggering complexity of the policy process, the analyst *must* find
some way of simplifying the situation in order to have any chance of understanding it. One simply cannot look for, and see, everything. Work in the philosophy of
science and social psychology has provided persuasive evidence that perceptions
are almost always mediated by a set of presuppositions. These perform two critical mediating functions. First, they tell the observer what to look for, that is, what
factors are likely to be critically important versus those that can be safely ignored.
Second, they define the categories in which phenomena are to be grouped (Kuhn,
1970; Lakatos, 1971; Brown, 1977; Lord, Ross, and Lepper, 1979; Hawkesworth,
1992). In understanding the policy process, for example, most institutional rational choice approaches tell the analyst (1) to focus on the leaders of a few critical
institutions with formal decisionmaking authority, (2) to assume that these actors are pursuing their material self-interest (e.g., income, power, security), and
(3) to group actors into a few institutional categories, for example, legislatures,
administrative agencies, and interest groups (Shepsle, 1989; Scharpf, 1997). In
contrast, the advocacy coalition framework tells the analyst to assume (1) that

belief systems are more important than institutional affiliation, (2) that actors may be pursuing a wide variety of objectives, which must be measured empirically, and (3) that one must add researchers and journalists to the set of potentially important policy actors (Sabatier and Jenkins-Smith, 1993). Thus analysts from these two different perspectives look at the same situation through quite different lenses and thus are likely to see quite different things—at least initially.

Given that we have little choice but to look at the world through a lens consisting of a set of simplifying presuppositions, at least two quite different strategies exist for developing such a lens. On the one hand, the analyst can approach the world in an implicit, ad hoc fashion, using whatever categories and assumptions have arisen from his or her experience. This is essentially the method of common sense. It may be reasonably accurate for situations important to the analyst's welfare in which she or he has considerable experience. In such situations, the analyst has both the incentive and the experience to eliminate clearly invalid propositions. Beyond that limited scope, the commonsense strategy is likely to be beset by internal inconsistencies, ambiguities, erroneous assumptions, and invalid propositions precisely because the strategy does not contain any explicit methods for error correction. Since its assumptions and propositions remain implicit and largely unknown, they are unlikely to be subjected to serious scrutiny. The analyst simply assumes they are, by and large, correct—insofar as he or she is even cognizant of their content.

An alternative strategy is that of science. Its fundamental ontological assumption is that a smaller set of critical relationships underlies the bewildering complexity of phenomena. For example, a century ago Darwin provided a relatively simple explanation—summarized under the processes of natural selection—for the thousands of species he encountered on his voyages. The critical characteristics of science are that (1) its methods of data acquisition and analysis should be presented in a sufficiently public manner that they can be replicated by others; (2) its concepts and propositions should be clearly defined and logically consistent and should give rise to empirically falsifiable propositions; (3) those propositions should be as general as possible and should explicitly address relevant uncertainties; and (4) both the methods and concepts should be self-consciously subjected to criticism and evaluation by experts in that field (Nagel, 1961; Lave and March, 1975; King, Keohane, and Verba, 1994). The overriding strategy can be summarized in the injunction: "Be clear enough to be proven wrong." Unlike "common sense," science is designed to be self-consciously, error seeking, and thus self-correcting.

A critical component of that strategy—derived from Principles 2–4 above—is that scientists should develop clear and logically interrelated sets of propositions, some of them empirically falsifiable, to explain fairly general sets of phenomena. Such coherent sets of propositions have traditionally been termed *theories*.

In several recent papers (including Chapter 3 of this volume and Ostrom et al., 1994), Elinor Ostrom has developed some very useful distinctions among three different sets of propositions. In her view, a *conceptual framework* identifies a set of variables and the relationships among them that presumably account for a set of phenomena. The framework can provide anything from a modest set of variables to something as extensive as a paradigm. It need not identify directions among relationships, although more developed frameworks will certainly specify some hypotheses. A *theory* provides a "denser" and more logically coherent set of relationships. It applies values to some of the variables and usually specifies how relationships may vary depending upon the values of critical variables. Numerous theories may be consistent with the same conceptual framework. A *model* is a representation of a specific situation. It is usually much narrower in scope, and more precise in its assumptions, than the underlying theory. Ideally, it is mathematical. Thus frameworks, theories, and models can be conceptualized as operating along a continuum involving increasing logical interconnectedness and specificity, but decreasing scope.

One final point: Scientists should be aware of, and capable of applying, several different theoretical perspectives—not just a single one (Stinchcomb, 1968). Knowledge of several different perspectives forces the analyst to clarify differences in assumptions across frameworks, rather than implicitly assuming a given set. Second, multiple perspectives encourage the development of competing hypotheses that should lead ideally to "strong inference" (Platt, 1964)—or at least to the accumulation of evidence in favor of one perspective more than another. Finally, knowledge and application of multiple perspectives should gradually clarify the conditions under which one perspective is more useful than another.

Consistent with this multiple-lens strategy, this volume discusses seven conceptual frameworks. A few of them—notably, institutional rational choice—have given rise to one or more theories, and virtually all have spawned a variety of models seeking to explain specific situations.

THEORETICAL FRAMEWORKS OF THE POLICY PROCESS

The Stages Heuristic

Until recently, the most influential framework for understanding the policy process—particularly among American scholars—has been the "stages heuristic," or what Nakamura (1987) termed the "textbook approach." As developed by Jones (1970), Anderson (1975), and Brewer and deLeon (1983), it divided the policy process into a series of stages—usually agenda setting, policy formulation and legitimation, implementation, and evaluation—and discussed some of the factors affecting the process within each stage. The stages heuristic served a useful purpose in the 1970s and early 1980s by dividing the very complex policy process into discrete stages and by stimulating some excellent research within specific stages—particularly agenda setting (Cobb, Ross, and Ross, 1976; Kingdon, 1984; Nelson, 1984) and policy implementation (Pressman and Wildavsky, 1973; Hjern and Hull, 1982; Mazmanian and Sabatier (1983).

In the past decade, however, the stages heuristic has been subjected to some rather devastating criticisms (Nakamura, 1987; Sabatier, 1991; Sabatier and Jenkins-Smith, 1993):

1. It is not really a causal theory since it never identifies a set of causal drivers that govern the process within and across stages. Instead, work within each stage has tended to develop on its own, almost totally without reference to research in other stages. In addition, without causal drivers there can be no coherent set of hypotheses within and across stages.

2. The proposed sequence of stages is often descriptively inaccurate. For example, evaluations of existing programs affect agenda setting, and policy formulation/legitimation occurs as bureaucrats attempt to implement vague legislation (Nakamura, 1987).

3. The stages heuristic has a very legalistic, top-down bias in which the focus is typically on the passage and implementation of a major piece of legislation. This focus neglects the interaction of the implementation and evaluation of numerous pieces of legislation—none of them preeminent—within a given policy domain (Hjern and Hull, 1982; Sabatier, 1986).

4. The assumption that there is a single policy cycle focused on a major piece of legislation oversimplifies the usual process of *multiple, interacting cycles* involving numerous policy proposals and statutes at multiple levels of government. For example, abortion activists are currently involved in litigation in the federal courts and most state courts, in new policy proposals in Washington and most states, in the implementation of other proposals at the federal and state levels, and in the evaluation of all sorts of programs and proposed programs. They're also continually trying to affect the conceptualization of the problem. In such a situation—which is common—focusing on "a policy cycle" makes very little sense.

The conclusion seems inescapable: The stages heuristic has outlived its usefulness and needs to be replaced with better theoretical frameworks.

More Promising Theoretical Frameworks

Fortunately, over the past fifteen years a number of new theoretical frameworks of the policy process have been either developed or extensively modified. This book seeks to present some of the more promising ones and to assess the strengths and limitations of each.[1]

Following are the criteria utilized in selecting the frameworks to be discussed. They strike me as relatively straightforward, although reasonable people may certainly disagree with my application of them:

1. Each framework must do a reasonably good job of meeting the criteria of a scientific theory; that is, its concepts and propositions must be relatively clear and internally consistent, it must identify clear causal drivers, it must give rise to falsifiable hypotheses, and it must be fairly broad in scope (i.e., apply to most of the policy process in a variety of political systems).
2. Each framework must be the subject of a fair amount of recent conceptual development and/or empirical testing. A number of currently active policy scholars must view it as a viable way of understanding the policy process.
3. Each framework must be a positive theory seeking to explain much of the policy process. The theoretical framework may also contain some explicitly normative elements, but these are not required.
4. Each framework must address the broad sets of factors that political scientists looking at different aspects of public policymaking have traditionally deemed important: conflicting values and interests, information flows, institutional arrangements, and variation in the socioeconomic environment.

By means of these criteria, seven frameworks have been selected for analysis. Following is a brief description and justification for each selection.

The Stages Heuristic.   Although I have doubts that the stages heuristic meets Criteria 1 and 2 above, there is certainly room for disagreement on the second. In particular, implementation studies may be undergoing a revival (Lester and Goggin, 1998). Even were that not the case, I have spent so much time criticizing the stages heuristic that simple fairness requires me to provide a forum for its defense. Peter deLeon, one of the earliest proponents of the heuristic, has volunteered to be the spokesperson.

Institutional Rational Choice.   Institutional rational choice is a family of frameworks focusing on how institutional rules alter the behavior of intendedly rational individuals motivated by material self-interest. Although much of the literature on institutional rational choice focuses on rather specific sets of institutions, such as the relationships between Congress and administrative agencies in the United States (Moe, 1984; Shepsle, 1989; Miller, 1992), the general framework is extremely broad in scope and has been applied to important policy problems in the United States and other countries (Ostrom, 1986, 1990; Ostrom et al., 1993, 1994; Scholz, Twombley, and Headrick, 1991; Schneider, Larason, and Ingram, 1995; Chubb and Moe, 1990; Dowding, 1995; Scharpf, 1997). It is clearly the most developed of all the frameworks in this volume and is arguably the most utilized in the United States and perhaps in Germany. Elinor Ostrom has agreed to write the chapter for this volume.

The Multiple-Streams Framework.   The multiple-streams framework was developed by John Kingdon (1984) based upon the "garbage can" model of organizational behavior (Cohen, March, and Olsen, 1972). It views the policy process as composed of three streams of actors and processes: a problem stream consisting of data about various problems and the proponents of various problem definitions; a policy stream involving the proponents of solutions to policy problems; and a politics stream consisting of elections and elected officials. In Kingdon's view, the streams normally operate independently of each other, except when a "window of opportunity" permits policy entrepreneurs to couple the various streams. If the entrepreneurs are successful, the result is major policy change. Although the multiple-streams framework is not always as clear and internally consistent as one might like, it appears to be applicable to a wide variety of policy arenas and is cited about eighty times annually in the Social Science Citation Index. John Kingdon is the obvious author for this chapter. He declined, however, and I then selected Nikolaos Zahariadis, who has utilized the multiple-streams framework extensively in his own research (Zahariadis, 1992, 1995).

Punctuated-Equilibrium Framework.   Originally developed by Baumgartner and Jones (1993), the punctuated-equilibrium (PE) framework argues that policymaking in the United States is characterized by long periods of incremental change punctuated by brief periods of major policy change. The latter come about when opponents manage to fashion new "policy images" and exploit the multiple policy venues characteristic of the United States. Originally developed to explain changes in legislation, this framework has recently been expanded to include some very sophisticated analyses of long-term changes in the budgets of the federal government (Jones, Baumgartner, and True, 1998). The PE framework clearly meets all four criteria, at least for systems with multiple policy venues. The chapter for this volume is coauthored by its original proponents, Frank R. Baumgartner and Bryan D. Jones, together with James L. True.

The Advocacy Coalition Framework.   Developed by Sabatier and Jenkins-Smith (1988, 1993), the advocacy coalition framework (ACF) focuses on the interaction of advocacy coalitions—each consisting of actors from a variety of institutions who share a set of policy beliefs—within a policy subsystem. Policy change is a function of both competition within the subsystem and events outside the subsystem. The framework spends a lot of time mapping the belief systems of policy elites and analyzing the conditions under which policy-oriented learning across coalitions can occur. It has stimulated considerable interest throughout the countries of the Organization for Economic Cooperation and Development (OECD)—including some very constructive criticism (Schlager, 1995). Paul Sabatier and Hank C. Jenkins-Smith are clearly qualified to assess the implications of these recent applications.

The frameworks discussed thus far have all focused on explaining policy change within a given political system or set of institutional arrangements (including efforts to change those arrangements). The next two frameworks seek to provide explanations of variation across a large number of political systems.

Policy Diffusion Framework.   The policy diffusion framework was developed by Berry and Berry (1990, 1992) to explain variation in the adoption of specific policy innovations, such as a lottery, across a large number of states (or localities). It argues that adoption is a function of both the characteristics of the specific political systems and a variety of diffusion processes. Recently, Mintrom and Vergari (1998) integrated it with the literature on policy networks. The diffusion framework has thus far been utilized almost exclusively in the United States. It should, however, apply to variation among countries or regions within the European Union, the OECD, or any other set of political systems. The authors of the chapter in this volume are Frances Stokes Berry and William D. Berry.

The Funnel of Causality and Other Frameworks in Large-N Comparative Studies. Finally, we turn to a variety of frameworks that were extremely important in the United States in the 1960s and 1970s in explaining variation in policy outcomes (usually, budgetary expenditures) across large numbers of states and localities (Dye, 1966; 1991; Sharkansky, 1970; Hofferbert, 1974). These began as very simple frameworks seeking to apportion the variance among background socioeconomic conditions, public opinion, and political institutions—although they became somewhat more sophisticated over time (Mazmanian and Sabatier, 1981; Hofferbert and Urice, 1985). Although interest in this approach has declined somewhat in the United States, it is still popular in OECD countries, particularly to explain variation in social welfare programs (Flora, 1986; Klingeman, Hofferbert, and Budge, 1994; Schmidt, 1996). The author for this chapter is William Blomquist. Although he has contributed to this literature (Blomquist, 1991), he is not a major proponent—and thus differs from all the other chapter authors. He was selected because I expected him to be critical of the "black box" features of this framework and to seek to integrate it with other literatures, particularly institutional rational choice. Although those expectations were never communicated to him, he wound up doing a superb job of fulfilling them.

Omitted Frameworks

Although this volume contains chapters on seven different frameworks of public policymaking, several other frameworks have been omitted. Following are a few, as well as brief explanations of my reasons for judging them to be less promising that those selected.

Arenas of Power.   Originally developed by Lowi (1964, 1972), the arenas-of power framework posits a set of three or four different types of policy—for example, regulatory, distributive, and redistributive—and argues that each is characterized by quite different processes. The original formulation was rife with ambiguous concepts and causal relationships. Although these were clarified during the 1970s (Mann, 1975; Ripley and Franklin, 1976, 1982), my perception is that the arenas-of-power framework has aroused very little interest over the past fifteen years (except for Kellow, 1988). In short, it does not appear to be a "progressive" research program (Lakatos, 1971).

Cultural Theory. Originally developed by Douglas and Wildavsky (1982), cultural theory views policy as essentially dominated by four different general ideologies (what the ACF would refer to as "deep core"): individualism, hierarchicalism, egalitarianism, and fatalism. It has generated a fair amount of empirical research (Coyle and Wildavksy, 1987; Hoppe and Peterse, 1993), but many of the critical concepts remain ambiguous, and the links to institutional arrangements and to socioeconomic conditions are still relatively undeveloped. In my view, then, it is too incomplete and unclear to be included.

Constructivist Frameworks. The constructivist frameworks all focus on the "social construction" of policy problems, policy belief systems, and/or frames of reference (Fischer and Forester, 1993; Papadopoulos, 1995; Faure, Pollet, and Warin, 1995; Schneider and Ingram, 1997). These tend to be more popular in Europe, particularly in France and the Netherlands, than in the United States. Although it is clear that much of social "reality" is "socially constructed," these frameworks generally (a) leave ideas unconnected to socioeconomic conditions or institutions and (b) conceive of ideas as free-floating, that is, unconnected to specific individuals and thus largely nonfalsifiable. Having said that, I am struck that Pierre Muller's (1995) conception of a "referentiel" (a belief system or frame of reference) within a policy sector is worth pursuing if it can be rendered more empirically concrete.

Policy Domain Framework. Developed by David Knoke and his colleagues over the past decade (Laumann and Knoke, 1987; Knoke, 1990; Knoke et al., 1996), the policy domain framework is a rather complex set of concepts for guiding network analysis. It argues that, within a given policy domain/subsystem, organizations with an interest in a given policy area develop patterns of resource exchange and seek to influence policy events. In many respects, this framework is a more empirical version of institutional rational choice (IRC). Like IRC, it assumes that organizations can be treated as unitary individuals that behave in an instrumentally rational fashion. Its model of the actor is less clear than in IRC, but the policy domain framework involves many more organizations. Although I find much of the conceptualization to be difficult to understand—one is tempted to say, "Teutonic"—in retrospect this framework probably should have been included because it meets the criteria fairly well, and much of the empirical work is quite impressive.[2]

None of these evaluations as "relatively less promising" is written in stone. In fact, the major flaws in all four frameworks are some combination of (a) incompleteness (i.e., omission of critical categories of variables) and/or (b) scientific clarity and falsifiability. These flaws are correctable. In fact, I hope to add one or more of these frameworks to the set of those discussed in future editions of this book.

PLAN OF THE BOOK

With respect to each of the seven theoretical frameworks selected for discussion, I have asked one of its principal proponents to present a brief history, to discuss its underlying principles and propositions, to analyze recent empirical evidence and revisions, to evaluate the strengths and limitations of the framework, and to suggest directions for future development.

The introductory section of the book contains Peter deLeon's review of the literature on the stages heuristic.

The next section contains analyses of two frameworks that differ substantially concerning their assumptions of individual and collective rationality. Institutional rational choice frameworks assume that policy actors are "intendedly rational"; that is, they seek to realize a few goals efficiently but must overcome some obstacles (including imperfect information) to do so. The assumption is that policy problems and options are relatively well defined, but ascertaining the probable consequences of those alternatives is problematic. In contrast, Kingdon's multiple-streams model assumes that most policy situations are cloaked in "ambiguity," that is, lacking clear problem definitions and goals. In addition, serendipity and chance play a major role in the multiple-streams framework.

The next section presents two frameworks that seek to explain policy change over fairly long periods of time within a policy subsystem/domain: the punctuated-equilibrium framework of Jones et al. and the advocacy coalition framework of Sabatier et al. Although these two frameworks have similar dependent variables, they differ in several respects—most notably, in the relative importance of the general public versus policy elites.

The fourth section contains two frameworks that typically seek to explain variation in policy decisions across large numbers of political systems. I had considered combining these into a single chapter but decided against it for two reasons. First, the diffusion models discussed by Berry and Berry are really a significant addition to the traditional set of state/local system variables discussed by Sharkansky/Dye/Hofferbert. Second, I very much wanted to have a critique of the "black box" character of the Sharkansky et al. models on the record, and Berry and Berry would probably not have given me such a critique.

The final section contains two concluding chapters. The first is a comparison of the various theoretical frameworks, including comparisons of their dependent variables, the critical independent variables, the strengths and weaknesses of each, and some speculations about how they might be integrated and/or more clearly differentiated. The author is Edella Schlager, who has already revealed herself to be extremely talented at this sort of comparative analysis (Schlager, 1995; Schlager and Blomquist, 1996). In the last chapter, I suggest several strategies for advancing the state of policy theory.

The goal of this book is to advance the state of policy theory by presenting several of the more promising frameworks and by inviting the reader to compare the strengths and limitations of each. At the end of the day, the reader will hopefully have a "repertoire" of two or three frameworks that she or he is familiar with and adept at employing.

NOTES

1. Just to show that my tastes are not totally idiosyncratic, the list of "synthetic theories" developed by Peter John (1998) includes the advocacy coalition framework, punctuated equilibrium, and multiple streams. Earlier in the book, he includes socioeconomic approaches, institutions, rational choice, and ideas. I have grouped most of the last into a constructivist paradigm in the next section. My list also overlaps considerably those of Parsons (1996) and Muller and Surel (1998).

2. For example, in Knoke et al. (1996), *interest* is used for both a "topic of concern" and a "goal" (p. 13), and the critical discussion of organizational interests in specific events (pp. 21–22) is quite confusing. The basic reason for exclusion, however, is that I was simply not sufficiently aware of Knoke's work when putting together this symposium in the spring of 1996.

REFERENCES

Anderson, James. 1975. *Public Policy-Making*. New York: Praeger.

Baumgartner, Frank, and Bryan Jones. 1993. *Agendas and Instability in American Politics*. Chicago: University of Chicago Press.

Berry, Frances Stokes, and William Berry. 1990. "State Lottery Adoptions as Policy Innovations: An Event History Analysis," *American Political Science Review* 84 (June):397–415.

_____. (1992). "Tax Innovation in the States: Capitalizing on Political Opportunity," *American Journal of Political Science* 36 (August):715–742.

Blomquist, William. 1991. "Exploring State Differences in Groundwater Policy Adoptions, 1980–89," *Publius* 21:101–115.

Brewer, Gary, and Peter deLeon. 1983. *The Foundations of Policy Analysis*. Monterey, Calif.: Brooks/Cole.

Brown, Harold. 1977. *Perception, Theory, and Commitment*. Chicago: University of Chicago Press.

Chubb, John, and Terry Moe. 1990. *Politics, Markets, and America's Schools*. Washington, D.C.: Brookings Institution.

Cobb, Roger, Jennie-Keith Ross, and Marc Ross. 1976. "Agenda Building as a Comparative Political Process," *American Political Science Review* 70 (March):126–138.

Cohen, Michael, James March, and Johan Olsen. 1972. "A Garbage Can Model of Organizational Choice," *Administrative Science Quarterly* 17 (March):1–25.

Coyle, Dennis, and Aaron Wildavsky. 1987. "Requisites of Radical Reform: Income Maintenance Versus Tax Preferences," *Journal of Policy Analysis and Management* 7 (Fall):1–16.

Derthick, Martha, and Paul Quirk. 1985. *The Politics of Deregulation*. Washington, D.C.: Brookings Institution.

Douglas, Mary, and Aaron Wildavsky. 1982. *Risk and Culture*. Berkeley: University of California Press.

Dowding, Keith. 1995. "Model or Metaphor? A Critical Review of the Policy Network Approach," *Political Studies* 43 (March):136–159.

Dye, Thomas. 1966. *Politics, Economics, and Public Policy*. Chicago: Rand McNally.

_____. 1991. *Politics in States and Communities*, 7th ed. Englewood Cliffs, N.J.: Prentice-Hall.

Eisner, Marc A. 1993. *Regulatory Politics in Transition*. Baltimore: Johns Hopkins University Press.

Faure, Alain, Gilles Pollet, et Phillipe Warin. 1995. *La construction du sens dan les politique publiques*. Paris: L'Harmattan.

Fischer, Frank, and John Forester, eds. 1993. *The Argumentative Turn in Policy Analysis*. Durham, N.C.: Duke University Press.

Flora, Peter, ed. 1986. *Growth to Limits: The Western European Welfare States Since World War II*. Berlin: deGruyter.

Hawkesworth, Mary. 1992. "Epistemology and Policy Analysis." In William Dunn and Rita Kelly, eds., *Advances in Policy Studies*, pp. 295–329. New Brunswick, N.J.: Transaction Books.

Hjern, Benny, and Chris Hull. 1982. "Implementation Research as Empirical Constitutionalism," *European Journal of Political Research* 10:105–115.

Hjern, Benny, and David Porter. 1981. "Implementation Structures: A New Unit of Administrative Analysis," *Organization Studies* 2:211–227.

Hofferbert, Richard. 1974. *The Study of Public Policy*. Indianapolis, Ind.: Bobbs-Merrill.

Hofferbert, Richard, and John Urice. 1985. "Small-Scale Policy: The Federal Stimulus Versus Competing Explanations for State Funding for the Arts," *American Journal of Political Science* 29 (May):308–329.

Hoppe, Rob, and Aat Peterse. 1993. *Handling Frozen Fire: Political Culture and Risk Management*. Boulder: Westview Press.

John, Peter. 1998. *Analyzing Public Policy*. London: Pinter.

Jones, Bryan, Frank Baumgartner, and James True. 1998. "Policy Punctuations: U.S. Budget Authority, 1947–1995," *Journal of Politics* 60 (February):1–33.

Jones, Charles. 1970. *An Introduction to the Study of Public Policy*. Belmont, Calif.: Wadsworth.

Jordan, A. G. 1990. "Sub-Governments, Policy Communities, and Networks," *Journal of Theoretical Politics* 2:319–338.

Kellow, Aynsley. 1988. "Promoting Elegance in Policy Theory: Simplifying Lowi's Arenas of Power," *Policy Studies Journal* 16 (Summer):713–724.

King, Gary, Robert Keohane, and Sidney Verba. 1994. *Designing Social Inquiry*. Princeton: Princeton University Press.

Kingdon, John. 1984. *Agendas, Alternatives, and Public Policies*. Boston: Little, Brown.

Kirst, Michael, and Richard Jung 1982. "The Utility of a Longitudinal Approach in Assessing Implementation." In Walter Williams, ed., *Studying Implementation*, pp. 119–148. Chatham, N.J.: Chatham House.

Klingemann, Hans-Dieter, Richard Hofferbert, and Ian Budge. 1994. *Parties, Policies, and Democracy*. Boulder: Westview Press.

Knoke, David. 1990. *Political Networks*. Cambridge, England: Cambridge University Press.

Knoke, David, Franz Urban Pappi, Jeffrey Broadbent, and Yutaka Tsujinaka. 1996. *Comparing Policy Networks: Labor Politics in the U.S., Germany, and Japan*. Cambridge, England: Cambridge University Press.

Kuhn, Thomas. 1970. *The Structure of Scientific Revolutions*, 2d ed. Chicago: University of Chicago Press.

Lakatos, Imre. 1971. "History of Science and Its Rational Reconstruction." In R. C. Buck and R. S. Cohen, eds., *Boston Studies in the Philosophy of Science*, pp. 91–122. Dordrecht: D. Reidel.

Laumann, Edward, and David Knoke. 1987. *The Organizational State: A Perspective on National Energy and Health Networks*. Madison: University of Wisconsin Press.

Lave, Charles, and James March. 1975. *An Introduction to Models in the Social Sciences*. New York: Harper & Row.

Lester, James, and Malcolm Goggin. 1998. "Back to the Future: The Rediscovery of Implementation Studies," *Policy Currents* 8(3):1–10.

Lord, Charles, Lee Ross, and Mark Lepper. 1979. "Biased Assimilation and Attitude Polarization: The Effects of Prior Theories on Subsequently Considered Evidence," *Journal of Personality and Social Psychology* 37:2098–2109.

Lowi, Theodore. 1964. "American Business, Public Policy, Case Studies, and Political Theory," *World Politics* 16 (July):677–715.

_____. (1972). "Four Systems of Policy, Politics, and Choice," *Public Administration Review* 32 (July/August):298–301.

Mann, Dean. 1975. "Political Incentives in U.S. Water Policy: Relationships Between Distributive and Regulatory Politics." In Matthew Holden and Dennis Dresang, eds., *What Government Does*, pp. 106–116. Beverly Hills, Calif.: Sage.

Mazmanian, Daneil, and Paul Sabatier. 1981. "A Multivariate Model of Public Policy-Making," *American Journal of Political Science* 24 (August):439–468.

_____. 1983. *Implementation and Public Policy*. Glenview, Ill.: Scott Foresman. (Reissued in 1989 by University Press of America.)

Miller, Gary. 1992. *Managerial Dilemmas*. Cambridge, England: Cambridge University Press.

Mintrom, Michael, and Sandra Vergari. 1998. "Policy Networks and Innovation Diffusion: The Case of State Educational Reform," *Journal of Politics* 60 (February):120–148.

Moe, Terry. 1984. "The New Economics of Organization," *American Journal of Political Science* 28 (November):739–777.

_____. 1990a. "Political Institutions: The Neglected Side of the Story," *Journal of Law, Economics, and Organization* 6:215–253.

_____. 1990b. "The Politics of Structural Choice." In Oliver Williamson, ed., *Organization Theory: From Chester Bernard to the Present and Beyond*, pp. 116–153. Oxford: Oxford University Press.

Muller, Pierre. 1995. "Les politiques publiques comme construction d'un rapport au monde." In Alain Faure et al., eds., *La construction du sens dans les politiques publiques*, pp. 153–179. Paris: L'Harmattan.

Muller, Pierre, and Yves Surel. 1998. *L'analyse des politiques publiques*. Paris: Montchrestien.

Nagel, Ernest. 1961. *The Structure of Science*. New York: Harcourt, Brace, & World.

Nakamura, Robert. 1987. "The Textbook Process and Implementation Research," *Policy Studies Review* 1:142–154.

Nelson, Barbara. 1984. *Making an Issue of Child Abuse*. Chicago: University of Chicago Press.

Ostrom, Elinor. 1983. "A Public Service Industry Approach to the Study of Local Government Structure and Reform," *Policy and Politics* 11:313–341.

_____. 1986. "An Agenda for the Study of Institutions," *Public Choice* 48:3–25.

_____. 1990. *Governing the Commons*. Cambridge, England: Cambridge University Press.

Ostrom, Elinor, Roy Gardner, and James Walker. 1994. *Rules, Games, and Common-Pool Resources*. Ann Arbor: University of Michigan Press.

Ostrom, Elinor, Larry Schroeder, and Susan Wynne. 1993. *Institutional Incentives and Sustainable Development*. Boulder: Westview Press.

Papadopoulos, Yannis. 1995. *Complexité sociale et politiques publiques*. Paris: Montchrestien.

Parsons, Wayne. 1996. *Public Policy: An Introduction to the Theory and Practice of Policy Analysis*. London: Elgar, Aldershot.

Platt, John, 1964. "Strong Inference," *Science* 146 (October): 347–353.

Pressman, Jeffrey and Aaron Wildavsky. 1973. *Implementation*. Berkeley: University of California Press.

Rhodes, R. A. W. 1988. *Beyond Westminster and Whitehall*. London: Unwin & Hyman.

Riker, William. 1986. *The Art of Political Manipulation*. New Haven: Yale University Press.

Ripley, Randall, and Grace Franklin. 1976. *Congress, the Bureaucracy, and Public Policy*. Homewood, Ill.: Dorsey.

_____. 1982. *Bureaucracy and Policy Implementation*. Homewood, Ill.: Dorsey.

Sabatier, Paul. 1986. "Top-Down and Bottom-Up Models of Policy Implementation: A Critical and Suggested Synthesis," *Journal of Public Policy* 6 (January): 21–48.

_____. 1991. "Toward Better Theories of the Policy Process," *PS: Political Science and Politics* 24 (June):147–156.

Sabatier, Paul, and Hank Jenkins-Smith. 1988. Symposium Issue, "Policy Change and Policy-Oriented Learning: Exploring an Advocacy Coalition Framework," *Policy Sciences* 21:123–272.

_____. 1993. *Policy Change and Learning: An Advocacy Coalition Approach*. Boulder: Westview Press.

Scharpf, Fritz. 1997. *Games Policy Actors Play*. Boulder: Westview Press.

Schlager, Edella. 1995. "Policy-Making and Collective Action: Defining Coalitions within the Advocacy Coalition Framework," *Policy Sciences* 28:243–270.

Schlager, Edella, and William Blomquist. 1996. "Emerging Political Theories of the Policy Process: Institutional Rational Choice, the Politics of Structural Choice, and Advocacy Coalitions," *Political Research Quarterly* 49 (September):651–672.

Schmidt, Manfred. 1996. "When Parties Matter," *European Journal of Political Research* 30 (September):155–183.

Schneider, Anne Larason, and Helen Ingram. 1997. *Policy Design for Democracy.* Lawrence: University Press of Kansas.

Schneider, Mark, Paul Teske, Michael Mintrom, and Sam Best. 1993. "Establishing the Micro Foundations for Macro-Level Theory," *American Political Science Review* 87:702–716.

Scholz, John, James Twombley, and Barbara Headrick. 1991. "Street Level Political Controls over Federal Bureaucrats," *American Political Science Review* 85 (September):829–858.

Sharkansky, Ira. 1970. *Policy Analysis in Political Science.* Chicago: Markham

Shepsle, Kenneth. 1989. "Studying Institutions: Some Lessons from the Rational Choice Approach," *Journal of Theoretical Politics* 1:131–147.

Stinchcombe, Arthur. 1968. *Constructing Social Theories.* Chicago: University of Chicago Press.

Zahariadis, Nikolaos. 1992. "To Sell or Not to Sell? Telecommunications Policy in Britain and France," *Journal of Public Policy* 12:355–376.

_____. 1995. *Markets, States, and Public Policy: Privatization in Britain and France.* Ann Arbor: University of Michigan Press.

2

The Stages Approach to the Policy Process

What Has It Done? Where Is It Going?

PETER DELEON

"I'm sorry Peter, but it seems that [policy research] has moved beyond the [policy process] stages heuristic."
—Participant at 1996 APSA meetings

More than forty-five years ago, Harold D. Lasswell articulated the first formal usage of the concept *policy sciences*. Although informal policy advice had been offered by advisers to rulers for centuries, Lasswell was the first to define in any coherent manner what composed this "new" approach to government and its characteristics (Lasswell, 1951; also Lasswell and Kaplan, 1950). Since then, the policy sciences—largely under the derivative rubrics of policy analysis and later public management—have made tremendous strides in terms of widespread acceptance, surely in the United States and increasingly in other nations. But as the policy sciences orientation approaches half a century, one can legitimately wonder what it has produced in terms of Lasswell's original vision, its everyday operation, and, most important, its capacity for future research, in short, its overall success. More pessimistic observers would agree with Donald Schön and Martin

The original version of this chapter was presented as part of the twentieth anniversary of the Centro de Investigacion y Docencia Economicas, in Mexico City, 3 June 1996. I am grateful for the insightful comments provided by Profs. Omas Guerrero (UNAM) and José Luis Méndez (Colegio de Mexico). Professor Paul A. Sabatier (University of California at Davis), as editor of this volume, forced an especially close attention to these arguments.

Rein (1994, p. xvi), who—although themselves sympathetic to the policy sciences—wrote that "the policy analytic movement begun by Harold Lasswell in the early 1950s has largely failed."

In this essay, I deal with one particular aspect of Lasswell's vision of the policy sciences. Lasswell operationalized—although rather abstractly—many of his ideas about improving the quality of governance by improving the quality of the information being rendered to government. He focused particular attention on the "policy process," or the functional stages or phases that a given government policy (or program) would go through during its "policy life." As we shall see, many observers have argued against the Lasswellian approach and have strongly suggested the shortcomings of the policy process/stages approach. In this context, we can examine Lasswell's (and others') policy framework to see if it has become as antiquated (some would claim dysfunctional) as its critics have charged. Alternatively, we can see if it still offers some utility as the art and craft of policy research continue to evolve as a tool to improve the quality of the information offered government.

KNOWLEDGE IN THE POLICY PROCESS

Lasswell gave special emphasis to what he termed "knowledge *of* the policy process" and "knowledge *in* the policy process," the former being more substantive (e.g., How much CO_2 can be released into the atmosphere without evoking a disastrous global warming condition?) and the latter being more procedural (How does a democratic polity publicly intervene in reducing its CO_2 emissions?). He framed a "conceptual map [that] must provide a guide to obtaining a generalistic image of the major phases of any collective act" (Lasswell, 1971, p. 28) and nominated seven "stages" of what he was later to call "the decision process" (Lasswell, 1956):

- Intelligence
- Promotion
- Prescription
- Invocation
- Application
- Termination
- Appraisal

This listing reflects the origin of what has arguably been the most widely accepted concept of the policy sciences, that is, the policy process, the procedure by which a given policy is proposed, examined, carried out, and perhaps terminated (see Lasswell, 1956). Later, one of Lasswell's students at Yale University, Garry D. Brewer (1974), proposed a derivative list (almost certainly with Lasswell's specific approval) that (with other very similar alternatives from other authors) has shaped much of the research agenda undertaken by policy scientists since the mid-1970s, in both substantive and practical terms:[1]

- Initiation
- Estimation
- Selection
- Implementation
- Evaluation
- Termination

These stages are not simply divined from the heady atmosphere of the academy. Both individually and in combination, they offer a way to think about public policy in concept and, just as important, in operation. Although they certainly can merge with one another, each does have a distinctive characteristic and mannerism and process that give the individual stage a life and presence of its own. Without denying that the stages can (and often should) share information and procedures, few observers would confuse the distinguishing set of activities that defines program estimation with those dealing with (say) policy termination. Angela Browne and Aaron Wildavsky (1984, p. 205) made the point with great cogency as they distinguished between the mutually supportive duality of implementation and evaluation:

> The conceptual distinction between evaluation and implementation is important to maintain, however much the two overlap in practice, because they protect against the absorption of analysis into action to the detriment of both.

The idea of a delineated, sequential policy process framework apparently was much admired, for, as stated above, numerous authors have availed themselves of the framework, either explicitly or implicitly. Charles Jones's *An Introduction to the Study of Public Policy* (1970/1977/1984) and James Anderson's *Public Policy Making* (1975/1979) were among the first "policy process" volumes; Anderson references both Lasswell and Jones in his description of the policy stages (although omitting termination). In 1983, Brewer and deLeon published their volume, which completely laid out the stages of and rationales for the policy process. All three volumes (and other analogous models, such as Judith May and Aaron Wildavsky, 1978, and Dennis Palumbo, 1988) focused the reader's attentions on "knowledge *of,*" that is, the workings of the policy process as a process-oriented event.

Just as important, these volumes and their advocacy (or at least their utilization) of the policy process model directed an entire generation of research by noted policy scholars, as they studied stages as stages (e.g., policy initiation) rather than as specific issue areas (e.g., energy resources).[2] These works include such unquestionable policy classics as:[3]

- Initiation: Nelson Polsby's *Political Innovation in Am*erica (1984), John Kingdon's *Agendas, Alternatives, and Public Policy* (1984/1996), and Barbara Nelson's *Making an Issue of Child Abuse* (1984).
- Estimation: Alice Rivlin's *Systematic Thinking for Social Action* (1971), Edward Quade's *Analysis for Public Decisions* (1983), and David Weimer and Aidan Vining's *Policy Analysis* (1989).
- Implementation: Jeffrey Pressman and Aaron Wildavsky's *Implementation ...* (1973), Eugene Bardach's *The Implementation Game* (1977), and Daniel Mazmanian and Paul Sabatier's *Implementation and Public Policy* (1983).
- Evaluation: Edward Suchman's *Evaluation Research* (1967) and Richard Titmuss's *The Gift Relationship* (1971).
- Termination: Herbert Kaufman's *Are Government Organizations Immortal?* (1976) and Fred Iklè's *Every War Must End* (1971/1991).

In his *Advice and Consent* (1988), deLeon compared the relative strengths and weaknesses of the segmentation of the policy stages/process framework as it affects the policy sciences research agenda. On the one hand, these works brought a new richness to the policy sciences, as Polsby and other policy scholars emphasized the intense complexity that theorists in political science and economics, in search of more rigorous, hypotheses-generating-models, might have overlooked. For instance, Pressman and Wildavsky's detailing of the high drama performed by the Economic Development Administration (EDA) and its incredibly cumbersome ballet with the city of Oakland, partially initiated to ward off potential urban violence (that surely was not part of the EDA's initial mission), demonstrated just how involved and actually convoluted policy implementation could be. Similarly, Titmuss's normatively oriented evaluation of comparative blood transfusion policies in *The Gift Relationship* forcefully argues against a reliance on standard benefit-cost analyses that were the growing standard of program evaluation.

Moreover, an emphasis on the policy process moved research away from a strict adherence to the study of public administration and institutions, which was increasing in political science, and of quasi-markets, which was the predilection of economics. Thus, it helped to rationalize a new problem-oriented perspective markedly different from its disciplinary predecessors. The cumulative analyses of the various stages clearly demonstrated Lasswell's insistence on a multidisciplinary approach to the policy sciences, as well as the interactive effects among the different stages. Finally, the policy process framework readily permitted the explicit inclusion of social norms and personal values, a component too often neglected or ignored in contemporary political and economic examinations.

But at the same time, these analyses of specific stages in the policy process model had a clear downside in that they oriented scholars toward looking at just one stage at a time (deLeon, 1988), thereby neglecting the entire process. Ultimately, many policy researchers (and policymakers[4]) came to view the process as a sharply differentiated set of activities: First, you define the problem; then, a completely different set of actors implements the chosen policy option; a third stage defines the evaluation; and so on. Likewise, they portrayed a disjointed, episodic process rather than a more ongoing, continuous one, as well as a policy phenomenon that seemingly took place in the relatively short term, one more suitable to the policymaker's rapidly changing schedule than the life span of a given policy. Finally, to many, the policy process/stages image implied a certain linearity—for example, first initiation, then estimation. . . . then (possibly) termination—as opposed to a series of feedback actions or recursive loops (e.g., estimation can lead back to initiation rather than the next step, selection, and implementation and evaluation insistently feed back and forth on each other) that characterize the operations and politics of the policy process.

Nevertheless, most (even subsequent critics) agree that the framework of the policy process and its various stages held center stage for at least the better part of the 1970s and 1980s. It was, for many, the "conventional wisdom" (Robert Nakaruma, 1987, referred to it as "the textbook policy process") that forced itself upon an emerging discipline, largely in disregard of Albert Hirschman's (1970) prescient warning that paradigms, unless closely considered, can become a hindrance to understanding. And arguably, that is exactly what happened as policy scholars began to inform their own interpretations of the policy process framework as if it were the target rather than the condition it sought to describe. Although certainly none would argue against a new statement of perspectives, one can openly question its basic assumptions. Let us therefore examine the thrust of these criticisms.

IN SEARCH OF A THEORY . . .

It was not until the late 1980s that Robert Nakamura (1987) began to question the conventional wisdom, asking if its "widespread use" suggested that the stages were anywhere near as precisely defined as their proponents proposed; if not, he claimed, the process/stages image could not be used as a "paradigm." Later, Paul Sabatier (see Sabatier, 1988, 1991), often in cooperation with Hank Jenkins-Smith (1993), proposed that the policy process "heuristic" (their term) has "serious limitations as a basis for research and teaching" (Jenkins-Smith and Sabatier, 1993, p. 3), and, more specifically, that the policy process neglects "the role of ideas—particularly ideas involving the relatively technical aspects of policy debates—in policy evolution" (Sabatier, 1993, p. 15).

Sabatier offered six very concrete complaints about the policy process as a unifying concept within the policy sciences (Jenkins-Smith and Sabatier, 1993, pp. 3–4; emphases in original):

1. "The stages model is not really a *causal model at all.*" That is, it did not lend itself to prediction, or even to indicating how one stage led to another.
2. "The stages model *does not provide a clear basis for empirical hypothesis testing.*" Hence it is not amenable to confirmation, amendment, or fabrication.
3. "The stages heuristic suffers from *descriptive inaccuracy* in posing a series of stages. . . . "
4. "The stages metaphor suffers from a built-in *legalistic, top-down focus.*"
5. "The stages metaphor inappropriately *emphasizes the policy cycle as the temporal unit of analysis.*" In other words, it neglects the concept of a system of intergovernmental relations.
6. "The stages metaphor fails to provide a good vehicle for integrating the roles of policy analysis and *policy-oriented learning throughout the public policy process.*"

Sabatier's criticisms were well couched and thoughtful, even though not always to the point of those who used the policy process/stages metaphor.[5] The primary shortcoming, according to Ronald Brunner (1991), is that Sabatier's criticisms reflected a worrisomely narrow use of *empirical* (e.g., a use conducive to specific hypothesis creation and prediction) theory; it overlooks the presence of what Lasswell called a *central* theory, which helps integrate (N.B.: not necessarily predict) policy events. As Brunner (1991, p. 70) posited, "An adequate body of central theory—composed of concepts as well as normative and empirical propositions—has been available for some time." Later, Brunner (1991, pp. 80–81) was even more explicit: "The purpose of the policy sciences as 'science' is to realize more of the potential for free choice through the sharing of insight [i.e., central theory]. The purpose is *not* prediction." (emphasis in original).

This narrowness is also present in more functional uses (to which Lasswell gave equal footing) of the policy process paradigm. For example, Brewer and deLeon (and, by implication, Lasswell) never proposed that the policy process comprised a theoretic *model* as ascribed by Sabatier, for they certainly realized that it was not suitable to formal hypothesis testing or prediction with much precision. Rather, they viewed the policy process as a device (a heuristic, as it were) to help dissaggregate an otherwise seamless web of public policy transactions, as was too regularly depicted in political science. They proposed that each segment and transition were distinguished by differentiated actions and purposes. For instance, policy estimation was primarily an analytic activity pursued by (usually) staff analysts within an agency; on the other hand, implementation was performed by an entirely different set of actors, generally acting outside the agency, having to interact with a defined set of external clients, and occasionally having to alter literally the policy purposes as a matter of local necessity (Groggin et al., 1990).

Still, the overall policy process metaphor implied a system. In Brewer and deLeon's (1983) simile, the policy process "model" was likened to that of a medical doctor; a physician might well examine a patient's blood circulation or hormonal balance but would never lose track of the fact that the body's circulation or biochemistry is contained within and vital to a system (i.e., the body). Nor did Brewer and deLeon ever claim that the stages are unidirectional or lacked feedback capabilities; indeed, quite the opposite. To claim that the policy process heuristic lacks *empirical* theoretic constructs and characteristics and is therefore empty, or even "dysfunctional," is somewhat akin to claiming that Tom Cruise's reputed lack of serious acting ability disqualifies him as a matinee idol and box office cash cow.

However, these reservations or rejoinders are not meant to diminish the importance of Sabatier and Jenkins-Smith's research agenda. Indeed, at its base, it is nowhere near as dismissive of the policy process/stages heuristic as the authors would have us believe. Rather, one could justifiably argue that in the articulation of their advocacy coalition framework (Sabatier and Jenkins-Smith, 1991), they were talking implicitly about a perceived lacuna in the policy process, in this case, policy initiation (or what others, such as David Dery, 1984, have termed "problem definition"). Their very title—*Policy Change and Learning*—speaks directly to their goals, that is, to explain how new (or seriously revised) programs are brought into being, sometimes over at least a decade and despite any number of opposition parties, which are not so much defeated as coopted or persuaded or cajoled into what Sabatier and Jenkins-Smith called an "advocacy coalition." Moreover, these authors' particular contributions to policy research—as opposed to, say, Kingdon's on agenda setting—are significant, as they focus explicitly on differences between dynamic and static policy elements. In this way, Sabatier and Jenkins-Smith provide greater awareness between (what they call) secondary versus core issues and try to incorporate changes in such "values" as they permit norms to become a formal part of the policy considerations.

We can identify analogous contributions on the part of Frank Baumgartner and Bryan Jones (1993), as they described events in terms of activities that they called regular "triggering events," resulting in "punctuated equilibria," leading naturally to the establishment of a new political status quo. They, too, fall easily into the area encompassed by issues of policy initiation—specifically, how the media serve as a surrogate for emerging policy issues.

Much the same set of arguments might be made about program evaluation. Although new approaches to program evaluation are constantly being proposed and tested (see, e.g., Fischer, 1995, for evaluation from a postpositivist perspective), these do not destroy the utility of the policy process framework or undermine the necessary role of program evaluation.

All of these areas have historically been under-attended by policy analysts (see Schön and Rein, 1994; also deLeon, 1994a), and this neglect has adversely affected the insights offered by the consensual policy framework. But Sabatier and

Jenkins-Smith do not necessarily undercut the legitimacy or viability of the policy process approach.

ON BALANCE

Regardless of the contributions of Sabatier and Jenkins-Smith, one still needs to ask if their charges regarding the, at best, marginal improvements for further research results in the policy process are commensurate with reduced research efforts in that vein. I propose a rather more positive response than Sabatier and Jenkins-Smith's gloomy prognostication of reduced research efforts, that the policy process framework will continue to serve as a valuable heuristic in both policy research and programmatic operations. First, as I have suggested, and despite Sabatier and Jenkins-Smith's repeated protestations, there is some doubt as to whether they and the advocacy coalition framework (ACF) have broken out of the paradigm created by the policy process orientation.[6] And to be fair, it is not clear that we should want them to, for it is apparent that a great deal of pivotal research is still to be done within that framework as long as one can admit that the policy process is *not* a model in the formal sense of the word.

Brewer and deLeon (and other "policy processers," I suspect) prefer to reflect upon the policy process/stages heuristic as a basis for viewing and categorizing actors and actions in ways that help unravel and elucidate given policies, both in retrospect (always, of course, the clearer view) and—more cautiously—in the future. As most observers fully know, these benefits are no small accomplishments, even if they do not create a clear view over the next policy mountain, let alone anticipate it. To argue over whether policy process represents a "model," a "metaphor," or a "heuristic" serves little purpose as long as we recognize its main strengths (i.e., that it is a means for categorizing policy actions as they vary from stage to stage) and attendant weaknesses (e.g., that it has a lack of predictive capabilities) and act accordingly. For instance, Steven Waldman's (1995) masterly account of the AmericaCorps legislation is perfectly clear in using the concepts developed within policy formulation, even though Waldman made no conscious appeal to the policy stages framework.

One can make the case that many of the more radical iterations of policy research—I mean the postpositivist themes, including research in hermeneutics and critical theory—could also be easily incorporated into the policy process paradigm (see Hawkesworth, 1988, and deLeon, 1997). Marie Danziger (1995) made the case (drawing from Foucault and others) that the "objective" basis of policy analysis is little more than a subjective judgment and cannot be used as if it were scientific "fact." Critical theory, as an example, makes the case that "systematically distorted communications" threaten the foundations of good policy and social legitimacy, that is, according to Jürgen Habermas, "communicative rationality" (see, e.g., Forester, 1985, 1993). It would be an easy transition from critical theory to describe a movement encompassing greater subjectivity or going toward greater communicative rationality in terms of improved problem definition. Lasswell originally called this stage the "intelligence" function, and later scholars (e.g., Brewer and deLeon, 1983) referred to it as the initiation stage. Other postpositivists, such as Fischer and Forester (1993), could be similarly located. A model as carefully structured as Sabatier and Jenkins-Smith's ACF would be unable to encompass these newer policy approaches, such as communicative rationality and postpositivism.

Likewise, new contributions to policy research, such as ethnography or mediated negotiation, can also be fitted into the policy process model without undermining—in fact, enhancing—its validity for understanding, working on, or, more to the point, improving the quality of information provided to government. This last task, of course, was one of Lasswell's original and enduring charges. In the above examples, if we attribute any credibility to the cited research approaches (and I propose few would entirely disown them), policy scholars such as Sabatier could be seen as possibly inhibiting the advancement of the policy sciences by clinging tenaciously to the problematic tenets of positivist thought and procedures. Conversely, these alternative concepts can readily be captured by the policy process framework.

The more pressing question is not "whither the policy process" but whether the policy process framework (or heuristic) can be useful in moving the policy sciences toward a set of policy-oriented theories. The quest for a policy theory was, after all, the clear intention of Sabatier and Jenkins-Smith and of Elinor Ostrom, not the denigration of the "straw man" policy process heuristic. To this particular question, the answer must be much more agnostic. Lasswell's (1971) proposed "maximization theorem" is a candidate (see Brunner, 1991, pp. 77–78); it

> holds that living forms are predisposed to complete acts in ways that are perceived to leave the actor better off than if he had completed them differently. The postulate draws attention to the actor's own perception of the alternative act completions open to him in a given situation.

However, the maximization postulate is less consonant with an empirical theory than it sounds. In the first place, it seems entirely too dependent on traditional economic reasoning; there are simply too many instances in which *imperium economia*—however convenient and enticing—does not prevail, as Amitai Etzioni, Robert Bellah, and the communitarians are quick to point out. Second, the maximization postulate is too prone to understandable ambiguity, depending, as it does, on "the actor's own perception." Nor does Yehezkel Dror's (1971) advocacy of metatheory seem particularly persuasive, even after twenty-five years.

Unfortunately, the standard disciplinary formulations are even more suspect and querulous in terms of theory building. For example, let us take the case of benefit-cost analysis: U.S. president Bill Clinton accepted an entirely new budget-busting component in 1996 when he ordered expanded disability benefits for U.S. Vietnam veterans who *might* have contracted prostrate cancer, basing his decision on scientifically inconclusive evidence linking prostrate cancer to the herbicide Agent Orange. Considering that close to 3 million men fought in Vietnam and that 10 percent of all men (regardless of their Vietnam experience) contract prostrate cancer, the relevant government benefits could be substantial (Purdum, 1996). More to our point, President Clinton's actions hardly seem to validate a strictly economic approach. Or institutional analysis: In a similarly iconoclastic manner, Paul Sabatier and his colleagues (1995) indicated that the standard institutional pressures seemed to be less than compelling in examinations of the operations of the U.S. Forest Service. Or even "objective" economic data: *The Economist* ("Damned Lies," 1996, p. 18) opined that "finding the right number is much harder than you might think. . . . Many of these activities cannot be seen and cannot be numbered." These and numerous other instances emphasize the complexity of policy actions that render analysis from a limited perspective less than useful (Bobrow and Dryzek, 1987) and, concomitantly, enhance the value of the policy process model.

In these cases, one can justifiably wonder if the policy sciences would be better served if they adopted more of a systems analysis perspective (read: policy process "model") as opposed to a general systems perspective, that is, if they accepted tentatively the policy stages/process for its constrained worth and leave it behind when bigger and better things materialize. The systems model is certainly more holistic in its approach, searching for, perhaps stumbling toward, the "big picture," replete with the requisite daunting big-picture complexities and linkages. In physics, a general systems perspective would be known as a *grand unifying theory,* in other words, most physicists' Holy Grail. However, systems *analysis* (from the Greek, "to loosen or break apart") attempts to answer the question of the disaggregated parts in lieu of the much more forbidding whole. In its defense, we can admit that linkages can remain elusive (or that the reconfigured whole is different from the earlier, unreconstructed body), but at least we have some idea as to what makes up (or, just as important, what does not make up) the parts. Although this information may appear as little more than isolated and unrelated, we know from Thomas Kuhn (1962) that these parts are the founding elements of "scientific revolutions." Given the idiosyncratic episodes addressed by most policy research, we might well be better served to devote ourselves to the quest for a series of mid-range theories, as Robert Merton (1968) set out to do some years ago, or even toward a better, generalized understanding, rather than a policy grand unifying theory.

In the case of the policy process, we still may be unable to grasp how the entire system works *in verifiable* (or, if one prefers Karl Popper's terminology, *falsifiable) theory,* but with the assistance of, for example, Eugene Bardach (1977), we have a much better idea of how agendas are formulated and policy alternatives presented. And as Charles Lindblom (1990; Lindblom and Cohen, 1971) has repeatedly advised us over the years, although Holy Grails are all well and good and fully warrant our lusting after them, still "usable knowledge," "lay probing," and "muddling through" do provide a valuable illumination of their own. Or in the famous phrase of John Maynard Keynes, "It is better to be roughly right than precisely wrong," especially when we know that the precisely wrong will surely find itself manifested with great certitude into public policies.

CONCLUSION

In short, before we discard a useful friend—in this instance, the policy process or policy stages framework—we need to make sure, first, that it really does warrant a place in the dustbin of abandoned paradigms; second, that we have a better, more robust framework on which to rely; and third, that even in our quest for the theoretical, we have little use for the operational. None of these criteria (or the alternative models) argues decisively or even very strongly for abandoning the policy stages framework.

The policy process paradigm has never given us everything we might have wanted from it, so we need to ask two additional questions: In lieu of alternative policy formulations, have we loaded an impossibly heroic stature upon the policy stages framework? And more centrally, exactly what are we asking it to provide? A theory of political change or occurrences? Perhaps, but what about other—and now neglected—stages of public policy? And, failing that, as we certainly must, then certainly operational insights or, as Lasswell observed, "better intelligence leading to better government" is an acceptable alternative to empty theorizing. In Lasswell's own words (quoted in Brunner, 1991, p. 81):

It is the growth of insight, not simply of the capacity of the observer to predict the future operation of an automatic compulsion, or of a non-personal factor, that represents the major contribution of the scientific study of interpersonal relations to policy.

It was, of course, F. Scott Fitzgerald—the consummate policy analyst for the Roaring Twenties—writing about the fatally deluded Jay Gatsby, who offered what could be an appropriate paean to the troubled and maligned policy stages framework, heuristic, or model:

Gatsby believed in the green light, the orgiastic future that year by year recedes before us. It eluded us then, but that's no matter—tomorrow we will run faster, stretch out our arms farther. . . . And one fine morning—

NOTES

1. In the early 1980s, when Garry Brewer and Peter deLeon were finalizing their *Foundations of Policy Analysis* (1983), they asked Lasswell if he might prepare a foreword. He chose not to, explaining that the book and its format were fine just as they were.

2. Perhaps of equal importance, these stages assisted in the design of a number of academic curricula, engendering a flurry of policy design, estimation, and evaluation courses.

3. Obviously this is meant to be a representative rather than an exhaustive listing; apologies to those missing are hereby given.

4. On 25 November 1986, President Ronald Reagan explained to the American public that although "our policy goals [in dealing with the revolutionary government of Iran] were to be well founded . . . information brought to my attention yesterday convinced me that, in one aspect, the *implementation* of the policy was seriously flawed" (emphasis added), thus announcing the denouement of the Iran-Contra scandal.

5. A more complete review of Sabatier and Jenkins-Smith's essay is deLeon (1994); also see Lawlor (1995). Sabatier (1991) drew on more than just the policy process/stages framework, as he also included Elinor Ostrom (1990) and Richard Hofferbert (1974, 1990) in his criticisms.

6. The source here is numerous conversations with Professor Sabatier on this subject. One can fairly cite Professor Sabatier's earlier mastery of the implementation literature as evidence that his disavowal of the policy process is recent at the very best.

REFERENCES

Anderson, James E. 1979. *Public Policy Making,* 2d ed. New Holt, Rinehart, & Winston. (Originally published in 1975.)

Bardach, Eugene. 1977. *The Implementation Game.* Chicago: University of Chicago Press.

Baumgartner, Frank R., and Bryan D. Jones. 1993. *Agendas and Instability in American Politics.* Chicago: University of Chicago Press.

Bellah, Robert, et al. 1985. *Habits of the Heart.* New York: Perennial Library of Harper & Row.

Bobrow, Davis B., and John S. Dryzek. 1987. *Policy Analysis by Design.* Pittsburgh: University of Pittsburgh Press.

Brewer, Garry D. 1974. "The Policy Sciences Emerge: To Nurture and Structure a Discipline." *Policy Sciences* 5(3) (September):239–244.

Brewer, Garry D., and Peter deLeon. 1983. *The Foundations of Policy Analysis.* Monterey, Calif.: Brooks/Cole.

Browne, Angela, and Aaron Wildavsky. 1984. "What Should Evaluation Mean to Implementation?" In Jeffrey L. Pressman and Aaron Wildavsky, eds., *Implementation . . . ,* 3d ed. Berkeley: University of California Press.

Brunner, Ronals D. 1991. "The Policy Movement as a Policy Problem, *Policy Sciences* 24(1) (February):65–98.

"Damned Lies." 1996. *The Economist* 341(7993) (November 23):18.

Danziger, Marie. 1995. "Policy Analysis Postmodernized," *Policy Studies Journal* 23(3) (Fall):435–450.

deLeon, Peter. 1988. *Advice and Consent: The Development of the Policy Sciences.* New York: Russell Sage Foundation.

_____. 1994a. "The Policy Sciences Redux: New Roads to Post-Positivism," *Policy Studies Journal* 22(2) (Summer):200–212.

_____. 1994b. "Reinventing the Policy Sciences: Three Steps Back to the Future," *Policy Sciences* 27(1):77–95.

_____. 1997. *Democracy and the Policy Sciences*. Albany: State University of New York Press.

Dery, David. 1984. *Problem Definition in Policy Analysis*. Lawrence: University of Kansas Press.

Dror, Yehezkel. 1971. *Design for the Policy Sciences*. New York: American Elsevier.

Etzioni, Amitai. 1988. *The Moral Dimension*. New York: Free Press.

Fischer, Frank. 1995. *Evaluating Public Policy*. Chicago: Nelson Hall.

Fischer, Frank, and John Forester, eds. 1993. *The Argumentative Turn in Policy Analysis and Planning*. Durham, N.C.: Duke University Press.

Forester, John, ed. 1985. *Critical Thinking and Public Life*. Cambridge, Mass.: MIT Press.

_____. 1993. *Critical Theory, Public Policy, and Planning Practice*. Albany: State University of New York Press.

Groggin, Malcolm L. et al. 1990. *Implementation Theory and Practice*. Glenville, Ill.: Scott, Foresman/Little, Brown.

Hawkesworth, M. E., 1988. *Theoretical Issues in Policy Analysis*. Albany: State University of New York Press.

Hirschman, Albert O. 1970. "The Search for Paradigms as a Hindrance to Understanding," *World Politics* 22(3) (April):329–343.

Hofferbert, Richard. 1974. *A Study of Public Policy*. Indianapolis, Ind.: Bobbs-Merrill.

_____. 1990. *The Reach and Grasp of Policy Analysis*. Tuscaloosa: University of Alabama Press.

Iklè, Fred Charles. 1991. *Every War Must End, rev. ed*. New York: Columbia University Press. (Originally published in 1971.)

Jenkins-Smith, Hank C., and Paul A. Sabatier. 1993. "The Study of the Public Policy Process." In Paul A. Sabatier and Hank C. Jenkins-Smith, eds., 1993. *Policy Change and Learning: An Advocacy Coalition Approach*. Boulder: Westview Press.

_____. 1995. "Evaluating the Advocacy Coalition Framework," *Journal of Public Policy* 14(2):175–203.

Jones, Charles. 1984. *An Introduction to the Study of Public Policy, 3d ed*. Belmont, Calif.: Wadsworth. (Originally published in 1970; 2d ed., 1977.)

Kaufman, Herbert. 1976. *Are Government Organizations Immortal?* Washington, D.C.: Brookings Institution.

Kingdon, John. 1996. *Agendas, Alternatives, and Public Policy* (2nd ed.). Boston: Little, Brown.

Kingdon, John. 1996. *Agendas, Alternatives, and Public Policy, 2d ed*. Boston: Little, Brown. (Originally published in 1984.)

Kuhn, Thomas. 1962. *The Structure of Scientific Revolutions*. Chicago: University of Chicago Press.

Lasswell, Harold D. 1951. "The Policy Orientation." In Daniel Lerner and Harold D. Lasswell, eds., *The Policy Sciences*. Stanford: Stanford University Press.

_____. 1956. *The Decision Process*. College Park: University of Maryland Press.

_____. 1971. *A Pre-View of Policy Sciences*. New York: American Elsevier.

Lasswell, Harold D., and Abraham Kaplan. 1950. *Power and Society*. New Haven: Yale University Press.

Lawlor, Edward F. 1996. "Book Review." *Journal of Policy Analysis and Management* 15(1) (Winter):110–121.

Lindblom, Charles E. 1990. *Inquiry and Change*. New Haven: Yale University Press.

Lindblom, Charles E., and David K. Cohen. 1971. *Usable Knowledge*. New Haven: Yale University Press.

May, Judith V., and Aaron B. Wildavsky, eds. 1978. *The Policy Cycle*. Beverly Hills, Calif.: Sage.

Mazmanian Daniel, and Paul A. Sabatier. 1983. *Implementation and Public Policy*. Glenview, Ill.: Scott Foresman. (Reissued in 1989 by University Press of America.)

Merton, Robert K. 1968. *Social Theory and Social Structure*. New York: Free Press. (Originally published in 1949.)

Nakaruma, Robert. 1987. "The Textbook Policy Process and Implementation Research," *Policy Studies Review* 7(2) (Autumn):142–154.

Nelson, Barbara. 1984. *Making an Issue of Child Abuse*. Chicago: University of Chicago Press.

Ostrom, Elinor. 1990. *Governing the Commons: The Evolutions of Institutions for Collective Action*. New York: Cambridge University Press.

Palumbo, Dennis. 1988. *Public Policy in America*. New York: Harcourt, Brace Jovanovich.

Polsby, Nelson W. 1984. *Political Innovation in America*. New Haven: Yale University Press.

Pressman, Jeffrey L., and Aaron B. Wildavsky. 1973. *Implementation* . . . Berkeley: University of California Press. (Revised in 1979 and 1984.)

Purdum, Todd S. 1996. "Clinton Orders Expanded Agent Orange Benefits," *New York Times* (May 29), pp. A1, A12.

Quade, Edward S. 1983. *Analysis for Public Decisions*. New York: American Elsevier.

Rivlin, Alice M. 1971. *Systematic Thinking for Social Action*. Washington, D.C.: Brookings Institution.

Sabatier, Paul A. 1988. "An Advocacy Coalition Framework of Policy Change and the Role of Policy-Oriented Learning Therein," *Policy Sciences* 21(2–3):129–168.

_____. 1991. "Towards Better Theories of the Policy Process," *PS: Political Science and Politics* 24(2) (June):147–156.

_____. 1993. "Policy Change over a Decade or More." In Paul A. Sabatier and Hank C. Jenkins-Smith, eds., *Policy Change and Learning: An Advocacy Coalition Approach*. Boulder: Westview Press.

Sabatier, Paul A., and Hank C. Jenkins-Smith, eds. 1993. *Policy Change and Learning: An Advocacy Coalition Approach*. Boulder: Westview Press.

Sabatier, Paul A., John Loomis, and Catherine McCarthy. 1995. "Hierarchical Controls, Professional Norms, Local Constituencies, and Budget Maximization: An Analysis of U.S. Forest Service Planning Decisions," *American Journal of Political Science* 39(1) (February):204–242.

Schön, Donald A., and Martin Rein. 1994. *Frame Reflection*. New York: BasicBooks.

Suchman, Edward A. 1967. *Evaluative Research*. New York: Russell Sage Foundation.

Titmuss, Richard. 1971. *The Gift Relationship*. New York: Pantheon Books of Random House.

Waldman, Steven. 1995. *The Bill*. New York: Penguin.

Weimer, David L., and Aidan R. Vining. 1989. *Policy Analysis: Concepts and Practice*. Englewood Cliffs, N.J.: Prentice-Hall.

PART II

Alternative Views of the Role of Rationality in the Policy Process

3

Institutional Rational Choice

An Assessment of the Institutional Analysis and Development Framework

ELINOR OSTROM

BACKGROUND

Paul Sabatier has asked me to do an assessment of institutional rational choice. Unfortunately, I think the field is now too broad for one person to do an assessment of all the work that might be covered by the term *institutional rational choice*. Instead of trying an assessment of such a broad array of literature, I will focus more specifically on the institutional analysis and development (IAD) framework that has evolved out of the work of many colleagues at the Workshop in Political Theory and Policy Analysis at Indiana University.

The publication of "The Three Worlds of Action: A Metatheoretical Synthesis of Institutional Approaches" (Kiser and Ostrom, 1982) represents the initial pub-

This chapter is based on a paper presented at the 1996 Annual Meetings of the American Political Science Association, San Francisco Hilton and Towers, San Francisco, 29 August–1 September 1996. An earlier version of part of this paper was presented to the Economic Development Institute of the World Bank, Curriculum Development Workshop, Washington, D.C., 6–7 December 1995. The author appreciates the support provided by the National Science Foundation (Grants SBR-93 19835 and SBR-95 21918) and the Ford Foundation (Grant 950-1160). Useful comments by Kathryn Firmin-Sellers, Maurice Garnier, Clark Gibson, Vincent Ostrom, Roger Parks, Margaret Polski, Eric Rasmusen, Paul Sabatier, Edella Schlager, James Walker, Tjip Walker, and Xin Zhang on earlier drafts are deeply appreciated. The thoughtful editing of Patty Dalecki is always appreciated.

lished attempt to develop a general framework to help integrate work undertaken by political scientists, economists, anthropologists, lawyers, social psychologists, and others interested in how institutions affect the incentives confronting individuals and their resultant behavior.[1] During the nearly fifteen years since this publication, the framework has been further developed and applied to the analysis of a diversity of empirical settings (E. Ostrom, 1986; E. Ostrom, Gardener, and Walker, 1994, ch. 2; Blomquist, 1992; Tang, 1992; Schlager, 1990; Oakerson, 1992). The elements involved in the framework are closely related to concepts that play an important role in related theories, such as those represented in the work of Douglass C. North, Oliver Williamson, and others in the "new institutional economics" tradition (see Eggertsson, 1990).

Two important aspects of the IAD framework were developed in the initial article. One aspect is the distinction among three tiers of decisionmaking and the relations among them: constitutional, collective choice, and operational decisions. The second is the elucidation of the fundamental elements that can be used for analysis of outcomes and their evaluation at any of the three tiers of decisionmaking. In this chapter, I will present an updated version of the framework in light of the additional work undertaken since 1982 and of theories and models consistent with this framework. I will conclude with a brief assessment of the utility of this tool for institutional analysis. Before I do this, however, I wish to indicate some of the difficulties that confront those interested in understanding incentives, institutions, and outcomes.

CHALLENGES

Various aspects of the IAD approach are clarified if one is aware of the difficulties to be overcome in undertaking any form of institutional analysis. Here is an initial list of what I consider the key difficulties involved in studying institutions:

1. The term *institution* refers to many different types of entities, including both organizations and the rules used to structure patterns of interaction within and across organizations.
2. Although the buildings in which organized entities are located are quite visible, institutions themselves are invisible.
3. To develop a coherent approach to studying diverse types of institutional arrangements, including markets, hierarchies, firms, families, voluntary associations, national governments, and international regimes, one needs multiple inputs from diverse disciplines.
4. Given the multiple languages used across disciplines, a coherent institutional framework is needed to allow for expression and comparison of diverse theories and models of theories applied to particular puzzles and problem settings.

5. Decisions made about rules at any one level are usually made within a structure of rules existing at a different level. Thus, institutional studies need to encompass multiple levels of analysis.

6. At any one level of analysis, combinations of rules, attributes of the world, and communities of individuals involved are combined in a configural rather than an additive manner.

Let us briefly discuss these issues before turning to the IAD approach.

Multiple Definitions of Institutions

It is hard to make much progress in the study of institutions if scholars define the term *institution* as meaning almost anything. A major confusion exists between scholars who use the term to refer to an organizational entity such as the U.S. Congress, a business firm, a political party, or a family and scholars who use the term to refer to the rules, norms, and strategies adopted by individuals operating within or across organizations. In this paper, I will use the term *institution* in the latter sense, to refer to the shared concepts used by humans in repetitive situations organized by rules, norms, and strategies (see Crawford and Ostrom, 1995). By *rules*, I mean shared prescriptions (must, must not, or may) that are mutually understood and predictably enforced in particular situations by agents responsible for monitoring conduct and for imposing sanctions. By *norms*, I mean shared prescriptions that tend to be enforced by the participants themselves through internally and externally imposed costs and inducements. By *strategies*, I mean the regularized plans that individuals make within the structure of incentives produced by rules, norms, and expectations of the likely behavior of others in a situation affected by relevant physical and material conditions.[2]

Invisibility of Institutions

One of the most difficult problems to overcome in the study of institutions is how to identify and measure them. Because institutions are fundamentally shared concepts, they exist in the minds of the participants and sometimes are shared as implicit knowledge rather than in an explicit and written form. One of the problems facing scholars and officials is learning how to recognize the presence of institutions on the ground. The primitive physical structures that embed property rights systems that farmers have constructed over time look flimsy to an engineer who considers real only structures built out of concrete and iron. These flimsy structures, however, are frequently used by individuals to allocate resource flows to participants according to rules that have been devised in tough constitutional and collective-choice bargaining situations over time.

In training researchers to identify and measure institutions, we stress the concept of rules-in-use rather than focusing on rules-in-form. Rules-in-use are referred to whenever someone new (such as a new employee or a child) is being socialized into an existing rule-ordered system of behavior. They are the dos and don'ts that one learns on the ground that may not exist in any written document. In some instances, they may actually be contrary to the dos and don'ts that are written in formal documents. Being armed with a set of questions concerning how X is done here and why Y is not done here is a very useful way of identifying rules-in-use, shared norms, and operational strategies.

Multiple Disciplines—Multiple Languages

Because regularized human behavior occurs within a wide diversity of rule-ordered situations that share structural features such as markets, hierarchies or firms, families, voluntary associations, national governments, and international regimes, there is no single discipline that addresses all questions important for the study of human institutions. Understanding the kinds of strategies and heuristics that humans adopt in diverse situations is enhanced by the study of anthropology, economics, game theory, history, law, philosophy, political science, psychology, public administration, and sociology. Scholars within these disciplines learn separate technical languages. Meaningful communication across the social sciences can be extremely difficult to achieve. When social scientists need to work with biologists and/or physical scientists, communication problems are even more difficult. One of the reasons for developing the IAD framework has been, therefore, to develop a common set of linguistic elements that can be used to analyze a wide diversity of problems.

Multiple Levels of Analysis

When individuals interact in repetitive settings, they may be in operational situations that directly affect the world, or they may be making decisions at other levels of analysis that eventually impinge on operational decisionmaking situations (Shepsle, 1989). Multiple sources of structure are located at diverse analytical levels as well as diverse geographic domains. Biologists took several centuries to learn how to separate the diverse kinds of relevant structures needed to analyze both communities and individual biological entities. Separating phenotypical structure from genotypical structure was part of the major Darwinian breakthrough that allowed biologists to achieve real momentum and cumulation during the past century. The nested structure of rules within rules, within still further rules, is a particularly difficult analytical problem to solve for those interested in the study of institutions. Studies conducted at a macro level (see Kaminski, 1992; V. Ostrom, 1997; Loveman, 1993; Sawyer, 1992) focus on constitutional structures. These, in turn, affect the type of collective-choice decisions as they eventually impinge on the day-to-day decisions of citizens and/or subjects. Studies conducted at a micro level (Firmin-Sellers, 1996; E. Ostrom, Gardner, and Walker, 1994) focus more on operational-level decisions as they are in turn affected by collective-choice and constitutional-choice rules, some, but not all, of which are under the control of those making operational decisions. Finding ways to communicate across these levels is a key challenge for all institutional theorists.

Configural Relationships

Successful analysis can cumulate rapidly when scholars have been able to analyze a problem by separating it into component parts that are analyzed independently and then recombining these parts additively. Many puzzles of interest to social scientists can be torn apart and recombined. Frequently, however, the impact on incentives and behavior of one type of rule is not independent of the configuration of other rules. Thus, the impact of changing one of the current rules that is part of a state "welfare system" depends on which other rules are also in effect. Changing the minimum outside income that one can earn before losing benefits from one program, for example, cannot be analyzed independently of the effect of income on benefits derived from other programs.[3] Similarly, analyzing the impact of changing the proportion of individuals who must agree prior to making an authoritative collective choice (e.g., 50 percent plus one) depends on the quorum rule in force. If a quorum rule specifying a low proportion of members is in effect, requiring two-thirds agreement may be a less stringent decision rule than a simple majority rule combined with a quorum rule requiring a high proportion of members. Ceteris paribus conditions are always essential for doing any theoretical work involving institutions. In the case of institutional analysis, one needs to know the value of other variables rather than simply asserting that they are held constant. This configural nature of rules makes institutional analysis a more difficult and complex enterprise than studies of phenomena that are strictly additive.

INSTITUTIONAL FRAMEWORKS, THEORIES, AND MODELS

Given the need for multiple disciplines, and hence multiple disciplinary languages, and given the multiple levels of analysis involved in studying configural relationships among rules, relevant aspects of the world, and cultural phenomena, the study of institutions does depend on theoretical work undertaken at three levels of specificity that are often confused with one another. These essential foundations are (1) frameworks, (2) theories, and (3) models. Analyses conducted at each level provide different degrees of specificity related to a particular problem.

The development and use of a general *framework* help to identify the elements and relationships among these elements that one needs to consider for institutional analysis. Frameworks organize diagnostic and prescriptive inquiry. They provide the most general list of variables that should be used to analyze all types of institutional arrangements. Frameworks provide a metatheoretical language that can be used to compare theories. They attempt to identify the *universal* elements that any theory relevant to the same kind of phenomena would need to include. Many differences in surface reality can result from the way these variables combine with or interact with one another. Thus, the elements contained in a framework help analysts generate the questions that need to be addressed when they first conduct an analysis.

The development and use of *theories* enable the analyst to specify which elements of the framework are particularly relevant to certain kinds of questions and to make general working assumptions about these elements. Thus, theories focus on a framework and make specific assumptions that are necessary for an analyst to diagnose a phenomenon, explain its processes, and predict outcomes. Several theories are usually compatible with any framework. Economic theory, game theory, transaction cost theory, social choice theory, covenantal theory, and theories of public goods and common-pool resources are all compatible with the IAD framework discussed in this chapter. In this chapter, I illustrate the framework primarily with reference to our work on the theory of common-pool resources.

The development and use of *models* make precise assumptions about a limited set of parameters and variables. Logic, mathematics, game theory, experimentation and simulation, and other means are used to explore systematically the consequences of these assumptions in a limited set of outcomes. Multiple models are compatible with most theories. A recent effort to understand the strategic structure of the games that irrigators play in differently organized irrigation systems, for example, developed four families of models just to begin to explore the likely consequences of different institutional and physical combinations relevant to understanding how successful farmer organizations arranged for monitoring and sanctioning activities (Weissing and Ostrom, 1991). This is one of the models we have developed for the precise analysis of a subpart of the theory of common-pool resources.

For policymakers and scholars interested in issues related to how different governance systems enable individuals to solve problems democratically, the IAD framework helps to organize diagnostic, analytical, and prescriptive capabilities. It also aids in the accumulation of knowledge from empirical studies and in the assessment of past efforts at reforms. Markets and hierarchies are frequently presented as fundamentally different "pure types" of organization. Not only are these types of institutional arrangements perceived to be different, but each is presumed to require its own explanatory theory. Scholars who attempt to explain behavior within markets use microeconomic theory, whereas scholars who attempt to explain behavior within hierarchies use political and sociological theory. Such a view precludes a more general explanatory framework and closely related theories that help analysts make cross-institutional comparisons and evaluations.

Without the capacity to undertake systematic, comparative institutional assessments, recommendations of reform may be based on naive ideas about which kinds of institutions are "good" or "bad" and not on an analysis of performance. One needs a common framework and family of theories in order to address questions of reforms and transitions. Particular models then help the analyst to deduce specific predictions about likely outcomes of highly simplified structures. Models are useful in policy analysis when they are well tailored to the particular problem at hand. Models can be used inappropriately when applied to the study of problematic situations that do not closely fit the assumptions of the model.

THE INSTITUTIONAL ANALYSIS
AND DEVELOPMENT FRAMEWORK

As indicated earlier, an institutional framework should identify the major types of structural variables that are present to some extent in *all* institutional arrangements, but whose values differ from one type of institutional arrangement to another. The IAD framework is a multitier conceptual map (see Figure 3.1). One part of the framework is the identification of an action arena, the resulting patterns of interactions and outcomes, and evaluating these outcomes (see right half of Figure 3.1). The problem could be at an operational tier where actors interact in light of the incentives they face to generate outcomes directly in the world. Examples of operational problems include:

- The task of designing the incentives of a voluntary environmental action group so as to overcome to some extent the free-rider problem;
- The challenge of organizing local users of a forest to contribute resources to the protection of local watersheds to improve soil quality and water storage; and
- The question of how to invest in irrigation infrastructures so that capital investments enhance, rather than detract from, the organizational capabilities of local farmers.

The problem could also be at a policy (or collective-choice) tier where decision-makers repeatedly have to make policy decisions within the constraints of a set of collective-choice rules. The policy decisions then affect the structure of arenas where individuals are making operational decisions and thus impacting directly on a physical world. The problem could as well be at a constitutional tier where decisions are made about who is eligible to participate in policymaking and about the rules that will be used to undertake policymaking.

The first step in analyzing a problem is to identify a conceptual unit—called an *action arena*—that can be utilized to analyze, predict, and explain behavior within institutional arrangements. Action arenas include an *action situation* and

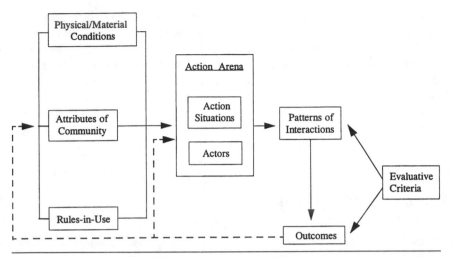

FIGURE 3.1   A Framework for Institutional Analysis
SOURCE: Adapted from Ostrom, Gardner, and Walker (1994, p. 37).

the *actors* in that situation. An action situation can be characterized by means of seven clusters of variables: (1) participants, (2) positions, (3) outcomes, (4) action-outcome linkages, (5) the control that participants exercise, (6) information, and (7) the costs and benefits assigned to outcomes. An actor (an individual or a corporate actor) includes assumptions about four clusters of variables:

1. The *resources* that an actor brings to a situation;
2. The *valuation* actors assign to states of the world and to actions;
3. The way actors acquire, process, retain, and use *knowledge contingencies and information;* and
4. The processes actors use for *selection* of particular courses of action.

The term *action arena* refers to the social space where individuals interact, exchange goods and services, solve problems, dominate one another, or fight (among the many things that individuals do in action arenas). A major proportion of theoretical work stops at this level and takes the variables specifying the situation and the motivational and cognitive structure of an actor as givens. Analysis proceeds toward the prediction of the likely behavior of individuals in such a structure.

An institutional analyst can take two additional steps after making an effort to understand the initial structure of an action arena. One step digs deeper and inquires into the factors that affect the structure of an action arena. From this vantage point, the action arena is viewed as a set of variables dependent upon other factors. These factors affecting the structure of an action arena include three clusters of variables: (1) the rules used by participants to order their relationships, (2) the attributes of states of the world that are acted upon in these arenas, and (3) the structure of the more general community within which any particular arena is placed (see Kiser and Ostrom, 1982). The next section of this chapter explicitly examines how shared understandings of rules, states of the world, and nature of the community affect the values of the variables characterizing action arenas.

Then one can move outward from action arenas to consider methods for explaining complex structures that link sequential and simultaneous action arenas to one another (see the left side of Figure 3.1).

DIAGNOSIS AND EXPLANATION WITHIN THE FRAME OF AN ACTION ARENA

As mentioned earlier, the term *action arena* refers to a complex conceptual unit containing one set of variables called an *action situation* and a second set of variables called an *actor*. One needs both components—the situation and the actors in the situation—to diagnose, explain, and predict actions and results.

An Action Situation

The term *action situation* is used to refer to an analytic concept that enables an analyst to isolate the immediate structure affecting a process of interest to the analyst for the purpose of explaining regularities in human actions and results, and potentially to reform them. A common set of variables used to describe the structure of an action situation includes (1) the set of participants, (2) the specific positions to be filled by participants, (3) the set of allowable actions and their linkage to outcomes, (4) the potential outcomes that are linked to individual sequences of actions, (5) the level of control each participant has over choice, (6) the information available to participants about the structure of the action situation, and (7) the costs and benefits—which serve as incentives and deterrents—assigned to actions and outcomes. In addition, whether a situation will occur once, a known finite number of times, or indefinitely affects the strategies of individuals. When one is explaining actions and cumulated results within the framework of an action arena, these variables are the "givens" that one works with to describe the structure of the situation. These are the common elements used in game theory to construct formal game models.

Most operational activities related to natural resources can be conceptualized as involving provision, production, appropriation, and assignment (see E. Ostrom, Gardner, and Walker, 1994; E. Ostrom, Schroeder, and Wynne, 1993). In an analysis of appropriation problems concerning overharvesting from a common-pool resource situation, for example, answers to the following questions are needed before analysis:

- *The set of participants:* Who and how many individuals withdraw resource units (e.g., fish, water, fodder) from this resource system?
- *The positions:* What positions exist (e.g., members of an irrigation association, water distributors-guards, and a chair)?
- *The set of allowable actions:* Which types of harvesting technologies are
  used? (E.g., are chain saws used to harvest timber? Are there open and
  closed seasons? Do fishers return fish smaller than some limit to the
  water?)
- *The potential outcomes:* What geographic region and what events in that
  region are affected by participants in these positions? What chain of
  events links actions to outcomes?
- *The level of control over choice:* Do appropriators take the above actions
  on their own initiative, or do they confer with others? (E.g., before en-
  tering the forest to cut fodder, does an appropriator obtain a permit?)
- *The information available:* How much information do appropriators
  have about the condition of the resource itself, about other appropriators' cost and benefit functions, and about how their actions cumulate
  into joint outcomes?
- *The costs and benefits of actions and outcomes:* How costly are various
  actions to each type of appropriator, and what kinds of benefits can be
  achieved as a result of various group outcomes?

The Actor: Theories and Models of the Individual

The *actor* in a situation can be thought of as a single individual or as a group
functioning as a corporate actor. The term *action* refers to those human behaviors to which the acting individual attaches a subjective and instrumental meaning. All analysts of microbehavior use an implicit or explicit theory or model of
the actors in situations in order to derive inferences about the likely behavior of
each actor in a situation (and thus about the pattern of joint results that may be
produced). The analyst must make assumptions about how and what participants value; what resources, information, and beliefs they have; what their information-processing capabilities are; and what internal mechanisms they use to decide upon strategies.

For many problems, it is useful to accept the classical political economy view
that an individual's choice of strategy in any particular situation depends on
how he or she perceives and weighs the benefits and costs of various strategies
and their likely outcomes (Radnitzky, 1987). The most well-established formal
model of the individual used in institutional analysis is *Homo economicus* as developed in neoclassical economics and game theory. To use *Homo economicus*,
one assumes that actors have complete and well-ordered preferences and complete information, and that they maximize the net value of expected returns to

themselves. All of these assumptions are controversial and are being challenged on many fronts. Many institutional analysts tend to use a broader conception of individual actors. Many stress that perceived costs and benefits include the time and resources devoted to establishing and maintaining relationships (Williamson, 1979), as well as the value that individuals attach to establishing a reputation for being reliable and trustworthy (Breton and Wintrobe, 1982).

Alternatively, one could assume that the individuals who calculate benefits and costs are fallible learners who vary in terms of the number of other persons whose perceived benefits and costs are important to them and in terms of their personal commitment to keeping promises and honoring forms of reciprocity extended to them (E. Ostrom, 1990). Fallible learners can, and often do, make mistakes. Settings differ, however, in whether the institutional incentives involved encourage people to learn from these mistakes. Fallibility and the capacity to learn can thus be viewed as assumptions of a more general theory of the individual. One can then presume that the various institutional arrangements that individuals use in governing and managing common-pool resources (or other problematic situations) offer them different incentives and opportunities to learn. In some settings, the incentives lead them to repeat the mistakes of the past. In others, the rate of effective learning about how to make a resource sustainable over time is rapid. In all cases, the repertoire of institutional design principles known to individuals also affects their capacity to change their institutions in order to improve learning and other outcomes when faced with repeated failures.

When fallible, learning individuals interact in frequently repeated and simple situations, it is possible to model them as if they had complete information about the variables relevant to making choices in those situations. In highly competitive environments, we can make the further assumption that the individuals who survive the selective pressure of the environment act as if they are maximizers of a key variable associated with survival in that environment (e.g., profits or fitness) (Alchian, 1950; Dosi and Egidi, 1987). When individuals face a relatively simple decision situation where institutions generate accurate information about the variables relevant to a particular problem, that problem can be adequately represented as a straightforward, constrained maximization problem.

The most fully developed, explicit theories of individual choice compatible with the IAD framework—game theory and neoclassical economic theory—involve extreme assumptions such as unlimited computational capability and full maximization of net benefits. For some field settings, these theories generate empirically confirmed explanatory and diagnostic results. When analyzing commodity auction markets that are run repeatedly in a setting where property rights are well defined and enforced at a relatively low cost to buyers and sellers, theories of market behavior and outcome based on complete information and maximization of profits predict outcomes very well. Using these assumptions about individual choice turns out to be a very useful way of doing institutional analysis when the problematic settings closely approximate this type of very constrained and competitive choice.

Many of the situations of interest in understanding common-pool resources, however, are uncertain and complex and lack the selective pressure and information-generating capabilities of a competitive market. Therefore, one can substitute the assumption of bounded rationality—that persons are intendedly rational but only limitedly so—for the assumptions of perfect information and utility maximization used in axiomatic choice theory (see Simon, 1947/1965, 1972; Williamson, 1985; E. Ostrom, Gardner, and Walker, 1994, ch. 9). Information search is costly, and the information-processing capabilities of human beings are limited. Individuals, therefore, often must make choices based on incomplete knowledge of all possible alternatives and their likely outcomes. With incomplete information and imperfect information-processing capabilities, all individuals may make mistakes in choosing strategies designed to realize a set of goals (V. Ostrom, 1986). Over time, however, they can acquire a greater understanding of their situation and adopt strategies that result in higher returns. Reciprocity may develop, rather than strictly narrow, short-term pursuit of self-interest (Hyden, 1990; Oakerson, 1993).

Individuals do not always have access to the same information known by others with whom they interact. For example, how much any one individual contributes to a joint undertaking is often difficult for others to judge. When joint outcomes depend on multiple actors contributing inputs that are costly and difficult to measure, incentives exist for individuals to behave opportunistically (Williamson, 1975). Opportunism—deceitful behavior intended to improve one's own welfare at the expense of others—may take many forms, from inconsequential, perhaps unconscious, shirking to a carefully calculated effort to defraud others with whom one is engaged in ongoing relationships. The opportunism of individuals who may say one thing and do something else further compounds the problem of uncertainty in a given situation. Moreover, the level of opportunistic behavior that may occur in any setting is affected by the norms and institutions used to govern relationships in that setting, as well as by attributes of the decision environment itself.

Predicting Outcomes Within an Action Arena

Depending upon the analytical structure of a situation and the particular assumptions about the actor used, the analyst makes strong or weak inferences about results. In tightly constrained, one-shot, action situations under conditions of complete information, where participants are motivated to select particular strategies or chains of actions that jointly lead to stable equilibria, an analyst can frequently make strong inferences and specific predictions about likely patterns of behavior and outcomes.

When there is no limit on the number of appropriators from a common-pool resource or on the amount of harvesting activities they undertake, for example, one can develop a mathematical model of an open-access, common-pool resource (see, for example, E. Ostrom et al., 1994). When the net benefits of harvesting to each entrant increase for the initial set of resource units sought and decrease thereafter, each appropriator acting independently tends to make individual decisions that jointly yield a deficient (but stable) equilibrium. A model of an open-access, common-pool resource generates a clear prediction of a race to use up the resource, leading to high social costs. Both field research and laboratory experimental research strongly support the predictions of overuse and potential destruction of open-access, common-pool resources where appropriators do not share access to collective-choice arenas in which to change the open-access structure they face (E. Ostrom et al., 1994).

Many arenas, however, do not generate such unambiguous results. Instead of making completely independent or autonomous decisions, individuals may be embedded in communities where initial norms of fairness and conservation may change the structure of the situation dramatically. Within these situations, participants may adopt a broader range of strategies. Further, they may change their strategies over time as they learn about the results of past actions. The institutional analyst examining these more open, less-constrained situations makes weaker inferences and predicts the patterns of outcomes that are more-or-less likely to result from a particular type of situation. In laboratory experiments, for example, giving subjects in a common-pool resource situation opportunities to communicate generally increases the joint outcomes they achieve (see E. Ostrom et al., 1994, and citations contained therein). In field settings, one can assume that helping individuals engage in face-to-face discussions will increase the probability of improved outcomes, but there are many historical factors that also affect this likelihood. Even weak inferences about likely results have an importance in specifying general tendencies. At times, it is possible to predict what will *not* occur. Predictions of impossibilities are very useful when one is contemplating reforms.

In field settings, it is hard to tell where one action arena starts and another stops. Life continues in what appears to be a seamless web as individuals move from home to market to work (action situations typically characterized by reciprocity, by exchange, or by team problem solving or command). Further, within arenas, choices of actions *within* a set of rules as contrasted to choices *among* future rules are frequently made without a recognition that the level of action has shifted. So, when a "boss" says to an "employee," "How about changing the way we do X?" and the two discuss options and jointly agree upon a better way, they have shifted from taking actions *within* previously established rules to making decisions *about* the rules structuring future actions. In other words, in IAD language, they have shifted to a collective-choice arena.

Evaluating Outcomes

In addition to predicting outcomes, the institutional analyst may evaluate the outcomes that are being achieved as well as the likely set of outcomes that could be achieved under alternative institutional arrangements. Evaluative criteria are applied to both the outcomes and the processes of achieving outcomes. Although there are many potential evaluative criteria, let us briefly focus on (1) economic efficiency, (2) equity through fiscal equivalence, (3) redistributional equity, (4) accountability, (5) conformance to general morality, and (6) adaptability.

Economic Efficiency. Economic efficiency is determined by the magnitude of the change in the flow of net benefits associated with an allocation or reallocation of resources. The concept of efficiency plays a central role in studies estimating the benefits and costs or rates of return to investments, which are often used to determine the economic feasibility or desirability of public policies. When considering alternative institutional arrangements, therefore, it is crucial to consider how revisions in the rules affecting participants will alter behavior and hence the allocation of resources.

Fiscal Equivalence. There are two principal means of assessing equity: (1) on the basis of the equality between individuals' contributions to an effort and the benefits they derive and (2) on the basis of differential abilities to pay. The concept of equity that underlies an exchange economy holds that those who benefit from a service should bear the burden of financing that service. Perceptions of fiscal equivalence or a lack thereof can affect the willingness of individuals to contribute toward the development and maintenance of resource systems.

Redistributional Equity. Policies that redistribute resources to poorer individuals are of considerable importance. Thus, although efficiency would dictate that scarce resources be used where they produce the greatest net benefit, equity goals may temper this objective, and the result is the provision of facilities that benefit particularly needy groups. Likewise, redistributional objectives may conflict with the goal of achieving fiscal equivalence.

Accountability. In a democratic polity, officials should be accountable to citizens concerning the development and use of public facilities and natural resources. Concern for accountability need not conflict greatly with efficiency and equity goals. Indeed, achieving efficiency requires that information about the preferences of citizens be available to decisionmakers, as does achieving accountability. Institutional arrangements that effectively aggregate this information assist in realizing efficiency at the same time that they serve to increase accountability and to promote the achievement of redistributional objectives.

Conformance to General Morality.   In addition to accountability, one may wish to evaluate the level of general morality fostered by a particular set of institutional arrangements. Are those who are able to cheat and go undetected able to obtain very high payoffs? Are those who keep promises more likely to be rewarded and advanced in their careers? How do those who repeatedly interact within a set of institutional arrangements learn to relate to one another over the long term?

Adaptability.   Finally, unless institutional arrangements are able to respond to ever-changing environments, the sustainability of resources and investments is likely to suffer. Rural areas of developing countries are often faced with natural disasters and highly localized special circumstances. If an institutional arrangement is too inflexible to cope with these unique conditions, it is unlikely to prosper. For example, if an irrigation system is centrally controlled and allocates only a specific amount of resources to annual and periodic maintenance, it may not be able to meet the special needs associated with a major flood that destroys a section of the canal system.

Trade-offs are often necessary in using performance criteria as a basis for selecting from alternative institutional arrangements. It is particularly difficult to choose between the goals of efficiency and redistributional equity. The trade-off issue arises most explicitly in considerations of alternative methods of funding public projects. Economically efficient pricing of the use of an existing resource or facility should reflect only the incremental maintenance costs and any external or social costs associated with its use. This is the well-known, efficiency pricing principle that requires that prices equal the marginal costs of usage. The principle is especially problematic in the case of goods with nonsubtractability attributes. In such instances, the marginal cost of another user's utilizing the good is zero; hence, the efficient price is also zero. Zero user prices, however, require that all sources of resource mobilization be tax-based and thereby induce other kinds of perverse incentives and potential inefficiencies. Evaluating how institutional arrangements compare across overall criteria is quite a challenge. Analytical examination of the likely trade-offs between intermediate costs is valuable in attempts to understand comparative institutional performance (see E. Ostrom, Schroeder, and Wynne, 1993, ch. 5).

EXPLANATION: VIEWING ACTION ARENAS
AS DEPENDENT VARIABLES

Underlying the way analysts conceptualize action arenas are implicit assumptions about the *rules* individuals use to order their relationships, about attributes of *states of the world and their transformations*, and about the *attributes of the com-*

munity within which the arena occurs. Some analysts are not interested in the role of these underlying variables and focus only on a particular arena whose structure is given. On the other hand, institutional analysts may be more interested in one factor affecting the structure of arenas than they are interested in others. Sociologists tend to be more interested in how shared value systems affect the ways humans organize their relationships with one another. Environmentalists tend to focus on various ways that physical and biological systems interact and create opportunities or constraints on the situation human beings face. Political scientists tend to focus more on how specific combinations of rules affect incentives. Rules, states of the world, and the nature of the community all jointly affect the types of actions that individuals can take, the benefits and costs of these actions and resulting outcomes, and the likely outcomes achieved.

The Concept of Rules

Rules are shared understandings among those involved that refer to enforced prescriptions about what actions (or states of the world) are *required, prohibited,* or *permitted.*[4] All rules are the result of implicit or explicit efforts to achieve order and predictability among humans by creating classes of persons (positions) that are then required, permitted, or forbidden to take classes of actions in relation to required, permitted, or forbidden states of the world (Crawford and Ostrom, 1995; V. Ostrom, 1991).

With governance, one needs to ask where the rules that individuals use in action situations originate. In an open and democratic governance system, there are many sources of the rules that individuals use in everyday life. It is not considered illegal or improper for individuals to organize themselves and craft their own rules, if the activities they engage in are legal. In addition to the legislation and regulations of a formal central government, there are apt to be laws passed by regional, local, and special governments. Within private firms and voluntary associations, individuals are authorized to adopt many different rules about who is a member of the firm or association, how profits (benefits) are to be shared, and how decisions will be made. Each family constitutes its own rule-making body.

When individuals genuinely participate in the crafting of multiple layers of rules, some of that crafting will occur using pen and paper. Much of it, however, will occur as problem-solving individuals interact trying to figure out how to do a better job in the future than they have done in the past. Colleagues in a work team are crafting their own rules when they might say to one another, "How about if you do A in the future, and I will do B, and before we ever make a decision about C again, we both discuss it and make a joint decision?" In a democratic society, problem-solving individuals do this all the time. They also participate in less fluid decisionmaking arrangements, including elections to select legislators.

Thus, when we do a deeper institutional analysis, we attempt first to understand the working rules that individuals use in making decisions. Working rules are the set of rules to which participants would make reference if asked to explain and justify their actions to fellow participants. Although following a rule may become a "social habit," it is possible to make participants consciously aware of the rules they use to order their relationships. Individuals can consciously decide to adopt a different rule and change their behavior to conform to such a decision. Over time, behavior in conformance with a new rule may itself become habitual (see Shimanoff, 1980; Toulmin, 1974; Harré, 1974). The capacity of humans to use complex cognitive systems to order their own behavior at a relatively subconscious level makes it difficult for empirical researchers to ascertain what the working rules for an ongoing action arena may be.

Once we understand the working rules, then, we attempt to understand where those rules come from. In a system governed by a "rule of law," the general legal framework in use will have its source in actions taken in constitutional, legislative, and administrative settings augmented by decisions taken by individuals in many different particular settings. In other words, the rules-in-form are consistent with the rules-in-use (Sproule-Jones, 1993). In a system that is not governed by a "rule of law," there may be central laws and considerable effort made to enforce them, but individuals attempt to evade rather than obey the law.

Rule-following or conforming actions are not as predictable as biological or physical behavior explained by scientific laws. All rules are formulated in human language. Therefore, rules share the problems of lack of clarity, misunderstanding, and change that typify any language-based phenomenon (V. Ostrom, 1980, 1997). Words are always more simple than the phenomenon to which they refer.

The stability of rule-ordered actions depends upon the shared meaning assigned to words used to formulate a set of rules. If no shared meaning exists when a rule is formulated, confusion will exist about what actions are required, permitted, or forbidden. Regularities in actions cannot result if those who must repeatedly interpret the meaning of a rule within action situations arrive at multiple interpretations. Because "rules are not self-formulating, self-determining, or self-enforcing" (V. Ostrom, 1980, p. 342), it is human agents who formulate them, apply them in particular situations, and attempt to enforce performance consistent with them. Even if shared meaning exists at the time of the acceptance of a rule, transformations in technology, in shared norms, and in circumstances more generally change the events to which rules apply: "Applying language to changing configurations of development increases the ambiguities and threatens the shared criteria of choice with an erosion of their appropriate meaning" (V. Ostrom, 1980, p. 342).

What rules are important for institutional analysis? A myriad of specific rules are used in structuring complex action arenas. Scholars have been trapped into endless cataloging of rules not related to a method of classification most useful for theoretical explanations. But classification is a necessary step in developing a science. Anyone attempting to define a useful typology of rules must be concerned that the classification is more than a method for imposing superficial order onto an extremely large set of seemingly disparate rules. The way we have tackled this problem using the IAD framework is to classify rules according to their impact on the elements of an action situation.

Rule Configurations

A first step toward identifying the working rules can be made, then, by overtly examining how working rules affect each of the variables of an action situation. A set of working rules that affect these variables should constitute the minimal but necessary set of rules needed to offer an explanation of actions and results based on the working rules used by participants to order their relationships within an action arena. Because states of the world and their transformations and the nature of a community also affect the structure of an action situation, working rules alone never provide both a necessary and a sufficient explanation of the structure of an action situation and results.

If this view of the task is adopted, seven types of working rules can be said to affect the structure of an action situation. These are *entry and exit rules, position rules, scope rules, authority rules, aggregation rules, information rules,* and *payoff rules.* The cumulative effect of these seven types of rules affects the seven elements of an action situation.

Entry and exit rules affect the number of *participants,* their attributes and resources, whether they can enter freely, and the conditions they face for leaving. Position rules establish *positions* in the situation. Authority rules assign sets of *actions* that participants in positions at particular nodes must, may, or may not take. Scope rules delimit the *potential outcomes* that can be affected and, working backward, the actions linked to specific outcomes. Authority rules, combined with the scientific laws about the relevant states of the world being acted upon, determine the shape of the decision tree, that is, the *action-outcome linkages.* Aggregation rules affect the level of *control* that a participant in a position exercises in the selection of an action at a node. Information rules affect the *knowledge-contingent information sets* of participants. Payoff rules affect the *benefits and costs* that will be assigned to particular combinations of actions and outcomes, and they establish the incentives and deterrents for action. The set of working rules is a *configuration* in the sense that the effect of a change in one rule may depend upon the other rules-in-use.

Let us return to the example of conducting an analysis of common-pool resources discussed earlier. Now we will focus on a series of questions that are intended to help the analyst get at the rules-in-use that help structure an action situation. Thus, to understand these rules, one would begin to ask questions such as:

- *Entry and exit rules:* Are the appropriators from this resource limited to local residents; to one group defined by ethnicity, race, caste, gender, or family structure; to those who win a lottery; to those who have obtained a permit; to those who own required assets (such as a fishing berth or land); or in some other way limited to a class of individuals that is bounded? Is a new participant allowed to join a group by some kind of entry fee or initiation? Must an appropriator give up rights to harvest upon migrating to another location?

- *Position rules*: How does someone move from being just a "member" of a group of appropriators to someone who has a specialized task, such as a water distributor-guard?
- *Scope rules*: What understandings do these appropriators and others have about the authorized or forbidden geographic or functional domains? Do any maps exist showing who can appropriate from which region? Are there understandings about resource units that are "off-limits" (e.g., the historical rules in some sections of Africa that particular acacia trees could not be cut down even on land owned privately or communally)?
- *Authority rules*: What understandings do appropriators have about mandatory, authorized, or forbidden harvesting technologies? For fishers, must net size be of a particular grossness? Must forest users use some cutting tools and not others? What choices do various types of monitors have related to the actions they can take?
- *Aggregation rules*: What understandings exist concerning the rules affecting the choice of harvesting activities? Do certain actions require prior permission from, or agreement of, others?
- *Information rules*: What information must be held secret, and what information must be made public?
- *Payoff rules*: How large are the sanctions that can be imposed for breaking any of the rules identified above? How is conformance to rules monitored? Who is responsible for sanctioning nonconformers? How reliably are sanctions imposed? Are any positive rewards offered to appropriators for any actions they can take? (e.g., is someone who is an elected official relieved of labor duties?)

The problem for the field researcher is that many rules-in-use are not written down. Nor can the field researcher simply be a survey worker asking a random sample of respondents about their rules. Many of the rules-in-use are not even conceptualized by participants as rules. In settings where the rules-in-use have evolved over long periods of time and are understood implicitly by participants, obtaining information about rules-in-use requires spending time at a site and learning how to ask nonthreatening, context-specific questions about rule configurations.[5]

Attributes of States of the World: Physical and Material Conditions

Although a rule configuration affects all of the elements of an action situation, some of the variables of an action situation are also affected by attributes of the physical and material world. What actions are physically possible, what outcomes can be produced, how actions are linked to outcomes, and what is contained in the actors' information sets are affected by the world being acted upon in a situation. The same set of rules may yield entirely different types of action situations depending upon the types of events in the world being acted upon by participants.

The attributes of states of the world and their transformation are explicitly examined when the analyst self-consciously asks a series of questions about how the world being acted upon in a situation affects the outcome, action sets, action-outcome linkages, and information sets in that situation. The relative importance of the rule configuration and states of the world in structuring an action situation varies dramatically across different types of settings. The rule configuration almost totally constitutes some games, like chess, where physical attributes are relatively unimportant. The relative importance of working rules to attributes of the world also varies dramatically within action situations considered part of the public sector. Rules define and constrain voting behavior inside a legislature more than attributes of the world. Voting can be accomplished by raising hands, by paper ballots, by calling for the ayes and nays, by marching before an official counter, or by installing computer terminals for each legislator, on which votes are registered. However, in regard to organizing communication within a legislature, attributes of the world strongly affect the available options. The principle that only one person can be heard and understood at a time in any one forum strongly affects the capacity of legislators to communicate effectively with one another (see V. Ostrom, 1987).

Let us consider several attributes that are frequently used to distinguish goods and services that are more effectively provided by diverse institutional arrangements. Goods that are generally considered "public goods" yield nonsubtractive benefits that can be enjoyed jointly and simultaneously by many people who are hard to exclude from obtaining these benefits. Common-pool resources yield benefits where beneficiaries are hard to exclude but each person's use of a resource system subtracts units of that resource from a finite total available for harvesting.

Excludability and the Free-Rider Problem.   When it is difficult or costly to exclude beneficiaries from a good once it is produced, it is frequently assumed that such a good must be provided publicly, rather than privately. When the benefits of a good are available to a group, whether or not members of the group contribute to the provision of the good, that good is characterized by problems with excludability. Where exclusion is costly, those wishing to provide a good or service face a potential free-rider or collective-action problem (Olson, 1965). Individuals who gain from the maintenance of an irrigation system, for example, may not wish to contribute labor or taxes to maintenance activities, hoping that others will bear the burden. This is not to say that all individuals will free-ride whenever they can. A strong incentive exists to be a free-rider in all situations where potential beneficiaries cannot easily be excluded for failing to contribute to the provision of a good or service.

When it is costly to exclude individuals from enjoying benefits from a common-pool resource or an infrastructure facility, private, profit-seeking entrepreneurs, who must recoup their investments through quid pro quo exchanges, have few incentives to provide such services on their own initiative. Excludability problems can thus lead to the problem of free riding, which in turn leads to underinvestment in capital and its maintenance.

Public sector provision of common-pool resources or infrastructure facilities raises additional problems in determining preferences and organizing finances. When exclusion is of low cost to the supplier, preferences are revealed as a result of many quid pro quo transactions. Producers learn about preferences through the consumers' willingness to pay for various goods offered for sale. Where exclusion is difficult, designing mechanisms that honestly reflect beneficiaries' preferences and their willingness to pay is complex, regardless of whether the providing unit is organized in the public or the private sphere. In very small groups, those affected are usually able to discuss their preferences and constraints face to face and to reach a rough consensus. In larger groups, decisions about infrastructure are apt to be made through mechanisms such as voting or the delegation of authority to public officials. The extensive literature on voting systems demonstrates how difficult it is to translate individual preferences into collective choices that adequately reflect individual views (Arrow, 1951; Shepsle, 1979; Buchanan and Tullock, 1962).

Another attribute of some goods with excludability problems is that once they are provided, consumers may have no choice whatsoever as to whether they will consume. An example is the public spraying of insects. If an individual does not want this public service to be provided, there are even stronger incentives not to comply with a general tax levy. Thus, compliance with a broad financing instrument may, in turn, depend upon the legitimacy of the public-choice mechanism used to make provision decisions.

Subtractability of the Flow.   Jointly used infrastructure facilities can generate a flow of services that is entirely subtractable upon consumption by one user; in other instances, consumption by one does not subtract from the flow of services available to others. The withdrawal of a quantity of water from an irrigation canal by one farmer means that there is that much less water for anyone else to use. Most agricultural uses of water are fully subtractive, whereas many other uses of water—such as for power generation or navigation—are not. Most of the water that passes through a turbine to generate power, for instance, can be used again downstream. When the use of a flow of services by one individual subtracts from what is available to others, and when the flow is scarce relative to demand, users will be tempted to try to obtain as much as they can of the flow for fear that it will not be available later.

Effective rules are required if scarce, fully subtractive service flows are to be allocated productively. Charging prices for subtractive services obviously constitutes one such allocation mechanism. Sometimes, however, it is not feasible to price services. In these instances, some individuals will be able to grab considerably more of the subtractive services than others, thereby leading to noneconomic uses of the flow and high levels of conflict among users.

Allocation rules also affect the incentives of users to maintain a system. Farmers located at the tail end of an irrigation system that lacks effective allocation rules have little motivation to contribute to the maintenance of that system because they only occasionally receive their share of water. Similarly, farmers located at the head end of such a system are not motivated to provide maintenance services voluntarily because they will receive disproportionate shares of the water whether or not the system is well maintained (E. Ostrom, 1996b).

Consequently, for common-pool resources whose flows are highly subtractive, institutional arrangements related to the allocation of the flow of services are intimately tied to the sustainability of the resource. It is highly unlikely that one can achieve sustainability without careful attention to the efficiency, fairness, and enforceability of the rules specifying who can appropriate how much of the service flow, at what times and places, and under what conditions. Furthermore, unless responsibilities are linked in a reasonable fashion to benefits obtained, the beneficiaries themselves will resist efforts to insist that they take responsibilities.

Additional Attributes.   In addition to these general attributes of physical and material conditions that affect the incentives of participants, resource systems are also characterized by a diversity of other attributes that affect how rules combine with physical and material conditions to generate positive or negative incentives. Whether resource units are *mobile* or *stationary* and whether *storage* is available somewhere in a system affect the problems that individuals governing and managing common-pool resources face (Schlager, Blomquist, and Tang, 1994). The problems of regulating a lobster fishery, for example, are much simpler than those of regulating a salmon fishery. Similarly, allocating water predictably and efficiently is easier to achieve when there is some storage in the system than when it is a run-of-the-river system.

If a natural resource system is renewable, such as many groundwater basins, the relevant time horizon for sustaining use is very long, and achieving appropriate rules may mean the difference between creating a sustainable conjunctive-use system and destroying a groundwater basin. Devising an effective set of rules for regulating the use of an oil pool, on the other hand, involves determining an optimal path for mining a resource. The cost of withdrawing the last units of oil will be much higher if producers have not coordinated their withdrawal patterns, but the lack of a future may produce insufficient incentives to achieve adequate regulation early in the development phase.

The size of a resource system can also have a major impact on the incentives facing participants. The length and slope of a main canal of an irrigation system affect not only the cost of its maintenance but also the strategic bargaining that exists between headenders and tailenders on an irrigation system (Lam, 1994; E. Ostrom, 1996b). Increasing the number of participants is associated with increased transaction costs. How steeply the costs rise depends, to a large extent, on the rules-in-use and the heterogeneity of the users.

The productivity, predictability, and patchiness of a resource affect the likelihood that private-property arrangements will be successful and enhance the likelihood that common-property arrangements will be necessary (Netting, 1982). Similarly, the resilience of a multispecies ecosystem affects the sensitivity of the system both to the rules used to govern the particular system and to changes in economic or environmental conditions elsewhere (Holling, 1994). These additional attributes are slowly being integrated into a body of coherent theory about the impact of physical and material conditions on the structure of the situations that individuals face and their resulting incentives and behavior. Analysts diagnosing resource problems need to be sensitive to the very large difference among resource settings and the need to tailor rules to diverse combinations of attributes rather than trying to achieve some assumed uniformity across all resources in a particular sector within a country.

Attributes of the Community

A third set of variables that affect the structure of an action arena relates to the community. The attributes of a community that are important in affecting the structure of an action arena include the norms of behavior generally accepted in the community, the level of common understanding that potential participants share about the structure of particular types of action arenas, the extent of homogeneity in the preferences of those living in a community, and the distribution of resources among those affected. The term *culture* is frequently applied to this bundle of variables.

For example, when all appropriators from a common-pool resource share a common set of values and interact with one another in a multiplex set of arrangements, the probabilities of their developing adequate rules and norms to govern resources are much greater (Taylor, 1987). The importance of building a reputation for keeping one's word is important in such a community, and the cost of developing monitoring and sanctioning mechanisms is relatively low. If the appropriators from a resource come from many different communities and are distrustful of one another, the task of devising and sustaining effective rules is substantially more difficult.

Whether individuals use a written vernacular language to express their ideas, develop a common understanding, share learning, and explain the foundation of their social order is also a crucial variable of relevance to institutional analysis (V.

Ostrom, 1997). Without a written vernacular language, individuals face considerably more difficulties in accumulating their own learning in a usable form to transmit from one generation to the next.

LINKING ACTION ARENAS

In addition to analysis that digs deeper into the factors affecting individual action arenas, an important development in institutional analysis is the examination of linked arenas. Whereas the concept of a "single" arena may include large numbers of participants and complex chains of action, most of social reality is composed of multiple arenas linked sequentially or simultaneously. The chapters in this volume that address policy subsystems examine multiple linked action arenas at all three levels of analysis (see Chapter 6 by Sabatier and Jenkins-Smith).

When individuals wish to intervene to change the structure of incentives and deterrents faced by participants in socially constructed realities to guide (or control) participants toward a different pattern of results, they do so by attempting to change the rules participants use to order their interactions within particular types of action arenas. Some interesting and important institutional arrangements for coordinating complex chains of actions among large numbers of actors involve multiple organizations competing with one another according to a set of rules. Markets are the most frequently studied institutional arrangements that achieve coordination by relying primarily on rule-governed competitive relationships among organizations. Rule-governed competition among two or more political parties is considered by many analysts an important requisite for a democratic polity. Less studied, but potentially as important a means for achieving responsiveness and efficiency in producing public goods and services, are arrangements that allow rule-ordered competition among two or more potential *producers* of public goods and services.

MULTIPLE LEVELS OF ANALYSIS

Besides multiple and nested action arenas at any one level of analysis, nesting of arenas also occurs across several levels of analysis. All rules are nested in another set of rules that define how the first set of rules can be changed. The nesting of rules within rules at several levels is similar to the nesting of computer languages at several levels. What can be done at a higher level will depend on the capabilities and limits of the rules (or the software) at that level and at a deeper level. Whenever one addresses questions about *institutional change*, as contrasted to action within institutional constraints, it is necessary to recognize the following:

1. Changes in the rules used to order action at one level occur within a currently "fixed" set of rules at a deeper level.

2. Changes in deeper-level rules usually are more difficult and more costly to accomplish; thus, there is an increased stability in the mutual expectations of individuals interacting according to a set of rules.

It is useful to distinguish three levels of rules that cumulatively affect the actions taken and outcomes obtained in any setting (Kiser and Ostrom, 1982). *Operational rules* directly affect day-to-day decisions made by the participants in any setting. *Collective-choice rules* affect operational activities and results through their effects in determining who is eligible and the specific rules to be used in changing operational rules. *Constitutional-choice rules* affect operational activities and their effects in determining who is eligible and the rules to be used in crafting the set of collective-choice rules that in turn affect the set of operational rules. There is even a "metaconstitutional" level underlying all the others that is not frequently analyzed. One can think of the linkages among these rules and the related level of analysis as shown in Figure 3.2.

At each level of analysis, there may be one or more arenas in which the types of decisions made at that level will occur. In the collective-choice, constitutional, and metaconstitutional situations, activities involve prescribing, invoking, monitoring, applying, and enforcing rules (Lasswell and Kaplan, 1950; Oakerson, 1994). The concept of an *arena*, as described earlier, does not imply a formal setting but can include such formal settings as legislatures and courts. Policymaking (or governance) regarding the rules that will be used to regulate operational-level choices is usually carried out in one or more collective-choice arenas, as shown in Figure 3.3.

USES OF THE IAD FRAMEWORK

The IAD framework is thus a general language about how rules, physical and material conditions, and attributes of community affect the structure of action arenas, the incentives that individuals face, and the resulting outcomes. It has been used extensively in teaching (see, for example, E. Ostrom, V. Ostrom, and McGinnis, 1996), as well as in the metalanguage for analyzing diverse theories. In the early 1970s, when the IAD framework was first being developed, we were trying to understand how the diverse paradigms in political science affected the way we conceptualized both public administration and metropolitan organization (see V. Ostrom and E. Ostrom, 1971; E. Ostrom, 1972). Then, for a decade and a half, we used the nascent framework as a foundation for the conduct of an extensive number of empirical studies of police service delivery in metropolitan areas. Since the late 1980s, the IAD framework has been used as the language to develop a theory of common-pool resources and to link formal models of appropriation and monitoring with empirical work conducted in an experimental laboratory and in field settings (see, for example, E. Ostrom et al., 1994).

In crafting empirical studies using the IAD framework, a key question has always been the appropriate units and levels of analysis for any particular type of

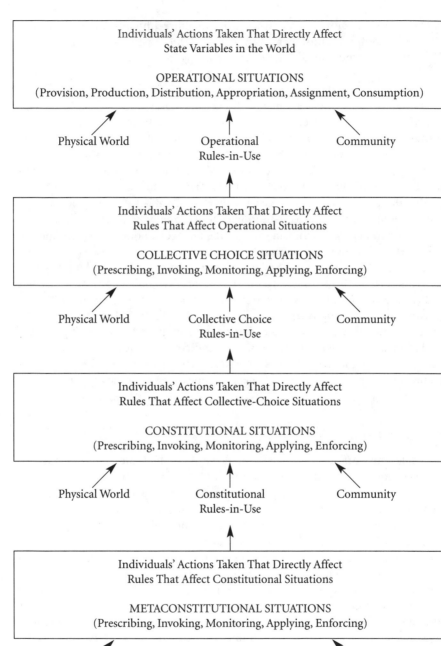

FIGURE 3.2   Levels of Analysis and Outcomes

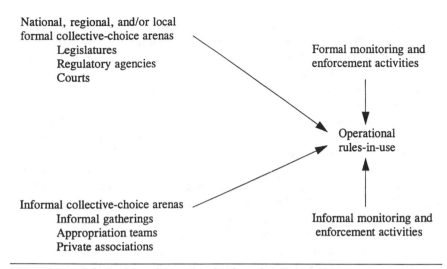

National, regional, and/or local
formal collective-choice arenas
    Legislatures
    Regulatory agencies
    Courts

Formal monitoring and
enforcement activities

Operational
rules-in-use

Informal collective-choice arenas
    Informal gatherings
    Appropriation teams
    Private associations

Informal monitoring and
enforcement activities

FIGURE 3.3   Relationships of Formal and Informal Collective-Choice Arenas

SOURCE: Ostrom (1990, p. 53).

question (see Gregg, 1974). For example, when we studied police services, the police department was only one of the units of analysis included in our work. Instead of assuming that the entire department was the appropriate unit, we tried to understand who the actors involved were in diverse service situations, such as immediate response services, homicide investigation, laboratory analysis, training, and communication services. We found different sets of actors involved in each of the service situations. In some, citizens as well as police officers as street-level bureaucrats were key participants. In others, we found participants from many different urban service agencies. We had to examine interorganizational arrangements to understand patterns of interaction and results. Using this perspective, we found highly structured patterns of relationships where others had found only chaos. The highest levels of police performance existed, for example, in those metropolitan areas where small-scale, immediate-response units worked along with large-scale investigatory, laboratory, and communication units (Parks, 1985). Ongoing research by Roger B. Parks in the Indianapolis area is providing strong evidence that many of the patterns we observed in the 1970s and 1980s were still in evidence in the 1990s. Efforts to understand who was involved in producing public safety led us to formulate a theory of coproduction of urban public services (Parks et al., 1982; Percy, 1984; Kiser, 1984; Lam, 1996; Whitaker, 1980). The theory of coproduction has now been applied to a wider set of phenomena (E. Ostrom, 1996b). In light of the extensive empirical research, colleagues were able to achieve a far better understanding of the patterns of metropolitan organization and local government more generally (Advisory Commission on Intergovernmental Relations—ACIR, 1987, 1988; V. Ostrom, Bish, and E. Ostrom, 1988; Oakerson and Parks, 1988; Parks and Oakerson, 1989; Stein, 1990).

The second broad area in which the IAD framework has played an important organizing role has been the study of common-pool resources. In the early 1980s, the National Academy of Sciences organized a research panel on the study of common property. Ronald Oakerson (1992) wrote a framework paper for the panel that was used in the organization of a series of case studies of how diverse people had devised institutional arrangements related to common-pool resources (see also Thomson, Feeny, and Oakerson, 1992; E. Ostrom, 1992). Oakerson's presentation of the framework has influenced an untold number of studies of common-property regimes in many diverse sectors in all regions of the world. The intellectual productivity stimulated by the work of the NAS panel has led to the formation of an International Association for the Study of Common Property (IASCP). More than five hundred scholars attended the 1996 meeting of the association held in Berkeley in June 1996.

Colleagues at Indiana University have developed a theory of common-pool resources and a series of theoretical models of appropriation from a common-pool resource and have tested these in experimental laboratory settings (see E. Ostrom et al., 1994; E. Ostrom, Walker, and Gardner, 1992; Walker and Gardner, 1992; Hackett, Schlager, and Walker, 1994). Weissing and Ostrom (1991, 1993) developed a series of models focusing on how actions taken by appropriators were monitored. Predictions from these models have been tested in an experimental lab by Moir (1995). When laboratory subjects are not allowed to communicate, their behavior closely approximates the behavior that is predicted by finitely repeated, noncooperative game theory. When subjects are allowed to communicate or to use sanctioning mechanisms, the behavior observed in the lab is not consistent with these theoretical models but is similar to what we have observed in field settings. We have consequently developed a theory of how boundedly rational individuals use heuristics such as "measured responses" to stabilize agreements achieved in settings where there are no external enforcers to impose rules on participants (E. Ostrom et al., 1994).

The IAD framework has now been used to develop three major databases related to the study of common-pool resources and diverse property regimes. The first "Common Pool Resource (CPR) Database" drew on the cases produced for the NAS panel and on the extremely large number of individual case studies that we discovered had been written by historians, sociologists, engineers, political scientists, anthropologists, and students of environmental science (Martin, 1989/1992; Hess, 1996). We used the IAD framework overtly to create a structured database for appropriation and collective-choice arenas. Schlager (1990, 1994) and Tang (1991, 1992) studied approximately fifty inshore fisheries and irrigation systems, respectively, and were able to isolate key rules that were positively associated with higher performance levels. In *Governing the Commons* (1990), I was able to draw on the framework and on an analysis of the extensive case studies we were all reading at that time to elucidate some aspects of a theory of common-pool resources. In particular, I examined the key design principles that characterized robust, self-organized institutions for achieving sustainable resource use of very long periods of time as well as for developing an initial theory of institutional change.

The second database focused entirely on irrigation systems and has been used to code more than 175 irrigation systems in Nepal (Benjamin et al., 1994). That database has enabled us to test many propositions growing out of both our own theoretical efforts and those of development scholars more generally (see Adhikari, Pandit, and Schweik, 1997; Lam, 1994; E. Ostrom, Lam, and Lee, 1994; E. Ostrom and Gardner, 1993; E. Ostrom, 1994, 1996a). We have been able to challenge many of the empirical assumptions used by development scholars who have presumed that farmers are unable to self-organize and engage in costly collective action without the imposition of rules from external authorities (see also Thomson, 1992). We have found that farmer-managed irrigation systems in Nepal are able to outperform agency-managed systems in regard to agricultural productivity when we have controlled for factors such as size of group, length of canal, and type of terrain (Lam, 1994).

The third database is an integral part of the International Forestry Resources and Institutions (IFRI) research program, which is a major ongoing research program of the Workshop on Political Theory and Policy Analysis and of the recently established Center for the Study of Institutions, Population, and Environmental Change (CIPEC). This research program is designed to address knowledge and information gaps about how institutions affect the incentives of forest users that result in substantial levels of deforestation in some locations, whereas forest conditions are improving in other locations. Six collaborative research centers have now been established in Bolivia, Ecuador, India, Mali, Nepal, and Uganda, and several more will be established during 1997 (E. Ostrom and Wertime, 1994; Jerrells and Ostrom, 1995). In Uganda, Banana and Gombya-Ssembajjwe (1996) showed in their initial studies that the only forests where deforestation is not extensive are those where local institutional arrangements are viewed by local residents as legitimate and are monitored extensively. In their study of a *comuna* in Ecuador, Becker and Gibson (1996) documented the importance of distance from a forest as it affects the costs that villagers would have to pay to actively monitor and enforce rules even when they have full authority to make and enforce their own rules. In India, Agrawal (1996) provided an empirical challenge to the presumption of many scholars that collective action becomes progressively more difficult as the size of the group increases from a very small face-to-face group. He showed that moderate-sized villages are better able to generate the labor needed to protect local forests than are very small villages. Schweik (1996) examined the geographic distribution of *Shorea robusta,* a highly valued species. He found that neither the population density of the villages adjacent to the three forests he studied in Nepal nor predictions by optimal foraging theory adequately predicted the spatial distribution of the species. The most robust explanation for the distribution of this species relates to the institutional rules that allow higher-caste villagers to access their "own" forests as well as forests located near the villages where lower-caste villagers live, but not vice versa.

In addition to the aforementioned research programs, the IAD framework has also influenced a variety of other studies, including those developing models of social-choice situations and then subjecting them to empirical tests in experimental laboratories (Herzberg, 1986; Wilson and Herzberg, 1987; Herzberg and Wilson, 1988; Herzberg and Ostrom, 1991); other empirical questions include the study of rural infrastructure in developing countries (E. Ostrom, Schroeder, and Wynne, 1993); privatization processes (S. Walker, 1994a, 1994b); development processes more generally (V. Ostrom, Feeny, and Picht, 1993; Wunsch and Olowu, 1995); constitutional dynamics in the American federal system (Jillson and Wilson, 1994; V. Ostrom, 1987, 1991) as well as in the Canadian federal system (Sproule-Jones, 1993); linking local and global commons (McGinnis and Ostrom, 1996; Keohane and Ostrom, 1995); and an analysis of how rules, norms, and equilibrium strategies are related (Crawford and Ostrom, 1995).

The IAD framework has thus influenced the analysis of a wide diversity of questions, including how institutions are organized for the provision and production of urban policing and education, primary health care, fertilizer, coffee, roads, irrigation, fisheries, forest resources, and common-pool resources more generally. Empirical work has been carried on in Bangladesh, Bolivia, Brazil, Cameroon, China, Ecuador, Ghana, Guatemala, Hong Kong, India, Indonesia, Ivory Coast, Liberia, Madagascar, Mali, Nepal, Nigeria, Norway, Poland, Taiwan, Uganda, and the United States.

ASSESSING THE VALUE OF A FRAMEWORK

It is hard to know exactly how to provide an assessment of a framework. The criteria for evaluating theories are relatively well known and accepted. Theories are evaluated for their capacity to generate predictions supported by empirical evidence and to provide coherent explanations for observed regularities. The criteria for evaluating frameworks or paradigms are not well established. The differences between frameworks, theories, and models are not even generally recognized. It is also difficult for someone who has been intimately involved in the evolution of a framework to make an unbiased assessment of its value. So, instead of providing an assessment as such, I will provide some of the key questions that would need to be addressed in such an assessment. These include questions related to three broad types of usefulness:

Usefulness for Theoretical Analysis

1. Does the framework provide a coherent language for identifying universal elements of theories attempting to explain an important range of phenomena?

2. Does the framework help scholars to identify the similarities and differences of diverse theories as well as to analyze the relative strengths and
weaknesses of theories in explaining particular types of phenomenon?
3. Does the framework stimulate new theoretical developments?

Usefulness for Empirical Research

4. Does the framework help organize empirical research in those areas
where well-specified theories are not yet formulated?
5. Does empirical research drawing on the framework lead to new discov-
eries and better explanations of important phenomena?
6. Can the framework be applied to multiple levels of analysis in empirical
research?

Usefulness for Relating to Other Disciplines and Frameworks

7. Does the framework encourage integration across other disciplines?
8. Is the framework consistent with other frameworks initially developed
to focus on a particular level of analysis?
9. Does the framework perform better than others in a similar range of
applications?

I would answer these questions positively, but the real assessment will be made
by other scholars over the next several decades.

NOTES

1. Elements of the framework have been used in teaching both graduate and under-
graduate courses at Indiana University since the mid–1970s (see historical file of materials
on the IAD framework, Workshop Library).

2. In formal game-theoretical analysis, such strategies would be those identified as
equilibrium strategies. Shared strategies may, however, take the form of heuristics adopted
by most individuals in a society when they find themselves in particular situations.

3. I am more appreciative of these configural relationships because of a very insightful
colloquium presentation made by Professor Lloyd Orr, Department of Economics, Indiana University, to the Workshop in Political Theory and Policy Analysis on November
1995.

4. This section draws heavily on E. Ostrom, Gardner, and Walker (1994, pp. 38–41).

5. The International Forestry Resources and Institutions (IFRI) research program has
faced this problem in developing research protocols that enable a network of research
scholars to gather the "same" information from a sample of forestry sites located in multiple countries of the world. The recording forms can be structured and filled in by the research teams in the evening after in-depth group and individual discussions, but there
cannot be a standard way of asking the questions. Anthropologists have looked upon the

individuals with whom they talk as "informants," and this is the stance that one has to take in any effort to elucidate any information about rules-in-use (see E. Ostrom and Wertime, 1994).

REFERENCES

Adhikari, Keshav R., Kala N. Pandit, and Charles M. Schweik. 1997. "Integration of GIS and GPS Techniques in Irrigation and Forest Resources Mapping: Lessons Learned." In Ganesh Shivakoti et al., eds., *Participation, People, and Sustainable Development*. Bloomington, Ind., and Rampur, Nepal: Indiana University and Institute of Agriculture and Animal Sciences.

Advisory Commission on Intergovernmental Relations (Ronald J. Oakerson). 1987. *The Organization of Local Public Economies*. Washington, D.C.: ACIR.

Advisory Commission on Intergovernmental Relations (Ronald J. Oakerson, Roger B. Parks, and Henry A. Bell). 1988. *Metropolitan Organization: The St. Louis Case*. Washington, D.C.: ACIR.

Agrawal, Arun. 1996. "Group Size and Successful Collective Action: A Case Study of Forest Management Institutions in the Indian Himalayas." Forests, Trees and People Programme, Phase II. Working paper. Rome, Italy: Food and Agriculture Organization of the United Nations.

Alchian, Armen A. 1950. "Uncertainty, Evolution, and Economic Theory," *Journal of Political Economy* 58(3):211–221.

Arrow, Kenneth. 1951. *Social Choice and Individual Values*. 2d ed. New York: Wiley.

Banana, Abwoli Y., and William Gombya-Ssembajjwe. 1996. "Successful Forest Management: The Importance of Security of Tenure and Rule Enforcement in Ugandan Forests." Forests, Trees and People Programme, Phase II. Working paper. Rome, Italy: Food and Agriculture Organization of the United Nations.

Becker, C. Dustin, and Clark C. Gibson. 1996. "The Lack of Institutional Supply: Why a Strong Local Community in Western Ecuador Fails to Protect its Forest." Forests, Trees and People Programme, Phase II. Working paper. Rome, Italy: Food and Agriculture Organization of the United Nations.

Benjamin, Paul, Wai Fung Lam, Elinor Ostrom, and Ganesh Shivakoti. 1994. *Institutions, Incentives, and Irrigation in Nepal*. Decentralization: Finance and Management Project Report. Burlington, Vt.: Associates in Rural Development.

Blomquist, William. 1992. *Dividing the Waters: Governing Groundwater in Southern California*. San Francisco: Institute for Contemporary Studies Press.

Breton, Albert, and Ronald Wintrobe. 1982. *The Logic of Bureaucratic Conduct: An Economic Analysis of Competition, Exchange, and Efficiency in Private and Public Organizations*. Cambridge, England: Cambridge University Press.

Buchanan, James M., and Gordon Tullock. 1962. *The Calculus of Consent*. Ann Arbor: University of Michigan Press.

Crawford, Sue E. S., and Elinor Ostrom. 1995. "A Grammar of Institutions." *American Political Science Review* 89(3) (September):582–600.

Dosi, Giovanni, and Massimo Egidi. 1987. "Substantive and Procedural Uncertainty: An Exploration of Economic Behaviours in Complex and Changing Environments." Paper prepared at the International Workshop on Programmable Automation and New Work Modes, Paris, April 2–4.

Eggertsson, Thráinn. 1990. *Economic Behavior and Institutions*. New York: Cambridge University Press.

Firmin-Sellers, Kathryn. 1996. *The Transformation of Property Rights in the Gold Coast: An Empirical Study Applying Rational Choice Theory*. New York: Cambridge University Press.

Gregg, Phillip M. 1974. "Units and Levels of Analysis: A Problem of Policy Analysis in Federal Systems," *Publius* 4(4) (Fall):59–86.

Hackett, Steven, Edella Schlager, and James Walker. 1994. "The Role of Communication in Resolving Commons Dilemmas: Experimental Evidence with Heterogenous Appropriators," *Journal of Environmental Economics and Management* 27:99–126.

Harré, R. 1974. "Some Remarks on 'Rule' as a Scientific Concept." In T. Mischel, ed., *Understanding Other Persons*. Oxford: Basil Blackwell.

Herzberg, Roberta. 1986."Blocking Coalitions and Policy Change." In Gerald C. Wright, Leroy Rieselbach, and Larry Dodd, eds., *Congress and Policy Change*, pp. 201–222. New York: Agathon Press.

Herzberg, Roberta, and Vincent Ostrom. 1991. "Votes and Vetoes." In Franz-Xaver Kaufmann, ed., *The Public Sector—Challenge for Coordination and Learning*, pp. 441–450. Berlin and New York: Walter de Gruyter.

Herzberg, Roberta, and Rick Wilson. 1988. "Results on Sophisticated Voting in an Experimental Setting," *Journal of Politics* 50(2):471–486.

Hess, Charlotte. 1996. *Common-Pool Resources and Collective Action: A Bibliography*, Vol. 3. Bloomington: Indiana University, Workshop in Political Theory and Policy Analysis.

Holling, C. S. 1994. "An Ecologist View of the Malthusian Conflict." In K. Lindahl-Kiessling and H. Landberg, eds., *Population, Economic Development, and the Environment*, pp. 79–103. New York: Oxford University Press.

Hyden, Goran. 1990. "Reciprocity and Governance in Africa." In James Wunsch and Dele Olowu, eds., *The Failure of the Centralized State: Institutions and Self-Governance in Africa*, pp. 245–269. Boulder: Westview Press.

Jerrells, Joby, and Elinor Ostrom. 1995. "Current Developments in a Relational Database for Biological and Social Science Research." Paper presented at the IUFRO World Congress conference, Tampere, Finland, August 8–11.

Jillson, Calvin C., and Rick K. Wilson. 1994. *Congressional Dynamics: Structure, Coordination, and Choice in the First American Congress, 1774–1789*. Stanford: Stanford University Press.

Kaminski, Antoni. 1992. *An Institutional Theory of Communist Regimes: Design, Function, and Breakdown*. San Francisco: Institute for Contemporary Studies Press.

Keohane, Robert O., and Elinor Ostrom, eds. 1995. *Local Commons and Global Interdependence: Heterogeneity and Cooperation in Two Domains*. London: Sage.

Kiser, Larry L. 1984. "Toward an Institutional Theory of Citizen Coproduction," *Urban Affairs Quarterly* 19(4) (June):485–510.

Kiser, Larry L., and Elinor Ostrom. 1982. "The Three Worlds of Action: A Metatheoretical Synthesis of Institutional Approaches." In Elinor Ostrom, ed., *Strategies of Political Inquiry*, pp. 179–222. Beverly Hills, Calif.: Sage.

Lam, Wai Fung. 1994. "Institutions, Engineering Infrastructure, and Performance in the Governance and Management of Irrigation Systems: The Case of Nepal." Ph.D. dissertation, Indiana University.

_____. 1996. "Institutional Design of Public Agencies and Coproduction: A Study of Irrigation Associations in Taiwan," *World Development* 24(6) (June):1039–1054.

Lasswell, Harold, and Abraham Kaplan. 1950. *Power and Society. A Framework for Political Inquiry*. New Haven: Yale University Press.

Loveman, Brian. 1993. *The Constitution of Tyranny: Regimes of Exception in Spanish America*. Pittsburgh: University of Pittsburgh Press.

Martin, Fenton. 1989/1992. *Common-Pool Resources and Collective Action: A Bibliography*, Vols. 1, 2. Bloomington: Indiana University, Workshop in Political Theory and Policy Analysis.

McGinnis, Michael, and Elinor Ostrom. 1996. "Design Principles for Local and Global Commons." In Oran R. Young, ed., *The International Political Economy and International Institutions*, Vol. 2, pp. 465–493. Cheltenham, United Kingdom: Edward Elgar.

Moir, Rob. 1995. "The Effects of Costly Monitoring and Sanctioning upon Common Property Resource Appropriation." Working paper. Saint John: University of New Brunswick, Department of Economics.

Netting, Robert McC. 1982. "Territory, Property, and Tenure." In R. McC. Adams, N. J. Smelser, and D. J. Treiman, eds., *Behavioral and Social Science Research: A National Resource*, pp. 446–501. Washington, D.C.: National Academy Press.

Oakerson, Ronald J. 1992. "Analyzing the Commons: A Framework." In Daniel W. Bromley et al., eds., *Making the Commons Work: Theory, Practice, and Policy*, pp. 41–59. San Francisco: Institute for Contemporary Studies Press.

_____. 1993. "Reciprocity: A Bottom-Up View of Political Development." In Vincent Ostrom, David Feeny, and Hartmut Picht, eds., *Rethinking Institutional Analysis and Development: Issues, Alternatives, and Choices*, pp.141–158. San Francisco: Institute for Contemporary Studies Press.

_____. 1994. "The Logic of Multi-Level Institutional Analysis." Paper presented at the "Workshop on the Workshop" conference, Indiana University, Workshop in Political Theory and Policy Analysis, Bloomington, June 15–19.

Oakerson, Ronald J., and Roger B. Parks. 1988. "Citizen Voice and Public Entrepreneurship: The Organizational Dynamic of a Complex Metropolitan County," *Publius* 18 (Fall): 91–112.

Olson, Mancur. 1965. *The Logic of Collective Action: Public Goods and the Theory of Groups*. Cambridge, Mass.: Harvard University Press.

Ostrom, Elinor. 1972. A Metropolitan Reform: Propositions Derived from Two Traditions," *Social Science Quarterly* 53 (December):474–493.

_____. 1986. "An Agenda for the Study of Institutions," *Public Choice* 48:3–25.

_____. 1990. *Governing the Commons: The Evolution of Institutions for Collective Action*. New York: Cambridge University Press.

_____. 1992. "The Rudiments of a Theory of the Origins, Survival, and Performance of Common-Property Institutions." In Daniel W. Bromley et al., eds., *Making the Commons Work: Theory, Practice, and Policy*, pp. 41–59. San Francisco: Institute for Contemporary Studies Press.

_____. 1994. "Neither Market Nor State: Governance of Common-Pool Resources in the Twenty-First Century." International Food Policy Research Institute Lecture Series No. 2, presented June 2, Washington, D.C.

_____. 1996a. "Crossing the Great Divide: Coproduction, Synergy, and Development," *World Development* 24(6) (June):1073–1087.

_____. 1996b. "Incentives, Rules of the Game, and Development." In *Proceedings of the Annual World Bank Conference on Development Economics 1995*, pp. 207–234. Washington, D.C.: World Bank.

Ostrom, Elinor, and Roy Gardner. 1993. "Coping with Asymmetries in the Commons: Self-Governing Irrigation Systems Can Work," *Journal of Economic Perspectives* 7(4) (Fall):93–112.

Ostrom, Elinor, Roy Gardner, and James Walker. 1994. *Rules, Games, and Common-Pool Resources.* Ann Arbor: University of Michigan Press.

Ostrom, Elinor, Wai Fung Lam, and Myungsuk Lee. 1994. "The Performance of Self-Governing Irrigation Systems in Nepal," *Human Systems Management* 14(3):87–108.

Ostrom, Elinor, Vincent Ostrom, and Michael McGinnis. 1996. "A Course of Study in Institutional Analysis and Development: 1995–96." Bloomington: Indiana University, Workshop in Political Theory and Policy Analysis.

Ostrom, Elinor, Larry Schroeder, and Susan Wynne. 1993. *Institutional Incentives and Sustainable Development: Infrastructure Policies in Perspective.* Boulder: Westview Press.

Ostrom, Elinor, James Walker, and Roy Gardner. 1992. "Covenants With and Without a Sword: Self-Governance is Possible," *American Political Science Review* 86(2) (June): 404–417.

Ostrom, Elinor, and Mary Beth Wertime. 1994. "IFRI Research Strategy." Working paper. Bloomington: Indiana University, Workshop in Political Theory and Policy Analysis.

Ostrom, Vincent. 1980. "Artisanship and Artifact," *Public Administration Review* 40 (July-August):309–317.

_____. 1986. "A Fallabilist's Approach to Norms and Criteria of Choice." In Franz-Xaver Kaufmann, Giandomenico Majone, and Vincent Ostrom, eds., *Guidance, Control, and Evaluation in the Public Sector,* pp. 229–249. Berlin and New York: Walter de Gruyter.

_____. 1987. *The Political Theory of a Compound Republic: Designing the American Experiment,* 2d ed. Lincoln: University of Nebraska Press.

_____. 1991. *The Meaning of American Federalism: Constituting a Self-Governing Society.* San Francisco: Institute for Contemporary Studies Press.

_____. 1997. *The Meaning of Democracy and the Vulnerability of Democracies: A Response to Tocqueville's Challenge.* Ann Arbor: University of Michigan Press.

Ostrom, Vincent, Robert Bish, and Elinor Ostrom. 1988. *Local Government in the United States.* San Francisco: Institute for Contemporary Studies Press.

Ostrom, Vincent, David Feeny, and Hartmut Picht, eds. 1993. *Rethinking Institutional Analysis and Development: Issues, Alternatives, and Choices,* 2d ed. San Francisco: Institute for Contemporary Studies Press.

Ostrom, Vincent, and Elinor Ostrom. 1971. "Public Choice: A Different Approach to the Study of Public Administration," *Public Administration Review* 13 (March-April): 203–216.

Parks, Roger B. 1985. "Metropolitan Structure and Systematic Performance: The Case of Police Service Delivery." In Kenneth Hanf and Theo A. J. Toonen, eds., *Policy Implementation in Federal and Unitary Systems,* pp. 161–191. Dordrecht, The Netherlands: Martinus Nijhoff.

Parks, Roger B., Paula C. Baker, Larry L. Kiser, Ronald J. Oakerson, Elinor Ostrom, Vincent Ostrom, Stephen L. Percy, Martha Vandivort, Gordon P. Whitaker, and Rick Wilson. 1982. "Coproduction of Public Services." In Richard C. Rich, ed., *Analyzing Urban-Service Distributions,* pp. 185–199. Lexington, Mass.: Lexington Books.

Parks, Roger B., and Ronald J. Oakerson. 1989. "Metropolitan Organization and Governance: A Local Public Economy Approach," *Urban Affairs Quarterly* 25(1) (September):18–29.

Percy, Stephen L. 1984. "Citizen Participation in the Coproduction of Urban Services," *Urban Affairs Quarterly* 19(4) (June):431–446.

Radnitzky, Gerard. 1987. "Cost-Benefit Thinking the Methodology of Research: The 'Economic Approach' Applied to Key Problems to the Philosophy of Science." In Gerard Radnitzky and Peter Bernholz, eds., *Economic Imperialism: The Economic Approach Applied Outside the Field of Economics*, pp. 283–334. New York: Paragon House.

Sawyer, Amos. 1992. *The Emergence of Autocracy in Liberia: Tragedy and Challenge.* San Francisco: Institute for Contemporary Studies Press.

Schlager, Edella. 1990. "Model Specification and Policy Analysis: The Governance of Coastal Fisheries." Ph.D. dissertation, Indiana University.

_____. 1994. "Fishers' Institutional Responses to Common-Pool Resource Dilemmas." In Elinor Ostrom, Roy Gardner, and James Walker, eds., *Rules, Games, and Common-Pool Resources*, pp. 247–66. Ann Arbor: University of Michigan Press.

Schlager, Edella, William Blomquist, and Shui Yan Tang. 1994. "Mobile Flows, Storage, and Self-Organized Institutions for Governing Common-Pool Resources," *Land Economics* 70(3) (Aug.):294–317.

Schweik, Charles M. 1996. "Social Norms and Human Foraging: An Investigation into the Spatial Distribution of *Shorea robusta* in Nepal." Forests, Trees and People Programme, Phase II. Working paper. Rome, Italy: Food and Agriculture Organization of the United Nations.

Shepsle, Kenneth A. 1979. "The Role of Institutional Structure in the Creation of Policy Equilibrium." In Douglas W. Rae and Theodore J. Eismeier, eds., *Public Policy and Public Choice*, pp. 249–283. Sage Yearbooks in Politics and Public Policy, Vol. 6. Beverly Hills, Calif.: Sage.

_____. 1989. "Studying Institutions: Some Lessons from the Rational Choice Approach," *Journal of Theoretical Politics* 1:131–149.

Shimanoff, Susan B. 1980. *Communication Rules: Theory and Research.* Beverly Hills, Calif.: Sage.

Simon, Herbert A. 1965. *Administrative Behavior: A Study of Decision-making Processes in Administrative Organization.* New York: Free Press. (Originally published in 1947.)

_____. 1972. "Theories of Bounded Rationality." In C. B. McGuire and Roy Radner, eds., *Decision and Organization: A Volume in Honor of Jacob Marschak*, pp. 161–176. Amsterdam: North Holland.

Sproule-Jones, Mark. 1993. *Governments at Work: Canadian Parliamentary Federalism and Its Public Policy* Effects. Toronto: University of Toronto Press.

Stein, Robert. 1990. *Urban Alternatives: Public and Private Markets in the Provision of Local Services.* Pittsburgh: University of Pittsburgh Press.

Tang, Shui Yan. 1991. "Institutional Arrangements and the Management of Common-Pool Resources," *Public Administration Review* 51 (January-February):42–51.

_____. 1992. *Institutions and Collective Action: Self-Governance in Irrigation.* San Francisco: Institute for Contemporary Studies Press.

Taylor, Michael. 1987. *The Possibility of Cooperation.* New York: Cambridge University Press.

Thomson, James T. 1992. *A Framework for Analyzing Institutional Incentives in Community Forestry.* Rome, Italy: Food and Agriculture Organization of the United Nations, Forestry Department, Via delle Terme di Caracalla.

Thomson, James T., David Feeny, and Ronald J. Oakerson. 1992. "Institutional Dynamics: The Evolution and Dissolution of Common-Property Resource Management." In

Daniel W. Bromley et al., eds., *Making the Commons Work: Theory, Practice, and Policy*, pp. 129–160. San Francisco: Institute for Contemporary Studies Press.

Toulmin, S. 1974. "Rules and Their Relevance for Understanding Human Behavior." In T. Mischel, ed., *Understanding Other Persons*. Oxford: Basil Blackwell.

Walker, James, and Ray Gardner. 1992. "Probabilistic Destruction of Common-Pool Resources: Experimental Evidence," *Economic Journal* 102(414) (September):1, 149–161.

Walker, S. Tjip. 1994a. *Crafting a Market: A Case Study of USAID's Fertilizer Sub-Sector Reform Program*. Decentralization: Finance and Management Project Report. Burlington, Vt.: Associates in Rural Development.

_____. 1994b. *Pitfalls of Privatization: A Case Study of the European Community's Programme Spécial d'Importation d'Engrais*. Decentralization: Finance and Management Project Report. Burlington, Vt.: Associates in Rural Development.

Weissing, Franz J., and Elinor Ostrom. 1991. "Irrigation Institutions and the Games Irrigators Play: Rule Enforcement without Guards." In Reinhard Selten, ed., *Game Equilibrium Models II: Methods, Morals, and Markets*, pp. 188–262. Berlin: Springer-Verlag.

_____ 1993. "Irrigation Institutions and the Games Irrigators Play: Rule Enforcement on Government- and Farmer-Managed Systems." In Fritz W. Scharpf, ed., *Games in Hierarchies and Networks: Analytical and Empirical Approaches to the Study of Governance Institutions*, pp. 387–428. Frankfurt am Main: Campus Verlag; Boulder: Westview Press.

Whitaker, Gordon P. 1980. "Coproduction: Citizen Participation in Service Delivery," *Public Administration Review* 40(4) (July-August):309–317.

Williamson, Oliver E. 1975. *Markets and Hierarchies: Analysis and Antitrust Implications*. New York: Free Press.

_____. 1979. "Transaction Cost Economics: The Governance of Contractual Relations," *Journal of Law and Economics* 22(2) (October): 233–261.

_____. 1985. *The Economic Institutions of Capitalism*. New York: Free Press.

Wilson, Rick, and Roberta Herzberg. 1987. "Negative Decision Powers and Institutional Equilibrium: Experiments on Blocking Coalitions," *Western Political Quarterly* 40(4) (Dec.):593–609.

Wunsch, James S., and Dele Olowu, eds. 1995. *The Failure of the Centralized State: Institutions and Self-Governance in Africa*, 2d ed. San Francisco: Institute for Contemporary Studies Press.

4

Ambiguity, Time, and Multiple Streams

NIKOLAOS ZAHARIADIS

Multiple streams (MS) is a lens or approach—I use the terms interchangeably—that explains how policies are made. Although it could conceivably be extended to cover the entire process of policymaking, it is examined here only in its capacity to explain policy formation (agenda setting and decisionmaking). The framework examines policy choice under conditions of ambiguity and assumes a temporal order: The adoption of specific alternatives depends on when policies are made. It provides answers to three essential questions: How is the attention of policymakers rationed? How are issues framed? And how and where is the search for solutions and problems conducted? At present, answers to attention and search are more fully developed than answers to framing.

The basic outline of the multiple-streams lens is put forth by Kingdon (1995). The first section contains Kingdon's ideas. The second discusses some modifications to them. The third addresses criticisms and limitations of the lens, and the concluding part charts an agenda for future research.

KINGDON'S MULTIPLE-STREAMS FORMULATION

Kingdon (1995) adapted the garbage can model, which was developed by Cohen, March, and Olsen (1972), to the U.S. federal government and used it to illuminate two predecision processes: agenda setting and alternative specification. Deriving his data mainly from interviews conducted in the period 1976–1979, the author concentrated on two broad policy areas: health and transportation. In the first portion of this section, I discuss the lens's fundamental elements, and then I discuss Kingdon's ideas.

Level and Unit of Analysis

MS draws inspiration from work on bounded rationality and organization theory as formulated by James March, Herbert Simon, and their colleagues. The lens theorizes at the systemic level, and it incorporates the entire system or a separate decision as the unit of analysis. Much as does systems theory, it views choice as collective output formulated by the push and pull of several factors. The lens is sensitive to the way information affects choice, which is at the heart of earlier theorizing on systems and political communication (e.g., Easton, 1964; Deutsch, 1966; Steinbruner, 1974). Unlike Easton's systems model, however, MS focuses on the process of transforming inputs into outputs, that is, the workings of the black box. Moreover, it shares common ground with chaos theories in being attentive to complexity, in assuming a considerable amount of residual randomness, and in viewing systems as constantly evolving and not necessarily settling into equilibria (Kingdon, 1994, p. 219).

Ambiguity

MS deals with policymaking only under conditions of ambiguity. *Ambiguity* refers to "a state of having many ways of thinking about the same circumstances or phenomena" (Feldman, 1989, p. 5). These ways may not be reconcilable and thus may create vagueness, confusion, and stress. Ambiguity is different from uncertainty, a related concept, in that the latter refers to the inability to accurately predict an event. Ambiguity may be thought of as ambivalence, whereas uncertainty may be referred to as ignorance or imprecision (March, 1994, pp. 178–179). Although more information may (or may not) reduce uncertainty (Wilson, 1989, p. 228), more information does not reduce ambiguity.[1] For example, more information can tell us how AIDS is spread, but it won't tell us whether AIDS is a health, educational, political, or moral issue.

At the heart of the lens lies a garbage can model of choice. In an insightful article, Cohen, March, and Olsen (1972) outlined such a model that explains decisionmaking in organizations—or decision situations—they term "organized anarchies," where ambiguity is rampant. These organizations, such as universities and national governments, are characterized by three general properties: fluid participation, problematic preferences, and unclear technology. First, participation in such organizations is fluid. Turnover is high, and participants drift from one decision to the next. Legislators come and go, and bureaucrats, especially high-level civil servants, often move from public service to private practice. Moreover, nongovernmental actors, such as employer associations, trade unions, and consumer groups, exercise a significant influence over the form certain decisions will take. Involvement in any one decision varies considerably, and so does the time and effort that participants devote to it.

Second, people often don't know what they want. To say that policymakers almost never make their objectives crystal clear is hardly novel, but it is true that quite often time constraints force politicians to make decisions without having formulated precise preferences. Decisions are made and may even be facilitated by opaqueness. This situation stands in stark contrast to that in most business firms, where the ultimate goal is clear: to make a profit. As Cohen, March, and Olsen (1972, p. 1) aptly put it, organized anarchies "can be described better as a collection of ideas than as a coherent structure."

Third, technology—that is, an organization's processes that turn inputs into products—is unclear. Members of an organized anarchy may be aware of their individual responsibilities, but they exhibit only rudimentary knowledge concerning the way their job fits into the overall mission of the organization. Jurisdictional boundaries are unclear, and turf battles between different ministries are a common occurrence. Members of parliament often complain of unaccountable ministers, who, in turn, frequently express their frustration with overburdening reporting rules and independent-minded public managers. Past experience often guides their actions, making trial-and-error procedures indispensable learning tools.

Temporal Sorting

Under such extreme conditions, theories based on rational behavior are of limited utility. Because problems and preferences are not well known, selecting the alternative that yields the most net benefits becomes an impossible task. The problem under conditions of ambiguity is that we don't know what the problem is; its definition is vague and shifting. Distinguishing between relevant and irrelevant information is problematic and can lead to false and misleading facts. Choice becomes less an exercise in solving problems and more an attempt to make sense of a partially comprehensible world (Weick, 1979, p. 175). Contradictions and paradoxes appear: State agencies are told to strengthen their oversight functions, and at the same time, their budgets are slashed in half. Information is requested and produced but not used in any decisions (Feldman and March, 1981). In contrast to models that stress rational action, the garbage can provides an alternative logic based on time.

Who pays attention to what and when is critical. Time is a unique, scarce resource. Because the primary concern of decisionmakers—policymakers, business executives, or top civil servants—is to manage time effectively rather than to manage tasks (Drucker, 1967, p. 25; Mackenzie, 1972, p. 2), it is reasonable to pursue a lens that accords significance to time rather than to rationality. The multiple-streams perspective translates into a process in which individuals are viewed as less capable of choosing the issues they would like to solve and more concerned about addressing the multitude of problems that are thrust upon them, largely by factors beyond their control. Attention to a particular issue is a function of opportunity, bias, formal position in an organization or government, and the number of issues competing for policymakers' attention (March and Romelaer, 1976).

Kingdon's Three Streams

Kingdon attempted to determine why some agenda items are prominent and others are neglected. He identified three streams flowing through the system: problems, policies, and politics. Each is conceptualized as largely separate from the others, with its own dynamics and rules. At critical points in time, the streams are coupled by policy entrepreneurs. The combination of all three streams into a single package enhances dramatically the chances that an issue will receive serious attention by policymakers.

The first stream contains problems. Why do policymakers pay attention to some problems and not others? The answer lies in the way officials learn about conditions and, more important, the way these conditions come to be defined as problems. There are three ways to identify conditions. First, indicators may be used to assess the existence and magnitude of a condition—for example, the cost of a program, infant mortality rates, or highway deaths. Indicators can be monitored either routinely or through special studies. For example, special studies occasionally seek to estimate the number of Americans without health insurance. The indicators then can be used to measure the magnitude of change in the hope of catching official attention. Second, dramatic events or crises can occasionally call attention to a problem. The crash of a Boeing 747 serves as a powerful stimulant for increased air safety. Third, feedback from existing programs can bring conditions to the fore. Letters from constituents and impact evaluation studies are two relevant examples. Of course, not all conditions become problems. As Kingdon (1995, p. 110) categorically asserted, problems contain a "perceptual, interpretive element." Some conditions come to be defined as problems and consequently receive more attention than others (Rochefort and Cobb, 1994). How is this done? People define conditions as problems by letting their values and beliefs guide their decisions, by placing subjects in one category rather than another, and by comparing conditions in different countries.

Policies constitute the second stream. They include a wide variety of ideas floating around in the "policy primeval soup." Ideas are generated by specialists in policy communities—networks that include bureaucrats, congressional staff members, academics, and researchers in think tanks who share a common concern in a single policy area, such as health or environmental policy. These ideas are tried out in various ways, including hearings, papers, and conversations. Some ideas survive this initial period basically unchanged, others are combined into new proposals, and still others just disappear. Although the number of ideas floating around is quite large, only a few ever receive serious consideration. Selection criteria include technical feasibility and value acceptability. Proposals that are or appear difficult to implement have fewer chances of surviving this process. Moreover, proposals that do not conform to the values of policymakers are less likely to be considered for adoption. Proposals to nationalize U.S. railroads, for instance, stand little chance of survival in Washington.

Kingdon labeled the third stream politics. It consists of three elements: the national mood, pressure group campaigns, and administrative or legislative turnover. *National mood* refers to the notion that a fairly large number of individuals in a given country tend to think along common lines and that the mood swings from time to time. Government officials sensing changes in this mood—through, say, monitoring public opinion polls—act to promote certain items on the agenda or to dim the hopes of others. In addition, politicians often view the support or opposition of interest groups as indicators of consensus or dissent in the broader political arena. For example, if all interest groups voice their support for deregulation, it is likely that government officials will hasten to include the item on the agenda. In case of conflicting views, which are frequent, politicians formulate an image of the balance of support and opposition. This perception that the balance is tilting one way or another directly affects the likelihood of the issue's prominence or obscurity. In addition to the aforementioned factors, legislative or administrative turnover frequently affects the agenda in quite dramatic ways. A sudden influx of new members of Congress ideologically predisposed against "big government" is likely to propel the issue of deregulation into high prominence. Moreover, turnover of key personnel in the administration has a significant impact. The advent of a new president or new Secretary of the Interior signifies potential changes. Certain issues, such as proposals to cut the budget, may receive more attention, and others, such as comprehensive national health insurance, may simply be pushed into obscurity. Of the three elements in the political stream, the combination of the national mood and turnover in government exerts the most powerful effect on agendas.

An important feature of Kingdon's argument is coupling. Issues rise on the agenda when these streams are joined together at critical moments in time. Kingdon (1995, p. 165) labeled these moments "policy windows" and defined them as fleeting "opportunity[ies] for advocates of proposals to push their pet solutions, or to push attention to their special problems." Such windows are opened by compelling problems or by events in the political stream. The crash of an airplane, for example, brings attention to air safety issues. In the political stream, a new administration may be ideologically committed to deregulation. Policy windows are of short duration and may be as predictable as annual budget allocations or as unpredictable as earthquakes.

When windows open, policy entrepreneurs, who are individuals willing to invest "time, energy, reputation, money—to promote a position for anticipated future gain in the form of material, purposive or solidary benefits" (Kingdon, 1995, p. 179), must immediately seize the opportunity to initiate action. Otherwise, the opportunity is lost and the policy entrepreneurs must wait for the next one to come along. Policy entrepreneurs must be not only persistent but also skilled at coupling. They must be able to attach problems to their solutions and find politicians receptive to their ideas. An issue's chances of gaining prominence in the agenda are enhanced when problems and solutions or solutions and politics are joined. The issue's chances dramatically increase when all three streams—problems, policies, and politics—are coupled in a single package.

Why do some issues receive prominence and others do not? Kingdon's answer can be summarized as follows: The agenda is set by events in the political stream, by compelling problems, and by such visible participants as elected officials. Alternative specification is guided by the selection process in the policy stream and the involvement of relatively hidden participants who are specialists in that policy area.

Kingdon's adaptation of the garbage can model to policymaking at the national level is particularly useful because it integrates policy communities with broader events and because it addresses the ideas-versus-interests dilemma. MS amends arguments concerning the study of public policy developed explicitly by reference to narrow policy communities (e.g., Hayward, 1991). Broad political events are connected to narrow sectoral developments in specific ways. Although one does not determine the other, political events outside specific sectors influence the types of solutions that will be examined when windows open. This conceptualization allows for a test of Freeman's (1985) hypothesis that sectoral policies are influenced less by national events or styles and more by the characteristics of the sectors themselves. Kingdon's work also addresses the issue of ideas in public policy. Although it does not deny the importance of self-interest, it does point to the significance of ideas in two ways. First, solutions are developed, Kingdon argued, not simply on the basis of efficiency or power, but also on the basis of equity. Argument, persuasion, and reasoning are central elements of public policy formation and not mere rationalizations after the fact. Second, political ideology is a good heuristic in an ambiguous and rapidly changing world (Kingdon, 1993, p. 79). It provides meaning to action or cues for floor voting, and it serves as an (imprecise) guide to what issues are important. Ideas may be used by politicians not only to define others, but also to define themselves. People, however, need not be motivated exclusively by ideas. Entrepreneurs whose purpose is to couple the three streams will occasionally bend ideological proclivities in order to take advantage of fleeting opportunities (Zahariadis, 1996). Kingdon's (1995) work is a good way of exploring the impact of ideas without necessarily denying the importance of self-interest.

MAJOR EXTENSIONS AND REVISIONS

Kingdon's work is useful because he has been able to adapt the original garbage can model to policymaking at the national level. However, his argument refers to predecision processes in the United States: agenda setting and alternative specification. Are his conclusions generalizable to other countries as well as to other stages of the policymaking process? Zahariadis (1995b) addressed these questions by making three extensions and one refinement/amendment to Kingdon's argument. His study explores the politics of privatization in Britain and France in three sectors: oil, telecommunications, and railroads.

First, Zahariadis used MS to explain the full policy formation process (agenda setting and decisionmaking). In this respect, it differs from Kingdon's original application to predecision processes. Although agenda setting—that is, the process by which certain issues gain prominence—is conceptualized as a separate process, alternative specification is not. Kingdon distinguished between the specification of a narrow list of alternatives from which a choice is to be made and the actual choice itself. Zahariadis viewed them as parts of the same process—decisionmaking—defined as the process by which policymakers make an authoritative choice from a limited set of previously generated alternatives.

Second, MS is useful in the comparative study of policy as well. Kingdon's emphasis on the U.S. federal level seems to approximate the conditions of rampant ambiguity well. Britain (or France, for that matter), however, deviates from these conditions in several aspects. First, the British system is not as anarchic or decentralized. Rather, executive power is fused with legislative majority and combined with strong partisan discipline; both minimize intergovernmental conflict. Hence, preferences among decisionmakers are likely to be less problematic. Second, British cabinet ministers normally are seasoned politicians with years of parliamentary experience and close partisan ties. Thus, their participation in policymaking is much less fluid than that of cabinet members in the United States, where department secretaries constantly move in and out of public office. Finally, vast differences in the size and the relative cohesiveness of bureaucracies, as well as the limited access that interest groups and other societal actors have to decisionmaking centers in Britain, help make technology clearer. Roles in Britain are less ambiguous and contested, links are tighter and more formalized, and fewer actors have an input into policy choice. For these reasons, the lens may be viewed as less applicable to Britain, but Zahariadis demonstrated this is not the case.

The third extension refers to a shift in the unit of analysis.[2] Kingdon's discussion of MS referred to the entire national government and a multiplicity of issues. Zahariadis attempted to model a single issue: privatization. Whereas Kingdon viewed the entire system as a giant receptacle of problems, solutions, and politics covering many issues, Zahariadis analyzed the tendency of one issue to become a temporary receptacle regardless of how other issues are addressed.

The refinement/amendment to Kingdon combines the three dimensions in the political stream labeled *national mood, interest groups,* and *turnover* into one conceptual variable—the ideology of governing parties—without losing much analytical power.[3] This amalgamation makes sense in countries with relatively centralized political systems and strong political parties. As mentioned earlier,

national mood refers to the notion that a large number of people in a given country think along "certain common lines." Government officials sense this mood
and frequently seek to capitalize on it. This is a nebulous definition, however. Of
what exactly does the national mood consist, and who are the people involved? In
theory, an index may be constructed, but in practice, it is very difficult to "put our
finger on it." Some analysts have argued that public opinion captures the essence
of the national mood, but Kingdon (1995, p. 148) warned that the national mood
"does not necessarily reside in the mass public." So exactly how can it be operationalized? Moreover, because of mood swings, how do we know when these
swings occur? Are they rooted in the outcomes of other policies? For example, the
failure of parties to successfully implement their programs may shape this mood;
in this case, party politics is the main determinant of mood change.

Interest groups and legislative or administrative turnover may be similarly
combined. Given the decentralized nature of U.S. politics, keeping interest
groups and government turnover analytically separate makes sense. Politics in
many other countries, however, takes place within more centralized confines, and
parties play a more important role in shaping policy choice. Members of parties
that have the majority of seats in legislative chambers also occupy key posts in the
executive branch; therefore, the process is centralized. The principal division in
British government, for example, is not between the legislative and the executive,
but "within the House of Commons separating the majority party in control of
both the Commons and Cabinet from the opposition" (Rose, 1989, p. 113).
Moreover, party discipline ensures that party preferences will often be translated
into actual legislation. The net result is that government-sponsored bills are usually approved in Parliament with minor modifications. The average proportion
of government bills, for example, approved by the House of Commons in Britain
during the period 1945–1987 was 97 percent (Rose, 1989, p. 113)! Control is
equally great in France, where the prerogative to initiate legislation is shared by
the prime minister and parliament. From the beginning of the Fifth Republic in
1959 to October 1985, an average of only 12.5 percent of all laws originated in
parliament (Duhamel, 1987, p. 148). Generally speaking, parties tend to dominate the political stream and exercise considerable control over the shape of policy choices. Consequently, focusing on the ideology of parties does not deviate
much from Kingdon's ideas because it does not bias the results.

As a result of this modification, parties loom more important in Zahariadis's
(1995b) study. The ideology of the governing party (or coalition) shapes the
kinds of issues that will rise to the agenda and demarcates the solutions available
for adoption. For example, British Conservative focus on the elimination of government deficits gave an occasion to think about ways to shrink government.
Margaret Thatcher's doctrinaire (and more generally Conservative) antipathy toward state-owned enterprises made privatization a particularly appealing option.
Of course, congruence of a policy with party ideology is not a sufficient condition for its adoption, but it is often a necessary one.

These extensions and refinements increase the scope and generalizability of the lens. MS can accommodate questions of agenda setting and policy choice in several national settings. The incorporation of policy windows gives the lens a dynamic quality that differentiates it from explanations of structurally determined policy styles or rational choice. Coupling suggests that the effects of the streams are not additive. Rather, only a combination of all three streams at the same time can produce the desired outcome. Moreover, the inclusion of policy windows implies that policies may change or be reversed as a result of different combinations of problems, solutions, and politics. This is not to suggest that choice is haphazard, only that serendipity and politics are crucial elements of the same process.

SPECIFIC ISSUES AND CONCERNS

The critics, however, point to several drawbacks. I will reflect upon five questions that have been posed in the literature and will point to further refinements. They are (1) Are the streams really independent? (2) What is the precise role of policy windows in coupling? (3) How does entrepreneurial strategy affect coupling? (4) Do solutions always follow an incremental evolution in the policy stream? And (5) is the lens merely a heuristic device? It is important to remember that although Kingdon's work refers exclusively to predecision processes, his ideas are treated here in more generalized form under the rubric of MS, which deals with the entire process of policy formation.

Are the Streams Really Independent?

MS argues that although the streams are not completely independent of one another, each can be viewed as having a life of its own. Participants drift in and out of decisions, making some choices more likely than others. Problems rise and fall on the government's agenda regardless of whether they are solvable or have been solved. Similarly, people generate solutions not necessarily because they have identified a particular problem, but because the solution happens to answer a problem that fits their values, beliefs, or material well-being. Changes in the political stream take place whether or not the problems facing the nation have changed. Thus, each stream seems to obey its own rules and flows largely independently of the others. The streams interact only during open windows when policy entrepreneurs attach problems to solutions and present them to receptive political audiences.

Critics disagree. Mucciaroni (1992) questioned the appropriateness of conceptualizing independent streams. The streams can be more fruitfully viewed as interdepedent, he maintained, and changes in one stream can trigger or reinforce changes in another, so that coupling is much less fortuitous and the process is more purposive and strategic. For example, the problem of U.S. tax reform was tied to the supply-side tax cuts proposed by conservatives in symbolic and substantive ways long before Reagan's coming to power opened a policy window.

There is certainly merit to the critique, but it is impossible to settle the question when one views stream independence as logically necessary. The advantage of independence is that it enables researchers to uncover rather than assume rationality; that is, one does not assume that solutions are always developed in response to clearly defined problems. Sometimes policies are in search of a rationale, or they solve no problems (Stone, 1988; Zahariadis, 1996). The key is to specify when there is little or no linking between problems and solutions.

What Is the Precise Role of Policy Windows in Coupling?

A policy window is a temporal stimulus for choice. Not only do windows signal the temporal limits of the coupling process to policy entrepreneurs, but they also help structure the search for appropriate problems or policies that may be palatable to the policymakers of the day. Kingdon (1995) mentioned two types of windows: those that open in the problem stream and those that open in the politics stream. The crash of an airplane is an example of a window opening in the problem stream, and the outcome of a national election is an example of a window opening in the politics stream. He maintained that some windows are predictable (e.g., budget cycles), others are unpredictable (e.g., rail crashes), and most are of limited duration. "Once a window opens," Kingdon (1995, p. 169) argued, "it does not stay open long. An idea's time comes, but it also passes. There is no irresistible momentum that builds for a given initiative." Windows close for several reasons: (1) policymakers feel they have addressed the issue sufficiently, (2) policymakers have failed to generate action, (3) there is no available alternative, (4) the persons whose presence opened the window are no longer in power, and (5) the crisis or focusing event has passed from the scene. Timing is important because when decisions are made is likely to affect what option will be selected. But the different properties of opportunities indicate that each window has a differential impact on coupling. For example, unpredictability may shorten the duration of windows and is thus likely to make the process even more time-dependent. Although Kingdon (1995, pp. 205–206) stated that coupling is likely to take the form of solutions chasing problems because "advocacy of solutions often precedes the highlighting of problems to which they become attached," he was unclear on the conditions that structure this paradoxical outcome. Clues that provide an answer focus on causal mechanisms that link opportunity to choice.

Using the quest to sell British Rail as a case study, Zahariadis (1996) proposed two hypotheses: When windows open in the problem stream, coupling is likely to be consequential (finding a solution to a given problem), and when windows open in the politics stream, coupling is likely to be doctrinal (finding a problem for a given solution).

Problem windows encourage a consequential search for fit. A problem window triggers a search with a problem already in mind, however vaguely it may be defined. For example, a plane crash will focus attention on safety issues that address the causes of at least that crash and possibly other safety hazards as well. Consequently, the process begins with a search for clues about appropriate solutions to an already existing problem. In the course of coupling, solutions and the problem are marginally redefined to ensure a good fit.

In contrast, windows in the politics stream promote the reverse. The search for fit will concentrate on finding or inventing a problem for an already existing solution. Several reasons explain this propensity. First, an electoral victory, however small it may be, is perceived by the incoming government as approval for enacting promised policies. Of course, the victory can be as much (or more) a punishment for the previous government as an approval of the opposition. But the victors will seek to emphasize that policies are adopted because the public demands change. Hence, adopting promised policies is far more important and politically beneficial than actually solving any problems.

Second, it is easier to scan for solutions than for problems. Policymakers typically face a large number of potentially serious problems but can offer only a few solutions because of the time and resources needed to think them through. As a result, raising problems first and seeking solutions later is far costlier than the reverse. Risk-averse policymakers are far more likely to espouse solutions first because they fear the reverse may create expectations they cannot meet because they cannot solve highly complex problems or because they risk being "forced" to adopt nonpreferred solutions. Raising solutions first satisfies the predilections of politicians and their supporters, gives politicians more control over what issues will be raised and how they will be defined, and makes it less costly for a problem to be found or invented to legitimize that solution.

Third, rapid technological change is likely to encourage the formulation of more sophisticated solutions, which will in turn stimulate awareness of previously unnoticed or unsalient problems. Bureaucrats will happily concur with this propensity for solutions because it provides them with a greater sense of competence.

Fourth, spillovers tend to promote doctrinal coupling. Success with a specific policy in one sector—say, telecommunications—is likely to create pressure to adopt the same solution in railroads in the hope of replicating success regardless of the actual rail problem(s) considered at the time. The literature on privatization is replete with references to spillovers either across sectors in the same country (Zahariadis, 1992) or across countries (Ikenberry, 1990).

One area of refinement involves the possibility that windows are sometimes not temporary. Sharp (1994) suggested that certain characteristics make an issue continuously activated (i.e., it is always on the agenda), but she did not elaborate on the implications for MS. An issue such as drugs and drug policy has dramatic potential, high visibility, a plethora of organized interests that constantly offer expert diagnoses and prescriptions, and a multitude of consequences—social, personal, political, economic, or physiological—that make it a favorite supplement to a variety of other issues. If certain windows are not fleeting, what are the effects on coupling over time? Do they lead to greater partisan conflict, more symbolic action, or more problem solving?

How Does Entrepreneurial Strategy Affect Coupling?

Coupling involves the matching of problems and solutions by policy entrepreneurs with receptive audiences. Zahariadis (1996) probed this idea further by examining the impact of two elements: entrepreneurial position and strategy. Entrepreneurial position is very important in coupling the streams. Well-connected and persistent entrepreneurs are more likely to be successful at coupling (Kingdon, 1995, pp. 180–181). For example, being a current member of parliament in the governing party, a minister, or an adviser to a minister increases the political clout of the entrepreneur's ideas. Higher administrative or partisan rank increases access and potential influence over decisionmakers. Being a member of multiple arenas or institutional venues (Baumgartner and Jones, 1993) also helps entrepreneurs skillfully move issues from one venue to another where success is more likely. Moreover, successful entrepreneurs are those who are willing to spend considerable amounts of resources (time, energy, money, etc.) to make their ideas and pet proposals palatable to various policymakers. In some instances, even mere presence at (or absence from) critical meetings can affect the outcome (March and Romelaer, 1976).

Entrepreneurs employ various strategies to join streams together. Successful entrepreneurs use strategies that contain one or more heresthetical devices: manipulation of dimensions, agenda control, or strategic voting (Riker, 1986).[4] Riker maintained that the most frequently employed strategies are those of dimension manipulation and agenda control. Dimension manipulation is important to coupling because it affects how policymakers come to think about problems and appropriate solutions. It is a strategy for upsetting a political equilibrium by introducing new or redefining old aspects of a given issue. Once a salient dimension is invoked to a target audience, it creates the potential for gain (or loss) among the actors to be manipulated. For example, once Lincoln raised the issue of slavery to Douglas in the Illinois senatorial campaign, Douglas could not ignore it because it was salient. Lincoln cleverly used this heresthetical device because he knew that the Democratic party was sorely divided on this issue and hence that any position Douglas might adopt would alienate some Democrats and hurt Douglas's future presidential aspirations. Entrepreneurs also seek to control the issues to be examined by suppressing those for which they don't have solutions or that they view as embarrassing or politically costly and by discussing those they are likely to win. For example, governing Conservatives in Thatcher's Britain were keen on keeping privatization on the agenda, knowing it was a politically rewarding policy. Although manipulation of dimensions can be part of any entrepreneur's strategy, agenda control is an activity usually restricted to political leaders and important media magnates. Entrepreneurs who can use both devices, such as governing political leaders, will be more successful at coupling.

So far, strategy has assumed that the level of ambiguity remains constant. Given that different policymakers have different propensities for ambiguity, one can envision a model of choice that examines the implications of different levels of ambiguity (e.g., Hogarth and Einhorn, 1986). Does the strategic manipulation of ambiguity create consensus, and if so how? Cognitive psychologists have presented strong evidence to suggest that "framing" or issue definition has significant implications for choice (Heath and Tversky, 1991; Tversky and Kahneman, 1981). Are there limits to the ability of entrepreneurs to manipulate ambiguity in their favor? Do precedent and feedback reduce the scope of manipulation?

Do Solutions Always Follow
an Incremental Evolution in the Policy Stream?

Critics argue that MS is ahistorical. Weir (1992, p. 191) and Mucciaroni (1992, pp. 470–472) contend that the approach does not pay enough attention to the way previous solutions affect contemporary debates and, ultimately, policy choice. In response to such criticism, modifications have been attempted, although empirical verification is still pending.

In describing the policy stream, Kingdon (1995) argued that the generation of specific alternatives in the policy stream remains incremental. He referred to the process as "softening up" and claimed that ideas are constantly recombined. Some critics, however, have argued that the process need not be only incremental and may not involve simply a recombination of old ideas. Building on this point, Durant and Diehl (1989) argued that the trajectory of alternatives varies considerably in tempo and mode. The gestation period (tempo) can range from rapid (swift movement from conception to prominence without prolonged softening) to protracted (glacial motion with extensive softening). The mode in which the evolution of alternatives takes place can range from phyletic transformation (marginal extensions of existing policies) to pure mutation (totally new proposals). Recombination of ideas, according to the authors, is a hybrid form along the mode continuum. Based on these criteria, Durant and Diehl developed a typology of evolutionary processes that characterize trajectories of alternatives. Quantum evolution consists of alternatives demonstrating breakthrough qualities and negligible softening. Emergent solutions rely mostly on conceptually new ideas whose tempo is protracted, and convergent evolution characterizes a trajectory of rapid propulsion to salience of persistently softened ideas. Finally, gradualist evolution involves a protracted softening process of marginal extensions of existing policies.

Zahariadis and Allen (1995) argued that the structure of policy networks affects variations in the trajectory of ideas in the policy stream. They adopted the term *network* to refer to what Kingdon called policy communities in the policy stream, and they defined networks as constellations of actors and their interaction in a policy sector. Network structure is conceptualized as integration, which means linkages among participants and is distinguished by variations in four dimensions: size, mode, capacity, and access. Based on these dimensions, networks can be classified as more or less integrated. Less integrated networks are larger in size and have a competitive mode, lower administrative capacity, and less restricted access. Conversely, more integrated networks are smaller in size and have a consensual mode, higher capacity, and more restricted access. In turn, this level of integration affects the trajectory of alternatives. Less integrated networks are more likely to facilitate a quantum leap to gradualist evolution, and more integrated networks are more likely to follow an emergent to convergent pattern. Of course, this is not to say that other combinations are not possible; instead, integration renders such evolutionary trajectories more-or-less likely.

There is considerable debate over the issue of incrementalism in public policy (Bendor, 1995; Hayes, 1992). Numerous studies in the United States have suggested that policy change is incremental, to be punctuated only occasionally by major shifts (Baumgartner and Jones, 1993; Sabatier and Jenkins-Smith, 1993). If this is so, Kingdon's formulation is somewhat inaccurate, and the refinement of tying structure in policy networks to the trajectory of solutions may unnecessarily complicate the argument in order to explain only a few infrequent cases. More empirical work is needed to examine the effects of path dependence and incrementalism in the policy stream.

Is the Lens Merely a Heuristic Device?

Policymaking lenses have two aims: description and prediction. Description aims to explain how policies are actually made, and prediction attempts to forecast future policies. In theory, the two aims should be symbiotic, but in practice, they are not. MS strives for understanding and explanation more than prediction. What is needed, MS concedes, is a more accurate picture of policymaking, which may in fact reduce predictive capability. It is not surprising, therefore, that one of the strongest criticisms leveled at MS is that it resembles more a heuristic device than an empirically falsifiable guide to policy analysis (King, 1985).

MS views the policymaking process as fluid and less predictable than other lenses in public policy (Zahariadis, 1995a). MS describes an environment within which policies are made by specifying the conditions under which its image of policymaking approximates reality. Consequently, in instances where the conditions of ambiguity are not met, MS cannot be adequately descriptive, let alone predictive. The complexity of the argument and the generous tolerance of serendipity have led some analysts to characterize MS as hypothesizing an essentially random process where prediction is impossible. Such criticisms are misplaced because MS does offer predictions, but more hypotheses certainly need to be generated and tested. Chance plays an important role in models of choice (Mandelbaum, 1987), and MS incorporates this notion. But the process of policymaking is not random. The dynamics internal to each stream, the limits on coupling possibilities, and general systemic constraints such as constitutional structure systematically affect outcomes (Kingdon, 1995, pp. 206–208). The lens predicts, for example, that the ideology of political parties will be an important factor in raising issues to the top of the government's agenda (Zahariadis, 1995b). And it predicts that bureaucrats will be more likely to shape alternative solutions than to manipulate the government's agenda (Kingdon, 1995). Studies of complexity in physics and biology may prove useful guides for further theoretical treatment and empirical refinements.

AN AGENDA FOR FUTURE RESEARCH

Multiple streams examines the process of making policies under conditions of ambiguity. Borrowing from Cohen, March, and Olsen's work on garbage cans, John Kingdon has drafted a framework that explains how issues rise on the agenda and how alternatives are specified. Zahariadis has extended Kingdon's ideas to the entire process of policy formation and to the comparative study of public policy. In the next paragraph, I reaffirm some of the lens's strengths, and then I chart a course for future research to further explore its weaknesses.

Multiple streams does not reject rationality, but it seeks to explain policy precisely when the assumptions of clarity and self-interest are inappropriate descriptors. The lens differs from rational choice in unit and level of analysis, in its relative emphasis on ideas and context, in rejecting the illusion of control, and in accepting the independence of solutions, problems, and politics (Zahariadis, 1995a). It describes a situation that traditional normative theories of choice condemn as pathological and usually treat as an aberration. Yet policymakers frequently face dynamic and shifting environments where ambiguity is rampant and where decision outcomes appear to be beyond anyone's control. Complexity, fluidity, and fuzziness are particularly appropriate characterizations of policymaking at the national level. The lens is robust because it can incorporate both mathematical and verbal formulations. It also demonstrates how profitable a dialogue can be between the disciplines or fields of organizational theory, policy studies, psychology, sociology, biology, and political science.

Future research might expand on the following areas. First, there is a need to generate more falsifiable hypotheses, to test them, to formulate formal models, and to develop quantitative applications of MS. Parsimony is a virtue in social science, and MS should be simplified to focus more attention on generating falsifiable hypotheses. Falsifiability presupposes operationalization of MS concepts. Some of these concepts have been measured successfully, but the measurement of others leaves much to be desired. For example, the notion of technical feasibility in the policy stream can be measured by firm profitability or demand growth when one is examining the issue of privatization of commercial assets (Zahariadis, 1992). Problems may include yawning government budget deficits, which increase the appeal of a sell-off as a way to increase revenues without raising taxes. Other concepts are more elusive. How can the national mood be operationalized? How does one know when successful coupling has occurred? Is coupling even necessary? That is, is political party ideology by itself sufficient to determine the policies to be adopted? Formalization will make the connections between variables more explicit and will shed light on implicit assumptions. Testing has so far relied heavily on qualitative studies. Although such probes are useful in their own right, quantitative assessments will add more weight to the lens and enhance its predictive capability. Additional experimental designs, such as computer simulations, will further illuminate similarities and differences between MS and the original garbage can model and will be used to investigate relations between variables that are too complex to be fully explored in verbal models.

Second, research may inquire into why some decisions tend to become garbage cans. Are there characteristics of issues that make some more likely candidates than others? Answers will circumscribe even more carefully the limits of MS and will lead to a better understanding of the policymaking process. Rommetveit (1976) suggested that prime candidates for garbage cans are those issues that involve changes in normative structures—basic value-priorities in a polity—and those that come up when no active participant dominates the policy process. When a society is in the process of reordering its values, established norms that underlie state-society relations are challenged. As a result, conventional wisdom is questioned, and dissenting groups are brought to the forefront of change. In turn, the activation of new groups and the wide disagreement as to the relevant values upon which to base the policy decision increase ambiguity and permit the evocation or appearance of new problems and solutions. Such desegmentation of previously established links between windows, problems, and politics complicates the process as new and perhaps unrelated elements are dumped into the can. In this light, the issue of privatization or government reform is indeed a good candidates for applying MS (Brunsson and Olsen, 1993; March and Olsen, 1983). Other characteristics of issues may be salient as well and may alter the behavior of the system in predictable ways (Mucciaroni, 1992).

On a slightly different note, analysis may inquire into the applicability of MS as a lens for explaining policy formation in areas other than educational organizations or whole national governments. Gordenker, Coate, Jönsson, and Söderholm (1995) applied the original garbage can model to the area of international cooperation, which is a broader area than a single organizational environment. Using the AIDS epidemic as a case study, they explored the applicability of the lens to much more fluid areas, called *regimes,* than had been hitherto discussed. Ambiguity is certainly a fact of life in such cases. Moreover, work on agenda setting in the European Community has shown that the process is highly complex and ambiguous, a solid candidate for garbage cans (Peters, 1994, p. 20). Further inquiry might profitably extend the application to the actual decisionmaking process as well.

Third, there is a need to anchor the framework within specific institutional contexts. Although the lens acknowledges the importance of structure, the impact of hierarchies, multiple levels of government and their interaction, or specific constitutional arrangements is not systematically explored. A profitable study may adapt Ostrom's institutional framework to the MS context and explore its implications.

Fourth, there is a need for a theory of action. How does one translate favorable responses elicited by framing into actual votes? Brunsson (1985) outlined some ideas that build on expectations, motivation, and commitment. Further research may model them within the MS framework or may borrow and adapt theories and models developed in the fields of marketing and social psychology that deal explicitly with such questions.

Fifth, how should policymakers cope with an ambiguous world? What lessons does MS have to offer to democratic governance? Research has barely touched on these issues. An earlier study in universities proposes, inter alia, that leaders should persist because decisions are partly fortuitous and merely the result of recurring episodes in different settings. They should also facilitate the involvement of opposition on the rationale that such involvement reduces the deleterious effect of exaggerated aspirations (Cohen and March, 1974). Looking specifically at bureaucratic hierarchies that exhibit garbage can characteristics, Padgett (1980) concluded that managers had better follow a "hands-off" approach, provided they tend to personnel policies and structural design. Crecine (1986, p. 116) added to this strategy the manipulation of windows, which alters the context of choice. Some windows are subject to manipulation, such those associated with budgets, public procurement, or elections in parliamentary democracies.

Finally, the multiple-streams approach may prove useful in linking the various stages of the policymaking process under the umbrella of a single lens. Current studies of policymaking adopt a stage heuristic framework that divides the process into subprocesses or stages (e.g., agenda setting or implementation). Although it is acknowledged that stage boundaries are arbitrary and that stages do not necessarily follow each other (Anderson, 1994), there have been few attempts to build a lens that links them into a causal whole. Politics (policy formation) and administration (implementation) are not so rigidly divorced (March, 1994, p. 109; Olsen, 1988). MS may be able to address this issue with appropriate revisions and qualifications (Skok, 1995).

CONCLUSION

Far from being a pathology or an aberration, ambiguity is a fact of policymaking. It has drawbacks because it makes policymaking messy, complex, and less comprehensible. Ambiguity requires analysts to have a lot of information. But more information will not necessarily resolve ambiguity; it will simply make the process more comprehensible. Serendipity plays a major role, and the ability to predict future events diminishes dramatically. Context rather than purpose becomes important. Decisions rarely solve problems; they merely process them.

But ambiguity also has its virtues. Innovation flourishes because ambiguity gives new ideas a chance to solve old problems. Ambiguity also permits conflict to be diffused because opposing parties can attach their own interpretations to the decision outcome (Huff, 1988). Ambiguity affords the luxury of attending to many issues simultaneously. Because preferences can be constructed as the process unfolds, the number of issues that can be addressed at any one time can be safely increased without a corresponding increase in prior planning, time, or cognitive capacity. In such a world, time, position, and resources are crucial advantages.

Policymaking assumes choice. Choice implies free will. Ambiguity enhances free will because more options can be considered and more or irrelevant but pressing issues addressed. A perfectly ambiguous world may well be intolerable because "anything goes." Fortunately, there are constraints and inhibitions. The multiple-streams lens studies the effects of these temporal and spatial constraints on policy choice. If the multiple streams approach indeed gives an accurate picture of policymaking, it can be fruitfully used to explain policymaking and perhaps to reform it, but, more important, to devise strategies to cope with it. The number and scope of phenomena are too great to be left unexplored.

NOTES

1. This definition differs from that of some psychologists, who view ambiguity as a special type of uncertainty. They define it as "the subjective experience of missing information relevant to a prediction" (Frisch and Baron, 1988, p. 152). Obviously, for them, more information reduces ambiguity.

2. This point draws inspiration from comments made by Mohr (1978) in his review of the differences between the original garbage can model and its subsequent adaptations.

3. An interesting empirical question is the extent to which party ideology actually corresponds to party policy. Klingemann, Hofferbert, and Budge (1994) showed that the two sometimes diverge. So the appropriateness of combining all elements of the politics stream may depend upon the political system or time period under examination.

4. Riker used the term "heresthetician," but I have chosen to retain the term *entrepreneur* in order to maintain consistency with Kingdon's terminology.

REFERENCES

Anderson, James E. 1994. *Public Policy Making: An Introduction,* 2d ed. Boston: Houghton Mifflin.

Baumgartner, Frank R., and Bryan D. Jones. 1993. *Agendas and Instability in American Politics*. Chicago: University of Chicago Press.

Bendor, Jonathan. 1995. "A Model of Muddling Through," *American Political Science Review* 89:819–830.

Brunsson, Nils. 1985. *The Irrational Organization*. New York: Wiley.

Brunsson, Nils, and Johan P. Olsen. 1993. *The Reforming Organization*. London: Routledge.

Cohen, Michael D., and James G. March. 1974. *Leadership and Ambiguity*. New York: McGraw-Hill.

Cohen, Michael D., James G. March, and Johan P. Olsen. 1972. "A Garbage Can Model of Organizational Choice," *Administrative Science Quarterly* 17:1–25.

Crecine, John P. 1986. "Defense Resource Allocation: Garbage Can Analysis of C3 Procurement." In James G. March and Roger Weissinger-Baylon, eds., *Ambiguity and Command*, pp. 72–119. Marshfield, Mass.: Pitman.

Deutsch, Karl W. 1966. *The Nerves of Government*. New York: Free Press.

Drucker, Peter. 1967. *The Effective Executive*. New York: Random House.

Duhamel, Olivier. 1987. "The Fifth Republic Under François Mitterrand: Evolution and Perspectives." In George Ross, Stanley Hoffmann, and Sylvia Malzacher, eds., *The Mitterrand Experiment*, pp. 140–160. New York: Oxford University Press.

Durant, Robert F., and Paul F. Diehl. 1989. "Agendas, Alternatives, and Public Policy: Lessons from the U.S. Foreign Policy Arena," *Journal of Public Policy* 9:179–205.

Easton, David. 1964. *A Systems Analysis of Political Life*. New York: Wiley.

Feldman, Martha S. 1989. *Order Without Design: Information Production and Policy Making*. Stanford: Stanford University Press.

Feldman, Martha S., and James G. March. 1981. "Information as Signal and Symbol," *Administrative Science Quarterly* 26:171–186.

Freeman, Gary P. 1985. "National Styles and Policy Sectors: Explaining Structural Variation," *Journal of Public Policy* 5:467–496.

Frisch, Deborah, and Jonathan Baron. 1988. "Ambiguity and Rationality," *Journal of Behavioral Decision Making* 1(3):149–157.

Gordenker, Leon, Roger A. Coate, Christer Jönsson, and Peter Söderholm. 1995. *International Cooperation in Response to AIDS*. New York: St. Martin's Press.

Hayes, Michael T. 1992. *Incrementalism and Public Policy*. New York and London: Longman.

Hayward, Jack. 1991. "The Policy Community Approach to Industrial Policy." In Dankwart A. Rustow and Kenneth Paul Erikson, eds., *Comparative Political Dynamics: Global Research Perspectives*, pp. 381–407. New York: HarperCollins.

Heath, Chip, and Amos Tversky. 1991. "Preference and Belief: Ambiguity and Competence in Choice Under Uncertainty," *Journal of Risk and Uncertainty*, 4:5–28.

Hogarth, and Einhorn. 1989.

Huff, Anne Sigismund. 1988. "Politics and Argument as a Means for Coping with Ambiguity and Change." In Louis R. Pondy, Richard J. Boland, Jr., and Howard Thomas, eds., *Managing Ambiguity and Change*, pp. 79–90. New York: Wiley.

Ikenberry, G. John. 1990. "The International Spread of Privatization Policies: Inducements, Learning, and Policy Bandwagoning." In Ezra N. Suleiman and John Waterbury, eds., *The Political Economy of Public Sector Reform and Privatization*, pp. 88–110. Boulder: Westview Press.

King, Anthony. 1985. "Agendas, Alternatives and Public Policies" (book review), *Journal of Public Policy* 5:281–283.

Kingdon, John W. 1993. "Politicians, Self-Interest, and Ideas." In George E. Marcus and Russell L. Hanson, eds., *Reconsidering the Democratic Public,* pp. 73–89. University Park: Pennsylvania State University.

———. 1994. "Agendas, Ideas, and Policy Change." In Lawrence C. Dodd and Calvin Jillson, eds., *New Perspectives on American Politics,* pp. 215–229. Washington, D.C.: Congressional Quarterly Press.

———. 1995. *Agendas, Alternatives and Public Policies,* 2d ed. New York: HarperCollins.

Klingemann, Hans-Dieter, Richard I. Hofferbert, and Ian Budge. 1994. *Parties, Policies, and Democracy.* Boulder: Westview Press.

Mackenzie, R. Alec. 1972. *The Time Trap.* New York: AMACOM.

Mandelbaum, Maurice. 1987. *Purpose and Necessity in Social Theory.* Baltimore and London: Johns Hopkins University Press.

March, James G. 1994. *A Primer on Decision Making.* New York: Free Press.

March, James G., and Johan P. Olsen. 1983. "Organizing Political Life: What Administrative Reorganization Tells Us About Government," *American Political Science Review* 77:281–297.

March, James G., and Pierre J. Romelaer. 1976. "Position and Presence in the Drift of Decision." In James G. March and Johan P. Olsen, eds., *Ambiguity and Choice in Organizations,* pp. 251–276. Bergen, Norway: Universitetforlaget.

Mohr, Lawrence B. 1978. "Ambiguity and Choice in Organizations" (book review), *American Political Science Review* 72:1033–1035.

Mucciaroni, Gary. 1992. "The Garbage Can Model and the Study of Policy Making: A Critique," *Polity* 24:459–482.

Olsen, Johan P. 1988. "Administrative Reform and Theories of Organization." In Colin Campbell and B. Guy Peters, eds., *Organizing Governance, Governing Organizations,* pp. 233–254. Pittsburgh: University of Pittsburgh Press.

Padgett, John F. 1980. "Managing Garbage Can Hierarchies," *Administrative Science Quarterly* 25:583–604.

Peters, B. Guy. 1994. "Agenda-Setting in the European Community," *Journal of European Public Policy* 1:9–26.

Riker, William. 1986. *The Art of Political Manipulation.* New Haven: Yale University Press.

Rochefort, David A., and Roger W. Cobb, eds. 1994. *The Politics of Problem Definition: Shaping the Policy Agenda.* Lawrence: University Press of Kansas.

Rommetveit, Kåre. 1976. "Decision Making Under Changing Norms." In James G. March and Johan P. Olsen, eds. *Ambiguity and Choice in Organizations,* pp. 140–155. Bergen, Norway: Universitetforlaget.

Rose, Richard. 1989. *Politics in England.* Glenview, Ill.: Scott, Foresman.

Sabatier, Paul A., and Hank Jenkins-Smith, eds. 1993. *Policy Change and Learning: An Advocacy Coalition Approach.* Boulder: Westview Press.

Sharp, Elaine B. 1994. "Paradoxes of National Antidrug Policymaking." In David A. Rochefort and Roger W. Cobb, eds., *The Politics of Problem Definition: Shaping the Policy Agenda,* pp. 98–116. Lawrence: University Press of Kansas.

Skok, James E. 1995. "Policy Issue Networks and the Public Policy Cycle: A Structural Functional Framework for Public Administration," *Public Administration Review* 55:325–332.

Steinbruner, John D. 1974. *The Cybernetic Theory of Decision.* Princeton: Princeton University Press.

Stone, Deborah. 1988. *Policy Paradox and Political Reason.* Boston: Little, Brown.

Tversky, Amos, and Daniel Kahneman. 1981. "The Framing of Decisions and the Psychology of Choice," *Science* 211:453–458.

Weick, Karl E. 1979. *The Social Psychology of Organizing,* 2d ed. New York: Random House.

Weir, Margaret. 1992. "Ideas and the Politics of Bounded Innovation." In Sven Steinmo, Kathleen Thelen, and Frank Longstreth, eds., *Structuring Politics: Historical Institutionalism in Comparative Analysis,* pp. 188–216. Cambridge: Cambridge University Press.

Weissinger-Baylon, Roger. 1986. "Garbage Can Decision Processes in Naval Warfare." In James G. March and Roger Weissinger-Baylon, eds., *Ambiguity and Command,* pp. 36–52. Marshfield, Mass.: Pitman.

Wilson, James Q. 1989. *Bureaucracy.* New York: BasicBooks.

Zahariadis, Nikolaos. 1992. "To Sell or Not to Sell? Telecommunications Policy in Britain and France," *Journal of Public Policy* 12:355–376.

_____. 1995a. "Comparing Lenses in Comparative Public Policy," *Policy Studies Journal* 23:378–382.

_____. 1995b. *Markets, States, and Public Policies: Privatization in Britain and France.* Ann Arbor: University of Michigan Press.

_____. 1996. "Selling British Rail: An Idea Whose Time Has Come?" *Comparative Political Studies* 29:400–422.

Zahariadis, Nikolaos, and Christopher S. Allen. 1995. "Ideas, Networks, and Policy Streams: Privatization in Britain and Germany," *Policy Studies Review* 14:71–98.

PART III

Frameworks Focusing on Policy Change over Fairly Long Periods

5

Punctuated-Equilibrium Theory

Explaining Stability and Change in American Policymaking

JAMES L. TRUE, BRYAN D. JONES,
AND FRANK R. BAUMGARTNER

Punctuated-equilibrium theory seeks to explain a simple observation: Political processes are often driven by a logic of stability and incrementalism, but occasionally they also produce large-scale departures from the past. Stasis, rather than crisis, typically characterizes most policy areas. However, crises often occur. Dramatic changes in public policies are constantly occurring in many areas of American politics and policymaking, as public understandings of existing problems change. Important governmental programs are sometimes altered dramatically, even if most of the time they continue as they did in the previous year. The observation, then, is that both stability and change are important elements of the policy process. Most policy models have been designed to explain, or at least have been more successful at explaining, either the stability or the change. The punctuated-equilibrium theory encompasses both.

How to explain punctuations and stasis in a single theory? Punctuated-equilibrium theory places the policy process on a double foundation of political institutions and boundedly rational decisionmaking. It emphasizes two related elements of the policy process: issue definition and agenda setting. As issues are defined in public discourse in different ways, and as issues rise and fall in the public agenda, existing policies can be either reinforced or questioned. Reinforcement creates great obstacles to anything but modest change, but the questioning of policies at the most fundamental levels creates opportunities for dramatic reversals in policy outcomes.

Neither boundedly rational theories of incrementalism nor globally rational theories of preference maximization fit well with the joint observations of stasis and dramatic change that are the dual foci of the punctuated-equilibrium approach. However, rather than centering on the problems of purely incremental policy theories or purely rational choice theories, punctuated-equilibrium theory extends current agenda-setting theories to deal with both policy stasis and policy punctuations.

Several loosely related approaches in political science have noted that although agenda setting and policymaking often proceed smoothly with marginal accommodations, they also are regularly torn by lurches and significant departures from the incremental past (Kingdon, 1984, 1985/1995; Baumgartner and Jones, 1991, 1993; Dodd, 1994; Kelly, 1994). A unifying theme of these approaches is that we observe the same institutional system of government organizations and rules producing both a plethora of small accommodations and a significant number of radical departures from the past.

For the authors of this chapter, the clearest explanation for both marginal and large-scale policy changes comes from the interaction of subsystem politics and behavioral decisionmaking, a combination that creates patterns of stability and mobilization or punctuated equilibria.[1] In this chapter, we examine punctuated-equilibrium theory and its foundations in the longitudinal study of political institutions and in political decisionmaking. Next, we extend the punctuated-equilibrium theory to national budgeting and provide some recent evidence of punctuations and equilibria in national government spending since World War II. We conclude with an assessment of the strengths and weaknesses of this approach to understanding policymaking in America.

PUNCTUATED EQUILIBRIA IN AMERICAN POLICYMAKING

Since the path-breaking work of E. E. Schattschneider (1960), theories of conflict expansion and agenda setting have stressed the difficulty that disfavored groups and new ideas have in breaking through the established system of policymaking (Cobb and Elder, 1983; Bosso, 1987). As opposed to smooth, moderate adjustments to changing circumstances, the conservative nature of the national political system often favors the status quo, thereby making conflict or an extraordinary effort necessary for a major change.

When Baumgartner and Jones (1993) analyzed a number of policymaking cases over time and over a variety of issue areas, they found (1) that policymaking both makes leaps and undergoes periods of near stasis as issues emerge on and recede from the public agenda; (2) that this tendency toward punctuated equilibria is exacerbated by American political institutions; and (3) that policy images play a critical role in expanding issues beyond the control of the specialists and special interests that occupy what they termed "policy monopolies."

Baumgartner and Jones (1991, 1993) saw that the separated institutions, overlapping jurisdictions, and relatively open access to mobilizations in the United States combine to create a dynamic between the politics of subsystems and the macropolitics of Congress and the presidency—a dynamic that usually works against any impetus for change but occasionally reinforces it. For example, mobilizations are often required to overcome entrenched interests, but once under way, they can engender large-scale changes in policy. The reason is that once a mobilization is under way, the diffuse jurisdictional boundaries that separate the various overlapping institutions of government can allow many governmental actors to become involved in a new policy area. Typically, the newcomers are proponents of changes in the status quo, and they often overwhelm the previously controlling powers. Institutional separation often works to reinforce conservatism, but it sometimes works to wash away existing policy subsystems.

In short, American political institutions were conservatively designed to resist many efforts at change and thus to make mobilizations necessary if established interests are to be overcome. The result over time has been institutionally reinforced stability interrupted by bursts of change. These bursts have kept the U.S. government from becoming a gridlocked Leviathan despite its growth in size and complexity in this century. Instead, the U.S. government has become a complex, interactive system. Redford (1969) differentiated between subsystem politics and macropolitics. Baumgartner and Jones extended Redford's insight and combined it with the issue expansion and contraction insights of Schattschneider (1960) and Downs (1972) to form this theory of long-term agenda change and policymaking.

Institutional structures provide an important basis for the punctuated-equilibrium idea, and the agenda-setting process provides another. No political system features continuous discussion over all issues that confront it. Rather, discussions of political issues are usually disaggregated into a number of issue-oriented policy subsystems. These subsystems can be dominated by a single interest, can undergo competition among several interests, can be disintegrating over time, or may be building up their independence from others (Meier, 1985; Sabatier, 1987; Browne, 1995). They may be called *iron triangles, issue niches, policy subsystems,* or *issue networks,* but any such characterization can be considered only a snapshot of a dynamic process (Baumgartner and Jones, 1993, p. 6). Whatever the name one gives to these communities of specialists operating out of the political spotlight, most issues most of the time are treated within such a community of experts. Nonetheless, within the spotlight of macropolitics, some issues catch fire, dominate the agenda, and result in changes in one or more subsystems.

Herbert Simon (1957, 1977, 1983, 1985) distinguished between parallel processing and serial processing in individual and organizational decisionmaking. Some decision structures are capable of handling many issues simultaneously, in parallel. Others handle issues seriatim, one or a few at a time. Political systems, like humans, cannot simultaneously consider all the issues that face them, so the existence of some form of policy subsystems can be viewed as a mechanism that allows the political system to engage in parallel processing (Jones, 1994). Thousands of issues may be considered simultaneously in parallel within their respective communities of experts. This equilibrium of interests does not completely lock out change. Issue processing within subsystems allows for a politics of adjustment, with incremental change resulting from bargaining among interests and marginal moves in response to changing circumstances. But parallel processing does operate against larger policy changes, because it tends to be insulated from the glare of publicity associated with high-agenda politics.

Sometimes the parallel processing of issues breaks down, and they must be handled serially. The macropolitical institutions of Congress and the public presidency constitute governmental serial processing where high-profile issues are considered, contended over, and decided one at a time or, at most, a few at a time. When an issue moves higher on the political agenda, it is usually because new participants have become interested in the debate: "When a policy shifts to the macropolitical institutions for serial processing, it generally does so in an environment of changing issue definitions and heightened attentiveness by the media and broader publics" (Jones, 1994, p. 185). It is then that major changes tend to occur. Issues cannot forever be considered within the confines of a policy subsystem; occasionally macropolitical forces intervene. It is the intersection of the parallel processing capabilities of the policy subsystems and the serial processing needs of the macropolitical system that creates the nonincremental dynamics of lurching that we often observe in many policy areas. Punctuated equilibria in politics stem from this requirement of politics: Politicians cannot simultaneously deal with all important issues, but governments must.

When dominated by a single interest, the subsystem is best thought of as a policy monopoly. A policy monopoly has a definable institutional structure responsible for policymaking in an issue area, and its responsibility is supported by some powerful idea or image. This image is generally connected to core political values and can be communicated simply and directly to the public (Baumgartner and Jones, 1993, pp. 5–7). Because a successful policy monopoly systematically dampens pressures for change, we say that it contains a negative feedback process. Yet policy monopolies are not invulnerable forever.

A long-term view of U.S. policymaking reveals that policy monopolies can be constructed, and they can collapse. Their condition has an important effect on policymaking within their issue areas. If the citizens excluded from a monopoly remain apathetic, the institutional arrangement usually remains constant, and policy is likely to change only slowly (the negative feedback process). As pressure for change builds up, it may be resisted successfully for a time. But if pressures are sufficient, they may lead to a massive intervention by previously uninvolved political actors and governmental institutions. Generally, this requires a substantial change in the supporting policy image. As the issue is redefined, or as new dimensions of the debate become more salient, new actors feel qualified to exert their authority where previously they stayed away. These new actors may insist on rewriting the rules, and on changing the balance of power that will be reinforced by new institutional structures as previously dominant agencies and institutions are forced to share their power with groups or agencies that gain new legitimacy. Thus, the changes that occur as a policy monopoly is broken up may be locked in for the future as institutional reforms are put in place. These new institutions remain in place after public and political involvements recede, often establishing a new equilibrium in the policy area that lasts well after the issue recedes back off the agenda and into the parallel processing of a (newly altered) policy community.

Punctuated-equilibrium theory includes periods of equilibrium or near stasis, when an issue is captured by a subsystem, and periods of disequilibrium, when an issue is forced onto the macropolitical agenda. When an issue area is on the macropolitical agenda, small changes in the objective circumstances can cause large changes in policy, and we say that the system is undergoing a positive feedback process. Bak and Chen's (1991) study of large interactive systems helps flesh out this process of positive feedback. Like earthquakes, these policy punctuations can be precipitated by a mighty blow or by relatively minor events. What determines whether an issue will catch fire with positive feedback or not? The interaction of changing images and venues of public policies does.

Policy images are a mixture of empirical information and emotive appeals. The factual content of any policy or program can have many different aspects, and it can affect different people in different ways. When a single image is widely accepted and generally supportive of the policy, it is usually associated with a successful policy monopoly. When there is disagreement over the proper way to describe or understand a policy, proponents may focus on one set of images while their opponents refer to a different set of images. For example, when the image of civilian nuclear power was associated with economic progress and technical expertise, its policymaking typified a policy monopoly. When opponents raised images of danger and environmental degradation, the nuclear policy monopoly began to collapse (Baumgartner and Jones, 1991, 1993, pp. 25–28, 59–82). As we see in the next section, Jones (1994) further analyzed the importance of policy images not only to issue definition and redefinition in policymaking, but also to the serial and parallel processes of individual and collective decisionmaking in a democracy.

A new image may attract new participants, and the multiple venues in the American political system constitute multiple opportunities for policy entrepreneurs to advance their case. Not only do federalism, separation of powers, and jurisdictional overlaps inhibit major changes during periods of negative feedback, but they also mean that a mobilization stymied in one venue may be successful in

another. A problem that has not advanced onto the national agenda can sometimes be acted on by the states, and vice versa. The U.S. system of multiple policy
venues is an important part of the process of disrupting policy monopolies during periods of positive feedback.

In summary, subsystem politics is the politics of equilibrium—the politics of
the policy monopoly, incrementalism, a widely accepted supportive image, and
negative feedback. Subsystem decisionmaking is decentralized to the iron triangles and issue networks of specialists in the bureaucracy, congressional sub-
groups, and interested parties. Established interests tend to dampen departures
from inertia (except perhaps for the annual marginal increase in the budget) until
a political mobilization, advancement on the governmental agenda, and positive
feedback occur. At that point, issues spill over into the macropolitical system of
Congress and the public presidency.

Macropolitics is the politics of punctuation—the politics of large-scale change,
competing policy images, political manipulation, and positive feedback. Positive
feedback exacerbates impulses for change: It overcomes inertia and produces ex-
plosions or implosions from former states (Baumgartner and Jones, 1991, 1993;
Jones, Baumgartner, and Talbert, 1993; Jones, 1994; Talbert, Jones, and Baumgartner, 1995; Jones, Baumgartner, and True, 1996).

Policymaking in the United States is not well characterized by gridlock and a
straitjacket view of government. Vast changes have occurred in U.S. policy over
the years. Some of the change has been incremental, and some of it has occurred
in bursts or punctuations. During quiet periods for an issue area, the issue is not
widely seen as a public problem. Or if it is, then its policymaking is in the hands
of a subsystem (often a policy monopoly) with a generally accepted and supportive image. Nonetheless, there almost always remains some possibility that conflict
expansion or a mobilization of enthusiasm will generate new images and attract
new participants. Then the issue area is no longer quiet. It advances on the
agenda, and the macropolitical institutions grapple with it and with each other in
an effort to resolve the new "hot" issue. Major policy changes may be initiated,
one or more policy subsystems may be disrupted, and a new agency or program
may be created: "Punctuated equilibrium, rather than stability and immobilism,
characterizes the American political system" (Baumgartner and Jones, 1993,
p. 236).

BOUNDEDLY RATIONAL FOUNDATIONS
AND THE CENTRALITY OF DECISIONMAKING

Embedded in the punctuated-equilibrium theory of policy change is an implicit
theory of individual and collective decisionmaking. From a decisionmaking perspective, large-scale punctuations in policy spring from either a change in preferences or a change in attentiveness. If we regard preferences as relatively stable,

how can we explain nonmarginal changes in government policy? Particularly, how can we explain apparent cases of choice reversal when later studies find no large changes in the external environment?

Baumgartner and Jones (1993) explained "bursts" of change and policy punctuations as arising from the interactions of images and institutions. When an agreed-upon image becomes contested, a policy monopoly is usually under attack, and the likelihood grows of a new mobilization (a wave of either criticism or enthusiasm) advancing the issue onto the macropolitical agenda. How can policy images play such a central role in government agenda setting? Part of the answer is found in Jones's (1994) analysis of serial attention and rational decisionmaking, both individually and collectively.

Jones (1994) argued that individual and collective decision changes, including choice reversals, do not spring from rapid flip-flops of preferences or from basic irrationality (choosing to go against our own preferences); they spring from shifts in attention. He called such rapid changes "serial shifts." Individually, our serial attentiveness means that the senses may process information in a parallel way, but attention is given serially to one thing, or at most a few things, at a time (Simon, 1977, 1983). This means that although reality may be complex, changing, and multifaceted, we cannot smoothly integrate competing concerns and perspectives. We focus usually on one primary aspect of the choice situation at a time (Simon, 1957, 1985; Jones, 1994; see also Tversky, 1972; Zaller, 1992). Collectively, a shift in the object of attention can lead to a disjointed change in preferred alternatives, even when the alternatives are well defined (Jones, 1994, 1996).

Bounded rationality was wedded early to incrementalism (Lindblom, 1959; Wildavsky, 1964), yet incrementalism proved to be, at best, an incomplete explanation of government policymaking and, at worst, a misleading one. The basic problem with incrementalism surfaced when it was tested empirically. For example, when Davis, Dempster, and Wildavsky (1966) made a longitudinal study of bureau-level budget results, they found and reported empirical evidence of both incremental decision rules and two types of nonincremental shifts. The first shift apparently happened when a decision rule was temporarily set aside for a short period (called a *deviant case*), and the second occurred when a new decision rule was adopted (called a *shift point*) (1966, pp. 537–542). Except for these punctuations, these authors found support for a relatively incremental view of the budgetary process. The punctuations themselves were excluded from the model, and the authors' conclusions pointed to the significance of finding equations for the budget process and to the central role that the prior-year "base" played in those equations.

Focusing solely on incremental changes caused early behavioral decision theorists to downplay empirical evidence of large-scale change, and it led boundedly rational decisionmaking into a theoretical cul-de-sac. Incrementalism did seem to explain much of what happened in the budgetary process, but it had nothing to say about major policy changes. Indeed, boundedly rational decisionmaking even had a difficult time determining when changes could no longer be considered incremental (Wanat, 1974; Padgett, 1980; Berry, 1990; Hayes, 1992).

With Jones's reconceptualization, however, boundedly rational decisionmaking is a foundation for both major and minor changes—for both punctuations and equilibria. In the case of policymaking in America, the twin foundations of conservative and overlapping political institutions and boundedly rational decisionmaking (especially the role of images in dampening or exacerbating mobilizations against entrenched interests) combine to create a system that is both inherently conservative and liable to occasional radical change.

PUNCTUATIONS AND STABILITY
IN U.S. GOVERNMENT SPENDING

We have recently extended the punctuated-equilibrium theory to produce an agenda-based model of national budgeting (Jones, Baumgartner, and True, 1995, 1996, 1998). Its foundation remains the boundedly rational process of human decisionmaking interacting with disaggregated political institutions, specifically serial attentiveness and parallel subsystems. Collectively, government decisionmakers usually process information in a parallel way through subsystems, policy monopolies, iron triangles, and issue networks. When that happens, budgets change only incrementally. However, sometimes issues move from subsystem politics to macropolitics, and national attention in the Congress and in the presidency is of necessity given to one or a few high-profile items at a time. In the attention limelight of the macropolitical institutions, policies and programs can make radical departures from the past, and budgets can lurch into large changes.

National budget decisions are as boundedly rational as the policymaking decisions discussed above. Choice situations are multifaceted, yet decisionmakers tend to understand choices in terms of a circumscribed set of attributes, and they tend to have considerable difficulties in making trade-offs among these attributes. If a given policy promotes economic growth but simultaneously has some negative consequences in terms of human rights, one or the other of those competing values may be in the forefront of decisionmakers' attention. If attentiveness to these two dimensions were to shift—say as a result of scandal or changes in the composition of the group of decisionmakers, as sometimes occurs—then the chosen policy might shift dramatically as well. In general terms, Jones (1996) noted that decisionmakers tend to stick with a particular *decision design* (a term that refers to the attributes used in structuring a choice) until forced to reevaluate the decision design.

Budgets react to both endogenous and exogenous forces. The forces that might cause a change in the decision design may be external to the decisionmaker. Such influences may include changing levels of public attention, striking and compelling new information, or turnover in the composition of the decisionmaking body (say, when an election changes control of Congress, and when committee leaderships are rotated from one party to the other). When changing external circumstances force us out of an old decision design, the result is often not a modest adjustment but a major change in choice. Yet subsystem politics and the bureaucratic regularity of annual budget submissions constitute endogenous forces that tend to favor continuing with the same decision design. As a consequence, budget decisions tend either to be static, arrived at by applying the current decision design and subsystem institutions to the new choice situation, or disjointed, arrived at by utilizing a different decision design and macropolitical institutions that may incorporate new attributes into the choice structure or shift attention from one dimension to another. Even these explanations do not exhaust the possible interactions among institutions, images, and the environment, for large changes can also arise from endogenous conflicts over the appropriate image and from shifts in attention when the external circumstances have changed little, if at all.

Because political institutions amplify the tendency toward decisional stasis interspersed with abrupt change (as opposed to smooth, moderate adjustments to changing circumstances), the agenda-based model of policymaking and the serial shift model of decisionmaking together produce a pattern of punctuations and equilibria in the budget processes. As attentiveness shifts to the new aspect or attribute, so, too, do outcomes shift, and this process is often not smooth. Occasionally, in almost every issue area, the usual forces of negative feedback and subsystem maintenance will be replaced by deviation-enhancing positive feedback forces. Positive feedback leads to episodic and sporadic change (as institutionally induced stability tends to reassert itself after the punctuation).

This attention-driven, agenda-based budget model encompasses both periods of punctuation and periods of stability. In contrast to earlier theories, the agenda-based model has an almost tectonic flavor. Like earthquakes and avalanches, modern budgets reflect many small tremors and occasional major upheavals. Applied to budgets, the punctuated-equilibrium theory continues to differentiate between serial and parallel policy processing in government, and it incorporates a role for public mobilizations on an issue or issues. In elaborating on the theory, this model calls for varying interactions between mobilization pressures and resource constraints over time, and it calls for punctuations to occur at all levels of the budget.

This view of the budget process leads us to expect that annual budget changes within a given spending category should not be distributed in the normal, bell-shaped curve. Rather, these changes should reflect the nonnormal distributions found in earthquakes and other large interactive systems (see Mandelbrot, 1963; Padgett, 1980; Midlarsky, 1988; Bak and Chen, 1991; Peters, 1991). The "earthquake" budget model anticipates many minuscule real changes, few moderate changes, and many large changes (Jones et al., 1996).

The model implies that punctuations ought to occur at all levels of policymaking and at all levels of the budget, not to be driven simply by external (exogenous) factors in a top-down manner. This is a consequence of two factors. First, budget decisions are hostage to the statics and dynamics of selective attention to the underlying attributes structuring a political situation. Second, the theory of punctuated policy equilibrium is based in part on a "bottom-up" process in which policy change may occur in isolated subsystems; may spill over into other, related subsystems; or may be affected by exogenous shocks (Jones et al., 1996, 1998). If punctuations did not occur at all levels of scale in the budget, from the program level to the macropolitical level, and if they did not occur during all time periods, then we would have to question the application of this theory to budgeting.

Yet, because national budget decisions take place within political institutions, we expect that hierarchy will produce an inequality in the transmission of punctuations from one level to another. This inequality of transmission is connected to the notion of parallel versus serial processing of issues. Both the president and Congress are capable of transmitting top-down budget changes to many agencies at once, and they do so when an issue affecting many agencies or programs reaches the national agenda and is processed serially. Such top-down punctuations from fiscal stress will be more easily transmitted to departments, agencies, and bureaus than bottom-up punctuations from within those institutions will be transmitted upward. The reason is that the insular nature of parallel processing within subsystems damps out the spillover effects among subsystems. As a result, we expect fewer punctuations at the top than at the bottom levels of governmental organization.

PUNCTUATIONS IN PREVIOUS BUDGET THEORIES

Many different models of the policy process have predicted abrupt change, but they have generally postulated exogenous change. In particular, in the empirical and theoretical literature on public budgeting there is ample precedent to expect budget punctuations, beginning as shown above with Davis, Dempster, and Wildavsky (1966). Their studies focused on the use by decisionmakers of budget decision rules. These rules, understood by participants and offering a stable organizational environment for decisionmaking, were based on the concepts of base and fair share, which led to incrementalism in both process and output. But these authors later added that "although it is basically incremental, the budget process does respond to the needs of the economy and society, but only after sufficient pressure has built up to cause abrupt changes precipitated by these events" (Davis et al., 1974, p. 427). Exogenously caused punctuations in budget results are consistent with Ostrom and Marra (1986), Kamlet and Mowery (1987), Kiewiet and McCubbins (1991), and Su, Kamlet, and Mowery (1993).

The "earthquake" budget model departs from all of the cybernetic, optimizing, and adaptive models in emphasizing stasis or large change but not moderate change. The policymaking literature is replete with models of exogenously forced policy change. In addition to the authors cited above, such models are also suggested in the work of comparativists (Krasner, 1984) and scholars who study public representation. They see changes in public policy as exogenously driven by changes in public opinion (Stimson, MacKuen, and Erikson, 1995) or, alternatively, both responding to opinion and causing changes in opinion through a thermostat-like device (Wlezien, 1995). These models call for punctuations only if there is a change in macrolevel exogenous forces.

Other authors have allowed for complex interactions between endogenous and exogenous budget changes. Kiel and Elliott (1992) approached budgeting from a perspective of nonlinear dynamics, incorporating both linear and nonlinear processes. They noted the existence of likely nonlinearities in the budgeting process in which "exogenous and endogenous forces simply have varying impacts on budget outlays over time" (Kiel and Elliott, 1992, p. 143). Nonlinear, interactive processes imply occasional punctuations. Thurmaier (1995) reported the results of experiments in budget scenarios in which decisionmakers shift from economic to political rationales for their decisions after being given new information about political calculations. Such shifts in the bases of decisions can lead to punctuations. True (1995) found that domestic political factors had more influence on spending for national defense than had the dissolution of the Soviet Union. The case for both endogenous and exogenous influences on national budgets seems to be a strong one.

Most modern work in this area (including our own) must reckon with the seminal work of John Padgett (1980, 1981) on budget decisionmaking. Padgett's serial judgment model of the budget process implies "the occasional occurrence of very radical changes" (1980, p. 366). Both Padgett's serial judgment model and our agenda-based approach allow for endogenous mobilizations as well as exogenous shocks. Davis, Dempster, and Wildavsky (1966) suggested only exogenous shocks, but all three sets of authors have suggested punctuations in the budget process. The "earthquake" budget model alone, however, ties budget making both to an embedded cognitive decision theory and to an explicit policymaking theory—the punctuated-equilibrium theory of governance.

Following Padgett's lead, our agenda-based budget model assumes that budgeting is a stochastic process. It remains extremely difficult (and perhaps impossible) to specify precise causal linkages among all of the variables that interact nonlinearly or interdependently to produce changes in all of the line items of annual national budgets (especially if, like us, one hopes to do so for the entire postwar period). However, it is possible to develop hypotheses about the distribution of budget changes that can be derived from our agenda-based model and that can be distinguished from previous budgeting models. And that is the strategy we have followed (Jones et al., 1995, 1996).

Because we expect budgets generally to change very little, but occasionally to change a great deal, we hypothesize that annual budget changes will be distributed leptokurtotically. That is, their univariate distribution should have a large, slender central peak (representing a stability logic), weak shoulders (representing the difficulty in making moderate changes), and big tails (representing episodic punctuations). Note that a normal or Gaussian distribution would be found if continuous dynamic adjustment were the primary decision mechanism (Davis et al., 1966; Padgett, 1980; for a careful examination of univariate distributions, see Johnson, Kotz, and Balakrishnan, 1994).

Because we expect the dynamics of budget decisionmaking to occur at all levels, we hypothesize scale invariance. That is, we expected the underlying, nonnormal distribution of annual changes to be evident at all levels of aggregation (program, function, subfunction, and agency). Yet, because we expect changes in budget decisions to be more easily transmitted down the organizational chain than up, we expect that punctuations will be more pronounced at the bottom of the hierarchy than at the top. That is, we expect subfunctions to be more leptokurtotic than functions, and functions to be more leptokurtotic than higher aggregations.

These expectations diverge from the predictions of other budget and decision models. The boundedly rational models of Davis et al. (1966, 1974) explicitly describe the normality of their residual terms. That is, year-to-year changes are usually normally distributed, and after an exogenous factor has caused a shift in parameters, the series will again be modeled with a normal residual term. The "cybernetic" models of Ostrom and Marra (1986), Kamlet and Mowery (1987), or Blais, Blake, and Dion (1993) depend upon the assumption of normality to justify their use of linear regressions and pooled-regression models.

Budget-maximizing models have made few particular predictions in this area (Niskannen, 1971), but it is reasonable to expect a normal distribution of first differences from them as well, and indeed most regression analyses and analyses of variance depend upon the central limit theorem for their justification. Maximizing models do not predict punctuations unless there is a shift in exogenous factors, but if such a shift occurs, most maximizing models assume that the accumulation of exogenous factors will asymptotically approach normality.

We tested our hypotheses of nonnormal changes with a new data set of budget authority for Office of Management and Budget (OMB) subfunctions from fiscal year 1947 through FY 1995. We used actual budget authority corrected for inflation. This measure is more accurate than appropriations, which can confuse the timing of contract spending and depend upon estimates for trust fund spending. And budget authority is closer to the congressional decisionmaking process than outlay data, which can be delayed for several years after the decision has been made. We constructed the relevant estimates from original contemporary budgets based upon our analysis of current budget categories. We focused primarily on OMB's subfunction level, which divides the seventeen core governmental functions into seventy-four groupings based on the national purposes they are supposed to serve. We have limited our data set to sixty-two programmatic subfunctions, eliminating twelve primarily financial subfunctions because of their heavy use of offsetting receipts and net, rather than complete, results. The budget data were converted to constant calendar year 1987 figures by means of the implicit deflator for the gross domestic product of the *National Income and Product Accounts of the United States* and the National Income and Product Tables of the *Survey of Current Business*. We compared the percentage changes in each category for each pair of years from FY 1947 to FY 1994, approximately 2,700 observations in all.

The Distribution of Budget Changes

If we take the simple indicator of annual percentage change for each of the sixty-two programmatic budget subfunctions from FY 1947 through FY 1995, we get the distribution shown in the histogram in Figure 5.1. The distribution is clearly leptokurtotic and positively skewed. It diverges widely from a normal curve even when we drop the top 5 percent of the outliers when computing the mean and standard deviation for the normal curve. (If we include all of the observations in computing the normal curve, it is even flatter and more positively skewed.) Note the leptokurtotic peak, indicating the great number of very small changes; the weak shoulders, indicating fewer than normal moderate changes; and the big tails, indicating more than normal radical departures from the previous year's budget. Changes greater than 300 percent are grouped at that point.

Whether we plot percentage changes, first differences, or changes in logged data, the distributions are leptokurtotic and not normal. When we compare annual changes in budget authority for functions and subfunctions, the characteristic leptokurtosis remains, although the subfunctions are more leptokurtotic than the functions. When we plot the distribution of annual changes by agency, leptokurtosis remains. We examined plots of the following: subfunction budget outlay data, 1962–1994; subfunction budget authority data, 1976–1994; and agency-level budget authority data, 1976–1994. These series were assembled by OMB, and all exhibited leptokurtosis. We even plotted outlay data for the U.S. government for the period 1800–1994, in this case adjusting for inflation using the Consumer Price Index. Again leptokurtosis was in evidence.

Conclusions from Our Stochastic Budget Study

First, we conclude that the distribution of annual changes in budget authority is consistent with the "earthquake" budget model (as called for by the punctuated-equilibrium theory), but not with the boundedly rational theories of Davis et al. (1966), with the models of Kamlet and Mowery (1987), or with our understanding of budget-maximizing or adaptive behavior models. Second, we note that an-

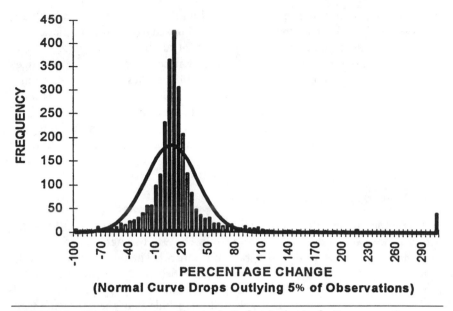

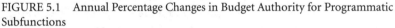

FIGURE 5.1   Annual Percentage Changes in Budget Authority for Programmatic Subfunctions

SOURCE: Frank R. Baumgartner and Bryan D. Jones Agenda Setting Project. Data are available from the Center for American Politics: <http://weber.u.washington.edu/~ampol.>

nual budget changes tend to be scale-invariant. The leptokurtotic distribution appears at the function level and the subfunction level; it appears in annual percentage changes and in annual first differences; and it survived logarithmic transformation. Leptokurtosis appears in the annual differences of budget authority for agencies and for outlay data of the government overall.

Third, we conclude that within this nearly universal leptokurtosis, there is nonetheless a hierarchical difference. As expected, punctuations are more pronounced at the bottom of the organizational ladder than at the top. Subfunctions are more leptokurtotic than functions. Agencies are more leptokurtotic than the budget as a whole. Although we view these results as support for our asymmetry hypothesis on the transmission of punctuations, there is a possibility that the observed differences may be more a function of the smaller N available from the more highly aggregated series (Mandelbrot 1963; Fama 1963). That is to say, there is a possibility that if we had 2,699 years of total budget data as we have 2,699 cases of annual subfunction changes, then we might observe as much leptokurtosis in the total budget as we do now in its parts.[2]

In summary, the extension of the punctuated-equilibrium model to national budgeting resulted in the following: (1) its elaboration into an agenda-based, attention-driven budgeting model; (2) hypotheses concerning the distribution of annual budget changes and its underlying structure; and (3) empirical evidence that conforms to the new theory but that is antithetical to the normal changes expected from incremental theory or from most other budget theories. Punctuated equilibrium, rather than incrementalism alone, characterizes national budgeting in America; just as punctuated equilibrium, rather than gridlock or marginalism, characterizes overall policymaking in the American political system.

EVALUATING THE STRENGTHS
AND WEAKNESSES OF PUNCTUATED EQUILIBRIUM

Founded on the bounded rationality of human decisionmaking and on the nature of U.S. government institutions, punctuated equilibrium can make a strong claim that its propositions closely accord with what we have observed about national policymaking. It accounts both for periods of stability and incremental change and for periods of upheaval and large-scale change. Incremental adjustments and even stasis will occur often, but not always. Punctuations and radical policy departures are not aberrations, and outliers to be discarded so that linear mathematics or the technology of the central limit theorem can function. Punctuations are a regular and important feature of U.S. budget making and U.S. policymaking.

The ubiquity of serial attentiveness and organizational routines of operation lead us to expect that stability and punctuations are a feature of policymaking in many governments. At the same time, the institutional aspect of multiple venues interacts with boundedly rational decisionmaking to make punctuated-equilibrium theory particularly apt for relatively open democracies. Indeed, the punctuated-equilibrium model is proving useful in understanding stability and change in British trunk roads policy (Dudley and Richardson, 1996), in congressional committee jurisdiction concentrations (Hardin, 1996), and in protracted interstate rivalries (Cioffi-Revilla, 1997).

Yet the utility of this theory and its accord with what is observed come at a price. A full appreciation of the complexity and changing interactions of the American policy process convinces us that individual-level predictions about policy outcomes will be possible only to the extent that either we can choose areas and periods for study that avoid the periods and areas of positive feedback and punctuations or we limit our "predictions" to periods when we can know after the fact what were the successful mobilizations. Nonlinearity, nonnormality, interdependencies, and high levels of aggregation for empirical data mean that clear causal chains and precise predictions will work only in some cases and for some times. To the extent that this is most of the cases and most of the times, scholars may be convinced that they have a good working model of the process. But a complete model will not be locally predictable, since we cannot predict the timing or the outcomes of the punctuations. What will cause the next big shift in attention, change in dimension, or new frame of reference? And when will any of these occur in a particular policy area? At the systems level, punctuated equilibrium, as a theory, leads us to expect that some policy punctuation is under way almost all of the time. And the theory joins institutional settings and decision-making processes to predict that the magnitude of local changes will be related to their systems-level frequency of occurrence. Punctuated-equilibrium theory predicts a form of systems-level stability, but it will not help us to make specific predictions for particular policy issues.

We can have a systems-level model of the policy process even though not having an individual-level model for each policy. Linear predictions about the details of future policies will fail each time they meet an unforeseen punctuation; they will succeed as long as the parameters of the test coincide with periods of equilibrium. This limitation means that it will be tempting to offer models applicable only to the more easily testable and confirmable periods of relative stability. In our view, a clearer, more complete, and more empirically accurate theoretical lens is that of punctuated equilibria in American political processes. But we understand that this theoretical completeness comes with a cost.

NOTES

1. Punctuated equilibrium was first advanced as an explanation of the development of differences among species, or speciation (Eldridge and Gould, 1972; Raup, 1991). Rather than changing smoothly and slowly as in the later Darwinian models, evolution and speciation were better characterized as a near stasis punctuated by large-scale extinctions and replacements. For example, there was a virtual explosion of diversity of life in the Pre-Cambrian Period, an explosion that has never been repeated on such an immense scale (Gould, 1989). The notion has been vigorously contested by evolutionary biologists, who claim that disconnects in evolution are not possible (although variations in the pace of evolution clearly are) (Dawkins, 1996). Interestingly, some of these scholars have argued that consciousness makes possible punctuations in human cultural evolution: What cannot occur via genes can occur via memes (Dawkins's term for the transmitters of cultural adaptive advantage) (Dawkins, 1989; cf. Boyd and Richerson, 1985).

2. The central limit theorem holds only for Gaussian distributions. As a consequence, we have no guarantee that a sample drawn from a leptokurtotic distribution (such as the Paretian) will produce sample statistics that are leptokurtotically distributed.

REFERENCES

Bak, Per, and Kan Chen. 1991. "Self-Organized Criticality," *Scientific American* 264:46–53.

Baumgartner, Frank R., and Bryan D. Jones. 1991. "Agenda Dynamics and Policy Subsystems," *Journal of Politics* 53:1044–1074.

_____. 1993. *Agendas and Instability in American Politics*. Chicago: University of Chicago Press.

Berry, William D. 1990. "The Confusing Case of Budgetary Incrementalism: Too Many Meanings for a Single Concept," *Journal of Politics* 52:167–196.

Blais, Andre, Donald Blake, and Stephane Dion. 1993. "Do Parties Make a Difference? Parties and the Size of Government in Liberal Democracies," *American Journal of Political Science* 37:40–62.

Bosso, Christopher J. 1987. *Pesticides and Politics: The Life Cycle of a Public Issue.* Pittsburgh: University of Pittsburgh Press.

Boyd, Robert, and Peter Richerson. 1985. *Culture and the Evolutionary Process.* Chicago: University of Chicago Press.

Browne, William P. 1995. *Cultivating Congress: Constituents, Issues, and Interests in Agricultural Policymaking.* Lawrence: University of Kansas Press.

Cioffi-Revilla, Claudio. 1997. "The Political Uncertainty of Interstate Rivalries: A Punctuated Equilibrium Model." In Paul F. Diehl, ed., *The Dynamics of Enduring Rivalries.* Urbana: University of Illinois Press.

Cobb, Roger W., and Charles D. Elder. 1983. *Participation in American Politics: The Dynamics of Agenda-Building.* Baltimore: Johns Hopkins University Press.

Davis, Otto A., M. A. H. Dempster, and Aaron Wildavsky. 1966. "A Theory of the Budget Process," *American Political Science Review* 60:529–547.

_____. 1974. "Towards a Predictive Theory of Government Expenditure: U.S. Domestic Appropriations," *British Journal of Political Science* 4:419–452.

Dawkins, Richard. 1989. *The Selfish Gene,* 2d ed. Oxford: Oxford University Press.

_____. 1996. *Climbing Mount Improbable.* New York: W. W. Norton.

Dodd, Lawrence C. 1994. "Political Learning and Political Change: Understanding Development Across Time." In *The Dynamics of American Politics.* Boulder: Westview Press.

Downs, Anthony. 1972. "Up and Down with Ecology: The Issue-Attention Cycle," *Public Interest* 28:38–50.

Dudley, Geoffrey, and Jeremy Richardson. 1996. "Why Does Policy Change over Time? Adversarial Policy Communities, Alternative Policy Arenas, and British Trunk Roads Policy 1945–95," *Journal of European Public Policy* 3:63–83.

Eldridge, Niles, and Stephen J. Gould. 1972. "Punctuated Equilibria: An Alternative to Phyletic Gradualism." In Thomas J. M. Schopf, ed., *Models in Paleobiology.* San Francisco: Freeman Cooper.

Fama, Eugene F. 1963. "Mandelbrot and the Stable Paretian Hypothesis." In Paul Cootner, ed., *The Random Character of Stock Market Prices.* Cambridge, Mass.: MIT Press.

Gould, Stephen Jay. 1989. *Wonderful Life: The Burgess Shale and the Nature of History.* New York: W. W. Norton.

Hardin, John W. 1996. "Fishing for Constituents, Promoting Certainty: The Dynamics of Committee Jurisdiction Concentration." Paper presented at the annual meeting of the Midwest Political Science Association, Chicago.

Hayes, Michael T. 1992. *Incrementalism and Public Policy.* New York: Longman.

Johnson, Norman L., Samuel Kotz, and N. Balakrishnan. 1994. *Continuous Univariate Distributions.* New York: Wiley.

Jones, Bryan D. 1994. *Reconceiving Decision-making in Democratic Politics: Attention, Choice, and Public Policy.* Chicago: University of Chicago Press.

_____. 1996. "Attributes, Alternatives, and the Flow of Ideas: Information Processing in Politics." Paper presented at the annual meeting of the American Political Science Association, San Francisco.

Jones, Bryan D., Frank Baumgartner, and Jeffrey Talbert. 1993. "The Destruction of Issue Monopolies in Congress," *American Political Science Review* 87:657–671.

Jones, Bryan D., Frank R. Baumgartner, and James L. True. 1995. "The Shape of Change: Punctuations and Stability in U.S. Budgeting, 1946–94." Working Paper 42, Program in American Politics, Texas A & M University.

_____. 1996. "The Shape of Change: Punctuations and Stability in U.S. Budgeting, 1946–94." Paper presented at the annual meeting of the Midwest Political Science Association, Chicago.

_____. 1998. "Policy Punctuations: U.S. Budget Authority, 1947–1995," *Journal of Politics* 60:1–33.

Kamlet, Mark S., and David C. Mowery. 1987. "Influences on Executive and Congressional Budgetary Priorities, 1955–1981," *American Political Science Review* 81:155–178.

Kelly, Sean. 1994. "Punctuated Change and the Era of Divided Government." In Lawrence C. Dodd and Calvin Jillson, eds., *New Perspectives on American Politics*. Washington, D.C.: Congressional Quarterly.

Kiel, Douglas, and Euel Elliott. 1992. "Budgets as Dynamic Systems: Change, Variation, Time, and Budgetary Heuristics," *Journal of Public Administration Theory* 2:139–56.

Kiewiet, Roderick, and Matthew McCubbins. 1991. *The Logic of Delegation: Congressional Parties and the Appropriations Process*. Chicago: University of Chicago Press.

Kingdon, John. 1995 *Agendas, Alternatives, and Public Policies*, 2d. ed. Boston: Little, Brown. (Originally published in 1985.)

Krasner, Stephen. 1984. "Approaches to the State: Alternative Conceptions and Historical Dynamics," *Comparative Politics* 16:223–246.

Lindblom, Charles. 1959. "The Science of Muddling Through," *Public Administration Review* 19:79–88.

Mandelbrot, Benoit. 1963. "New Methods in Statistical Economics," *Journal of Political Economy* 71:421–440.

Meier, Kenneth. 1985. *Regulation: Politics, Bureaucracy, and Economics*. New York: St. Martin's Press.

Midlarsky, Manus I. 1988. "Rulers and the Ruled: Patterned Inequality and the Onset of Mass Political Violence," *American Political Science Review* 82:491–509.

Niskannen, William A. 1971. *Bureaucracy and Representative Government*. Chicago: Aldine.

Ostrom, Charles W., Jr., and Robin F. Marra. 1986. "A Reactive Linkage Model of the U.S. Defense Expenditure Policymaking Process," *American Political Science Review* 72:941–957.

Padgett, John F. 1980. "Bounded Rationality in Budgetary Research," *American Political Science Review* 74:354–372.

_____. 1981. "Hierarchy and Ecological Control in Federal Budgetary Decision Making," *American Journal of Sociology* 87:75–128.

Peters, Edgar E. 1991. *Chaos and Order in the Capital Markets*. New York: Wiley.

President's Commission on Budget Concepts. (1967). *Report of the President's Commission on Budget Concepts*. Washington, D.C., October

Raup, David M. 1991. *Extinction: Bad Genes or Bad Luck?* New York: W. W. Norton.

Redford, Emmette S. 1969. *Democracy in the Administrative State*. New York: Oxford University Press.

Sabatier, Paul A. 1987. "Knowledge, Policy-Oriented Learning, and Policy Change," *Knowledge: Creation, Diffusion, Utilization* 8:649–692.

Schattschneider, E. E. 1960. *The Semi-Sovereign People.* New York: Holt, Rinehart & Winston.

Simon, Herbert A. 1957. *Models of Man.* New York: Wiley.

_____. 1977. "The Logic of Heuristic Decision-Making." In R. S. Cohen and M. W. Wartofsky, eds., *Models of Discovery.* Boston: D. Reidel.

_____. 1983. *Reason in Human Affairs.* Stanford: Stanford University Press.

_____. 1985. "Human Nature in Politics: The Dialogue of Psychology with Political Science," *American Political Science Review* 79:293–304.

Stimson, James A. Michael B. MacKuen, and Robert S. Erikson. 1995. "Dynamic Representation," *American Political Science Review* 89:543–565.

Su, Tsai-Tsu, Mark S. Kamlet, and David Mowery. 1993. "Modeling U.S. Budgetary and Fiscal Outcomes: A Disaggregated, Systemwide Perspective," *American Journal of Political Science* 37:213–245.

Talbert, Jeffrey, Bryan Jones, and Frank Baumgartner. 1995. "Nonlegislative Hearings and Policy Change in Congress," *American Journal of Political Science* 39:383–406.

Thurmaier, Kurt. 1995. "Decisive Decision-making in the Executive Budget Process: Analyzing the Political and Economic Propensities of Central Budget Bureau Analysts." *Public Administration Review* 55:448–460.

True, James L. 1995. "Is the National Budget Controllable?" *Public Budgeting and Finance* 15:18–32.

Tversky, Amos. 1972. "Elimination by Aspects: A Theory of Choice," *Psychological Review* 79:281–299.

U.S. Department of Commerce. 1990. *National Income and Product Accounts of the United States* Washington, D.C.: U.S. Department of Commerce.

U.S. Department of Commerce. *Survey of Current Business* Washington, D.C.: U.S. Department of Commerce (serial).

U.S. Office of Management and Budget. *Budget of the United States Government* (serial, fiscal year 1948 through 1996).

Wanat, John. 1974. "Bases of Budgetary Incrementalism," *American Political Science Review* 68:1221–1228.

Wildavsky, Aaron. 1964. *The Politics of the Budgetary Process.* Boston: Little, Brown.

Wlezien, Christopher. 1995. "The Public as Thermostat: Dynamics of Preferences for Spending," *American Journal of Political Science* 39:981–1000.

Zaller, John R. 1992. *The Nature and Origins of Mass Opinion.* New York: Cambridge University Press.

6

The Advocacy Coalition Framework

An Assessment

PAUL A. SABATIER AND HANK C. JENKINS-SMITH

The initial version of the advocacy coalition framework (ACF) was developed by Sabatier over a number of years, starting with a year-long research seminar (1981–1982) at the University of Bielefeld and culminating in two very similar papers (Sabatier, 1987, 1988).[1] It emerged out of (1) a search for an alternative to the stages heuristic (Jones, 1977) that was then dominating policy studies, (2) a desire to synthesize the best features of the top-down and bottom-up approaches to policy implementation (Sabatier, 1986), and (3) a commitment to incorporate technical information into a more prominent role in our understanding of the policy process.

In the mid-1980s, Sabatier developed a collaboration with Jenkins-Smith, who had, quite independently, developed very similar conceptions of the role of scien-

The authors would like to thank Chris Hood, Lin Ostrom, John Grinn, Robert Hoppe, Neil Pelkey, Yves Surel, Pierre Muller, Yannis Papadopoulos, and Fritz Scharpf for their constructive comments on previous versions presented at the 1996 American Political Science Association Meetings, at the University of Amsterdam (February 1997), and at several European universities (November 1998). We would also like to thank the scholars—many of them Ph.D. students—whose interest in the ACF has stimulated many of the revisions since 1993. Among the more important scholars have been Bill Blomquist, Dorothy Daley, Jan Eberg, Chris Elliot, Menno Fenger, Bill Freudenburg, Daniel Kuebler, Anne Loeber, Michael Mintrom, Edella Schlager, Gerald Thomas, Rinie van Est, Sonja Waelti, and Matt Zafonte. Like any viable theory, the ACF has become a collective enterprise to whom numerous scholars of varying ages have contributed. Throughout this chapter, we try to acknowledge those responsible for specific contributions.

tific information in public policy (Jenkins-Smith, 1988, 1990). Jenkins-Smith and Sabatier devised a strategy of encouraging other scholars to critically evaluate relevant portions of the ACF on policy domains and data sets at their disposal. The result was two symposia involving a total of nine applications of the ACF, which, in turn, led to several amendments (Sabatier and Jenkins-Smith, 1988, 1993; Jenkins-Smith and Sabatier, 1994). Since 1993, the ACF has been applied by a number of scholars in the United States, Canada, Australia, and western Europe, largely on their own initiative.

This chapter first lays out the foundations of the original (1987–1988) version of the ACF. The bulk of the chapter explores a variety of topics on which considerable research has been conducted since the late 1980s. On some topics—most notably, the existence of advocacy coalitions—the evidence has confirmed the basic arguments of the ACF. On several others, the evidence has pointed to the need to revise and/or elaborate the framework. The final section concludes with an assessment of the strengths and limitations of the framework, as well as suggestions for future research.

THE INITIAL (1987–1988) VERSION OF THE ACF

Premises

The initial version of the advocacy coalition framework was based on five basic premises, arising largely out of the literatures on policy implementation and the role of technical information in public policy.

First, theories of the policy process or policy change need to address the role played in the process by technical information concerning the magnitude and facets of the problem, its causes, and the probable impacts of various solutions. Such information clearly plays an important role in many administrative agency decisions (Sabatier, 1978; Crandall and Lave, 1981; Mazur, 1981). Many legislators want to have some knowledge of the severity of the problem and the probable benefits and costs of the proposed statutory or budgetary solutions before they impose those costs (Kingdon, 1984; Krehbiel, 1992; Whiteman, 1995). Finally, the rise of think tanks and policy analysis units both inside and outside government suggests there is a growing market for technical analysis (Jenkins-Smith, 1990; J. A. Smith, 1991).

Second, understanding the process of policy change—and the role of technical information therein—requires a time perspective of a decade or more. This argument for an extended time period comes directly from findings concerning the importance of the "enlightenment function" of policy research. Weiss (1977) argued persuasively that a focus on short-term decisionmaking will underestimate the influence of policy analysis because such research is used primarily to alter the belief systems of policymakers over time. The literature on policy implementation also points to the need for utilizing time frames of a decade or more in order to complete at least one formulation/implementation/reformulation cycle, to obtain a reasonably accurate portrait of success and failure, and to appreciate the variety of strategies actors pursue over time (Bernstein, 1955; Kirst and Jung, 1982; Mazmanian and Sabatier, 1989).

A third basic premise is that the most useful unit of analysis for understanding policy change in modern industrial societies is not any specific governmental organization or program, but a policy subsystem (or domain). A subsystem consists of those actors from a variety of public and private organizations who are actively concerned with a policy problem or issue, such as air pollution control, and who regularly seek to influence public policy in that domain. Policymaking in virtually any subsystem is of sufficient complexity—in terms of understanding the relevant laws and regulations, the magnitude of the problem and the influence of various causal factors, and the set of concerned organizations and individuals— so that actors must specialize if they are to have any influence. An additional rationale for focusing on subsystems as the unit of analysis—rather than on specific organizations or programs—is the repeated finding from bottom-up implementation studies that there is seldom a single dominant program at the local/operational level. Instead, one usually finds a multitude of programs initiated at different levels of government that local actors seek to utilize in pursuit of their own goals (Hjern, Hanf, and Porter, 1978; Hjern and Porter, 1981; Sabatier, 1986).

Fourth, within the subsystem, the ACF argues that our conception of policy subsystems should be broadened from traditional notions of iron triangles—limited to administrative agencies, legislative committees, and interest groups at a single level of government—to include two additional categories of actors: (1) journalists, researchers, and policy analysts, who play important roles in the generation, dissemination, and evaluation of policy ideas (Heclo, 1978; Jordan and Richardson, 1983; Kingdon, 1984; Hall, 1993), and (2) actors at *all* levels of government active in policy formulation and implementation. In many countries, policy innovations often occur first at a subnational level and are then expanded into nationwide programs (Walker, 1969; Nelson, 1984). Two decades of implementation research have conclusively demonstrated that subnational implementing officials have substantial discretion in deciding exactly how national policy gets translated into thousands of concrete decisions in very diverse local situations (Pressman and Wildavsky, 1973; Rhodes, 1988; Mazmanian and Sabatier, 1989; Scholz et al., 1991). Finally, international treaties and the European Union have increasingly provided an international dimension in many policy domains (Richardson, 1996; Sewell, 1999).

The fifth important premise is that public policies/programs incorporate implicit theories about how to achieve their objectives (Pressman and Wildavsky, 1973; Majone, 1980) and thus can be conceptualized in much the same way as belief systems. They involve value priorities, perceptions of important causal relationships, perceptions of world states (including the magnitude of the problem), and perceptions/assumptions concerning the efficacy of various policy instruments. This ability to map beliefs and policies on the same "canvas" provides a vehicle for assessing the influence of various actors over time, particularly the role of technical information in policy change.

Structural Overview of the ACF

Figure 6.1 presents a general overview of the 1988 version of the ACF. On the left side are two sets of exogenous variables—one quite stable, the other more dynamic—that affect the constraints and opportunities of subsystem actors (Sabatier, 1988, p.132).

The former variables include the basic constitutional structure, sociocultural values, and natural resources of a political system. Being extremely difficult to change, they are seldom the subject of coalition strategies (except in the very long term). Nevertheless, they clearly affect behavior. For example, Moe (1990) argued that changing the law is typically the focus of coalition strategies in separation-of-powers systems simply because, in such systems, a law once enacted is extremely difficult to overturn. On the other hand, in Westminster-style systems, where the majority party can change any law anytime it wishes, coalitions are more likely to rely upon a variety of more informal, and longer-lasting, arrangements. Likewise, Ashford (1981) argued that policy-oriented learning is more difficult in Britain than in many other countries because of the norms of secrecy that so permeate the civil service.

The second set of factors exogenous to the subsystem are more likely to change over the course of a decade or so. The ACF argues they are a critical prerequisite to major policy change. They include (1) major socioeconomic changes, such as economic dislocations or the rise of social movements (Eisner, 1993); (2) changes in the systemic governing coalition, including "realigning" elections (Burnham, 1970; Brady, 1988); and (3) policy decisions and impacts from other subsystems (Muller, 1995). Changes in tax law, for example, often have major impacts on all sorts of policy subsystems.

Within the subsystem, the ACF assumes that actors can be aggregated into a number (usually one to four) of "advocacy coalitions," each composed of people from various governmental and private organizations that both (1) share a set of normative and causal beliefs and (2) engage in a nontrivial degree of coordinated activity over time. The ACF explicitly argues that most coalitions will include not only interest group leaders, but also agency officials, legislators from multiple levels of government, applied researchers, and perhaps even a few journalists. At any given point in time, the subsystem will usually contain a number of individuals and organizations unassociated with any coalition, but the ACF assumes that most will not be important over the long term because they will either leave (out of frustration or lack of interest) or get incorporated into one of the coalitions.

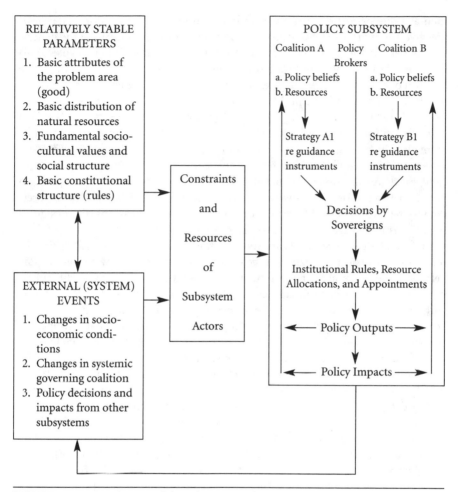

FIGURE 6.1   1988 Diagram of the Advocacy Coalition Framework

SOURCE: Sabatier (1988, p. 132).

The belief systems of each coalition are organized into a hierarchical tripartite structure, with higher/broader levels often constraining more specific beliefs (Peffley and Hurwitz, 1985). At the highest/broadest level, the *deep core* of the shared belief system includes basic ontological and normative beliefs, such as the relative valuation of individual freedom versus social equality, which operate across virtually all policy domains. The familiar left/right scale, which has proven to be a good predictor of political behavior on Congressional roll call votes (Poole and Daniels, 1985), operates at this level. At the next level are *policy core beliefs,* which represent a coalition's basic normative commitments and causal perceptions across an entire policy domain or subsystem. They include fundamental value priorities, such as the relative importance of economic development versus environmental protection, basic perceptions concerning the general seriousness of the problem (e.g., air pollution) and its principal causes, and strategies for realizing core values within the subsystem, such as the appropriate division of authority between governments and markets, the level of government best suited to deal with the problem, and the basic policy instruments to be used. The ACF assumes that policy core—not deep core—beliefs are the fundamental glue of coalitions because they represent basic normative and empirical commitments within the domain of specialization of policy elites.[2] Finally, the *secondary aspects* of a coalition's belief system comprise a large set of narrower (i.e., typically less than subsystemwide) beliefs concerning the seriousness of the problem or the relative importance of various causal factors in specific locales, policy preferences regarding desirable regulations or budgetary allocations, the design of specific institutions, and the evaluations of various actors' performance.

In general, deep core beliefs are very resistant to change—essentially akin to a religious conversion. A coalition's policy core beliefs are somewhat less rigidly held. Although several are almost exclusively normative and thus very difficult to modify, most involve empirical elements that may change over a period of time with the gradual accumulation of evidence (Weiss's "enlightenment function"). For example, whereas all environmental groups in the United States supported command-and-control regulation in the early 1970s, a few have gradually come to prefer economic incentives as a policy instrument in situations where the marginal costs of further environmental improvements are very high (Liroff, 1986). Beliefs in the secondary aspects are assumed to be more readily adjusted in light of new data, new experience, or changing strategic considerations.[3]

At any particular time, each coalition adopts one or more strategies involving the use of guidance instruments (changes in rules, budgets, personnel, or information) as a means of altering the behavior of various governmental authorities in an effort to realize its policy objectives. Conflicting strategies from various coalitions may be mediated by a third group of actors, here termed *policy brokers,* whose principal concern is to find some reasonable compromise that will reduce intense conflict.[4] The end result is one or more governmental programs, which in turn produce policy outputs at the operational level (e.g., agency permit decisions). These outputs—mediated by a number of other factors—result in a variety of impacts on targeted problem parameters (e.g., ambient air quality), as well as side effects. On the basis of perceptions of the adequacy of governmental decisions and/or the resultant impacts, as well as new information arising from search processes and external dynamics, each advocacy coalition may revise its beliefs (primarily in the secondary aspects) and/or alter its strategies. Altering strategies may involve seeking major institutional revisions at the collective choice level, more minor revisions at the operational level (Kiser and Ostrom, 1982), or even going outside the subsystem by seeking changes in the dominant coalition at the systemic level.

Policy-Oriented Learning and Policy Change

Within the general process of policy change, the ACF has a particular interest in understanding policy-oriented learning. Following Heclo (1974, p. 306), the term *policy-oriented learning* refers to relatively enduring alterations of thought or behavioral intentions that result from experience and/or new information and that are concerned with the attainment or revision of policy objectives. Policy-oriented learning involves increased knowledge of problem parameters and the factors affecting them, the internal feedback loops depicted in Figure 6.1 concerning policy effectiveness, and changing perceptions of the probable impacts of alternative policies.[5] The framework assumes that such learning is instrumental, that is, that members of various coalitions seek to better understand the world in order to further their policy objectives. Given the perceptual filtering discussed below, coalition members will resist information suggesting that their deep core or policy core beliefs may be invalid and/or unattainable, and they will use formal policy analyses to buttress and elaborate those beliefs (or attack their opponents).

Such learning, however, is only one of the forces affecting policy change. In addition to this cognitive activity, there are two other sources. The first involves changes in the real world, particularly the realm of system dynamics depicted in Figure 6.1. Changes in relevant socioeconomic conditions and systemwide governing coalitions—such as the 1973 Arab oil boycott or the 1974 election of the Thatcher wing of the British Conservative Party—can dramatically alter the composition and the resources of various coalitions and, in turn, public policy within the subsystem (Hoppe and Peterse, 1993; Hall, 1993; Richardson, 1994). Turnover in personnel—sometimes resulting from external conditions, sometimes merely from death or retirement—constitutes a second noncognitive source of change that can substantially alter the political resources of various coalitions and thus policy decisions. The basic argument of the ACF is that, although policy-oriented learning often alters secondary aspects of a coalition's belief system, changes in the policy core aspects of a governmental program require a perturbation in noncognitive factors external to the subsystem.

Hypotheses

Figure 6.2 lists the original set of hypotheses drawn from the ACF regarding advocacy coalitions, policy change, and policy learning (Sabatier, 1988).

The three hypotheses concerning coalitions are based on the premise that the principal glue holding a coalition together is agreement over policy core beliefs. Since these are very resistant to change, the lineup of allies and opponents within a subsystem will remain stable over periods of a decade or more (Coalition Hypothesis 1). Hypotheses 2 and 3 are essentially a restatement of the underlying premise.[6]

Given the arguments concerning the stability of a coalition's policy core beliefs and its desire to translate those beliefs into governmental programs, Policy

Hypotheses Concerning Advocacy Coalitions

Hypothesis 1/Coalition Hypothesis 1: On major controversies within a policy subsystem when policy core beliefs are in dispute, the lineup of allies and opponents tends to be rather stable over periods of a decade or so.

Hypothesis 2/Coalition Hypothesis 2: Actors within an advocacy coalition will show substantial consensus on issues pertaining to the policy core, although less so on secondary aspects.

Hypothesis 3/Coalition Hypothesis 3: An actor (or coalition) will give up secondary aspects of his or her (its) belief system before acknowledging weaknesses in the policy core.

Hypotheses Concerning Policy Change

Hypothesis 4/Policy Change Hypothesis 1: The policy core attributes of a governmental program in a specific jurisdiction will not be significantly revised as long as the subsystem advocacy coalition that instituted the program remains in power within that jurisdiction—except when the change is imposed by a hierarchically superior jurisdiction.

Hypothesis 5/Policy Change Hypothesis 2: The policy core attributes of a governmental action program are unlikely to be changed in the absence of significant perturbations external to the subsystem, i.e., changes in socio-economic conditions, public opinion, system-wide governing coalitions, or policy outputs from other subsystems.

Hypotheses Concerning Learning *Across* Coalitions

Hypothesis 6/Learning Hypothesis 1: Policy-oriented learning across belief systems is most likely when there is an intermediate level of informed conflict between the two coalitions. This requires that
   a) Each have the technical resources to engage in such a debate.
   b) The conflict be between secondary aspects of one belief system and core elements of the other or, alternatively, between important secondary aspects of the two belief systems.

Hypothesis 7/Learning Hypothesis 2: Problems for which accepted quantitative data and theory exist are more conducive to policy-oriented learning across belief systems than those in which data and theory are generally qualitative, quite subjective, or altogether lacking.

Hypothesis 8/Learning Hypothesis 3: Problems involving natural systems are more conducive to policy-oriented learning across belief systems than those involving purely social or political systems because, in the former, many of the critical variables are not themselves active strategists and because controlled experimentation is more feasible.

Hypothesis 9/Learning Hypothesis 4: Policy-oriented learning across belief systems is most likely when there exists a forum that is
   a) Prestigious enough to force professionals from different coalitions to participate and
   b) Dominated by professional norms.

FIGURE 6.2   Hypotheses in the Original Version of the ACF

NOTE: This figure contains both the original numbering (1–9) and the new numbering, which divides the hypotheses into three broad topics.

Change Hypothesis 1 contends that the policy core attributes of such programs in a jurisdiction will not change as long as the dominant coalition that instituted that policy remains in power—although the secondary aspects of those programs may well change. Given the logic thus far, it follows that the only way to change the policy core attributes of governmental policy in that jurisdiction is through some shock originating *outside* the subsystem that substantially alters the distribution of political resources or the views of coalitions within the subsystem. Such a shock can come either from external system events (Policy Change Hypothesis 2) or from attempts by hierarchically superior jurisdiction to change policy within a subordinate jurisdiction (Policy Change Hypothesis 1).[7]

The last four hypotheses deal with the conditions conducive to policy-oriented learning *across* belief systems (i.e., between coalitions). These are based upon the premise that coalitions resist changing their policy core beliefs or important secondary aspects of their belief systems, and thus that only very solid empirical evidence is likely to lead them to do so. It is hypothesized that such evidence is most likely to be developed and accepted in fields where accepted quantitative data and consensual theories are available (Learning Hypothesis 2), in the natural sciences more than the social sciences (Learning Hypothesis 3), when there exists a prestigious professional forum requiring the participation of experts from various coalitions (Learning Hypothesis 4), and in situations involving an intermediate level of conflict, that is, high enough to be worth expending analytical resources but not involving direct normative conflict (Learning Hypothesis 1).

ASSESSING THE EVIDENCE: 1987–1998

Since its initial publication in 1987–1988, the ACF has been applied in a critical fashion to at least the thirty-four cases listed in Table 6.1: six by the authors, eight by other scholars on their own databases but requested by the authors, and twenty by other scholars on their own initiative.[8] Twenty-three of the cases—including six by the authors—involve environmental or energy policy, suggesting the ACF may be particularly applicable to cases involving substantial political conflict and high technical complexity. The remaining eleven involve a variety of policy domains, including education, national defense, telecommunications regulation, drugs, infrastructure (roads), and gender discrimination in wages. Thirteen of the cases—all unsolicited—involve work by non-U.S. scholars on non-U.S. policy domains. Although the initial set of ACF cases dealt largely with energy and environmental policy in the United States, the ACF has increasingly been applied to western Europe, Canada, and Australia, and several of the most recent cases deal with eastern Europe (Andersson), developing countries (Elliot), and social policy (Mintrom and Vergari, Kuebler). The ACF thus appears to be applicable to a variety of policy domains and political systems, particularly—but not limited to—countries in the Organization for Economic Cooperation and Development (OECD).

TABLE 6.1   Published Cases Applying the ACF in a Critical Fashion, 1987–1998

Author(s) and Institutional Affiliation	Topic
A. Research by the Authors	
1. Jenkins-Smith (1988, 1990), Univ. New Mexico	U.S. energy policy
2. Jenkins-Smith, St. Clair, and Woods (1991, 1993)	Outer Continental Shelf (OSC) leasing policy
3. Jenkins-Smith (1991); Herron et al. (1999)	Nuclear waste and weapons (U.S.)
4. Sabatier et al. (1987, 1989, 1990, 1993)	Environmental policy at Lake Tahoe
5. Sabatier and Zafonte (1995, 1997, 1998, 1999)	San Francisco Bay/Delta water policy
6. Sabatier, Zafonte, and Gjerde (1999)	U.S. auto pollution control
B. Applications by Other Scholars but Solicited by the Authors	
7. Ted Heintz (1988), U.S. Dept. of Interior	OCS leasing (U.S.)
8. John Weyent (1988), Stanford Univ.	U.S. natural gas policy
9. Tony Brown, Oklahoma State, and Joe Stewart, Univ. New Mexico (1993)	U.S. airline regulation
10. John Munro (1993), UCLA/BDM	California water supply policy
11. Richard Barke (1993), Georgia Tech.	U.S. telecommunications regulation
12. Joe Stewart (1991), Univ. New Mexico	U.S. school desegregation, 1950–1985
13. Bill Freudenburg, Wisconsin, and Robert Gramling, SW Louisiana (1997)	OCS leasing (U.S.)
14. Miles Burnett and Charles Davis (1999), Colorado State	U.S. forest policy
C. Applications by Other Scholars on Their Own Initiative	
15. Charles and Sandra Davis (1988), Colorado State Univ.	U.S. public lands policy
16. James Lester and Michael Hamilton (1988), Colorado State Univ.	Ocean waste disposal (U.S.)
17. Marie-Louise van Muijen (1993), Erasmus University	National security policy in Europe
18. Hanna Mawhinney (1993), Univ. Ottawa	Canadian education policy
19. Wyn Grant (1995), Univ. of Warwick, UK	Auto pollution control in California
20. G. Dudley and J. Richardson (1996), Univ. of Essex	British roads policy, 1945–1995
21. Ken Lertzman et al. (1996), Simon Fraser Univ.	Forestry policy in British Columbia
22. M. Mintrom and S. Vergari (1996), Michigan State Univ.	Educational reform in Michigan
23. Anne Loeber and John Grin (1999), Univ. Amsterdam	Dutch water quality, 1977–1989
24. Jan Eberg (1997), Univ. Amsterdam	Hazardous waste in Netherlands and Bavaria
25. Tom Leschine et al. (1999), Univ. Washington	Water pollution in Puget Sound (U.S.)
26. Granville Sewell (1999), MIT	Climate change in U.S. and Netherlands
27. Adam Wellstead (1996), Univ. Toronto	Forestry policy in Ontario and Alberta
28. Elizabeth Shannon (1997), Univ. Tasmania	Gender discrimination in wage policy in Australia and Ireland
29. C. Radaelli and a. Martini (1997), Univ. of Bradford, UK	Professional forums in Italy
30. Robert Duffy (1997), Rider University	Nuclear power (U.S.)
31. Magnus Andersson (1998), Free Univ. of Amsterdam	Environmental policy in Poland
32. Chris Elliot (1998), Swiss Technical University	Forestry policy in Indonesia, Canada, and Sweden
33. Daniel Kuebler (1998), University of Lausanne	Drug policy in Switzerland
34. Gerald Thomas (1998), Colorado State Univ.	Communication satellite policy (U.S.)

The remainder of this section represents our reflections on the ACF since 1987 arising from three sources: (1) empirical applications in the thirty-four cases listed in Table 6.1; (2) criticisms by other authors, particularly Schlager (1995), Schlager and Blomquist (1996), Mintrom and Vergari (1996), and Grin and Hoppe (1997); and (3) the authors' own ruminations on the framework, particularly as stimulated by graduate students and other colleagues.[9] These reflections are organized around seven basic themes:

1. Advocacy coalitions: Composition, stability, and methods of analysis
2. Model of the individual and belief system structure
3. Subsystems: Delimitation, development, and interaction
4. Coalition behavior: Solving the collective action problem
5. Multiple intergovernmental venues and coalition strategies for influencing policy
6. Across-coalition learning and professional forums
7. Major policy change

Advocacy Coalitions: Composition, Stability, and Methods of Analysis

One of the ACF's most innovative features is that it challenges the implicit assumption of most political scientists that an actor's organizational affiliation is primordial—that there is something fundamentally different between legislators, administrative agency officials, interest group leaders, researchers, and journalists. In the traditional view, interest group leaders and legislators are politically active in seeking to influence public policy, whereas agency officials, researchers, and journalists tend to be perceived as more passive and/or policy-indifferent.[10] The ACF, in contrast, encourages us to think of agency officials, researchers, and journalists as potential members of advocacy coalitions—as having policy beliefs very similar to those of interest group leaders and their legislative allies, and as engaging in some nontrivial degree of coordinated activity in pursuit of their common policy objectives.

Virtually all the case studies have identified coalitions composed of interest groups, agencies, and usually a few legislators and researchers. For example, the Brown and Stewart (1993) analysis of airline regulation in the United States revealed three coalitions, two of which remained remarkably stable over several decades: (1) a proregulation coalition composed of the major airlines, most airline unions, many smaller airports, and their congressional allies; (2) an antiregulation coalition composed of the smaller airlines, the larger airports, most consumer groups, some economists, and their congressional allies; and (3) a deregulation coalition, which probably didn't emerge until the late 1960s and was composed largely of academic economists, Alfred Kahn (an economist who became Civil Aeronautics Board chair in the mid–1970s), some consumer groups, and a few critical members of Senator Edward Kennedy's staff in the mid-1970s.

The Civil Aeronautics Board (CAB) was usually in the proregulation coalition, although it could be moved around for a few years depending upon presidential appointments. In fact, Kahn moved the CAB officially into the deregulation coalition in the late 1970s.

Most of the case studies have not, however, *systematically* gathered data on actors' beliefs and behavior. Thus, the skeptical reader is unsure if the alleged members of a coalition really do share a set of policy core beliefs and engage in some degree of coordinated behavior or if coalition composition really does remain stable over time. Fortunately, surveys have been used to systematically gather data on beliefs and some aspects of coordinating behavior, and Sabatier and Jenkins-Smith (1993, Appendix) have developed techniques for systematically coding testimony at legislative and administrative hearings. Studies employing more systematic methods of data acquisition and analysis have (1) confirmed the existence of advocacy coalitions and (2) suggested several amendments to the framework.

First, survey data have repeatedly demonstrated that scientists are not necessarily "neutral" or "policy-indifferent"; instead, they are often members of coalitions. The evidence is probably clearest on San Francisco Bay water policy, where a 1992 survey demonstrated that university scientists as a whole were clearly members of the environmental coalition, in terms of both their policy core beliefs and their networks of sources and perceived allies (Sabatier and Zafonte, 1995, 1999; Zafonte and Sabatier, 1998). Surveys by Jenkins-Smith and his colleagues have revealed that (1) on nuclear waste disposal, biologists have views much closer to those of environmental groups than do physicists and engineers, and (2) on nuclear weapons policy, scientists working for the national laboratories have views quite different from those of members of the Union of Concerned Scientists (Barke and Jenkins-Smith, 1993; Herron, Jenkins-Smith, and Silva, 1999).[11] Finally, recall the major role that academic economists, most notably Alfred Kahn, played in airline and trucking deregulation (Derthick and Quirk, 1985; Robyn, 1987; Brown and Stewart, 1993).

Second, the higher resolution provided by systematic quantitative analysis reveals that there may well be more coalitions than first appear. Virtually all the *qualitative* applications of the ACF have found one to three coalitions, with most perceiving two. And our original quantitative work on San Francisco Bay water policy revealed two: an environmental/fishery coalition and a utilitarian-view-of-nature coalition (Sabatier and Zafonte, 1995). But that analysis dealt only with similar beliefs. When we reanalyzed the data to include the second criterion of a coalition—namely, coordinated behavior—four coalitions emerged, as the utilitarians split into several functional areas: water exporters, waste dischargers, and those concerned with fill and shoreline development (Zafonte and Sabatier, 1998).[12]

Third, more systematic analysis can provide a more accurate portrait of coalition composition and stability over time. Much of the work on both U.S. automotive pollution control and Lake Tahoe has suggested very stable environmental versus development coalitions (Mazmanian and Sabatier, 1989, ch. 4; Sabatier, Hunter, and McLaughlin, 1987). But systematic coding of hearing testimonies involving auto pollution control (Sabatier, Zafonte, and Gjerde, 1999) and Lake Tahoe (Sabatier and Brasher, 1993) have revealed two quite distinct periods. First came an initial period of very fluid and amorphous coalitions during the latter 1960s, in which virtually everyone was in favor of "clean air" or "environmental planning." This alignment changed dramatically in the early 1970s, probably because a watershed event clarified the benefits and costs of stringent environmental regulation. Afterward, the coalitions became very distinct and very stable for fifteen to twenty years. This higher resolution suggests the need to distinguish "nascent" from "mature" subsystems and to make a clarifying amendment to Coalition Hypothesis 1:

> Coalition Hypothesis 1 (revised): On major controversies within a *mature* policy subsystem, when policy core beliefs are in dispute, the lineup of allies and opponents tends to be rather stable over periods of a decade or so.

The distinction between "nascent" and "mature" subsystems will be further discussed below.

Fourth, the systematic analysis of testimonies at 1969–1987 Outer Continental Shelf (OCS) leasing hearings by Jenkins-Smith, St. Clair, and Woods (1991; Jenkins-Smith and St. Clair, 1993) suggests a potentially important amendment to our understanding of different types of actors within a coalition. The companies and industry trade groups most directly involved in OCS development were always in the preleasing coalition, and environmental groups were always in the environmental (antileasing) coalition. The involved federal agencies—Energy, Interior, the Environmental Protection Agency (EPA), and the National Oceanographic and Atmospheric Administration (NOAA)—were sandwiched between the competing interest groups. Over the course of the policy debate, the federal agencies—at least in their official pronouncements before congressional committees—shifted toward one coalition or the other in response to exogenous political and economic events. Energy and Interior were consistently closer to the preleasing side, however, whereas NOAA and EPA tended to be closer to the environmental side. The OCS case suggests the following hypothesis:[13]

> Coalition Hypothesis 4: Within a coalition, administrative agencies will usually advocate more moderate positions than their interest group allies.

The reasoning here is fairly straightforward: On the one hand, the ACF assumes that most administrative agencies have missions that make them part of a specific coalition. That mission is generally grounded in a statutory mandate and reinforced by the professional affiliation of agency personnel and the agency's need to provide benefits to the dominant coalition in its subsystem (Meier, 1985; Knott and Miller, 1987). On the other hand, most agencies have multiple sovereigns/principals (sources of money and legal authority) with somewhat different policy views. Thus, agencies need to find some way to adhere to their traditional mission without antagonizing important sovereigns. Interest groups—particularly those funded primarily by member contributions—are not normally confronted with such cross-cutting constraints and thus are free to adopt more extreme positions (Jenkins-Smith et al., 1991).

The evidence to date is quite mixed. The OCS hearing testimony inspired the new hypothesis and thus obviously supports it. Survey data from Lake Tahoe also tend to support it (Sabatier et al., 1987, Figure 1), but the Tahoe *hearing testimony* data are quite mixed (Sabatier and Brasher, 1993). The survey data on the San Francisco Bay water policy are also quite mixed. Personnel from most federal and state agencies expressed somewhat more moderate views than their interest group allies, but personnel from the federal fishery agencies tended to be at least as extreme as their allies from environmental and sportsmen's groups (Sabatier and Zafonte, 1999). Clearly, this is one aspect of the framework in need of additional empirical and theoretical work.[14]

On the whole, however, we are convinced that the existence of advocacy coalitions—defined as actors from a wide variety of institutions who share policy core beliefs and coordinate their behavior in a variety of ways—has been demonstrated for numerous policy subsystems in several OECD countries. This would seem to contradict many political scientists' assumption that institutional differences are primordial. The evidence to date suggests that the policy beliefs shared by members of different institutions may be at least as important in explaining their behavior as the institutional rules that apply to members of a given institution.

Model of the Individual and Belief System Structure

The model of the individual—and, by extension, the coalition as a corporate actor—in the ACF has been greatly clarified by the work of Schlager (1995; Schlager and Blomquist, 1996) and by discussions with colleagues, particularly Matt Zafonte. Although the ACF clearly assumes that actors are instrumentally rational—that is, that they seek to use information and other resources to achieve their goals—it draws much more heavily on research in cognitive and social psychology than on work in economics. In particular, the ACF assumes that goals are usually complex and that an individuals' ability to perceive the world and to process that information is affected by cognitive biases and constraints.

With respect to goals, all versions of the ACF have assumed that actors are driven by a set of policy-oriented goals comprising value priorities and conceptions of whose welfare should be of greatest concern. The most important beliefs are those in the policy core—that is, those that relate to the subsystem as a whole—

because these are more salient to the individual than deep core beliefs and serve as more efficient guides to behavior than specific policy preferences in the secondary aspects. The ACF does *not* assume that actors are driven primarily by simple goals of economic/political self-interest, nor does it assume that self-interested preferences are easy to ascertain (for confirming evidence, see Marcus and Goodman, 1986; Green and Shapiro, 1994; Martin, 1995; for a dissent, see Scharpf, 1997). Instead, it assumes that actors' goals (their "objective functions") are normally complex and should be ascertained empirically.

The attention to policy-oriented learning clearly implies that specific policy preferences, particularly in the secondary aspects, are endogenous to the sets of behavior to be explained. Policy core beliefs are also subject to change over periods of a decade or more and are thus partially endogenous. On the other hand, deep core values are basically given; that is, they are exogenous to the behavior being explained.

In processing information, the ACF assumes that actors suffer from a variety of cognitive biases and constraints. First, following Simon (1985) and many other scholars, we assume that actors' ability to process and analyze information is limited by time and computational constraints. This limitation produces substantial incentives to utilize a variety of heuristics as guides to complex situations. One of the implications is that policy core beliefs—because they are fairly general in scope yet very salient—provide more efficient guides to behavior over a wide variety of situations than do secondary aspects. This, in turn, contributes to the ACF's assumption that the policy core provides the principal glue of coalitions (Zafonte and Sabatier, 1998).

Second, the ACF assumes, consistent with prospect theory, that actors weigh losses more heavily than gains (Quattrone and Tversky, 1988). A logical corollary is that they remember defeats more than victories. This tendency to overemphasize defeats contributes to the tendency of policy actors, particularly in situations involving frequent conflict, to view opponents as more powerful than they probably are (Sabatier et al., 1987).

Third, the ACF assumes—consistent with attribution and cognitive dissonance theories—that on salient topics, actors' perceptions are strongly filtered by their preexisting normative and perceptual beliefs (Schiff, 1962; Smith, 1968; Tesser, 1978; Lord, Ross, and Lepper, 1979; Fiske and Taylor, 1984; Scholz and Pinney, 1995). Preexisting beliefs constitute a lens through which actors perceive the world.

This model of the individual, in turn, has important implications for coalition dynamics. In particular, the latter two assumptions concerning cognitive bias provide much of the underpinning for Coalition Hypothesis 1, concerning coalition stability over time (see Table 6.1). Since coalition actors (by definition) share a set of policy core beliefs, actors in different coalitions will perceive the world through different lenses and thus will often interpret a given piece of evidence in different ways. This contributes to in-group cohesion. It also produces distrust of people in other coalitions who, since they come to conclusions so different from ours on "factual" issues, must have questionable motives. When this is combined with the tendency to remember losses more than victories, it becomes easy in high-conflict situations for a mutual "devil shift" to take place, as each coalition views the others as more evil and more powerful than they probably are (Sabatier et al., 1987). As a result, conflict resolution among coalitions is more difficult than classic rational actor models would predict. Also, coalitions tend to be re-main more differentiated and more stable in composition over time (contrast the ACF, for example, with Riker, 1962).

In addition to a general clarification of the ACF's model of the individual and its implications for coalition stability, events since 1993 have led to several clarifi-cations of the policy core of belief systems.

First, the 1987–1988 (and even the 1993) versions of the ACF were ambiguous about the defining characteristics of policy core beliefs. In particular, they were not very not clear about whether the critical difference between deep core, policy core, and secondary aspects was based upon *scope* of belief or whether it was de-termined by *degree of abstraction.* The ambiguity arose largely because of the as-sumption borrowed from Converse (1964) and Peffley and Hurwitz (1985) that abstract beliefs constrain more specific ones. Subsequent work by Jenkins-Smith on OCS drilling and by Sabatier on Lake Tahoe environmental quality suggests, however, that the most fundamental (and probably least changing) beliefs of ma-terial groups are not very abstract. Instead, they tend to be quite concrete: mater-ial self-interest, operationalized as profit or market share (Jenkins-Smith and St.Clair, 1993; Jenkins-Smith and Sabatier, 1994, pp. 195–196). This finding, in turn, suggests that scope and topic should be the defining characteristics of pol-icy core beliefs. *Scope* means that the belief should apply to virtually all aspects of subsystem policy, rather than to only rather narrow ranges (which are covered by secondary aspects). *Topic* means that it should pertain to one of the subjects listed under "policy core" in Table 6.2. Of those topics, the fundamental norma-tive precepts are the most critical: (1) orientation on basic value priorities and (2) identification of groups/entities whose welfare is of concern. The ACF assumes that agreement on these two normative precepts applied on a subsystemwide ba-sis is the most important defining characteristic of an advocacy coalition.

Second, the set of topics covered by the policy core keeps undergoing revision. The list in Table 6.2 is intended to cover all the really critical aspects of policy on which salient, persistent cleavages might develop across coalitions, but our un-derstanding of what is "really critical" keeps changing slightly. The latest version contains several revisions over previous lists (Sabatier, 1988, p. 145; Sabatier and Jenkins-Smith, 1993, p. 221):

A. Basic causes of the problem: This is critical because the perceived causes obviously affect the set of plausible solutions and, in turn, who is likely to bear the costs of those solutions.

TABLE 6.2 Revised Structure of Belief Systems of Policy Elites,[a] 1998

	Deep Core	Policy Core	Secondary Aspects
Defining characteristics	Fundamental normative and ontological axioms	Fundamental policy positions concerning the basic strategies for achieving core values within the subsystem	Instrumental decisions and information searches necessary to implement policy core
Scope	Across all policy subsystems.	Subsystemwide	Usually only part of subsystem
Susceptibility to change	Very difficult; akin to a religious conversion.	Difficult, but can occur if experience reveals serious anomalies	Moderately easy; this is the topic of most administrative and even legislative policymaking

Illustrative components	1. Human nature:
	  a. Inherently evil vs. socially redeemable
	  b. Part of nature vs. dominion over nature
	  c. Narrow egoists vs. contractarians
	2. Relative priority of various ultimate values: Freedom, security, power knowledge, health, love, beauty, etc.
	3. Basic criteria of distributive justice: Whose welfare counts? Relative weights of self, primary groups, all people, future generations, nonhuman beings, etc.
	4. Sociocultural identity (e.g., ethnicity, religion, gender, profession)
		Fundamental normative precepts:
		1. Orientation on basic value priorities
		2. Identification of groups or other entities whose welfare is of greatest concern
		
		Precepts with a substantial empirical component:
		3. Overall seriousness of the problem
		4. Basic causes of the problem
		5. Proper distribution of authority between government and market
		6. Proper distribution of authority among levels of government
		7. Priority accorded various policy instruments (e.g., regulation, insurance, education, direct payments, tax credits)
		8. Ability to society to solve the problem (e.g., zero-sum competition vs. potential for mutual accommodation; technological optimism vs. pessimism)
		10. Participation of public vs. experts vs. elected officials
		11. Policy core policy preferences
			1. Seriousness of specific aspects of the problem in specific locales
			2. Importance of various causal linkages in different locales and over time
			3. Most decisions concerning administrative rules, budgetary allocations, disposition of cases, statutory interpretation, and even statutory revision
			4. Information regarding performance of specific programs or institutions

[a] The "Policy Core" and "Secondary Aspects" columns also apply to governmental programs.

SOURCE: Sabatier (1998a, p. 113).

B. Method of financing programs: This is obviously critical because it determines who will pay for problem solutions.
C. Desirability of participation by public versus experts versus elected officials: This choice is clearly critical in some policy domains, for example, nuclear power (Barke and Jenkins-Smith, 1994) and forestry (Wellstead, 1996). It also helps link the ACF to cultural theory (Thompson, Ellis, and Wildavsky, 1990).
D. Policy core policy preferences: Although policy preferences generally fall within the secondary aspects of belief systems, they can fall within the policy core if they (i) are subsystemwide in scope, (ii) are highly salient, and (iii) have been a major source of cleavage for some time.

The first three revisions represent relatively minor extensions of the basic logic of the policy core.[15] The fourth is a result of the work of Zafonte and Sabatier (1998), which first clarified the attributes of policy core items that make them the glue of coalitions and then sought to empirically determine the types of beliefs that were, in fact, most highly correlated with indicators of coordinated behavior in San Francisco Bay/Delta water policy. The logical analysis identified subsystemwide scope, salience, and source of long-term conflict as the critical attributes of policy core beliefs, and the empirical analysis demonstrated that several classic policy core items plus several "policy core policy preferences" were the beliefs most strongly related to indicators of coordinated behavior.

Third, the work of Jenkins-Smith and St. Clair (1993, p. 152) on OCS drilling has led to a new hypothesis concerning the degree of constraint/cohesion in the belief systems of different types of interest groups (and probably, by extension, the other members of their advocacy coalition):

Coalition Hypothesis 5: Elites of purposive groups are more constrained in their expression of beliefs and policy positions than elites from material groups.

The reasoning here is that purposive groups are espousing a tightly integrated set of beliefs, and thus, group leaders will be selected on the basis of their adherence to those beliefs and will be encouraged to espouse all aspects of the belief system, lest they risk losing members. In contrast, material groups focus on promoting their members' material self-interest, and members seem willing to give their leaders a fair amount of latitude in determining exactly how to promote that objective (Moe, 1980).

Fourth, John Grin and his colleagues (Loeber and Grin, 1999; Grin and Hoppe, 1997) have criticized the ACF for focusing solely on actors' beliefs relating to *public policy*. They argue that the ACF forgets that most actors have a more fundamental belief system relating to the basic goals of their organization or profession (which they refer to as "professional beliefs"). Understanding corporate behavior, for example, presumably requires knowledge of the company's goals concerning market share, its strategies for attaining these goals, and so on. We agree. But corporations that *regularly* get involved in public policy disputes almost certainly have a policy belief system that presumably is congruent with their more fundamental professional belief system. The same could be said of labor unions, many environmental groups, and religious organizations. In short, professional beliefs become important only insofar as they are *not* consistent with policy core beliefs—which, we suspect, happens very infrequently.

Finally, the ACF's model of the individual needs to be modified to include individual (and/or organizational) welfare in addition to the policy belief system (Schlager and Blomquist, 1996, pp. 661–664). The leader of an environmental group, for example, must be concerned about her or his group's organizational needs as well as with transforming the organization's policy belief system into governmental policy. Failure to recognize the role of individual/organizational self-interest is one of the critical reasons why previous versions of the ACF have underestimated the difficulty of forging effective coalitions among like-minded actors (Schlager, 1995; Schlager and Blomquist, 1996)—a topic to which we shall return shortly.

Subsystems: Delimitation, Development, and Interaction

The 1988 and 1993 versions of the ACF defined *policy subsystem* very loosely, as the group of actors interacting with some regularity in a functional policy domain (such as air pollution control).[16] In recent years, however, a number of cases have arisen in which scholars have sought to apply the ACF to something narrower than a classic policy domain and have wondered whether this narrower domain constituted a "subsystem" for ACF purposes.[17]

In addition to these rather practical concerns, the clarification of the policy core as being *subsystemwide* in scope obviously requires that subsystem boundaries be delineated with greater precision than has heretofore been the case. This clarification is critical to the internal logic of the ACF, since Coalition Hypotheses 1–3 and Policy Change Hypotheses 1 and 2 all depend upon distinguishing policy core from secondary aspects. In turn, greater precision in delineating subsystem boundaries has resulted in greater attention to changes in subsystem composition over time and to the interaction of related subsystems. These are among the areas where different aspects of the ACF have become more internally related, and hopefully consistent, over time.

For ACF purposes, the concept of a subsystem needs to focus on the group of people and/or organizations interacting regularly over periods of a decade or more to influence policy formulation and implementation within a given policy area/domain. Thus, one needs to distinguish a *nascent* subsystem (i.e., one in the process of forming) from a *mature* one (i.e., one that has existed for a decade or more). Following is the set of necessary and sufficient criteria for the existence of a mature policy subsystem:

1. The participants regard themselves as a semiautonomous community who share a domain of expertise.
2. They have sought to influence public policy within the domain over a fairly long period of time (i.e., seven to ten years). This criterion stems from the ACF's assumption that such an interval is necessary for doing meaningful policy analysis that can deal with learning and real-world impacts.
3. There exist specialized subunits within agencies at all relevant levels of government to deal with the topic. This criterion follows from our assumption that without such units at all levels, implementation will be exceedingly problematic and coalitions will come to realize this. A persisting subsystem needs to have some "organizational residue."
4. There exist interest groups, or specialized subunits within interest groups, that regard this as a major policy topic.

These criteria stem directly from the ACF's focus on long-term policy change, which, we assume, requires some organizational residue for at least administrative agencies and interest groups. The ACF is not interested in debating societies (which don't seek to influence policy over the long term) or in policy pronouncements that lack any serious effort at effective implementation and at changing problem conditions in the world.

The above characteristics of a mature subsystem should encourage studies of the conditions under which new subsystems emerge (see, for example, Thomas, 1998). Early versions of the ACF tended to assume that most new subsystems were spin-offs of existing ones and arose when a group of actors became dissatisfied with the neglect of a particular problem by an existing subsystem and sought to develop new venues (Baumgartner and Jones, 1993). In such cases—for example, the emergence of the food-and-drug safety subsystem out of the agricultural policy subsystem at the turn of the nineteenth century (Nadel, 1971)—one would expect clearly differentiated coalitions (mirroring preexisting groupings) from the birth of the new subsystem.

Subsystems may also emerge out of a new issue or a new conceptualization of a situation (Stone, 1988). In such cases, one might expect an initial situation characterized by great fluidity. For example, the coding of hearing testimony at Lake Tahoe (1960–1984) and U.S. automotive pollution control (1960–1990) suggests that subsystems arising because of concern about a relatively new issue—in this case, environmental quality—may initially be characterized by rather amorphous situations in which almost everyone espouses some "motherhood" ideal, such as "environmental planning" or "clean air." But as information develops concerning the seriousness of the problem, its causes, and the costs of remedying the situation, actors tend to coalesce into distinct coalitions, often around some watershed event(s) that clarifies the underlying conflicts (Downs, 1972; Sabatier and

Brasher, 1993; Sabatier et al., 1999).[18] In both the Tahoe and the air pollution cases, the subsystem began forming in the early 1960s but did not become "mature"—in the sense defined previously—until the late 1960s, largely with the organization of an environmental interest group focused on this subsystem. The watershed event occurred a few years thereafter, and after that event, coalitions were very stable for the next ten to fifteen years.

We now consider the interaction among related subsystems, which occurs along both functional and territorial lines (Zafonte and Sabatier, 1998). A subsystem may be nested within another (i.e., the former is a subset of the latter). In the United States, for example, a fully developed (by this definition) automotive pollution control subsystem has been nested within a larger air pollution subsystem since the early 1970s. Or two subsystems may overlap with each other (i.e., they interact with each other frequently enough so that a subset of actors is part of both). In the United States, for example, the transportation subsystem partially overlaps with the automotive pollution control subsystem on issues such transportation control plans (e.g., efforts to reduce vehicle miles traveled). But the transportation control actors are involved in only a *subset* of the entire range of automotive pollution control issues. Thus, some actors in a subsystem are "regulars" (i.e., they are involved in virtually all issues), whereas those from overlapping subsystems are "periodic" members (i.e., they are involved only in a distinct subset of topics) (see also Lindquist, 1992).

Policy domains that are intergovernmental in scope—whether between national and local units within a nation-state or between international organizations and specific nation-states—raise important issues about subsystem delineation: Does one put all of the actors—irrespective of governmental level—into a single (undifferentiated) subsystem, or does one assume that each territorial level is a separate subsystem? In Sabatier's work at Lake Tahoe and San Francisco Bay, he opted for the former, whereas Mawhinney (1993) and Sewell (1999) have chosen the latter approach. The choice should be based primarily upon empirical considerations regarding the degree of (1) legal autonomy of each level and (2) actor integration across levels. At Tahoe and the Bay/Delta, Sabatier put all the actors into the same subsystem because that placement mirrored their interaction patterns: No one level of government operates independently of the others, and the hierarchical distinctions between officials at different levels of government are blurred in practice. In the implementation of international treaties, however, autonomy by nation-states is jealously guarded, and the actors who negotiated the treaty usually comprise only a small percentage of those involved in its implementation (Sewell, 1999). The same could be said of the implementation of most federal legislation in the United States, Canada, and Germany, as well as in the European Union (EU). In these cases, one would probably envisage multiple nested subsystems representing different territorial units (e.g., a Bordeaux transportation subsystem nested within a French one, which is, in turn, nested within an EU one).

Coalition Behavior: Solving the Collective Action Problem

Advocacy coalitions have been consistently defined as "people from a variety of positions (elected and agency officials, interest group leaders, researchers) who (1) share a particular belief system—i.e., a set of basic values, causal assumptions, and problem perceptions—and who (2) show a non-trivial degree of coordinated activity over time" (Sabatier, 1988, p. 139; Sabatier and Jenkins-Smith, 1993, p. 25).

In two very interesting papers, Schlager (1995) and Schlager and Blomquist (1996) have argued, quite correctly, that most applications to date of the ACF by both Sabatier and Jenkins-Smith have implicitly assumed that actors who hold similar policy core beliefs will *act* in concert, that is, that the first condition of coalition formation is sufficient for the second.[19] Anyone familiar with the literature on collective action will realize the dubiousness of this assumption (see, for example, Olson, 1965; Ostrom, 1990; and, most embarrassingly, Sabatier, 1992). In particular, the ACF has been assuming that shared goals and beliefs plus a recognition that pooling resources increases the probability of success will be sufficient to overcome (1) the transaction costs involved in coming to a common understanding of the policy problem and the proper means of addressing it, (2) the difficulty of finding policies that fairly address distributional conflicts among coalition members, and (3) the temptation of each individual and organization to free-ride (Schlager, 1995, pp. 261–262; Schlager and Blomquist, 1996, pp. 663–666; Robyn, 1987).

We suspect that distributional conflicts and free riding are more serious problems for material groups—whose members are self-consciously seeking to maximize their own material self-interest—than for purposive groups, whose members are more committed to an ideology stressing the collective welfare and who often perceive themselves as David fighting Goliath (Berry, 1977; Sabatier, 1992). Nevertheless, the problems of developing a set of policy proposals that resolve distributional and other conflicts and of avoiding temptations to free-ride in actually pursuing a lobbying strategy affect all coalitions and can no longer be assumed away. In addition, by focusing on shared policy beliefs within a coalition, the ACF has neglected the interest that all individuals and organizations have in maintaining and increasing their viability/welfare. Environmental groups may agree on a general policy agenda, but each must also maintain (and even enhance) its budget and membership. Because, to some extent, such groups compete with each other for members and grant funds, they must also compete for credit concerning policy successes. How interest groups within potential coalitions overcome these difficulties is, to the best of our knowledge, a neglected topic.[20] In addition, although different members of a coalition may bring different resources to the table, institutional heterogeneity may create coordination problems. As Schlager (1995, p. 263) noted, "The institutional differences among a legislator, a journalist, a director of a material interest group, and an academic may very well limit their ability, and their willingness, to cooperate with one another, even if they share similar beliefs."

There have been three somewhat different responses to the challenge of revising the ACF to deal with these collective action problems.

The first has been to follow Schlager (1995) by incorporating principles from the Ostroms' IAD (institutional analysis and development) framework to deal with coordination problems within coalitions (see Chapter 3 on the IAD). Elinor Ostrom distinguishes short-term coordination (developing a common lobbying strategy in a specific controversy) from long-term coordination. From Schlager (1995, p. 262), we borrow the following hypothesis regarding short-term coordination:[21]

Schlager Coordination Hypothesis #1: Actors who share [policy core] beliefs are more likely to engage in short-term coordination if they (1) interact repeatedly, (2) experience relatively low information costs, and (3) believe that there are policies that, while not affecting each actor in similar ways, at least treat each fairly.

Repeated interaction and low information costs are important for developing a shared perspective on the policy problem, for developing a coordinated lobbying strategy, and for enforcing that strategy. "Fair" policies are necessary to resolve distributional conflicts among members. Long-term coordination—which can range from repeated informal interaction to the creation of a peak association— requires a rather similar set of conditions (Schlager, 1995, p. 264):

Schlager Coordination Hypothesis #2: Coalitions are more likely to persist if (1) the major beneficiaries of the benefits that a coalition produces are clearly identified and are members of the coalition, (2) the benefits received by coalition members are related to the maintenance costs of each member, and (3) coalition members monitor each others' actions to ensure compliance.

Although this is an extremely sensible approach, incorporating it intact into the ACF has one very serious problem:[22] It is based on the IAD's general model of the individual—rational and self-interested, although with limited information capabilities—rather than the ACF's model of the individual. In contrast to the former, the latter assumes (1) that individuals are not necessarily preoccupied with maximizing their material self-interest and (2) that perceptual filters are at least as important as information constraints.

Schlager's approach focuses on the *costs* of coordinating behavior and on the strategies for meeting those transaction costs—with the underlying assumption that the costs are difficult to overcome. Sabatier and his students have recently pursued an alternative approach that seeks, first, to reduce the costs and, second, to use the ACF's model of the individual to magnify the perceived *benefits* of coordination.

In a recent paper, Zafonte and Sabatier (1998) distinguished "strong" from "weak" coordination. The former requires the development of a common plan of action, the communication of that plan to potential coalition members, the monitoring of member compliance, and the imposition of sanctions for noncompliance. These requirements are what Schlager has in mind, and the transaction costs are usually quite substantial. In contrast, "weak" coordination simply requires that "organizational actors monitor each other's political behavior, and then alter their actions to make their political strategies complementary with respect to a common goal" (p. 480). Weak coordination does not require any elaborate decisionmaking or monitoring process. It simply requires the potential members of a coalition to monitor each others' behavior and alter their own to make it complementary. Assuming that the actors share policy core beliefs and generally trust each other, such alterations of behavior should not be very difficult (except when distributional conflicts among members are significant). The most likely cases of weak coordination are when actors defer to coalition members on issues of greater salience to the other or when other members have superior information or legal mandates. Weak (informal) coordination is likely to be particularly important among members coming from different organizations with legal impediments to more formalized (strong) coordination.

In addition to pointing to relatively low-cost methods of coordination, Sabatier has sought to use the ACF's model of the individual to augment the perceived benefits, and to lower the costs, of coordination. The basic argument flows directly from the "devil shift," that is, the tendency of actors in high-conflict situations to perceive their opponents as more evil and more powerful than they probably are. If the opponent is evil, then its victory is likely to result in very substantial costs to the members of a coalition. And if the opponent is very powerful, the only way to preclude its victory is to achieve very effective coordination among coalition members. This is not a novel insight. Interest group leaders commonly portray their opponents as "devils" in order to rally members. The ACF simply applies the same logic to coalitions consisting of members from different sorts of organizations. Thus, one can easily develop an analogue to Schlager's first coordination hypothesis:

> Coalition Hypothesis 6: Actors who share policy core beliefs are more likely to engage in short-term coordination if they view their opponents as (a) very powerful and (b) very likely to impose substantial costs upon them if victorious.

The ACF's model of the individual would also imply that the costs of coordination within an advocacy coalition are less than Schlager assumed: First, the belief system shared by the members of a coalition reduces the transaction costs involved in coming to a common understanding of the problem and identifying the means to resolve it because the members will be interpreting the evidence through a similar set of preexisting beliefs. Second, the temptation to free-ride should be reduced among coalition members. Actors who share policy core beliefs are more likely to trust each other, that is, to take each other's interests into account when deciding what to do, in large part because, by definition, many of those interests will be shared. Third, a shared belief system should also increase the willingness to distribute fairly the costs of pursing the common goals—and thus to decrease the temptation to free-ride. This is particularly true in coalitions involving purposive groups whose ideology values collective goods, rather than material self-interest. In sum, although coordination of coalition members remains a problem, the ACF's model of the individual implies less of a problem than the IAD's general model of the individual.

In a recent paper, Fenger and Klok (1998) helped clarify the coordination/collective action problem by examining the relationship between beliefs and organizational interdependencies. Beliefs are categorized as congruent, divergent, and unrelated. Competitive interdependency occurs when the functional tasks (and resources) of Actor A interfere with Actor B's ability to take action consistent with B's goals (and often vice versa). For example, fishery agencies and dam-building agencies are usually competitively interdependent. In contrast, symbiotic interdependency occurs when the functional tasks and resources of Actor A contribute to Actor B's ability to pursue B's goal (and often vice versa). In such a situation, actors have an incentive to exchange their respective resources in order for each to attain its goals. When two actors have congruent beliefs and symbiotic interdependencies, they will be members of the same coalition, and coordination should be relatively easy. In contrast, divergent beliefs plus competitive interdependencies will lead actors to be in different coalitions. The interesting cases occur in the cross-diagonals. When two actors have congruent beliefs but are competitively interdependent—for example, two agricultural water districts that compete with each other for Bureau of Reclamation water and with fishery agencies/groups for all water—Fenger and Klok interpreted the ACF as arguing that they would be members of the same agricultural water coalition but would face significant distributional conflicts within that coalition. The reason for putting them into the same coalition is that the ACF assumes that policy core beliefs are the principal glue of coalitions, and members of different agricultural water districts tend to have similar views on water development and environmental protection (Sabatier and Zafonte, 1999). By the same logic, when two actors have divergent beliefs but are symbiotically interdependent—for example, a fishery agency heavily reliant upon the fish ladders provided by a dam—Fenger and Klok interpreted the ACF as arguing that they would be in different coalitions but would be relatively moderate members of their respective coalitions and would seek to depoliticize their interdependencies. We find this analysis very helpful in predicting (1) the strong members of coalitions (congruent beliefs and symbiotic interdependencies), (2) the members with distributional conflicts (congruent beliefs, but competitive interdependencies), and (3) the moderate members (congruent beliefs, but symbiotic interdependencies with members of an opposing coalition).

Multiple Intergovernmental Venues
and Coalition Strategies for Influencing Policy

The ACF assumes that coalitions seek to alter the behavior of governmental institutions in order to achieve the policy objectives in their respective policy cores. In an intergovernmental system, coalitions have a multitude of possible venues, including legislatures, chief executives, administrative agencies, and the courts at all relevant levels of government. The means (guidance instruments) at their disposal include (1) seeking to influence legislatures to alter the budgets and the legal authority of administrative agencies through testimony and campaign contributions; (2) trying to change the incumbents of various positions, whether they be agency political appointees, agency civil servants, or elected legislators and chief executives; (3) trying to affect public opinion (a potentially powerful exogenous factor) via the mass media; (4) attempting to alter target group behavior via demonstrations or boycotts (Wellstead, 1996; Loeber and Grin, 1999); and (5) trying to gradually alter the perceptions of a variety of actors through research and information exchange.

Both Schlager (1995) and Mintrom and Vergari (1996) have criticized the authors of the ACF for focusing their attention almost exclusively on coalition beliefs, thereby neglecting coalition behavior. Although generally correct, this criticism overlooks the authors' efforts to address the strategies that coalition actors pursue within an intergovernmental subsystem (or set of nested subsystems). The ACF begins by assuming that coalitions will seek to utilize their resources efficiently, that is, to produce the most policy benefits for the cost incurred. In an earlier analysis, Sabatier and Jenkins-Smith (1993, pp. 227–230) suggested that

1. In general the costs of an instrument are usually proportional to its benefits. Changing a statute brings great benefits but is extremely difficult in a separation-of-powers system (Moe, 1990). Convincing an agency to alter one of its rules is easier but also produces benefits that are lower in scope and duration. Changing a line item in an agency's budget is even easier but usually produces even smaller benefits.
2. It is usually easier to alter the rules or budget of a state agency by appealing to its federal agency sovereign than by appealing to the state authorities. The former involves only one major veto point (the federal agency), whereas the latter involves the legislative process plus the governor.
3. In virtually all cases, the critical factor affecting costs is the policy predisposition of the responsible official: If she or he is sympathetic to (or a member of) the coalition, the costs are comparatively low. If she or he is hostile (i.e., a member of an opposing coalition), the costs are extremely high—if not out of the question. If she or he is neutral, they may be feasible.

4. Some types of resources work better in some institutions than in others. Solid technical analyses are more likely to influence administrative agencies or courts than legislatures. Conversely, mobilizing public/constituency support may be more influential with a legislative committee than with an agency.

The bottom-line conclusion is that coalitions should (and do) spend an enormous amount of time "venue shopping," to use a term coined by Baumgartner and Jones (1993) with a lineage going back to Schattschneider (1960). Most of the recent discussion has focused on shopping among different legislative committees, or the legislature versus the chief executive versus the courts, at a single level of government. But the choices are much broader than those in any intergovernmental policy subsystem. In fact, there is considerable evidence that coalitions pursue multiple venues at multiple levels, often simultaneously, in a constant effort to find some that will bear fruit.

For example, Figure 6.3 lists some of the major strategies pursued by members of the environmental coalition since 1984 in an effort to arrest the decline of numerous fisheries in the San Francisco Bay/Delta (Sabatier and Zafonte, 1999). The data reveal that, over a fourteen-year period, this coalition pursued at least fifteen different strategies aimed at the legislatures, courts, and multiple agencies at both federal and state levels. In general, the strategies pursued were consistent with the first and third principles developed by Sabatier and Jenkins-Smith (1993).[23] Most of the efforts were directed at agencies or courts, as such efforts tend to be less costly and more likely to succeed than strategies aimed at legislatures. Most of the efforts by the environmental coalition were directed at presumably sympathetic officials, for example, the EPA or the endangered-species agencies. The clearest example of selecting relatively sympathetic venues was the Central Valley Project Improvement Act (CVPIA). Environmentalists pushed it for three years while a sympathizer, Congress member George Miller, chaired the House Interior Subcommittee on Water, and both houses were Democratic. As soon as both houses of Congress went Republican (after the 1994 elections), farmers appealed for a drastic revision of the CVPIA—but their efforts failed amid multiple Congressional vetoes.

One final note: A frequent result of venue shopping is policy stalemate: Coalition A dominates one venue, and Coalition B dominates another. When approval from both is required, the result is a stalemate. Dudley and Richardson (1996) provided a nice example from British roads policy. During the 1980s, the highway lobby controlled the Department of Transportation, although environmentalists received a sympathetic hearing at many public inquiries regarding specific location decisions. The end result was a stalemate until a neutral/environmentally sympathetic Minister of Transportation managed to broker a temporary compromise.

1. *1984–1985:* Invoked international migratory bird treaties to convince the Bureau of Reclamation to close the Kesterson Wildlife Refuge and the San Luis Drain (which eventually discharges into San Francisco Bay) because of selenium contamination.
2. *1986–1988:* Presented testimony at hearings of the State Water Resources Control Board (SWRCB) in an unsuccessful effort to convince it to issue more stringent water quality standards.
3. *1987–1990:* Convinced the federal EPA to initiate the San Francisco Estuary Project under the Clean Water Act in an effort to reach a policy consensus (largely failed).
4. *1989–1992:* Joined with agricultural and urban water users in informal negotiations known as the Three Way Process (with very mixed success).
5. *1989:* Successfully petitioned the California Fish and Game Commission to list the winter-run salmon as a threatened species under the California Endangered Species Act. Soon thereafter, the species was also listed under federal law by the National Marine Fisheries Service (NMFS).
6. *1991:* Successfully sued the federal EPA for failing to force the SWRCB to issue new water quality standards for the Delta, as required by the Federal Clean Water Act.
7. *1991:* Unsuccessfully petitioned the California Fish and Game Commission to list the Delta smelt as a threatened species under the California Endangered Species Act.
8. *1992–1993:* Unsuccessfully petitioned the SWRCB to issue more stringent water quality standards for the Delta under state water quality legislation.
9. *1989–1992:* After a long battle, convinced Congress to fundamentally alter the statute governing the federal Central Valley Project (CVP) to provide more water for fish, increase water rates to farmers, and encourage voluntary water transfers from agriculture to urban areas.
10. *1992–1993:* Successfully petitioned the U.S. Fish and Wildlife Service to list the Delta smelt as a threatened species under the Federal Endangered Species Act.
11. *1993:* Successfully sued the EPA to force it to issue water quality standards for the Delta under federal law by December 1994.
12. *1994:* Engaged in successful negotiations with all the affected interests to come up with a basic agreement for dealing with the Delta's problems (the 1994 Bay/Delta Accord), which was then approved by the EPA and the SWRCB.
13. *1995–1996:* Successfully fought efforts by agricultural interests to convince the Republican-dominated Congress to (a) revise the CVPIA and (b) sell the CVP to its users.
14. *1995–1999:* Engaged in negotiations with a variety of federal and state agencies over a long term solution to the Delta's problems (the CALFED process).
15. *1996:* Successfully joined with ag and urban water users to convince the California Legislature to propose a bond issue to help fund some of those solutions. With no opposition, the bond (Prop 204) was easily approved by the electorate.

FIGURE 6.3   Strategies Pursued by the Environmental Coalition to Protect San Francisco Bay/Delta Fisheries Since 1984

Across-Coalition Learning and Professional Forums

One of the most influential aspects of the 1987–1988 version of the ACF was its contention that policy change is not simply the result of competition among various interests in which financial resources and institutional rules are critical, but that "policy-oriented learning" within and between coalitions is an important aspect of policy change (Sabatier, 1987, 1988; Jenkins-Smith, 1988, 1990). Learning about a topic is, however, filtered through preexisting beliefs. In particular, actors tend to accept information confirming existing beliefs and to screen out dissonant information. This is even more true of policy core beliefs than of secondary aspects (Coalition Hypothesis 3).

Several recent studies have tended to confirm this argument. Eberg's (1997, pp. 208–209) summary of learning processes regarding waste management in Bavaria and the Netherlands found that (1) learning was far more frequent in secondary aspects than in the policy core (thus, Coalition Hypothesis 3 was supported) and (2) that actors occasionally altered policy core learning on the basis of information coming from others within the same coalition. In addition, Freudenburg and Gramling (1997) provided a great example of how strong perceptual filters can be.[24]

Because learning among members of the same coalition is relatively unproblematic, attention has focused on identifying the conditions for learning *across* coalitions. Since 1988, we have made two sets of revisions in the framework on this topic.

First, the OCS leasing case revealed a situation in which there was very little across-coalition learning but in which there was considerable learning by a policy broker, Secretary of the Interior Cecil Andrus. He became convinced that drilling posed fewer risks than he had previously thought, and he had the legal authority to fundamentally alter the content of the administrative regulations regarding drilling (Heintz, 1988; Jenkins-Smith and St. Clair, 1993). This case led to the following hypothesis (Sabatier and Jenkins-Smith, 1993, p. 219):

> Learning Hypothesis 5: Even when the accumulation of technical information does not change the views of the opposing coalition, it can have important impacts on policy—at least in the short term—by altering the views of policy brokers or other important government officials.

The impact of such learning depends upon how much influence that official has to actually change policy and make the change stick. Andrus, for example, certainly had the authority, and his changes stuck because he was succeeded as Secretary of the Interior by James Watt, who was extremely proleasing. Had he been succeeded by an environmentally sympathetic person, the residue left by his learning might have been more ephemeral.

Second, given the role of professional forums in supposedly facilitating learning between coalitions (Learning Hypothesis 4), Sabatier and Zafonte (1997) developed a number of supplemental hypotheses concerning the characteristics of successful forums (see also Sabatier, 1998b). A successful forum is defined as one (1) in which consensus is reached among previously disagreeing scientists on whatever technical and policy issues are placed before it, and (2) in which the forum's decisions are accepted by the major coalitions involved. Following is a brief enumeration of the critical characteristics:

1. *Composition:* The forum should be composed of both (a) scientists clearly associated with each of the major coalitions and (b) neutral scientists (one of whom should be chair). The former are necessary because coalition leaders need to have representatives whom they trust, and the latter are needed to remind participants of professional norms regarding acceptable evidence, methodologies, and so on, and to indicate to the advocacy scientists when a professional consensus is beginning to emerge.

2. *Funding:* For the forum to be credible, funding must *not* come from sources dominated by a specific coalition. Instead, funding should come from (a) a foundation, (b) a legislative body in which all coalitions are represented, or (c) multiple agencies representing the various coalitions.

3. *Duration:* A forum should meet at least a half dozen times over a year or so. The assumption here is that it takes time for scientists from different coalitions to analyze their hidden assumptions, to critically evaluate the evidence, and to begin to trust each other.

4. *Context of a mutually unacceptable policy stalemate*: A forum will be successful only when each of the coalitions views a continuation of the status quo as unacceptable. Anyone who regards the status quo as acceptable will be unwilling to take the risks involved in changing important policy beliefs. Real compromise—or "true" success for a forum—requires both that scientists be willing to alter their relevant perceptions (concerning, for example, the seriousness of various causes of a problem) and that the coalitions make the relevant change in their policy preferences. A necessary, but not sufficient, condition for this result to occur is that all coalitions view a continuation of the status quo as unacceptable.

Because meeting all four conditions is quite difficult, we conclude that successful professional forums should be relatively rare. This would be particularly true in decentralized political systems like the United States, where coalitions that do not agree with the conclusions of a professional forum have *numerous* points of appeal (courts, legislatures, agencies at different levels of government) that have different biases. Thus dissatisfied coalitions can almost always find at least one route of appeal (venue) that will substantially block or delay implementation of the new policy. In more centralized systems—such as England—where routes of appeal are restricted, it may be possible for a coalition to change policy simply by convincing a policy broker of the merits of its point of view without having to change the views of the other coalition(s).

Major Policy Change

One of the major strengths of the ACF is that it provides a relatively clear-cut criterion for distinguishing major from minor policy change: Major change is change in the policy core aspects of a governmental program, whereas minor change is change in the secondary aspects.[25] Thus, it is the *topic* and the *scope* of policy change that determine whether it is major or minor. Linking change to scope also makes it clear that the same change may be "minor" for one subsystem but "major" for a subsystem nested within it. For example, changing automotive emission standards may be "major" for the automotive pollution control subsystem but relatively minor (i.e., dealing with secondary aspects) for the larger air pollution control subsystem. The ACF thus provides a clear reference point for determining the magnitude of change.

On the other hand, Mintrom and Vergari (1996, p. 425) are quite correct when they fault the ACF for neglecting the conditions under which major policy change occurs:

> [The ACF] directs our attention to thinking about the ways that belief structures arise and adjust over time to bring stability to a policy subsystem.... [But] it does not direct our attention to exploring the processes that determine when [major, i.e., policy core] policy change will actually take place. Clearly, not all exogenous shocks and not all instances of policy learning translate into policy change. We need to better understand why particular policy changes materialize.

How do we respond?

First, one needs to remember that changes in the policy core of governmental programs are infrequent events. The vast majority of changes occur in the secondary aspects. Like any large-scale, infrequent events, they are difficult to predict.[26]

Second, the cases by Brown and Stewart (1993) on airline deregulation and by Mawhinney (1993) on Canadian education have led to a revision of Hypothesis 5/Policy Change Hypothesis 2:

> Hypothesis 5/Policy Change Hypothesis 2 (revised): Significant perturbations external to the subsystem (e.g., changes in socioeconomic conditions, public opinion, systemwide governing coalitions, or policy outputs from other subsystems) are a *necessary, but not sufficient,* cause of change in the *policy core* attributes of a governmental program.

The basic argument is that such perturbations provide an opportunity for major policy change, but that such change will not occur unless that opportunity is skillfully exploited by proponents of change, that is, the heretofore minority coalition(s). [27]

Third, the 1993 version of the ACF separated "changes in public opinion" from the broader category of "changes in socioeconomic conditions" in order to give public opinion greater emphasis (see Figure 6.4). The basic argument is that although public opinion is seldom knowledgeable enough to affect policy specifics, it can certainly alter general spending priorities and the perceived seriousness of various problems (Sabatier and Jenkins-Smith, 1993, p. 223).

Fourth, Jan Eberg, Sonja Waelti, Pierre Muller, and several other European scholars have reminded us that the degree of consensus needed to institute a major policy change varies considerably across countries. The range is (1) from less than a majority (in nondemocratic countries and in strong states such as France; cf. Jobert and Muller, 1987, pp. 80–100); (2) to a bare majority (in Westminster systems like the UK and New Zealand); (3) to a supermajority (as in separation-of-powers systems like the United States); (4) to a consensus (as in Switzerland or the Netherlands). The degree of consensus required is a function of basic constitutional structure and cultural norms. It clearly affects the constraints and strategies of subsystem actors, as well as the probability that major policy change will actually occur. In fact, the degree of consensus required to institute a major policy change is so important that it should be added to the basic structural diagram of the ACF (see Figure 6.4).

Fifth, we must remember that a hierarchically superior unit of government may attempt to change the policy core of a "subordinate" level (Mawhinney, 1993; Sewell, 1999). Anyone familiar with the implementation literature is likely to view this as an exceedingly problematic enterprise that is strongly dependent upon the relative resources of coalitions at the two levels (Rodgers and Bullock, 1976; Van Horn, 1979: Mazmanian and Sabatier, 1989; Stewart, 1991).

Sixth, we suspect there may be two very different processes of major policy change within a given policy subsystem at a specific level of government (i.e., one that is *not* hierarchically imposed). On the one hand is the replacement of one dominant coalition by another. Sometimes a tremendous surge of public concern about a problem leads to a process of competitive policy escalation by elected officials (or political parties) and thus the replacement of one coalition by another virtually overnight. The 1970 Clean Air Amendments in the United States are an example (Jones, 1975). On the other hand, and far more frequent, we suspect, is a scenario in which the minority coalition increases in importance and attempts to take advantage of an opportunity afforded by an external perturbation but doesn't have the votes in the legislature to push through a substantial change in the policy core of governmental policy. This circumstance is particularly likely in systems where much more than a simple majority vote is required for major change. In such a situation, the minority coalition is likely to resort to *any* tactic that will garner additional votes, including offering pork barrel benefits, trying to

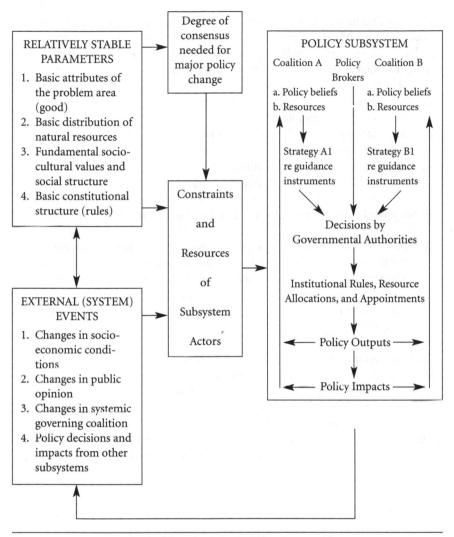

FIGURE 6.4   1998 Diagram of the Advocacy Coalition Framework

manipulate the dimensions of the issue to appeal to different constituencies, giving bribes, and attaching the bill as a waiver to other legislation (Evans, 1994; Mintrom and Vergari, 1996). In short, obtaining major policy change in super-majoritarian systems usually requires that an advocacy coalition augment its resources by developing short-term coalitions of convenience (Sabatier and Jenkins-Smith, 1993, p. 27) with a variety of other groups.

But there is at least one alternative that has been neglected by many policy scholars until recently. In situations in which *all major coalitions view a continuation of the current situation as unacceptable,* they may be willing to enter negotiations in the hope of finding a compromise that is viewed by everyone as superior to the status quo. We suspect that the conditions for such a successful consensus process (i.e., one that results in legally binding agreements viewed by everyone as an improvement) are similar to those for a successful professional forum discussed previously:

A. A stalemate exists wherein all coalitions view a continuation of the status quo as unacceptable.
B. Negotiations are conducted in private and last a relatively long time (e.g., at least six months).
C. Negotiations are led by a facilitator (policy broker) respected by all parties and viewed as relatively neutral.

In addition, Daniel Kuebler (1999) suggested a fourth condition:

A. Major conflicts must not be purely normative. If they are normative, the facilitator can do very little because most actors will be extremely reluctant to compromise on policy core norms. Instead, there must be some reasonably important empirical questions that can be used to alter beliefs or at least to point to areas of uncertainty that facilitate compromise.

The end result of such a process is not a dominant coalition and several minority coalitions but what might be regarded as power sharing among coalitions (analogous to a grand coalition in parliamentary systems). But the perceptual biases that are part of the ACF's model of the individual suggest that such grand coalitions are likely to be quite unstable unless (1) the arrangement produces a continuously "fair" distribution of benefits to all coalitions and (2) new leaders committed to consensus replace old warriors within the coalitions.

CONCLUSIONS

The ACF has been around for ten years now—which should be long enough, according to the ACF, to allow a reasonably accurate assessment. During that period, it has generated considerable interest by a variety of scholars in the United States and other OECD countries. In addition to the thirty-four cases mentioned in Table 6.2, there are at least a half dozen other major studies under way that seek to apply it critically. [28]

A Preliminary Assessment

The ACF does a reasonably good job of meeting the criteria for a scientific theory outlined in Chapter 1, which are largely drawn from Lave and March (1975) and King, Keohane, and Verba (1994):

1. Most of the *critical terms are clearly defined,* and most of the ACF's propositions appear to be clearly stated and internally consistent. At any rate, the definition of "advocacy coalition" was clear enough for Schlager (1995) to criticize us for ignoring the portion dealing with co-ordinated behavior.

2. It has *two causal drivers*: (a) the core values of coalition members and (b) external perturbations. In this sense, it is similar to theories of population dynamics in biology, where population levels are a function of (a) competition among individuals and species seeking to maximize inclusive fitness and (b) external perturbations.

3. It certainly has lots of *falsifiable hypotheses.*

4. It is fairly *broad in application;* that is, it appears to apply reasonably well to most policy domains in at least OECD countries.

The ACF has also aroused interest, and constructive criticism, from a wide variety of scholars, including those trained in institutional rational choice (Edella Schlager, Bill Blomquist, Michael Mintrom) and those predisposed toward cognitive explanations of policy (Robert Hoppe, Pierre Muller, Yves Surel). It has stimulated research by a large number of young scholars, some of whom will hopefully continue to work on it for years to come. In short, the ACF thus far appears to be a "progressive research program" (Lakatos, 1978), that is, one that stimulates interest and generates improvements.

Generalizability

The ACF was originally developed with a largely American context in mind, and most of the initial applications were to energy and environmental policy in the United States. Since the late 1980s, it has been applied to a fairly wide variety of policy areas in European and Commonwealth countries. But its generalizability is still unclear in a number of areas.

First, although it seems to work well in OECD countries, a couple of clarifications are called for when one is dealing with parliamentary systems (Sabatier, 1998a, pp. 120–122):

A. What constitutes a "change in the systemic governing coalition"? Does it require a complete change in the parties in government—in which case, it virtually never happens—or does it require simply a change in the most important party or even a change in the minor parties?

B. Policy documents in parliamentary systems often take the form of white papers or reports, whose legal status is much more ambiguous than that of the changes in statute that are the usual indicator of policy core change in separation-of-power systems (Moe, 1990; Wellstead, 1996; Loeber and Grin, 1999). In addition, the less frequent elections in many parliamentary systems (compared to the frequency of elections in the United States)

> provide governing coalitions with the time to dribble out major reforms over a period of years: first a white paper, then a framework law, and finally more detailed implementing laws or decrees (Casey et al., 1997).

This tendency of parliamentary systems to dribble out reforms is not a problem peculiar to the ACF, of course; it affects any theory attempting to distinguish major from minor policy change.

Second, its applicability to Eastern Europe and to developing countries is currently being explored. The minimal condition for the ACF to apply is that some degree of coordinated dissent from the policies of the dominant coalition must be possible—although not necessarily legal. Dissertations currently being written by Magnus Andersson (Free University of Amsterdam) on Polish environmental policy since 1980 and by Chris Elliot (Swiss Technical University) on Indonesian forestry policy suggest that the ACF can be applied without difficulty in these countries, but we'll have to see the complete results from these studies.

Third, several people have wondered whether the ACF applies to policy domains—such as abortion, gun control, human rights, gay rights, school prayer, and gender politics—in which technical issues are completely dominated by normative and identity concerns.[29] Our own perception is that it should work very well. These subsystems seem to be characterized by well-defined coalitions driven by belief-driven conflict, which resort to a wide variety of guidance instruments at multiple levels of government. In fact, the perceptual distortions in the ACF's model of the individual contributing to the "devil shift" should be particularly strong in such policy arenas. Thus far, there have been three case studies over which we have had no control—Mawhinney's (1993) analysis of linguistic conflict in Ontario education, Shannon's (1997) study of gender discrimination in wages in Australia and Ireland, and Kuebler's (1999) study of drug policy in Swiss cities—where the authors found the ACF applied quite well. But a more definite judgment will have to wait additional cases.

Directions for Future Research

What are the critical areas in need of elaboration, refinement, and testing? Most are a continuation of themes addressed in the previous section.

First, and most important, we need empirical research that systematically relates ACF variables to actual policy changes. Almost all the systematic, quantitative analysis thus far has dealt with coalition beliefs and coordination and has neglected the impact of these variables on actual policy changes. Since the ACF is a theory of policy change, we need to start addressing the principal dependent variable.[30] Within this general rubric, at least two specific areas come to mind:

A. The conditions conducive to successful professional and stakeholder forums, building upon the work of Kuebler (1999) and Sabatier and Zafonte (1997)

B. The role of coalitions in diffusing policy innovations and ideas among units of government, building upon the work of Berry and Berry (cf. Chapter 7) and Mintrom and Vergari (1996, 1998).

A second general topic involves the seriousness of collective action and coordination problems within coalitions and the conditions under which they can be overcome. This topic would be an excellent opportunity to develop, and test, competing hypotheses generated from IAD, ACF, and other approaches. It would also be very interesting to know if there are differences in coalition composition across countries. For example, the ACF assumes that legislators are members of coalitions only if they have considerable expertise in a specific policy area. This assumption might suggest that they would less frequently be members in countries with weak legislative committees at the national and regional levels. Another, and perhaps more important, area of study would be to look at variation across countries in the extent to which agency officials and researchers are members of coalitions.

A third area involves the scenarios of, and the factors affecting, subsystem development over time. Of particular interest is the role of watershed events in the transition from nascent to mature subsystems.

Fourth, there is still lots of work to be done on the belief systems of coalitions. In particular, most of the research to date has involved cross-sectional surveys. We need longitudinal and panel surveys to examine the factors affecting elite belief change over time. These surveys would also be a means of testing Hypothesis 3, that policy core beliefs are more stable than secondary aspects. Finally, Pierre Muller and Yves Surel (1998) have urged more attention to the processes by which belief system are constructed over time. In particular, to what extent can the development of a belief system be traced to an individual or small group of individuals—what Muller (1995) terms a "mediateur"?

Finally, on a conceptual level, the role of institutions in the ACF needs greater attention. And the implications of the ACF for various stages of the policy process—particularly implementation—need to be developed.[31]

Core Aspects of the ACF

A scientific theory or framework needs to be internally coherent. In responding to case studies that suggest various revisions in the ACF, we must resist the temptation of adding amendments that, although plausible, would be inconsistent with its fundamental principles. Our strategy should be to develop a relatively coherent theory that will explain 70 percent of policy change over periods of a decade or more rather than to add a hodgepodge of amendments in a misleading effort to explain 100 percent.

This requires that we identify those fundamental principles, or what Lakatos (1978) termed the "core" of a scientific research program. Following is our first attempt at such a list:[32]

1. *Reliance upon the policy subsystem as the principal aggregate unit of analysis:* Not only is such a reliance justified by multiple pressures for policy specialization, but subsystem scope has become critical to the ACF's conception of the structure of belief systems, the difference between major and minor policy change, and the factors affecting such change.

2. *A model of the individual based upon (a) the possibility of complex goal structures and (b) information-processing capabilities that are limited and, most important, involve perceptual filters:* This model is critical for understanding coalition stability and conflict, as well as for policy-oriented learning.

3. *Concern with policy-oriented learning as an important source of policy change, particularly in the secondary aspects.*

4. *The concept of advocacy coalitions as a means of aggregating large numbers of actors from different institutions at multiple levels of government into a manageable number of units:* This concept is both the defining characteristic of the ACF and one of its most innovative features.

5. *Conceptualizing both belief systems and public policies as sets of goals, perceptions of problems and their causes, and policy preferences that are organized in multiple tiers:* Mapping beliefs and policies on the same canvas facilitates analysis of the role of scientific and other information in policy. Providing a tiered and rather detailed concept of belief system structure encourages falsification.

6. *Coalitions that seek to manipulate governmental and other institutions to alter people's behavior and problem conditions in an effort to realize the coalition's belief system:* Coalitions seek to accomplish this kind of manipulation in an instrumentally rational fashion by moving among multiple venues in an intergovernmental system.

Once these core elements of the ACF have been identified, it becomes clear that the Schlager coordination hypotheses—although very plausible—should probably not be included in the ACF because they are based on an alternative model of the individual.

Framework or Theory?

The introductory and concluding chapters of this book borrow Elinor Ostrom's distinctions among frameworks, theories, and models. In our view, the ACF started as a framework (with a set of hypotheses) and is developing into the more integrated and denser set of relationships characteristic of a theory. Clearly, its model of the individual is much clearer now than in 1987 and much more integrated with other aspects of the theory, particularly coalition dynamics and belief change. The concept of a subsystem is much more clearly defined and much better integrated with belief system structure and policy change. The problems of achieving coordinated behavior among actors with similar beliefs are now explicitly acknowledged, and several relevant hypotheses have been proposed. Coalition strategies are much better developed. The factors affecting learning across coalitions—particularly the characteristics of professional forums—have been further elaborated. And at least a beginning has been made with respect to the processes underlying major policy change. If the ACF is not yet a theory, it is fairly close to becoming one.

NOTES

1. The year at Bielefeld (in the German Federal Republic) was notable for (1) the exposure it afforded Sabatier to two of the more committed and articulate bottom-uppers, Benny Hjern and Ken Hanf; (2) the opportunity to interact extensively with Lin Ostrom, a proponent of institutional rational choice who also served as a model of how to develop a coherent research program; (3) a walk in the woods with Martin Shubik, who convinced him that critics of rational choice would fail unless they developed an alternative theoretical framework; and (4) exposure to Heclo's (1974) classic work on social policy in Britain and Sweden, which, as much as anything, served as the basic inspiration for the ACF.

2. The ACF assumes that deep core and policy core beliefs will generally—but not always—be congruent. The deep core provides a very general set of principles—a heuristic—to guide political behavior on a very wide variety of topics. Policy core beliefs pertain within the subsystem, that is, the person's area of expertise. When the two conflict, the policy core will dominate because that is the area that is most salient to the person and in which she or he has thought the most deeply. In the United States, for example, conservatives are strong proponents of the market allocation of resources. But in the area of environmental policy, some conservatives recognize market limitations—such as externalities—and are willing to support a greater role for governmental intervention. For legislatures with strong committee systems, the ACF predicts that deep core beliefs would best predict floor votes, and policy core beliefs would best predict votes of specialists in committee.

3. For example, for an environmentalist who has a policy core belief that air quality poses a serious health problem throughout most of the United States, evidence that this is not the case in, for example, Boston poses no serious challenge. She or he simply changes a secondary aspect regarding problem seriousness for Boston. Information that air quality is no longer a hazard in a second locale will also pose no serious problem to the *policy core* belief; the analyst will simply change a specific secondary aspect for this second locale. But it will take very persuasive evidence from a high percentage of sites to produce a change in the policy core belief because the policy core is much broader in scope (the U.S. air pollution subsystem).

4. In their ongoing study of drug policy in a dozen European cities, Daniel Kuebler and his colleagues at the University of Lausanne have found very few cases of "neutral" brokers. Instead, most of the successful negotiations have been led by moderate members of the various coalitions (personal communication, November 1998; also Kuebler, 1999).

5. As originally conceived, "policy-oriented learning" focused largely on what might be termed substantive rather than political learning. It dealt with the severity of the policy

problem, its causes, and the probable impacts of alternative solutions on policy objectives rather than on the efficient political means of achieving those substantive objectives. We remain convinced of the general utility of distinguishing substantive from political learning, and of focusing policy-oriented learning on the former. For other discussions of policy learning, see May (1992), Bennett and Howlett (1992), Hall (1993), Goldstein and Keohane (1993), Radaelli (1995), and Lebovic (1995). For a discussion of the methodological difficulties in ascertaining whether learning has occurred, see King et al. (1994, pp. 191–192).

6. In fact, Hypothesis 2 is partially true by definition, as a coalition is defined as people who agree on policy core items. Thus, it is highly likely, although not logically required, that they will agree more on the policy core than on secondary aspects.

7. This listing of hypotheses follows the 1993, rather than the 1988, version of the framework (Sabatier and Jenkins-Smith, 1993, p. 217) because we have not included intergovernmental relations as a major category of framework development in this paper.

8. The middle set involves authors with established expertise in a particular policy domain, but no vested interest in supporting the ACF (i.e., none involved our students or colleagues). The vast majority of the thirty-four cases involve either journal articles or book chapters, although a few involve Ph.D. dissertations. All of them apply the ACF in a relatively serious and critical—not cursory—fashion.

9. There have also been a number of essays discussing the ACF, often comparing it with other approaches. These include Bennett and Howlett (1992), Lindquist (1992), deLeon (1994), Zahariadis (1995), Dowding (1995), Radaelli (1995b), Peterson (1995), Capano (1996), Parsons (1995), John (1998), and Bergeron, Surel, and Valluy (1998). Finally, there have been several papers (e.g., Radaelli, 1995a), that apply the ACF to a case(s) in a more cursory fashion than those listed in Table 6.1.

10. The situation is more complex than suggested here. On the one hand, the entire literature on iron triangles, closed subsystems, and corporatism suggests that many political scientists view administrative agency officials as active policy participants. And there has been some work on journalists as political actors (Rothman and Lichter, 1987; Iyengar, 1991). On the other hand, there is substantial evidence that many political scientists are reluctant to see agency officials, scientists, and journalists as potential members of advocacy coalitions. The following are three examples: (1)) A number of people, including Meier and Garman (1995), tend to view advocacy coalitions as virtually synonymous with interest groups. Although recognizing that agencies have policy goals, they are reluctant to see that agency officials often form active coalitions with sympathetic interest groups. They also neglect journalists and researchers as potential members of coalitions. (2) Most of the literature on principal agent models—particularly the work of Wood and Waterman (1991, 1994)—views agency officials as passive blanks who respond to stimuli from principals. (3) In his influential article on the change in British macroeconomic policy from Keynesianism to monetarism in the 1980s, Hall (1993) recognized the roles played by journalists and economists in popularizing monetarism but never admitted that they may have been active allies of the Thatcherites (rather than "neutral" chroniclers of the debate). For variations across countries in the extent to which agencies are expected to be neutral or policy-indifferent, see Aberbach et al. (1981).

11. Although neither of Jenkins-Smith's surveys contain measures of coordinated behavior—and thus are subject to Schlager's (1995) criticism that they have assumed that common beliefs lead to coordinated behavior—Duffy (1997, chs. 2, 3) provided evidence that national lab and UCS scientists were active members of opposing coalitions.

12. Although environmental groups tended to specialize a little, most were involved in at least two (and sometimes all three) of the major functional areas. The 1992 Bay/Delta questionnaire contained two indicators of coordinated behavior: (1)"Who do you rely upon for information and advice concerning Bay/Delta water policy issues?" and (2) "Who do you regard as allies/opponents?"

13. This hypothesis is "new" only with respect to the 1988 version of the framework. It was in the 1993 version (Sabatier and Jenkins-Smith, 1993, p. 213).

14. One possibility is that studies using testimony at public hearings will support the moderation hypothesis, whereas those based on (confidential) surveys are more likely to reveal relatively extreme views. The evidence to date, however, does not consistently support this argument.

15. Since (a) was in the text (but not the table) in the 1993 version and (c) was in the 1988 version, there is less change over time in the list of policy core topics than would first appear. For analyses of the importance of causal perceptions, see Sabatier and Hunter (1989) and Sabatier and Zafonte (1995, 1999).

The discerning reader will notice that "sociocultural identity" (e.g., ethnicity, religion, gender, identity) has been added to the *deep* core because it can obviously have a significant impact across a wide variety of policy areas (Schmidt, 1996). For the moment, we have decided not to add it to the policy core because the second normative precept (identification of groups whose welfare is critical) would seem to cover it. But we are impressed by Pierre Muller's (Jobert and Muller, 1987, pp. 80–100) argument that in a specific policy sector, groups can construct a new identity—for example, the image of "the young farmer, dynamic and moderniser"—that helped transform French agricultural policy in the 1960s.

16. This section is based largely upon conversations with (1) Gerald Thomas, John Grin, Anne Loeber, Tom Leschine, and Matt Zafonte at the 1996 Western Political Science Association meetings and (2) Grin and Rob Hoppe in Amsterdam in February 1997. See also the papers by Thomas (1996) and Grin and Hoppe (1997).

17. The problem cases include: (1) Is landsat a subsystem separate from the broader science and technology subsystem in the United States (Thomas, 1998)? (2) Is eutrophication a subsystem separate from the broader water quality subsystem in the Netherlands (Loeber and Grin, 1999)? (3) Is automotive pollution control a subsystem separate form the air pollution subsystem in the United States (Sabatier, Zafonte, and Gjerde, 1999)?

18. At Tahoe, those watershed events were approval of a fairly stringent regional plan in 1972 (opposed by many property owners) and the approval of several casinos in 1973–1974, which emasculated support for the agency by environmental groups and resource agencies (Sabatier and Pelkey, 1990). In air pollution control, the watershed event was the debate over the very stringent amendments to the Clean Air Act in 1970 (Ingram, 1978).

19. Interestingly, Haas (1992) made precisely the same mistake with respect to epistemic communities.

20. As Baumgartner and Leech (1998, ch. 7) observed, the literature on lobbying strategies consists of a series of case studies, and often, little effort is made to link case studies to existing theories or to accumulate evidence on specific topics. From our perspective, the most interesting work includes Hojnacki's (1997) analysis of the factors responsible for American interest groups' decisions to act alone or in concert in lobbying Congress. She found that groups are more likely to work together (1) on broad, rather than narrow, is-

sues, (2) when some organization is perceived as pivotal to success, or (3) when the groups perceive a strong organized opposition. In addition, niche theory suggests that one way to minimize competition for credit is to specialize, that is, to occupy a narrow niche (Gray and Lowery, 1996).

21. We have modified Schlager's "minimal levels of cooperation" hypothesis because it deals only with beliefs (i.e., agreement upon a definition of the problem and the content of policies used to address it) and does not involve any actual *behavior* (such as the development of a coordinated lobbying strategy). Schlager developed these criteria from Ostrom's (1990, p. 221) analysis of the conditions necessary for the formation of institutions to manage common property resources.

22. It was temporarily incorporated into the ACF in Sabatier (1998, p. 116), but this was before the incongruity in the two models of the individual became apparent.

23. Lack of data keeps us from addressing the second and fourth principles. Note that Figure 6.3 applies only to the federal and state levels and thus doesn't even try to list a multitude of local initiatives.

24. In their study of OCS leasing during the Reagan and Bush administrations, Freudenburg and Gramling (1997) found that the Department of Interior was so convinced of the evidence concerning the negligible environmental impacts of expanded drilling that they convinced President Bush to turn the issue over to the National Academy of Sciences for a judgment. Imagine their surprise when the academy ruled that the evidence was very mixed concerning the environmental risks of drilling.

25. On the other hand, we are not yet prepared to say whether a change in only one of the eleven topics in the policy core (see Table 6.2) would constitute "major" change, or whether it might require changes in several topics.

26. Baumgartner and Jones's punctuated-equilibrium framework (see Chapter 5) does no better than the ACF on this point. Just as the ACF points to exogenous shocks, they point to changes in "public image" and "venue" as precursors of major change, but both theories treat these precursors as exogenous to the phenomena being explained.

27. The 1993 revised version of the ACF attempted to revise Hypothesis 5 to deal with these criticisms, but it did so in a manner that made it virtually nonfalsifiable. This version is much better.

28. These include (1) Nigel Boyle, Claremont Graduate School, British labor market policy; (2) Rinie van Est, University of Amsterdam, wind energy policy in Denmark, the Netherlands, and California; (3) Laura Sims, University of Maryland, U.S. nutrition policy; (4) someone who recently submitted a paper to the *Journal of Politics* applying the ACF to welfare reform in the United States; (5) Mark Lubell and John Scholz, State University of New York at Stony Brook, coastal watershed partnerships in the United States; (6) Dorothy Daley, University of California at Davis, Superfund implementation; and (7) several colleagues at the University of California at Davis who are presently applying the ACF to 100 watershed partnerships in California and Washington. In addition, Larry Susskind (MIT) and John Power (University of Melbourne) have groups of students applying the ACF in graduate seminars (Casey et al., 1997).

29. We would like to thank Neil Pelkey for raising this issue particularly forcefully.

30. The ongoing study of 100 watershed partnerships at the University of California at Davis promises to do precisely this, and the ongoing study of European drug policy by Kuebler et al. should also produce some interesting conclusions on this subject.

31. Edella Schlager and Jim Lester are only two of the colleagues who have criticized the ACF for neglecting institutions and implementation. A first try at a response was made in presentations by Sabatier at several European universities in November 1998, but more work clearly needs to be done.

32. We are indebted to Chris Hood for reminding us to value internal coherence and to resist the temptation to synthesize a wide variety of approaches into a single "theory."

REFERENCES

Aberbach, Joel, Robert Putnam, and Bert Rockman. 1981. *Bureaucrats and Politicians in Western Democracies.* Cambridge, Mass.: Harvard University Press.

Andersson, Magnus. 1998. "An Advocacy Coalition Approach to Long-Term Environmental Policy Change in Poland." Ph.D. dissertation, Department of Political Science, Free University of Amsterdam.

Ashford, Douglas. 1981. *British Dogmatism and French Pragmatism.* London: George Allen & Unwin.

Barke, Richard. 1993. "Managing Technological Change in Federal Communications Policy: The Role of Industry Advisory Groups." In P. Sabatier and H. Jenkins-Smith, eds., *Policy Change and Learning*, pp. 129–146. Boulder: Westview Press.

Barke, Richard, and Hank Jenkins-Smith. 1993. "Politics and Scientific Expertise: Scientists, Risk Perceptions, and Nuclear Waste Policy," *Risk Analysis* (October).

Baumgartner, Frank, and Bryan Jones. 1993. *Agendas and Instability in American Politics.* Chicago: University of Chicago Press.

Baumgartner, Frank, and Beth Leech. 1998. *Basic Interests.* Princeton: Princeton University Press.

Bennett, Colin, and Michael Howlett. 1992. "The Lessons of Learning: Reconciling Theories of Policy Learning and Policy Change," *Policy Sciences* 25:275–294.

Bergeron, Henri, Yves Surel, and Jerome Valluy. 1998. "L'Advocacy Coalition Framework," *Politix*, No. 41:195–223.

Bernstein, Marver. 1955. *Regulating Business by Independent Commission.* Princeton: Princeton University Press.

Berry, Jeffrey. 1977. *Lobbying for the People.* Princeton: Princeton University Press.

Brady, David. 1988. *Critical Elections and Congressional Policy Making.* Stanford: Stanford University Press.

Brown, Anthony E., and Joseph Stewart. 1993. "Competing Advocacy Coalitions, Policy Evolution, and Airline Deregulation." In P. Sabatier and H. Jenkins-Smith, eds., *Policy Change and Learning*, pp. 83–104. Boulder: Westview Press.

Burnett, Miles, and Charles Davis 1999. "Getting Out the Cut: Politics and National Forest Timber Harvesting, 1960–96." In Paul Sabatier, ed., *An Advocacy Coalition Lens on Environmental Policy.* Cambridge, Mass.: MIT Press.

Burnham, Walter Dean. 1970. *Critical Elections and the Mainsprings of American Politics.* New York: W. W. Norton.

Capano, Giliberto. 1996. "Political Science and the Comparative Study of Policy Change in Higher Education," *Higher Education* 31:263–282.

Casey, Sue, et al. 1997. "Placing Post-Graduate Research in an Advocacy Coalition Framework." Paper presented at the Conference of the Public Policy Network, Melbourne, January.

Converse, Philip. 1964. "The Nature of Belief Systems in Mass Publics." In David Apter, ed., *Ideology and Discontent.* New York: Free Press.

Crandall, Robert, and Lave, Lester, eds. 1981. *The Scientific Basis of Health and Safety Regulation.* Washington, D.C.: Brookings Institution.

Davis, Charles, and Sandra Davis. 1988. "Analyzing Change in Public Lands Policymaking: From Subsystems to Advocacy Coalitions," *Policy Studies Journal* 17 (Fall):3–24.

deLeon, Peter. 1994. "The Policy Sciences Redux: New Roads to Post-Positivism," *Policy Studies Journal* 22(1):176–184.

Derthick, Martha, and Paul Quirk. 1985. *The Politics of Deregulation.* Washington, D.C.: Brookings Institution.

Dowding, Keith. 1995. "Model or Metaphor: A Critical Review of the Policy Network Approach," *Political Studies* 43 (March):136–158.

Downs, Anthony. 1972. "Up and Down with Ecology—The Issue Attention Cycle," *Public Interest* No. 28:38–50.

Dudley, Geoffrey, and Jeremy Richardson. 1996. "Why Does Policy Change over Time? Adversarial Policy Communities, Alternative Policy Arenas, and British Trunk Roads Policy, 1945–95," *Journal of European Public Policy* 3 (March):63–83.

Duffy, Robert. 1997. *Nuclear Politics in America.* Lawrence: University Press of Kansas.

Eberg, Jan. 1997. "Waste Policy and Learning." Ph.D. dissertation, Department of Political Science, University of Amsterdam.

Eisner, Marc A. 1993. *Regulatory Politics in Transition.* Baltimore: Johns Hopkins University Press.

Elliot, Chris. 1998. "Forest Certification in Indonesia, Canada, and Sweden." Ph.D. dissertation, Department of Environmental Management, Swiss Federal Institute of Technology, Lausanne.

Evans, Diana. 1994. "Policy and Pork: The Use of Pork Barrel Projects to Build Policy Coalitions in the House of Representatives," *American Journal of Political Science* 38 (November): 894–917.

Fenger, H. J. M., and P-J. Klok. 1998. "Interdependency, Beliefs, and Coalition Behavior: A Contribution to the Advocacy Coalition Framework." Paper presented at the University of Twente, November.

Fiske, Susan, and Shelley Taylor. 1984. *Social Cognition.* Reading, Mass.: Addison-Wesley.

Freudenburg, William, and Robert Gramling 1997. "How Crude: Advocacy Coalitions, Offshore Oil, and the Self-Negating Belief." Paper presented at the Annual Meeting of the American Association for the Advancement of Science, Seattle, February.

Goldstein, Judith, and Robert Keohane, eds. 1993. *Ideas and Foreign Policy.* Ithaca: Cornell University Press.

Grant, Wyn. 1995. *Autos, Smog, and Pollution Control.* Aldershot, England: Edward Elgar.

Gray, Virginia, and David Lowery. 1996. "A Niche Theory of Interest Representation," *Journal of Politics* 58 (February):91–111.

Green, David, and Ian Shapiro,, 1994. *Pathologies of Rational Choice Theory.* New Haven: Yale University Press.

Grin, John, and Robert Hoppe 1997. "Towards a Theory of the Policy Process: Problems, Premises, and Prospects of the ACF." Paper presented at the Polybios Workshop, University of Amsterdam, February.

Haas, Peter. 1992. "Introduction: Epistemic Communities and International Policy Coordination," *International Organization* 46 (Winter):1–35.

Hall, Peter. 1993. "Policy Paradigms, Social Learning, and the State: The Case of Economic Policymaking in Britain," *Comparative Politics* 25 (April):275–296.

Heclo, Hugh. 1974. *Social Policy in Britain and Sweden.* New Haven: Yale University Press.

_____. 1978. "Issue Networks in the Executive Establishment" In A. King, ed., *The New American Political System.* Washington, D.C.: American Enterprise Institute.

Heintz, Theodore. 1988. "Advocacy Coalitions an the OCS Lesing Debate: A Case Study in Policy Evolution," *Policy Sciences* 21:213–238.

Herron, Kerry, Hank Jenkins-Smith, and Carol Silva. 1999. "Scientists, Belief Systems, and Advocacy Coalitions in Environmental Policy" In Paul Sabatier, ed., *An ACF Lens on Environmental Policy.* Cambridge, Mass.: MIT Press.

Hjern, Benny, Kenneth Hanf, and David Porter. 1978. "Local Networks of Manpower Training in the Federal Republic of Germany and Sweden." In Kenneth Hanf and Fritz Scharpf, eds., *Interorganizational Policy Making: Limits to Coordination and Control*, pp. 303–344. London: Sage.

Hjern, Benny, and David Porter. 1981. "Implementation Structures: A New Unit of Administrative Analysis," *Organization Studies* 2:211–227.

Hoberg, George. 1998. "Distinguishing Learning from Other Sources of Policy Change." Paper presented at the Annual Meeting of the American Political Science Association, Boston, September.

Hojnacki, Marie. 1997. "Interest Groups' Decisions to Join Alliances or Work Alone," *American Journal of Political Science* 41 (January):61–87.

Hoppe, Robert, and Aat Peterse 1993. *Handling Frozen Fire.* Boulder: Westview Press.

Ingram, Helen. 1978. "The Political Rationality of Innovation: The Clean Air Act Amendments of 1970." In A. Friedlaender, ed., *Approaches to Controlling Air Pollution*, pp. 12–67. Cambridge, Mass.: MIT Press.

Iyengar, Shanto. 1991. *Is Anyone Responsible? How Television Frames Political Issues.* Chicago: University of Chicago Press.

Jenkins-Smith, Hank. 1988. "Analytical Debates and Policy Learning: Analysis and Change in the Federal Bureaucracy," *Policy Sciences* 21:169–212.

_____. 1990. *Democratic Politics and Policy Analysis.* Pacific Grove, Calif.: Brooks/Cole.

_____. 1991 "Alternative Theories of the Policy Process: Reflections on Research Strategy for the Study of Nuclear Waste Policy," *PS: Political Science and Politics* 24 (June):157–166.

Jenkins-Smith, Hank, and Paul Sabatier. 1994. "Evaluating the Advocacy Coalition Framework," *Journal of Public Policy* 14:175–203.

Jenkins-Smith, Hank, and Gilbert St. Clair. 1993. "The Politics of Offshore Energy: Empirically Testing the Advocacy Coalition Framework." In P. Sabatier and H. Jenkins-Smith, eds., *Policy Change and Learning*, pp. 149–176. Boulder: Westview Press. Jenkins-Smith, Hank, Gilbert St. Clair, and Brian Woods. 1991. "Explaining Change in Policy Subsystems: Analysis of Coalition Stability and Defection over Time," *American Journal of Political Science* 35 (4):851–872.

Jobert, Bruno, and Pierre Muller 1987. *L'Etat en action*. Paris: Presses Universitaires de France.

John, Peter. 1998. *Analysing Public Policy*. London: Pinter.

Jones, Charles. 1975. *Clean Air: The Policies and Politics of Pollution Control*. Pittsburgh: University of Pittsburgh Press.

_____. 1977. *An Introduction to the Study of Public Policy*, 2d ed. Belmont, Calif.: Wadsworth.

Jordan, A. G., and J. J. Richardson, 1983. "Policy Communities: British and European Style," *Policy Studies Journal*, 11 (June): 603–615.

King, Gary, Robert Keohane, and Sidney Verba. 1994. *Designing Social Inquiry*. Princeton: Princeton University Press.

Kingdon, John. 1984. *Agendas, Alternatives, and Public Policies*. Boston: Little Brown.

Kirst, Michael, and Richard Jung. 1982. "The Utility of a Longitudinal Approach in Assessing Implementation: Title I, ESEA." In W. Williams, ed., *Studying Implementation*, pp. 119–148. Chatham, N.J.: Chatham House.

Kiser, Larry, and Elinor Ostrom. 1982. "The Three Worlds of Action." In E. Ostrom, ed., *Strategies of Political Inquiry*, pp. 179–222. Beverly Hills, Calif.: Sage.

Knott, Jack, and Gary Miller. 1987. *Reforming Bureaucracy*. Englewood Cliffs, N.J.: Prentice-Hall.

Krehbiel, Keith. 1992. *Information and Legislative Organization*. Ann Arbor: University of Michigan Press.

Kuebler, Daniel. 1998. "Ideas as Catalytic Elements for Policy Change: Advocacy Coalitions and Drug Policy in Switzerland." In D. Braun and A. Busch, eds., *The Power of Ideas: Policy Ideas and Policy Change*. London: Routledge.

Lakatos, Imre. 1978. "The Methodology of Scientific Research Programmes." In J. Worrall and G. Currie, eds., *Philosophical Papers*, Vol. 1, pp. 1–101. Cambridge: Cambridge University Press.

Lave, Charles, and March, James. 1975. *An Introduction to Models in the Social Sciences*. New York: Harper & Row.

Lebovic, James. 1995. "How Organizations Learn: U.S. Government Estimates of Foreign Military Spending," *American Journal of Political Science* 39 (November):835–863.

Lertzman, Ken, Jeremy Rayner, and Jeremy Wilson. 1996. "Learning and Change in the British Columbia Forest Policy Sector: A Consideration of Sabatier's Advocacy Coalition Framework," *Canadian Journal of Political Science* 29 (March):111–133.

Leschine, Tom, Kent Lind, and Rishi Sharma. 1999. "Beliefs, Values, and Technical Assessments in Environmental Management: Contaminated Sediments in Puget Sound." In P. Sabatier, ed., *An Advocacy Coalition Lens on Environmental Policy*. Cambridge, Mass.: MIT Press.

Lester, James, and Michael Hamilton. 1988. "Intergovernmental Relations and Marine Policy Change: Ocean Dumping and At-Sea Incineration of Hazardous Waste." In *Ocean* Maynard Silva, ed., *Resources and U.S. Intergovernmental Relations in the 1980s*, pp. 197–220. Boulder: Westview Press.

Lindquist, Evert. 1992. "Public Managers and Policy Communities: Learning to Meet New Challenges," *Canadian Public Administration* 35 (Summer):127–159.

Liroff, Richard. 1986. *Reforming Air Pollution Regulation: The Toil and Trouble of EPA's Bubble*. Washington, D.C.: Conservation Foundation.

Loeber, Anne, and John Grin 1999. "From Phosphate Policy to Eutrophication Control: Policy Change and Learning in the Netherlands, 1977–89." In P. Sabatier, ed., *An Advocacy Coalition Lens on Environmental Policy.* Cambridge, Mass.: MIT Press.

Lord, Charles, Lee Ross, and Mark Lepper. 1979. "Biased Assimilation and Attitude Polarization: The Effects of Prior Theories on Subsequently Considered Evidence," *Journal of Personality and Social Psychology* 37:2098–2109.

Majone, Giandomenico. 1980. "Policies as Theories," *Omega* 8:151–162.

Marcus, Alfred, and Robert Goodman. (986. "Airline Deregulation: Factors Affecting the Choice of Firm Political Strategy," *Policy Studies Journal* 15 (Dec.):231–246.

Martin, Cathie Jo. 1995. "Nature or Nurture? Sources of Firm Preference for National Health Reform," *American Political Science Review* 89 (Dec.):898–913.

Mawhinney, Hanne. 1993. "An Advocacy Coalition Approach to Change in Canadian Education." In P. Sabatier and H. Jenkins-Smith, eds., *Policy Change and Learning*, pp. 59–82. Boulder: Westview Press.

May, Peter. 1992. "Policy Learning and Failure," *Journal of Public Policy* 12(4):331–354.

Mazmanian, Daniel, and Paul Sabatier. 1989. *Implementation and Public Policy.* Lanham, MD: University Press of America. (Reprint of 1983 book published by Scott Foresman and Co.)

Mazur, Alan. (1981). *The Dynamics of Technical Controversy.* Washington, D.C.: Communications Press.

Meier, Kenneth. 1985. *Regulation.* New York: St. Martin's Press.

Meier Kenneth, and E. Thomas Garman. 1995. *Regulation and Consumer Protection*, 2d ed. Houston: DAME Publications.

Mintrom, Michael, and Sandra Vergari. 1996. "Advocacy Coalitions, Policy Entrepreneurs, and Policy Change," *Policy Studies Journal* 24 (Fall):20–434.

_____. 1998. "Policy Networks and Innovation Diffusion: The Case of State Education Reforms," *Journal of Politics* 60 (Feb.):126–148.

Moe, Terry. 1980. *The Organization of Interests.* Chicago: University of Chicago Press.

_____. 1990. "Political Institutions: The Neglected Side of the Story," *Journal of Law, Economics, and Organization* 6:213–253.

Muller, Pierre. 1995. "Les politiques publiques comme construction d'un rapport au monde." In A. Faure, G. Pollet, and P. Warin, eds., *La construction du sens dans les politiques publiques,* pp. 1532–1179. Paris: L'Harmattan.

Muller, Pierre, and Yves Surel. 1998. *L'analyse des politiques publiques.* Paris: Montchrestien.

Munro, John. 1993. "California Water Politics: Explaining Policy Change in a Cognitively Polarized Subsystem." In P. Sabatier and H. Jenkins-Smith, eds., *Policy Change and Learning,* pp. 105–128. Boulder: Westview Press.

Nadel, Mark. 1971. *The Politics of Consumer Protection.* Indianapolis, Ind.: Bobbs-Merrill.

Nelson, Barbara. 1984. *Making an Issue of Child Abuse.* Chicago: University of Chicago Press.

Olson, Mancur. 1965. *The Logic of Collective Action.* Cambridge, Mass.: Harvard University Press.

Ostrom, Elinor. 1990. *Governing the Commons.* Cambridge: Cambridge University Press.

Parsons, Wayne. 1995. *Public Policy.* Cheltenham, England: Edward Elgar.

Peffley, Mark, and Jon Hurwitz. 1985. "A Hierarchical Model of Attitude Constraint," *American Journal of Political Science* 29 (November):871–890.

Peterson, John. 1995. "Decision-Making in the European Union: Towards a Framework of Analysis," *Journal of European Public Policy* 2 (March):69–93.

Poole, Keith, and R. Steven Daniels. 1985. "Ideology, Party, and Voting in the U.S. Congress," *American Political Science Review* 79 (June):373–399.

Pressman, Jeffrey, and Aaron Wildavsky. 1973. *Implementation.* Berkeley: University of California Press.

Quattrone, George, and Amos Tversky. 1988. "Contrasting Rational and Psychological Analyses of Political Choice," *American Political Science Review* 82 (Sept.):719–736.

Radaelli, Claudio. 1995a. "Corporate Direct Taxation in the European Union," *Journal of Public Policy* 15 (2):153–181.

_____. 1995b. "The Role of Knowledge in the Policy Process," *Journal of European Public Policy* 2 (June):159–183.

Radealli, Claudio, and Alberto Martini. 1997. "Think Tanks, Advocacy Coalitions, and Policy Change: A First Look at the Italian Case." In D. Stone, M. Garnett, and A. Denham, eds., *Think Tanks in Comparative Perspective: Insiders or Outsiders?* Manchester, England: Manchester University Press.

Rhodes, R. A. W. 1988. *Beyond Westminster and Whitehall.* London: Unwin & Hyman.

Richardson, J. J. 1994. "Doing Less by Doing More: British Government, 1979–1993," *West European Politics* 17 (July):178–197.

Richardson, J. J., ed. 1996. *European Union: Power and Policy-Making.* London: Routledge.

Riker, William 1962. *The Theory of Political Coalitions.* New Haven: Yale University Press.

Robyn, Dorothy. 1987. *Braking the Special Interests: Trucking Deregulation and the Politics of Policy Reform.* Chicago: University of Chicago Press.

Rodgers, Harrell, and Charles Bullock. 1976. *Coercion to Compliance.* Lexington, Mass.: D. C. Heath.

Rose, Richard. 1993. *Lesson-Drawing in Public Policy.* Chatham, N.J.: Chatham House.

Rothman, Stanley, and S. Robert Lichter. 1987. "Elite Ideology and Risk Perception in Nuclear Energy Policy," *American Political Science Review* 81 (June):383–404.

Sabatier, Paul. 1978. "The Acquisition and Utilization of Technical Information by Administrative Agencies," *Administrative Science Quarterly* 23 (Sept.):386–411.

_____. 1986. "Top-Down and Bottom-Up Models of Policy Implementation: A Critical Analysis and Suggested Synthesis," *Journal of Public Policy* 6 (January):21–48.

_____. 1987. "Knowledge, Policy-Oriented Learning, and Policy Change," *Knowledge* 8 (June): 649–692.

_____. 1988. "An Advocacy Coalition Framework of Policy Change and the Role of Policy-Oriented Learning Therein," *Policy Sciences* 21:129–168.

_____. 1992. "Interest Group Membership and Organization: Multiple Theories." In M. Petracca, ed., *The Politics of Interests*, pp. 99–129. Boulder: Westview Press.

_____. 1998a. "The Advocacy Coalition Framework: Revisions and Relevance for Europe," *Journal of European Public Policy* 5 (March):98–130.

_____. 1998b. "The Political Context of Evaluation Research: An Advocacy Coalition Perspective." In M.-C. Kessler, P. Lascoumes, M. Setbon, and J.-C. Thoenig, eds., *Evaluation des politiques publiques*, pp. 129–146. Paris: L'Harmattan.

Sabatier, Paul, ed. 1999. *An Advocacy Coalition Lens on Environmental Policy.* Cambridge, Mass.: MIT Press.

Sabatier, Paul, and Anne Brasher. 1993. "From Vague Consensus to Clearly-Differentiated Coalitions: Environmental Policy at Lake Tahoe, 1964–85." In P. Sabatier and H. Jenkins-Smith, eds., *Policy Change and Learning*, pp. 149–176. Boulder: Westview Press.

Sabatier, Paul, and Susan Hunter. 1989. "The Incorporation of Causal Perceptions into Models of Elite Belief Systems," *Western Political Quarterly* 42 (Sept.):229–261.

Sabatier, Paul, Susan Hunter, and Susan McLaughlin. 1987. "The Devil Shift: Perceptions and Misperceptions of Opponents," *Western Political Quarterly* 41 (Sept.):449–476.

Sabatier, Paul, and Hank Jenkins-Smith, eds. 1988. "Special Issue: Policy Change and Policy-Oriented Learning: Exploring an Advocacy Coalition Framework," *Policy Sciences* 21:123–278.

_____. 1993. *Policy Change and Learning: An Advocacy Coalition Approach*. Boulder: Westview Press.

Sabatier, Paul, and Susan McLaughlin. (1988). "Belief Congruence of Interest Group Elites with Their Constituencies," *American Politics Quarterly* 16 (Jan.):61–98.

Sabatier, Paul, and Neil Pelkey. 1990. *Land Development at Lake Tahoe*. Davis, Calif.: Institute of Ecology.

Sabatier, Paul, and Matthew Zafonte. 1995. "The Views of Bay/Delta Water Policy Activists on Endangered Species Issues," *Hastings West-Northwest Journal of Environmental Law and Policy* 2 (Winter):131–146.

_____. 1997. "Policy Oriented Learning Between Coalitions: Characteristics of Successful Professional/Scientific Fora." Paper presented at the AAAS meetings, Seattle, February.

_____. 1998. "Who Do Policy Elites Look to for Advice and Information?" Paper presented at the Max Planck Institut für Gesellschaftsforschung, Koln, November.

_____. 1999. "Are Bureaucrats and Scientists Members of Advocacy Coalitions?" In Paul Sabatier, ed., *An Advocacy Coalition Lens on Environmental Policy*. Cambridge, Mass.: MIT Press.

Sabatier, Paul, Matthew Zafonte, and Michael Gjerde. 1999. "Coalition Stability in U.S. Automotive Pollution Control Policy." In Paul. Sabatier, ed., *An Advocacy Coalition Lens on Environmental Policy*. Cambridge, Mass.: MIT Press.

Scharpf, Fritz. 1997. *Games Real Actors Play: Actor-Centered Institutionalism and Policy Research*. Boulder: Westview Press.

Schattschneider, E. E. 1960. *The Semi-Sovereign People*. New York: Holt, Reinhart & Winston.

Schiff, Ashley 1962. *Fire and Water: Scientific Heresy in the Forest Service*. Cambridge, Mass.: Harvard University Press.

Schlager, Edella. 1995. "Policy Making and Collective Action: Defining Coalitions within the Advocacy Coalition Framework," *Policy Sciences* 28:242–270.

Schlager, Edella, and William Blomquist. 1996. "A Comparison of Three Emerging Theories of the Policy Process," *Political Research Quarterly* 49 (Sept.):651–672.

Schmidt, Manfred. 1996. "When Parties Matter," *European Journal of Political Research*, 30 (Sept.):155–183.

Scholz, John, and Neil Pinney. 1995. "Duty, Fear, and Tax Compliance: The Heuristic Basis of Citizenship Behavior," *American Journal of Political Science* 39 (May):490–512.

Scholz, John, Neil Pinney, James Twombly, and Barbara Headrick. 1991. "Street-Level Political Controls over Federal Bureaucracy," *American Political Science Review* 85 (Sept.):829–850.

Sewell, Granville. 1999. "Advocacy Coalitions and the Implementation of the Framework Convention on Climate Change: A Preliminary Analysis." In P. Sabatier, ed., *An Advocacy Coalition Lens on Environmental Policy.* Cambridge, Mass.: MIT Press.

Shannon, Elizabeth. 1997. "Inching Towards Equality: Equal Pay in Australia and Ireland, 1969–1996." Ph.D. dissertation, Department of Political Science, University of Tasmania.

Simon, Herbert. 1985. "Human Nature in Politics: The Dialogue of Psychology with Political Science," *American Political Science Review* 79 (June):293–304.

Smith, Don. 1968. "Cognitive Consistency and the Perception of Others' Opinions," *Public Opinion Quarterly* 32:1–15.

Smith, James A. 1991. *The Idea Brokers.* New York: Free Press.

Stewart, Joseph. 1991. "Policy Models and Equal Educational Opportunity," *PS: Political Science and Politics* 26 (June):167–173.

Stone, Deborah. 1988. *Policy Paradox and Political Reason.* New York: HarperCollins.

Tesser, Abraham. 1978. "Self-Generated Attitude Change," *Advances in Experimental Social Psychology* 11:289–338.

Thomas, Gerald. 1996. "Policy Subsystems, the Advocacy Coalition Framework, and U.S. Civilian Land Remote Sensing (Landsat) Policy." Paper presented at the Annual Meeting of the Western Political Science Association, San Francisco, March.

_____. 1998. "Analyzing Environmental Policy Change: U.S. Landsat Policy, 1964–98." Ph.D. dissertation, Colorado State University, Ft. Collins.

Thompson, Michael, Richard Ellis, and Aaron Wildavsky. 1990. *Cultural Theory.* Boulder: Westview Press.

Van Horn, Carl. 1979. *Policy Implementation in the Federal System.* Lexington, Mass.: D. C. Heath.

van Muijen, Marie-Louise. 199. *Better Safe Than Provocative.* Amsterdam: VU University Press.

Walker, Jack. 1969. "The Diffusion of Innovations Among the American States," *American Political Science Review* 63 (Sept.):880–899.

Weiss, Carol. 1977. "Research for Policy's Sake: The Enlightenment Function of Social Research," *Policy Analysis* 3 (Fall):531–545.

Wellstead, Adam. 1996. *The Role of the Advocacy Coalition Framework in Understanding Forest Policy Changes: Alberta and Ontario.* Unpublished master's thesis, Graduate Department of Forestry, University of Toronto.

Weyent, John. 1988. "Is There Policy-Oriented Learning in the Analysis of Natural Gas Policy Issues?" *Policy Sciences* 21 (Fall):239–262.

Whiteman, David.1995. *Communication in Congress.* Lawrence: University Press of Kansas.

Wood, B. Dan. and Richard Waterman. 1991. "The Dynamics of Political Control of the Bureaucracy," *American Political Science Review* 85 (September):801–828.

_____. 1994.*Bureaucratic Dynamics.* Boulder: Westview Press.

Zafonte, Matthew, and Paul Sabatier. 1998. "Shared Beliefs and Imposed Interdependencies as Determinants of Ally Networks in Overlapping Subsystems," *Journal of Theoretical Politics* 10(4): 473–505.

Zahariadis, Nikolaos. 1995. "Comparing Lenses in Comparative Public Policy," *Policy Studies Journal* 23(2):378–382.

PART IV

Frameworks Comparing Policies Across a Large Number of Political Systems

7

Innovation and Diffusion Models in Policy Research

FRANCES STOKES BERRY AND WILLIAM D. BERRY

Although most actions by governments are incremental in the sense that they marginally modify existing programs or practices, and much research about policymaking seeks to explain why policymaking tends to be incremental, ultimately every government program can be traced back to some nonincremental *innovation*.[1] Thus, one cannot claim to understand policymaking unless one can explain the process through which governments adopt new programs. Recognizing this fact, public policy scholars have conducted extensive inquiry into policy innovation.

When people speak of innovation in common parlance, they usually refer to the introduction of something new. But when should a government program be termed "new"? The dominant practice in the policy innovation literature is to define an innovation as a program that is new to the government adopting it (Walker, 1969, p. 881). Thus, a governmental jurisdiction can innovate by adopting a program that numerous other jurisdictions established many years ago. By embracing this definition, students of policy innovation explicitly choose not to study policy *invention*—the process through which *original* policy ideas are conceived. To flesh out the distinction via illustration, a single policy *invention* can prompt numerous American states to *innovate*, some many years after the others.

This chapter reviews the dominant theories of government innovation in the public policy literature. However, we will see that these theories borrow heavily from ones developed to explain innovative behavior by *individuals*, for example, teachers using a new method of instruction (studied by education scholars), farmers adopting hybrid seeds and fertilizers (studied by rural sociologists), and

---

We are grateful to Henry Glick, Michael Mintrom, and Paul Sabatier for their very helpful and detailed comments on an earlier version of this paper.

consumers purchasing new products (studied by marketing scholars).[2] We will also see that theories of government innovation share many commonalities with models that seek to explain *organizational* innovation.

Some studies of government innovation have been cross-national, investigating how nations develop new programs and how such programs have diffused across countries (Collier and Messick, 1975; Heclo, 1974; Brown et al., 1979; Kraemer, Gurbaxani, and King, 1992). Other studies have focused on innovation by local governments within the United States (Aiken and Alford, 1970; Crain, 1966; Bingham, 1977; Midlarsky, 1978). But the vast majority of empirical research on government innovation has examined policymaking by the American states. For this reason, we will devote our primary attention to state-level research. Although most models of policy innovation we describe can be extended to national and local governments, some of these models hinge at least partially on the competitive nature of states within a federal system and thus must be modified when applied to local or regional governments within a unitary system, or to nations in an international system or an organization like the European Economic Community.

Despite the extensive number of studies of state government innovation at a general level, there are two principal forms of explanation for the adoption of a new program by a state: internal determinants and diffusion models. *Internal determinants models* posit that the factors leading a jurisdiction to innovate are political, economic, or social characteristics internal to the state. In these models, states are not conceived of as being influenced by the actions of other states. In contrast, *diffusion models* are inherently intergovernmental; they view state adoptions of policies as emulations of previous adoptions by other states. Both types of models were introduced to political scientists in Walker's (1969) seminal study of state government innovation across a wide range of policy areas.[3]

This chapter begins with separate discussions of the central features of the internal determinants and diffusion models. We then turn to the methodologies that have been used to test them. Although most scholars acknowledge that few policies' adoptions can be explained purely as a function of (1) internal determinants (with no diffusion effects) or (2) policy diffusion (with no impact by internal factors), most *empirical* research—and virtually *all* empirical research conducted before the 1990s—focused on one type of process or the other. At the time of their introduction during the late 1960s and early 1970s, the "single-explanation" methodologies developed were highly creative approaches using advanced quantitative techniques. However, recent research has shown that these traditional methodologies are severely flawed.

In the 1990s, more realistic models reflecting the simultaneous effects of both internal determinants and policy diffusion on state adoption behavior have been developed and tested by means of a technique called *event history analysis*. Such models hold great promise for advancing our understanding of government innovation. We discuss the gains that have already been achieved and offer suggestions for further enhancement of these models.

DIFFUSION MODELS

Rogers (1983, p. 5) defined diffusion as "the process by which an innovation is communicated through certain channels over time among the members of a social system." Students of state policy innovation positing diffusion models conceive of a social system consisting of the governments of the fifty American states and maintain that the pattern of adoption of the policy by the states results from states' emulating the behavior of other states. Various alternative diffusion models have been developed (each of which will be discussed below), the primary difference being the channels of communication and influence assumed to exist. However, we argue that all these models hypothesize that states emulate each other for one of three basic reasons.

First, states learn from one another as they borrow innovations perceived as successful elsewhere. Relying on the classic model of incremental decisionmaking (Lindblom 1965; Simon 1947), Walker (1969) hypothesized that state policymakers faced with complex problems seek decisionmaking shortcuts. Lindblom (1965) maintained that one critical method of simplification is the restriction by decisionmakers to consideration of only those alternatives that are marginally different from the status quo. Walker argued that another simplification method is to choose alternatives that, although not minor modifications of current policy, have been pursued and have proven effective or promising in other states. In effect, by showing how emulation of other states' innovations can be an aid to simplifying complex decisions, policy diffusion theorists have demonstrated how the adoption of *non*incremental policies can be consistent with the logic underlying incrementalism.[4]

Second, states compete with each other. Walker (1969, p. 891) argued that despite the autonomy that states possess in a federal system, there is pressure on all states to conform to nationally or regionally accepted standards. Such pressure leads states to adopt programs that have already been adopted widely by other states. Apart from a general pressure to conform, it is often rational for states to emulate other states to try to (1) achieve a competitive advantage or (2) avoid being disadvantaged. For instance, states may decrease welfare benefits to match the levels of their neighbors to keep from becoming a welfare magnet for the poor (Peterson and Rom, 1990). Similarly, a state may adopt a lottery to reduce the incentive for its own citizens living near a boundary to cross the border to play in another state's game (Berry and Berry, 1990). In a final example, states may adopt economic development incentive programs already present in other states to prevent an exodus of businesses from the state (Gray, 1994, p. 241).[5]

Third, apart from competition among policy elites across states, public officials can experience public pressure from their own citizens to adopt policies initiated in other states. News of the adoption of a popular policy by other states can create pressure on a state's public officials—especially elected officials planning to seek another term—to adopt the same policy.[6] To the extent that this is true, the news media play a large role in the diffusion process by publicizing successful new programs outside the borders of the states in which the programs were initiated.

As we review the various diffusion models developed in the policy innovation literature, each focusing on a different channel of communication and influence across government jurisdictions, we will see that each of the models relies on one or more of these three reasons to justify why states emulate other states when making public policy. We begin with the two models most commonly proposed in the literature—the national interaction model and the regional diffusion model—and finish with two other models positing different channels of influence.

The National Interaction Model

The national interaction model assumes a national communication network among state officials regarding public sector programs, in which officials learn about programs from their peers in other states. It is presumed that officials from states that have already adopted a program interact freely and mix thoroughly with officials from those states that have not yet adopted it, and that each contact by a not-yet-adopting state with a previous adopter provides an additional stimulus for the former to adopt. Thus, it is predicted that the probability that a state will adopt a program is proportional to the number of interactions its officials have had with officials of already-adopting states (Gray, 1973a). There are, indeed, formal institutional arrangements that encourage the thorough mixing of states. Chief among these are various associations of state officials that allow individuals with similar positions across the fifty states to meet periodically in national conferences. These include associations of elected generalist officials such as the National Governors' Association and the National Conference of State Legislatures, each of which have numerous committees on specific policy areas, as well as organizations of functionalist officials such as the National Association of General Service Administrators.

This learning model was developed and formalized by communication theorists analyzing the diffusion of an innovation through a social system (assumed to be of fixed size) consisting of individuals. In equation form, the model can be expressed as

Equation 1:
$$\Delta N_t = N_t - N_{t-1} = bN_{t-1}[L - N_{t-1}]$$

In this model, L is the proportion of individuals in the social system that are potential adopters (a value assumed to remain constant over time) and serves as a ceiling on possible adoptions. If every person in the system is unconstrained and may adopt, L equals 1. N_t is the cumulative proportion of adopters in the social system at the end of time period t, $N_t[\text{th}]\_[\text{th}]_1$ is the cumulative proportion at the end of the previous period; thus, ΔN_t is the proportion of new adopters during period t.[7] With some algebraic manipulation, the terms in Equation 1 can be rearranged to yield

Equation 2:

$$N_t = (bL + 1)\, N_{t-1} - bN^2_{t-1}$$

Then, since Equation 2 is linear, given data on the timing of adoptions by all potential adopters, the parameters b and L can be estimated by regressing N_t on N_{t-1} and N^2_{t-1}.[8]

When the cumulative proportion of adopters is graphed against time, Equation 1 yields an S-shaped curve, like that reflected in Figure 7.1. Early in the diffusion process, adoptions occur relatively infrequently. The rate of adoptions then increases dramatically but begins to taper off again as the pool of potential adopters that have not yet adopted becomes small.

In an important early effort to enhance the theoretical precision of state government innovation research and to explain states' adoptions of new policies with a widely applicable general theory of innovation, Virginia Gray (1973a; see also Menzel and Feller, 1977; Glick and Hays, 1991) employed Equation 2, assuming that the social system is the community of American states. Setting the time period as the calendar year, her regression analyses show that adoptions of several state policies—including Aid to Families with Dependent Children (AFDC), education policies, and civil rights laws—fit the equation very closely. But several factors limit the utility of the national interaction model—as traditionally conceived of in Equations 1 and 2—for students of government innovation.

First, the model assumes that during any time period, all potential adopters that have not yet adopted are equally likely to adopt; the only variable influencing the probability that a potential adopter will adopt during any time period is the cumulative number of adopters prior to that period. Indeed, the model treats all potential adopters as totally undifferentiated actors who interact randomly, that is, who are equally likely to have contact with all other members of the social system. Thus, the theory is well suited to a case in which the social system is a large society of individuals, and the scholarly interest is in a macrolevel description of the diffusion process. Although certainly in any society, friendships and work and family relations guarantee that an individual's interactions with other members of the society will be nonrandom, when studying the diffusion of a new consumer product through a large society, for instance, it may suffice to employ a model assuming random interaction. But when studying the diffusion of a policy through the fifty states, it seems less reasonable to treat the states as undifferentiated units; we know that Mississippi differs in many ways from New York, and

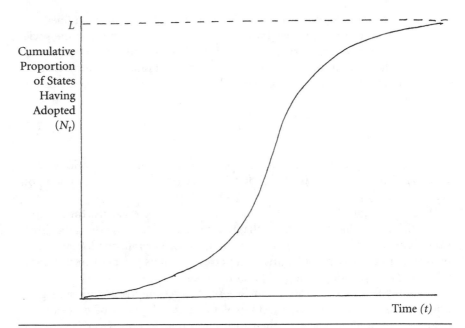

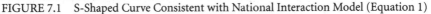

FIGURE 7.1   S-Shaped Curve Consistent with National Interaction Model (Equation 1)

our theory should probably take some of these differences into account. It is also likely that contacts between officials from different states are patterned rather than random.[9] It makes sense, for example, that politicians and bureaucrats in New York have more contact with their counterparts in New Jersey than with officials in Mississippi, and that state officials who choose to be active in their national associations interact more frequently with other state officials than those who choose to stay home.

Gray (1973a; see also Menzel and Feller, 1977) did not start with an a priori assumption about the value of the constant *L*—the ceiling on total possible adoptions—in Equation 1. Instead, she estimated *L* and did not view a value substantially less than 1 as inconsistent with the national interaction model. Yet nothing in the logic underlying the model explains why some states would not be potential adopters. Indeed, since states are completely undifferentiated within the model, by definition, there can be no accounting for the fact that some states have a chance of adopting whereas others do not. We believe that any analyst specifying a national interaction model should, at a minimum, assume that all states are potential adopters (and thus that *L* equals 1) or should introduce a priori predictions about which states will never adopt (and for what reasons these states are immune), thereby offering a testable prediction about the value of *L*.

Finally, Equation 1 is a time series model having as its dependent variable the proportion of new adopters in a time period (ΔN_t). This dependent variable limits sharply the scope of the phenomena to be explained. If we assume, contrary to the assumption of the national interaction model, that the probability of adoption of a policy varies across states, a more interesting dependent variable is the conditional probability that a particular state, *S*, will adopt the policy during a specified time period, given (1) the characteristics of the state and (2) other states' actions that might influence the choice by *S*. A model with this dependent variable could continue to specify interaction between states on a national basis, but the random pattern of contact assumed by the national interaction model can be replaced with a more structured process of state interaction.

The Regional Diffusion Model

Whereas the national interaction model assumes that states interact thoroughly with each other on a national basis, the regional diffusion model posits that states are influenced primarily by those states that are geographically proximate. Some models, which we call *neighbor models,* assume that states are influenced primarily by those states with which they share a border; for example, Berry and Berry (1990) hypothesized that the probability that a state will adopt a lottery is positively related to the number of states bordering it that have already adopted one (see also Lutz, 1987). Other models, which we term *fixed-region models,* assume that the nation is divided into multiple regions (of contiguous states) and that states tend to emulate the policies of other states within the same region (Mooney and Lee, 1995). Although not usually specified with such precision, a fixed-region model might hypothesize that the probability that a state will adopt a program is directly related to the percentage of states within its region that have previously adopted.

All three reasons for states' emulating each other—learning, competition, and public pressure—can be the basis for assuming that diffusion channels are regional in nature. States are more likely to "learn" from nearby states than from those far away because states can more easily analogize to proximate states, which tend to share economic and social problems, and which have environments similar enough so that policy actions may have similar effects (Mooney and Lee, 1995, p. 605; Elazar, 1972).[10] Public pressure to adopt a policy initiated by a different state may be especially great when that state is nearby, as actions in that state are likely to be more familiar and visible to the public than those occurring in more distant states. However, it is when policy adoptions are attempts to *compete* with other states that the likelihood of regionally focused, rather than nationally based, diffusion seems greatest. Because of constraints on the mobility of most individuals and firms, states are more likely to compete with nearby states than with those far away. For example, states worried about losing revenue—especially those with large population centers near a border—are likely to be very concerned about whether their immediate neighbors have lotteries, but unconcerned about lotteries in remote states. Similarly, a state fearful of becoming a welfare magnet may make immediate responses to policy changes by neighbors with large concentrations of poor people near their borders but may pay no attention to policy adjustments in faraway states.

Although fixed-region and neighbor models are similar to the degree that their emphasis is on the emulation of nearby states, the models are subtly different in their specified channels of influence. Fixed-region models presume (if only implicitly) that all states within the same region experience the same channels of influence. In contrast, neighbor models—by avoiding fixed regional groupings of states, and instead pointing to the influence of all bordering states—assume that each state has a unique set of reference states for cues on public sector innovations. Although one can discern policies where a neighbor model makes more sense that a fixed-region formulation (e.g., in the case of lottery adoptions), and vice versa, neither pure model is likely to be entirely realistic. Fixed-region models imply implausibly that some states—those bordering another region—are completely unaffected by some of their neighbors. Neighbor models assume that states that are close but share no border (e.g., Vermont and Maine) have no influence on one another. A more realistic regional diffusion model might assume that states are influenced most by their neighbors, and also by other states that are nearby. One simple specification consistent with this assumption is that the level of influence of one state on another is proportional to the distance between the two states.[11]

Leader-Laggard Models

Leader-laggard models assume that certain states are pioneers in the adoption of a policy, and that other states emulate these leaders (Walker, 1969, p. 893). Most often, scholars presume that leadership is regional, with states taking cues from one or more pioneer states within their geographic region (Walker, 1969, 1973; Grupp and Richards, 1975; Foster, 1978). However, this model can be modified easily to reflect the notion of national leaders: states that, when they adopt a new program, increase the likelihood that other states, regardless of their geographic location, will adopt. Leader-laggard models are consistent with the presumption that in any policy area, some states' personnel are more highly regarded by their peers than other states', and that policymakers are more likely to turn to these states for cues.[12] Therefore, these models assume that states emulate other states in a learning process rather than because of interstate competition or public pressure.

Although there are certainly strong reasons to expect leader states to emerge, thus forming the groundwork for leader-laggard diffusion, such models are often flawed by their failure to identify a priori (1) the states (or even the types of states) that are expected to be pioneers and (2) the predicted order of adoption of the states that are expected to follow. Indeed, without an a priori theoretical prediction of which state(s) will lead and the order in which the remaining states will follow, a leader-laggard model is virtually nontestable, as any adoption pattern will involve some state(s)—which ex-post-facto could be designated the pioneer(s)—adopting a policy first, and other states adopting afterward.

One leader-laggard model that clearly specifies the channels of diffusion is the hierarchical model developed by Collier and Messick (1975). Studying the pattern of social security adoptions by nations around the world, these authors hypothesized that the pioneers in social security were highly (economically) developed nations and that social security programs diffused down a hierarchy of nations from most developed to least developed.[13] Such a hypothesis specifies (in a testable fashion) the characteristics of leaders (high economic development) and a clear ordering of successive adoptions (from most developed to least developed countries). But note that although the hierarchical model specifically posits the diffusion of a policy across jurisdictions, its empirical prediction of a strong relationship between economic development and earliness of adoption is indistinguishable from that of an internal determinants model that assumes no influence of states on one another and assumes instead that the sole determinant of the propensity of a state to adopt is its level of development.

Vertical Influence Models

The vertical influence model sees states as emulating not the policies of other states—as part of a horizontal diffusion process—but the policies of the national government. One might argue that this model is conceptually similar to a leader-laggard model that specifies that there is a single pioneer state; in effect, the national government serves in the same role as a state-level pioneer. To the extent that states emulate the national government as a result of a learning process, the similarity between models is indeed quite strong; the national government is analogous to a widely respected leader state. But the reasons states are influenced by the national government to adopt policies extend beyond learning. In some cases, the national government can simply mandate certain activities by the states (e.g., the federal motor voter bill that requires states to allow people to register to vote at the same time that they register their vehicle). Although one might label such a process *diffusion*, it is a highly uninteresting form of diffusion, as nearly all state discretion is eliminated by national-level fiat. A more interesting theoretical process results when the states retain discretion, but the national government provides incentives for the adoption of a policy by the states. Typically, there are financial incentives resulting from the provisions of a federal grant-in-aid program, as in the case of Medicaid and its associated administration provisions. In another example, Derthick (1970) showed how the Social Security Act of 1935 shaped state welfare programs through the AFDC grant to the states. Moreover, Welch and Thompson (1980; see also Brown, 1975) found that policies for which the federal government offers incentives diffuse faster than state preserve policies.[14]

INTERNAL DETERMINANTS MODELS

Internal determinants models presume that the factors causing a state to adopt a new program or policy are political, economic, and social characteristics of the state. Thus, in their pure form, these models preclude diffusion effects in which a state is influenced by the actions of other states or the national government. Certainly, once a policy is adopted by one state, it is extremely unlikely that another state's adoption of the policy would be completely independent of the previous adoption. Unless the two states' arrival at the same (or very similar) policies was a highly improbable coincidence, at a minimum there must have been a diffusion from one state to the other of the idea for the policy. Thus, we believe that internal determinants models must acknowledge that when a state adopts a policy new to the American states, media coverage and institutionalized channels of communication among state officials make it likely that knowledge of the policy will spread to other states.[15] However, such models assume that once a state is aware of the policy, it is internal characteristics of the state that determine if and when an adoption will occur—instead of pressure created by other states' adoptions or explicit evaluations of the impacts of the policy in earlier-adopting states.

The Choice of a Dependent Variable

One important theoretical issue in the construction of internal determinants models is how the dependent variable—the propensity of a state to adopt a policy or a set of policies—is defined. Historically, most internal determinants models have made the American state the unit of analysis and have employed a dependent variable that assumes that the earlier a state adopts, the greater is its innovativeness. Empirical analysis is cross-sectional, and the dependent variable is generally measured at the interval level by the year of adoption (or some linear transformation thereof), or at the ordinal level by the rank of a state when states are ordered by their time of adoption (Canon and Baum, 1981; Glick, 1981; Gray, 1973a; Walker, 1969). However, a dichotomous version of this variable, which indicates whether a state has adopted a policy by a specified date, is also used (Filer, Moak, and Uze, 1988; Glick, 1981; Regens, 1980).

In the past decade, several internal determinants models in the state policy innovation literature have conceptualized the propensity of a state to adopt differently. The unit of analysis is still the American state but is now the state in a particular year. More precisely, the unit of analysis is the American state still eligible to adopt in a particular year.[16] The dependent variable is the probability that a state that is eligible to adopt will do so during that year (Berry and Berry, 1990, 1992; Hays and Glick, 1997; Mintrom, 1997). Empirical analysis is pooled (cross-sectional/time series) where states are observed over multiple years.

One important distinction between the two dependent variables is that the probability of adoption is a concept that is (1) defined for each state at any point in time and (2) free to change over time, whereas the earliness of adoption takes on a single fixed value for each state and is determined by the year it adopts. A second distinction is that although the timing of a state's adoption relative to adoption by other states is fundamental to the state's score on the earliness-of-adoption variable, relative timing is not necessarily relevant to a determination of a state's propensity to adopt when a probability-of-adoption conception is utilized. A state adopting a policy decades later than most other states is not necessarily deemed to have had a (stable) low propensity to adopt; it is possible that the state had a low probability for many years, but that changing conditions led to an increased probability of adoption.

Although we are reluctant to declare either of these dependent variables—earliness of adoption or probability of adoption—unambiguously best for internal determinants models, we believe that greater theoretical advances will come from models having the latter dependent variable, a position we will elaborate in the concluding section of this chapter. Furthermore, our discussion of the theory underlying internal determinants models in this section will emphasize conceptualizations in which the dependent variable is the probability of adoption.

When propensity to adopt is conceived of as the probability of adoption, the focus of research must be a single policy.[17] However, when one is studying the innovativeness of the states as reflected in their earliness of adoption, attention can focus on either one policy or a set of policies. At one extreme are studies designed to explain states' adoptions of a single policy or program (e.g., Berry and Berry's 1990 analysis of the lottery, and Hays and Glick's 1997 research on state living wills). Other internal determinants models have focused on multiple policy instruments in a single issue area (e.g., Sigelman and Smith's 1980 research on consumer protection, covering twenty-eight different kinds of consumer legislation). At the other extreme is Walker's (1969) analysis of the determinants of a state innovativeness index reflecting the earliness of adoption of a set of eighty-eight policies spanning a wide range of economic and social issue areas and Savage's (1978) innovativeness measure based on sixty-nine policies.

Implicit in the Walker and Savage measures of innovativeness is the claim that it is reasonable to conceive of a general proclivity of a state to innovate across a wide range of issue areas. Some are skeptical of this claim; in a classic exchange with Walker, Gray (1973a, 1973b) claimed that states can be highly innovative in one program area, but less innovative in others, thereby rendering any general innovativeness score useless. Of course, whether there is a tendency for a state to be innovative generally and across a range of policy areas is an empirical question, and if the evidence is supportive, it is useful to develop models explaining generic innovativeness.

But even the variation already documented in state innovativeness across issue areas makes it obvious that for any individual policy, the propensity of states to adopt the policy cannot be explained fully by a general proclivity to innovate (Gray, 1973a). For this reason, if generic innovativeness is a useful concept, we still ought not treat it as the ultimate dependent variable. A good alternative is to take the course of Mooney and Lee (1995) and Hays and Glick (1997), who have conceived of a state's general proclivity to innovate as just one of a set of independent variables that influence the probability that a state will adopt a particular policy. The idea is that states vary in their general receptivity to new ideas, and that this is one factor that accounts for their differential probabilities of adopting any specific program analyzed. The strength of the role played by general receptivity relative to other specific determinants of the probability of adoption is assessed empirically.

Hypotheses from Internal Determinants Models

Much of the theory underlying internal determinants models of state government innovation can be traced to research about the causes of innovativeness at the individual level. For example, a tremendous level of support has been generated for the proposition that persons with greater socioeconomic status—higher levels of education, income, and wealth—are more likely to innovate than persons with less status.[18] A high level of education provides individuals access to knowledge about innovative practices and an openness to new ideas. Many innovations cost money or involve financial risks for those that adopt them; greater income and wealth provide people the resources necessary to absorb these costs. Similar hypotheses have been developed about innovation in organizations. Organizations of greater size and with greater levels of slack resources are assumed to be more innovative than smaller organizations and those with fewer resources (Rogers, 1983; Cyert and March, 1963; F. S. Berry, 1994b). In turn, Walker (1969, pp. 883–884) explicitly drew on these organizational-level propositions to support the hypothesis that larger, wealthier, and more economically developed states are more innovative.

Indeed, we can turn to the literature on organizational innovation for a framework useful for assessing the variety of internal determinants likely to influence the probability that states will innovate. Lawrence Mohr (1969, p. 114) proposed that the probability that an organization will innovate is inversely related to the strength of the obstacles to innovation and is directly related to (1) the motivation to innovate and (2) the availability of resources for overcoming the obstacles. This proposition suggests a valuable organizational device, since among the hypotheses frequently reflected in internal determinants models are those concerning the motivation to innovate, as well as the obstacles to innovation and the resources available to surmount them.

We will review these hypotheses, emphasizing those that seem to be applicable to a wide range of policies. However, we recognize that explaining the adoption of any specific policy is likely to require attention to a set of variables that are ad hoc from the point of view of innovation theory but critical given the character of the politics surrounding the issue area in question. For example, states with strong teacher unions are less likely to adopt school choice reforms (Mintrom, 1997), and states with large fundamentalist populations are less likely to adopt policies considered immoral by many fundamentalists, such as state lotteries and state reforms (in the pre-*Roe* period) making abortions more accessible (Mooney and Lee, 1995; Berry and Berry, 1990). A strong presence of religious fundamentalists in a state does not diminish the likelihood of adoptions of every policy, just those raising moral issues central to their religious beliefs.

An explanation of the adoption of any specific policy is also likely to require independent variables that are relevant not because they are determinants of the propensity of a state to adopt a new policy, but because they influence the preferences of policymakers concerning the substantive issues raised by the new policy. For instance, a legislator's response to a proposal for a new welfare program should be driven partially by the same factors determining the legislator's reaction to a proposal to make an incremental change in existing welfare programs, such as increasing benefit levels. In a more extreme example, research by Berry and Berry (1992, 1994) on state tax policy found that the factors explaining states' adoptions of new tax instruments are virtually identical to the variables accounting for decisions to increase the rates in existing taxes—even though the imposition of a tax new to a state can unambiguously be termed a policy innovation, whereas an increase in the rate of an existing tax would probably be conceived of as an incremental policy choice. What seems to drive the politics of taxation in the American states is the unpopularity of taxes, and this affects both tax adoptions and tax increases.[19]

Our review of hypotheses from internal determinants theories of government innovation will emphasize variables that seem especially relevant to explaining the adoption of new programs. This means that we will not discuss a wide range of factors widely believed to influence both innovative and routine policymaking.[20] For example, citizen and elite ideology are frequently hypothesized to influence the adoption of many programs that reflect traditional liberal-conservative cleavages (Mooney and Lee, 1995; Berry and Berry, 1992). But their influence is not relevant to an understanding of policy innovation per se, because ideology is widely perceived as influencing routine or incremental policy choices as well (Hill, Leighly, and Hinton-Andersson, 1995; Clingermayer and Wood, 1995).[21]

Factors Reflecting the Motivation to Innovate

Social scientists often assume that the principal goal of elected officials is to win reelection (Mayhew, 1974; Kiewiet and McCubbins, 1985). This assumption suggests that elected officials should be responsive to public opinion when deciding whether to adopt a new policy (Hays and Glick, 1997). But the response should be expected to vary with the level of electoral security of state officials: The more insecure they feel, (1) the more likely they are to adopt new policies that are popular with the electorate, and (2) the less likely they are to adopt new policies that are widely unpopular, or at least sufficiently unpopular with some segment of the electorate to be deemed controversial. Two corollaries of this proposition have frequently been introduced in the state innovation literature. One relates to inter-party competition; Walker (1969) argued that politicians anticipating closely contested elections are especially likely to embrace new programs to try to broaden their electoral support. Implicit in this hypothesis is the idea that the new programs are popular with the public; in the case of unpopular programs (like the imposition of a new tax), electoral competition is likely to reduce the probability that a state's politicians will support the program.

Politicians' levels of electoral security also vary with the amount of time until their next election. Reasoning similar to the above suggests that the closer it is to the next statewide election, the more likely a state is to adopt a new popular pro-gram, and the less likely it is to adopt an unpopular new policy or one that is highly controversial. This proposition has received support in the case of highly popular state lotteries (Berry and Berry, 1990), very unpopular mandatory taxes (Mikesell, 1978; Berry and Berry, 1992), and controversial school choice initia-tives (Mintrom, 1997).

Obstacles to Innovation and
the Resources Available to Overcome Them

Theories of individual and organizational innovation have stressed the impor-tance of financial resources (i.e., wealth and income levels for individuals and slack resources for an organization) and other characteristics reflecting the capa-bility of the potential adopter (e.g., a high level of education for an individual and large size for an organization) as contributors to innovation. Similar kinds of resources are often held to be critical for government innovation.

Some new government programs require major expenditures, and therefore, the availability of financial resources is a prerequisite for adoption. Thus, one can hypothesize that the fiscal health of a state's government often has a positive im-pact on the propensity of a state to adopt a new policy.[22] Analogous to the notion of highly capable individuals or organizations is the concept of states with strong governmental capacity. Walker (1969) and Sigelman and Smith (1980) have maintained that states having legislatures that give their members generous staff support and extensive research facilities should be more likely to adopt new poli-cies than states with less professionalized legislatures. Alternatively, it can be ar-gued that it is the capacity of a state's economy to finance both extensive public services and a professional legislature that is the ultimate determinant of the propensity to innovate. Such capacity is reflected by several measures of eco-nomic development common in the literature, including per capita income, gross domestic product, and level of urbanization.

Walker's (1969, p. 884) reasoning suggests that states with high levels of eco-nomic development can be expected to have a greater probability of adopting even those policies that do not require large budgets (e.g., enabling legislation for zoning in cities or a state council on the arts), as he attributed part of the greater propensity of highly developed states to adopt new policies to their greater adaptivity and tolerance of change. Furthermore, Wagner (1877; see also Mann, 1980; Berry and Lowery, 1987) hypothesized that economic development prompts increased demand for government services. Greater personal income of a state's citizens leads them to demand governmental services that might be considered luxuries when personal income is low. Similarly, greater urbanization and industrialization lead to social problems that often require collective governmental solutions (Hofferbert, 1966).

Others have argued that although adequate financial resources are a prerequisite for government innovation, individuals who advocate policy ideas and are willing to devote their energies to pushing these ideas can be critical to the adoption of a new policy. Most of the scholarly attention to the importance of so-called policy entrepreneurs, both inside and outside government, has focused on their role in agenda setting (Kingdon, 1984; Baumgartner and Jones, 1993; Schneider, Teske, and Mintrom, 1995). But recently, Mintrom (1997; see also Mintrom and Vergari, 1996) offered evidence of the importance of policy entrepreneurs in facilitating the adoption of school choice initiatives in the states. Similarly, Sabatier and Jenkins-Smith (1998) argue that advocacy coalitions—that is, coordinated groups of governmental officials, activists, journalists, researchers, and policy analysts—can be crucial in paving the way for policy adoptions.[23]

Indeed, several theorists, recognizing the rarity of government innovation, have argued that innovation can be expected to occur only in the unusual case in which various independent conditions happen to occur simultaneously. Kingdon (1984, ch. 8) wrote of policy windows—rare periods of opportunity for innovation—that are created when a new political executive takes office, an important congressional committee chair changes hands, and/or some event or crisis generates an unusual level of public attention to some problem. He argued that policy entrepreneurs consciously wait for such windows of opportunity to press their policy demands. In their study of tax adoptions, Berry and Berry (1992; see also Hansen, 1983) argued that taxes tend to be adopted when several unrelated political and fiscal conditions converge to create a rare political opportunity for an adoption: the presence of a fiscal crisis in government occurring when the next election is not near and when one or more neighboring states has recently adopted a new tax.

TRADITIONAL APPROACHES TO TESTING
INTERNAL DETERMINANTS AND DIFFUSION MODELS

We have argued that nearly all explanations of government innovation have taken the form of either diffusion or internal determinants models. It is clear that these two forms of models are not mutually exclusive. The existence of internal factors that influence the probability of adoption of some policy by a state does not preclude the possibility that this probability is also affected by the actions of other states, and vice versa. But the literature on state government innovation is dominated by empirical research that tests (1) internal determinants explanations that assume no diffusion impacts or (2) diffusion models that assume no effects of internal determinants (F. S. Berry, 1994a). We will argue below that the major task of innovation scholars is to follow the course of several recent studies by developing and testing more realistic models that specify the simultaneous impacts of internal determinants and influences by other states. However, a preliminary task is to evaluate the success of traditional approaches in testing the single-explanation models that have dominated the literature.

Frances Stokes Berry (1994a) argued that each of three major models of government innovation—internal determinants, national interaction, and regional diffusion—has been associated with a distinct methodology for empirical testing, and she explored the ability of these techniques to detect the true innovation process underlying policy adoptions. She did this by applying the methodologies to data generated from simulated innovation processes with known characteristics. Berry's results, which we will summarize here, paint a very pessimistic picture of the ability of the traditional methodologies to help us understand state government innovation.[24]

Testing Internal Determinants Models

Internal determinants models have traditionally been tested with cross-sectional regression (or probit or discriminant) analysis (Regens, 1980; Glick, 1981; Canon and Baum, 1981; Filer, Moak, and Uze, 1988). The dependent variable is a measure of how early a state adopts one or more policies (or whether some policy has been adopted by a certain date), and the independent variables are political and socioeconomic characteristics of the states.[25]

Several problems with this cross-sectional regression strategy are immediately apparent. The first pertains to the year for observing independent variables. If one measures the values of the independent variables in a year that is later than some states' adoptions, one winds up attempting to account for the behaviors of these states with variables measured after the behavior has occurred. Thus, the only logical alternative is to measure the values of the independent variables in the year that the first state adopts (or some earlier year). But when adoptions of the policy are spread over many years, this approach requires the implausible assumption that late-adopting states' behavior can be explained by the characteristics of those states many years prior. Moreover, the cross-sectional approach to testing an internal determinants model does not permit an assessment of the effects of variables that change substantially over time; each state is a single case in the analysis, having a fixed value for the independent variables. Finally, the cross-sectional approach is suitable for testing only an internal determinants model in which the propensity to adopt is defined as the "earliness of adoption." A cross-sectional model cannot be used if the dependent variable is conceptualized as the probability of adoption in a particular year.

In addition to these limitations, Berry found that the cross-sectional approach to testing internal determinants models cannot be trusted to discern whether the adoptions of a policy by states are actually generated by internal determinants. She found, for example, that simulated policy adoptions generated out of a pure regional diffusion process—with no impact at all by internal state characteristics—tend to exhibit evidence of the effects of internal determinants when a traditional cross-sectional model containing independent variables frequently used in the literature is estimated. The empirical problem is that states near each other tend to have similar values on many political and socioeconomic characteristics of states. Thus, policies that diffuse regionally—say, by being passed to bordering states—tend to yield an order of adoption by states that correlates highly with these internal characteristics.

Testing the National Interaction Model

As noted earlier, the national interaction model is traditionally tested by means of time series regression to estimate a model in the form of Equation 2. But Berry found that this regression approach cannot reliably discern whether a policy's adoptions are the result of national interaction. In particular, when data for simulated policy adoptions generated either (1) by a pure regional diffusion process or (2) solely as a result of internal determinants are used to estimate Equation 2, the results often support the hypothesis that the policies spread via a national interaction process.

The empirical problem here is that for any policy for which a graph of the cumulative proportion of states having adopted against time approximates an S shape similar to that in Figure 7.1, the regression approach will generate support for the national interaction model. Unfortunately, this S shape will result from *any* process that produces a period of infrequent adoptions followed by a period of more frequent adoptions (which is inevitably followed by a tapering off in the rate of adoptions as the number of remaining potential adopters declines). Policies that diffuse regionally can produce this adoption pattern. Even policies that are adopted as independent responses to internal state conditions can. Consider, for example, a policy that is most likely to be adopted by states with healthy economies. If a national economic boom cycle lifts the economies of all states, adoptions by many states may be clumped together to produce a period of frequent adoptions sandwiched between periods with less frequent adoptions.

Testing Regional Diffusion Models

The classic approach to testing the regional diffusion model is Walker's (1969; see also Canon and Baum, 1981) factor-analytic technique. Walker used factor analysis to isolate groupings of states that had similar orders of adoption for eighty-eight policies. He then observed that the groupings coincided with regional clusters of states, which he interpreted as empirical evidence for regional diffusion.

F. S. Berry (1994a) simulated state adoptions of 144 policies, each diffusing regionally based on a pure neighbor model. When the data for these 144 policies were factor-analyzed according to Walker's procedure, there was strong support for the regional diffusion proposition. Thus, Berry found clear evidence that Walker's methodology correctly identifies neighbor-to-neighbor diffusion when it exists. Our hunch is that the methodology also successfully shows support for the regional diffusion hypothesis when employed with policies that diffuse via fixed-region diffusion. If we are correct, the good news would be that factor analysis reliably detects diffusion when it exists in either of two prototypical forms: neighbor to neighbor or in fixed regions. But the bad news would be that the technique is not able to distinguish the two similar—but still distinct—types of regional diffusion. More disconcerting, however, is that Berry found that Walker's methodology yields support for the regional diffusion hypothesis when applied to simulated policies known to diffuse via a pure national interaction model with no regional element whatsoever. She also found evidence that policy adoptions generated purely as a result of internal determinants can indicate the presence of regional diffusion when an alternative single-explanation methodology is used.[26]

Testing Any Diffusion Model

A critical problem with all traditional quantitative methodologies in studying diffusion processes is that they rely strictly on information about the timing of state adoptions. The methodologies take State B's adoption of a policy soon after State A's as evidence that A had an influence on B. However, B's adopting after A, although a necessary condition for A's influencing B, is not a sufficient condition; the similar timing of A's and B's adoptions may be coincidental. One way to overcome this problem is to supplement data about the timing of adoptions with survey data collected by asking state policymakers to identify the leaders in a particular policy area or which officials in other states they consult for advice (Freeman, 1985; Grupp and Richards, 1975; Light, 1978). If the responses are accurate, they can be used to help distinguish true influence from coincidentally timed adoptions resulting from the impacts of other forces. However, when adoptions of a policy are spread out over many years, it is impractical to interview officials in all states at times when their memories about the nature of policy formulation are fresh.

Another way to reduce the chances that coincidentally timed policy adoptions by states are mistaken as evidence of diffusion is to use methodologies that control the indicator of the impacts of diffusion for other potential causal factors, namely, internal determinants. The more fully a research design can control for alternative explanations of innovation, the more trustworthy is a conclusion that states that adopt a policy are emulating adoptions by other states. The next section of this chapter suggests a framework for analysis that accomplishes this kind of control.

AN AGENDA FOR THE FUTURE

Students of government innovation have developed a number of explanations for the adoptions of new policies by the American states. These include both internal determinants models and a range of diffusion models pointing to the influence of states on one other. Dating back to the early path-breaking studies on policy innovation and diffusion—by Walker (1969) and Gray (1973a), scholars have recognized that these various models are not mutually exclusive, and that a state may adopt a new policy in response to both conditions internal to the state and the actions of other states. When conducting empirical analysis, however, these same scholars have generally ignored the nonexclusive nature of these explanations by analyzing them in isolation. Of course, such analysts did not purposely misspecify their models; rather, the arsenal of methods commonly used by social scientists prior to the 1990s did not permit proper specification.

Unfortunately, F. S. Berry's (1994a) simulation results show that the discipline's compartmentalized approach to testing the various explanations of government innovation, which was dominant until the 1990s, calls into question the bulk of the existing body of evidence about these explanations. Berry found no evidence of false negatives—no reason to believe that the traditional tests for the presence of regional diffusion, national interaction, and the impact of internal determinants fail to discern these processes when they are present. But she found a disturbing pattern of false positives—a tendency for the methodologies to find regional diffusion, national interaction, or the effect of internal determinants when no such influence actually exists. Thus, we believe that the key to progress in research on state innovation is the development of models sensitive to the diversity of potential influences on a state's propensity to adopt a new policy—including forces both internal and external to the states.

A General Model of State Government Innovation

We propose that models of state government innovation should take the following general form:

Equation 3:
$$ADOPT_{i,t} = f(MOTIVATION_{i,t}, RESOURCES/OBSTACLES_{i,t},$$
$$OTHER\ POLICIES_{i,t}, EXTERNAL_{i,t})$$

The unit of analysis for this equation is the American state eligible to adopt a policy in a particular year (*t*, by virtue of the fact that it has not already adopted that policy). The dependent variable—$ADOPT_{i,t}$—is the probability that state i will adopt the policy in year t. $EXTERNAL_{i,t}$ denotes variables reflecting diffusion effects on state i at time t; thus, they would measure the behavior of other states at time t, or in the recent past.

The remainder of the terms in the function f are internal determinants. $MOTIVATION_{i,t}$ represents variables indicating the motivation to adopt the policy of public officials in state i at time t; they would include the character of public opinion and electoral competition in the state and other ad hoc motivation factors. $RESOURCES/OBSTACLES_{i,t}$ denotes variables reflecting obstacles to innovation and the resources available for overcoming them. For many policies, the state's level of economic development and the professionalism of its legislature would be included. Variables indicating the presence (and skill) of interested policy entrepreneurs or the strength of advocacy coalitions in a state could also be included.[27] Finally, $OTHERPOLICIES_{i,t}$ is a set of dummy variables indicating the presence or absence in state i of other policies that have implications for the likelihood that the state will adopt the new policy.

The impacts of previous policy choices on the probability of adopting a new policy have been virtually ignored in the empirical literature on state government innovation, but we contend that our models of policy innovation must recognize the effects of one policy choice on another. Mahajan and Peterson (1985, pp. 39–40) identified four types of innovation interrelationships; innovations may be (1) independent, (2) complementary, (3) contingent, or (4) substitute. This typology has relevance to explaining state policy adoptions.

If we are seeking to explain the adoption of Policy B, and Policy A is largely independent of B (in the sense that a state's probability of adopting B is unaffected by whether the state has already adopted A), obviously we need not concern ourselves at all with Policy A. But policies of the other three types are not so safely ignored. Sometimes two policies are complementary: The adoption of Policy A increases the probability that a state will adopt Policy B. For example, a state that has previously chosen to license one type of auxiliary medical practitioner (such as physician assistants) may have created a precedent that would make it more likely that advocates of licensing other auxiliary personnel (such as nurse practitioners) will be successful. If so, a model designed to explain state licensing of one type of medical practitioner should include a dichotomous explanatory variable indicating whether a state has previously adopted licensing of some other type of auxiliary medical personnel.

Note that a positive relationship between the probability of adoption of Policy B and the presence of Policy A can exist without A and B's being complementary, if the relationship is spurious—resulting from both policies' adoptions being influenced by a common set of variables. For example, if the probability that a state will adopt one type of welfare reform is positively related to the presence of another, similar type of reform, yet that relationship is due exclusively to the fact that the same kinds of causal forces are at work in the adoption of both policies, the two welfare reforms should not be conceived of as complementary. It is only when theory suggests that the adoption of one policy will change conditions in a state so as to make the state more receptive to the other policy that we would call the two policies complementary.

Another possibility is that Policy B's adoption is contingent on the previous adoption of Policy A, in which case the probability that a state will adopt B is zero until the state adopts A. Brace and Barrilleaux (1995) presented a theory of state policy reform designed to explain changes in existing programs in a variety of policy areas. The adoption of many of these policy changes is contingent on a state's previous adoption of the program being reformed. In this case, the units of analysis must exclude each state in all years prior to its adoption of the initial legislation.[28]

A final alternative is that Policy A is a substitute for Policy B. When A is an exact substitute for B, completely precluding the possibility of the adoption of B, the solution is excluding from the units of analysis in those state-years in which A is present. However, exact policy substitutes are rare; partial substitutes are more likely. In this case, the adoption of A does not totally preclude the adoption of B; it only reduces the adoption's likelihood. For instance, it may be that different school choice plans currently being considered by states are partial substitutes. One possibility is that states will create charter schools in an attempt to diminish the prospects that a more radical program—such as school vouchers—will be adopted. In this case, a state's previous adoption of a charter school program would lower the probability that the state would establish a voucher program.[29]

A recognition that some policies are substitutes suggests that we should also entertain models that involve more complex dependent variables than the probability that an individual policy will be adopted ($ADOPT$, in Equation 3). Sometimes it might be best to assume that a state makes a choice between multiple alternatives. For example, Berry and Berry (1992) studied the adoption of sales and income taxes separately, assuming for each, that states without the tax may choose to adopt or not in any year. But it may more accurately reflect the process of decisionmaking to conceptualize states that have neither tax in any year as having three choices: to adopt a sales tax, to adopt an income tax, or to adopt neither.[30]

Another way in which a conceptualization of the dependent variable as the probability of adopting a policy often oversimplifies reality is that it fails to distinguish between what Glick and Hays (1991, p. 836; see also Downs and Mohr, 1976) referred to as "superficial" and "deep" adoption. For example, two states might adopt an antidiscrimination program (e.g., in housing or the workplace); one adoption is largely symbolic, whereas the other involves an extensive commitment of resources through investigatory and enforcement actions. Calling both adoptions antidiscrimination programs, and treating them as functionally equivalent, may mask variations essential for understanding the innovation process at work.

Some of the variation in the depth of adoptions of a policy may be due to what Glick and Hays (1991; see also Clark, 1985) called policy "reinvention." Implicit in the notion of reinvention is a diffusion model that justifies the states' emulation of other states' policies by an assumption that states learn from each other. Yet the learning model is more sophisticated than those discussed above, because it assumes that states use information about the impacts of a policy in other states not only to assist them in deciding whether to adopt the policy, but also to help them refine the policy in the light of the other states' experiences. In turn, early adopters can reform their policies to take advantage of the experiences of late adopters who have passed a modified version of the initial policy. Unfortunately, models that allow for variation across states and over time not only in the probability of the adoption of a policy, but also in the content of the policy, are beyond the bounds of the framework for research reflected in Equation 3.

Testing the Model of State Government Innovation: Event History Analysis

Event history analysis is an ideal methodology for estimating the coefficients of an innovation model taking the form of Equation 3. In event history analysis, we conceive of a risk set, that is, the states that (at any point) are at risk of adopting the policy in question because they have not previously adopted. In a discrete time model, the period of analysis is divided into a set of discrete time periods, typically years. The dependent variable—being the probability that a state in the risk set will adopt during year t—is not directly observable. However, we can observe for each state in the risk set whether the state adopts the policy in the given year (typically coded 1) or not (scored 0). Since states fall out of the risk set after they adopt the policy, for each state that adopts during the period of analysis the time series for the dependent variable is a string of zeros followed by a single 1 in the year of adoption. Given data for the states in the risk set over a period of years, the event history model, having a dichotomous observed variable, can be estimated by means of logit or probit maximum likelihood techniques.[31]

The maximum likelihood estimates of the coefficients for the independent variables in the event history model offer information on the predicted impacts of these variables on the propensity of states in the risk set to adopt the policy. By the use of procedures common in the analysis of probit and logit results, the co-efficient estimates can, in turn, be used to generate predictions of the probability that a state with any specified combination of values on the independent variables will adopt the policy in a given year. Furthermore, one can estimate the change in the probability of adoption associated with a specified increase in the value of any independent variable, when the remaining independent variables are held constant. Such estimated changes in probability yield easily interpretable estimates of the magnitude of the effect of the independent variable. Additionally, event history analysis has proven capable of yielding meaningful results even when utilized to explain adoptions of a policy that are very rare among the American states (Berry and Berry, 1990; see also F. S. Berry, 1994b; Mooney and Lee, 1995; Hays and Glick, 1997; Mintrom, 1997). Indeed, in Berry and Berry's study of lottery adoptions, only 3 percent of the units in the risk set experienced an adoption during the period of analysis. Thus, the technique can be applicable with a surprisingly small amount of variation in the observed dependent variable.

Although event history analysis has for the first time allowed scholars of state government innovation to develop models that simultaneously incorporate internal determinants and diffusion impacts, thus far the diffusion effects specified have been limited to very simple forms of regional diffusion. The most common has been neighbor-to-neighbor influence (assuming that all states that border state i have equal influence on i), specified by including as an independent variable the number (or alternatively, the percentage) of neighboring states that have previously adopted (Berry and Berry, 1990, 1992; Hays and Glick, 1997). Also, Mooney and Lee (1995) specified a form of fixed-region diffusion (attributing equal influence on state i to all states in i's region), by including in their event history analysis model of abortion regulation an index measuring the average level of abortion permissiveness across the states in i's census region. However, more complex types of regional diffusion can also be specified. Our earlier suggestion of a conception allowing for the greatest influence by i's neighbors, yet also some influence by other nearby states (an effect that diminishes with the distance from i), can be operationalized by constructing a dummy variable for each state (1 if a state has adopted the policy, 0 if not) and taking a weighted average of these dummies across states, where the weights are proportional to the distance from state i.

The other forms of diffusion theorized in the literature can also be incorporated in event history models. Leader-laggard diffusion can be modeled with a dummy variable indicating whether state i's presumed leader has already adopted the policy. Vertical influence resulting from the incentives inherent in a federal grant-in-aid program can be specified by including an independent variable reflecting the potential monetary gain resulting from i's adoption of the policy. Even the thorough mixing of states assumed by the national interaction model can be specified in an event history model; the independent variables would include the percentage of the fifty states that have previously adopted the policy. However, we do not recommend this approach, preferring that scholars develop more realistic formulations of national interaction. For instance, one might hypothesize that the interaction of state officials in the National Association of State Personnel Executives will contribute to the diffusion of a new civil service reform policy, so that states whose officials are most active in the organization are the most likely to adopt. This proposition can be tested by including a measure of the extent of participation of officials from state i in the national association.

Perhaps the greatest weakness of extant studies of state policy innovation relying on event history analysis is their assumption of the independence of observations across time. Event history analysis assumes that the probability that a state will adopt in one year is unrelated to its probability of adoption in prior years. It is unlikely that the true policy process occurring in states conforms to this assumption. For instance, the pressure to adopt a new policy—and hence, the probability of adoption—can increase gradually over time as coalitions designed to promote the policy are built. Similarly, when intense efforts to secure adoption of a policy fail in a year, the probability of adoption may be reduced in the year following, as advocates of the policy tire of the battle and decide to marshal their resources for the future. Thus, the development of models that allow for memory in the policy process from one year to the next, and thus that can overcome the limitations imposed by the assumption of independence over time, is an important item on the research agenda.

CONCLUSION

Since the late 1960s, social scientists have proposed numerous theories to explain policy adoptions by the American states. These theories include internal determinants explanations and a variety of diffusion models that point to cross-state channels of influence. In isolation, these theories are drastically oversimplified models of policy innovation. Unfortunately, the vast majority of empirical research has tested these models individually and thus has yielded conclusions about these models that are of questionable value. However, the logic of internal determinants models and the logic of the various diffusion explanations are not incompatible, and recent studies have developed models that allow for the simultaneous impacts of internal political, economic, and social characteristics of states as well as multiple channels of regional and national cross-state influence. In this chapter, we have proposed a framework for analysis to guide the further development and refinement of these more realistic models.

Nevertheless, even achieving the greatest imaginable success in the development and testing of innovation models taking the form of Equation 3 would not yield a satisfactory theory of the overall policymaking process. Our proposed approach to policy innovation and diffusion research can be distinguished from some of the other theoretical approaches discussed in this volume, especially the advocacy coalition framework (ACF). By proposing that innovation models take the form of Equation 3, we are recommending that scholars deemphasize the analysis of the global concept of innovativeness concerning a wide range of policies and focus attention on explaining the propensity of states to adopt specific policies and programs. Although we believe that explanations for adoptions must recognize the complexity of the policy process (the importance of intergovernmental influences and the key roles played by policy activists inside and outside government), our focus is inherently more narrow than the ACF's focus on the comprehensive analysis of policy changes within a policy subsystem.

Is our narrow focus an advantage or a disadvantage? The debate will be settled only as scholars conduct research about policymaking at varied levels of generality, and we see what insights the different approaches yield. But we note that the complexity faced by students of policymaking is not unique. For instance, there is no widely accepted general theory of the political behavior of individual citizens. It would be difficult to argue that an individual's vote choice in a single election (whether to vote and, if so, for whom) is a discrete event independent from a larger longitudinal process of attitude development in which ideology, partisan identification, candidate evaluations, and specific issue positions change. Yet this recognition does not prevent scholars from investigating the factors that influence vote choice by doing research on specific individual elections. Similarly, the independence of states' discrete policy adoption events from a larger longitudinal and intergovernmental process of policymaking should not deter us from studying discrete policy adoptions as a vehicle for understanding the broader process.

When models in the form of Equation 3 are tested, they are capable of answering important questions about the conditions that promote and impede the adoption of new government policies. For example, those interested in the impact of electoral security on the policymaking behavior of public officials can learn from Berry and Berry's (1992) analysis of state tax innovation that when other independent variables are held constant at central values within their distributions, the probability that a state not yet having a gasoline tax will adopt one is only .03 during a gubernatorial election year but grows to .42 in the year immediately following an election.[32] When accompanied by similar findings regarding the adoption of other types of taxes, this finding is powerful evidence that elected officials establish their tax policies with an eye toward electoral security. Moreover, the specific empirical finding about probabilities of adoption offers an easily interpretable measure of the strength of the effect of politicians' electoral security on state tax policy.

We do recognize that the data requirements for our approach to innovation research are substantial. Testing a model in the form of Equation 3 requires pooled data; independent variables must be observed for each state in each year during the period of analysis. Data collection is especially challenging when the independent variables go beyond aggregate state characteristics to include the nature and behavior of policy entrepreneurs, interest groups, and advocacy coalitions; however, recent research by Mintrom (1997) shows that the collection costs are not insurmountable.

When key concepts central to one's theory of government innovation cannot be observed for all states over a period of years, what should be done? Berry's (1994a) simulation results show clearly that a return to the more traditional research strategies is unacceptable. Although the traditional methodologies (cross-sectional analysis to test internal determinants models, time series regression to test national interaction models, and factor analysis to test regional diffusion models) are less demanding in their need for data, they yield empirical results that are untrustworthy. When it is unfeasible to measure important variables for as many units as pooled state data analysis requires, the only reasonable alternative is to sacrifice the benefits available from large-sample quantitative research for the gains secured by intensive analysis of a small number of cases, via case studies or small-sample comparative designs. The theories need not change— only the approach to empirical testing.

NOTES

1. For a review of the literature on incremental decisionmaking, see W. D. Berry (1990).

2. Rogers (1983, ch. 2) discussed numerous examples of research on innovation at the individual level of analysis.

3. Walker (1969) called what we term his *internal determinants model* an analysis of the "correlates of innovation."

4. For a provocative discussion of the role of political learning in the diffusion of social policy across Western nations, see Heclo (1974).

5. Whether firms do indeed move in response to various financial incentives and whether poor people actually move in search of greater welfare benefits are empirical issues. But note that state officials may *perceive* that such behaviors occur and may make policy choices for this reason, even if the behaviors do not occur.

6. Berry and Berry (1990) argued that the great popularity of lotteries with the public was partially responsible for the diffusion of lotteries across the American states.

7. Since ΔN_t denotes the proportion of new adopters during time period t and $L - N_{t-1}$ is the proportion of potential adopters who have not adopted by the beginning of time period t, bN_{t-1} must represent the proportion of remaining potential adopters that actually adopt in time period t. Alternatively, $bN_{t}-\hat{A}_1$ can be viewed as the probability that an individual who has not yet adopted prior to time period t will do so during t.

Those familiar with calculus should note that Equation 1 can be cast in "continuous" terms if $N(t)$ is defined as the cumulative number of adopters at time t and L as the total number of potential adopters, and if it is specified (see Mahajan and Peterson, 1985) that

$$dN(t)/dt = bN(t-1)\,[L - N(t)].$$

8. Since there is no "constant" term in Equation 2, the model predicts that the regression intercept will be zero.

9. Gray (1973b) recognized that the national interaction model's assumption of a thorough mixing of states is unrealistic but adopted a position of methodological nominalism (Friedman, 1953), arguing that the essential issue is not whether the assumption is realistic, but whether it sufficiently approximates reality to be useful for explanation.

10. This reasoning parallels individual-level diffusion models that assume that people are most likely to emulate the innovations of persons who share their beliefs, education, and social status (Rogers, 1983, pp. 274–275).

11. The "distance" between states is admittedly an ambiguous concept. Does one measure distance from geographic centers of states, capitals, nearest points, or other locations? The answer should depend on the hypothesized reason for geographic diffusion. But for many applications, the distance between two states ought to reflect the distance between

major population centers. For example, assume that State A, which does not have a lottery, is bordered by two states—B and C—with lotteries. A has its largest urban area very near the border with B but has only a small share of its population within 100 miles of the border with C. An appropriate measure of distance from A in a model of the influence of other states on A's propensity to adopt a lottery would place B very close and C much farther away even though both B and C are neighbors.

12. This "inequality of esteem" across states was observed by Grupp and Richards (1975) in their survey of upper-level state administrators.

13. Hierarchical models—based on population, rather than economic development—originated in geographers' theories of the diffusion among individuals of product and cultural innovations that predict that such innovations tend to flow from more populated cities to less populated rural areas (Hagerstrand, 1967; Blaikie, 1978).

14. Implicitly presenting an alternative vertical influence model that reverses the standard direction of influence, Nathan (1993, pp. 16–17) pointed out that various national New Deal programs were copies of 1930s state-level programs. Rockefeller (1968) and Boeckelman (1992) also used historical evidence to support the claim that the federal government uses states as learning laboratories.

15. Rogers (1983, p. 20) viewed *knowledge* as the first stage in the "innovation decision process."

16. We employ the term *eligible* to eliminate from the units of analysis states in all years after they have adopted the policy and thus are no longer at risk of adopting.

17. This is also true of diffusion models, which by their very nature focus on the spread of a single policy.

18. For a review of the research on the determinants of individual innovativeness, see Rogers (1983, pp. 251–263).

19. Taxation may be unique in this regard. Adopting a new tax instrument may be closer to routine policymaking than adopting most other major new policies, since most proposals for new policies face the difficult task of finding a spot on a crowded governmental agenda, but governments' need for revenue gives the issue of tax policy a permanent place on the agenda.

20. For a review of a variety of factors found to influence state public policy outputs in cross-sectional quantitative studies, see Blomquist's chapter in this volume.

21. Moreover, the effect of ideology on innovation varies across policies. For example, a high level of liberalism should promote the adoption of new social welfare initiatives but should impede the adoption of conservative criminal justice programs inconsistent with liberal ideology.

22. For some policies, it is actually *poor* fiscal health that contributes to an increase in the likelihood of adoption. This has been found to be the case with state taxes (Berry and Berry, 1992) and industrial policies designed to attract new business to a state (Gray and Lowery, 1990). For conceptual and operational definitions of *fiscal health*, see Reeves (1986), Ladd and Yinger (1989), and Berry and Berry (1990).

23. The character and activities of advocacy coalitions—which are presumed to consist of numerous individuals across the American states—might be conceived of as factors influencing state government innovation that are neither purely internal nor external to states.

24. The rest of this section of the paper draws extensively from F. S. Berry's (1994a) results.

25. Note that Collier and Messick's (1975) hierarchical diffusion model could be tested with a similar kind of cross-sectional model, in which level of economic development would be the independent variable.

26. The method is an event history model (like those described in the concluding section of this chapter) with a single independent variable: the number of bordering states that have previously adopted.

27. Some might argue that it is not feasible to measure accurately the presence or strength of entrepreneurs and advocacy coalitions when doing fifty-state analysis. But Mintrom (1997) developed such measures for school choice entrepreneurs in the American states.

28. Mintrom (1997) exhibited similar reasoning by constructing an equation predicting the probability that a state will *consider* a school choice proposal and then a second equation predicting the probability that a state considering the proposal will actually *adopt* it. In our terminology, Mintrom assumed that policy adoption is contingent on preliminary policy consideration.

29. An alternative proposition is that a charter school program and a school voucher policy are complementary: When a state adopts one type of school choice reform, the political environment is changed, and the state becomes more amenable to other school choice· initiatives. Presumably, empirical analysis could resolve these competing hypotheses.

30. Innovation processes that allow for the adoption of multiple competing polices can be specified by means of a multiple logit model (Greene, 1993).

31. For a more detailed discussion of event history analysis, see Allison (1984).

32. The period of analysis is historical: 1919–1929.

REFERENCES

Aiken, M., and R. Alford. 1970. "Community Structure and Innovation: The Case of Public Housing," *American Political Science Review* 64:843–864.

Allison, Paul D. 1984. *Event History Analysis Data.* Beverly Hills, Calif.: Sage.

Baumgartner, Frank R., and Bryan D. Jones. 1993. *Agendas and Instability in American Politics.* Chicago: University of Chicago Press.

Berry, Frances Stokes. 1994a. "Innovation in Public Management: The Adoption of State Strategic Planning," *Public Administration Review* 54: 322–29.

_____. 1994b. "Sizing Up State Policy Innovation Research," *Policy Studies Journal* 22:442–456.

Berry, Frances Stokes, and William D. Berry. 1990. "State Lottery Adoptions as Policy Innovations: An Event History Analysis," *American Political Science Review* 84:395–415.

_____. 1992. "Tax Innovation in the States: Capitalizing on Political Opportunity," *American Journal of Political Science* 36:715–742.

_____. 1994. "The politics of Tax Increases in the States," *American Journal of Political Science* 38:855–859.

Berry, William D. 1990. "The Confusing Case of Budgetary Incrementalism: Too Many Meanings for a Single Concept?" *Journal of Politics* 52:167–196.

Berry, William D., and David Lowery. 1987. *Understanding United States Government Growth: An Empirical Assessment of the Postwar Era.* New York: Praeger.

Bingham, Richard D. 1977. "The Diffusion of Innovation Among Local Governments," *Urban Affairs Quarterly* 13:223–232.

Bingham, R. D., B. W. Hawkins, and F. T. Hebert. 1978. *The Politics of Raising State and Local Revenues.* New York: Praeger.

Blaikie, P. 1978. "The Theory of the Spatial Diffusion of Innovativeness: A Spacious Cul de Sac," *Progress in Human Geography* 2:268–295.

Boeckelman, Keith. 1992. "The Influence of States on Federal Policy Adoptions," *Policy Studies Journal* 20:365–375.

Brace, Paul, and Charles Barrilleaux. 1995. "A Model of Policy Reform in the American States." Paper presented at the Annual Meeting of the American Political Science Association, Chicago.

Brown, L., R. Schneider, M. Harvey, and B. Ridell. 1979. "Innovation Diffusion and Development in a Third World Setting: The Cooperative Movement in Sierra Leone," *Social Science Quarterly* 60:249–268.

Brown, L. A. 1975. "The Market and Infrastructure Context of Adoption: A Spatial Perspective on the Diffusion of Innovations," *Economic Geography* 51:185–216.

Brown, L. A., and K. Cox. 1971. "Empirical Regularities in the Diffusion of Innovation," *Annuals of the Association of American Geographers* 61:551–559.

Canon, Bradley C., and Lawrence Baum. 1981. "Patterns of Adoption of Tort Law Innovations," *American Political Science Review* 75:975–987.

Collier, D., and R. E. Messick. 1975. "Prerequisites Versus Diffusion: Testing Explanations of Social Security Adoption," *American Political Science Review* 69:1299–1315.

Clark, Jill. 1985. "Policy Diffusion and Program Scope: Research Directions," *Publius* 15:61–70.

Clingermayer, James C. 1991. "Administrative Innovations as Instruments of State Legislative Control," *Western Political Quarterly* 44:389–403.

Clingermayer, James, and B. Dan Wood. 1995. "Disentangling Patterns of State Debt Financing," *American Political Science Review* 89:108–120.

Crain, R. L. 1966. "Fluoridation: The Diffusion of Innovation Among Cities," *Social Forces* 44:467–476.

Cyert, R. M., and J. C. March. 1963. *A Behavioral Theory of the Firm.* Englewood Cliffs, N.J.: Prentice-Hall.

Derthick, Martha. 1970. *The Influence of Federal Grants.* Cambridge, Mass.: Harvard University Press.

Downs, George W., Jr., and Lawrence B. Mohr. 1976. "Conceptual Issues in the Study of Innovation," *Administrative Science Quarterly* 21:700–713.

Elazar, Daniel. 1972. *American Federalism: A View from the States.* New York: Thomas Crowell.

Filer, John E., Donald L. Moak, and Barry Uze. 1988. "Why Some States Adopt Lotteries and Others Don't," *Public Finance Quarterly* 16:259–283.

Foster, John. 1978. "Regionalism and Innovation in the American States," *Journal of Politics* 40:179–187.

Freeman, Patricia K. 1985. "Interstate Communication Among State Legislators Regarding Energy Policy Innovation," *Publius* 15:99–111.

Friedman, Milton. 1953. *Essays in Positive Economics.* Chicago: University of Chicago Press.

Glick, Henry. 1981. "Innovation in State Judicial Administration: Effects on Court Management and Organization," *American Politics Quarterly* 9:49–69.

Glick, Henry R., and Scott P. Hays. 1991. "Innovation and Reinvention in State Policymaking: Theory and the Evolution of Living Will Laws," *Journal of Politics* 53:835–850.

Gow, James Iain. 1992. "Diffusion of Administrative Innovations in Canadian Public Administrations," *Administration and Society* 23:430–454.

Gray, Virginia. 1973a. "Innovation in the States: A Diffusion Study." *American Political Science Review* 67: 1174–85.

_____. 1973b. "Rejoinder to 'Comment' by Jack L.Walker." *American Political Science Review* 67: 1192–93.

_____. 1994. "Competition, Emulation and Policy Innovation". In *New Perspectives in American Politics*, eds. Lawrence Dodd and Calvin Jillson. Washington, D.C.: Congressional Quarterly Press.

Gray, Virginia, and David Lowery. 1990. "The Corporatist Foundations of State Industrial Policy," *Social Science Quarterly* 71:3–24.

Greene, William H. 1993. *Econometric Analysis*, 2d ed. New York: Macmillan.

Grupp, Fred W., Jr., and Alan R. Richards. 1975. "Variations in Elite Perceptions of American States as Referents for Public Policy Making," *American Political Science Review* 69:850–858.

Gujarati, Damodar N. 1988. *Basic Econometrics*, 2d ed. New York: McGraw-Hill.

Hagerstrand, T. 1967. *Innovation Diffusion as a Spatial Process*. Chicago: University of Chicago Press.

Hansen, Susan. 1983. *The Politics of Taxation*. Westport, Conn.: Praeger.

Hays, Scott P., and Henry R. Glick. 1997. "The Role of Agenda Setting in Policy Innovation: An Event History Analysis of Living Will Laws," *American Politics Quarterly* 25:497–516.

Heclo, Hugh. 1974. *Modern Social Politics in Britain and Sweden*. New Haven: Yale University Press.

Hill, Kim Quaile, Jan Leighly, and Angela Hinton-Andersson. 1995. "Lower Class Mobilization and Policy Linkage in the United States," *American Journal of Political Science* 39:75–86.

Hofferbert, Richard. 1966. "The Relation Between Public Policy and Some Structural and Environmental Variables in the American States," *American Political Science Review* 60:83–92.

Kiewiet, D. Roderick, and Matthew D. McCubbins. 1985. "Congressional Appropriations and the Electoral Connection," *Journal of Politics* 47:59–82.

Kingdon, John W. 1984. *Agendas, Alternatives, and Public Policies*. Boston: Little, Brown.

Kraemer, Kenneth I., Vijay Gurbaxani, and John Leslie King. 1992. "Economic Development, Government Policy, and the Diffusion of Computing in Asia-Pacific Countries," *Public Administration Review* 52:146–156.

Ladd, Helen F., and John L. Yinger. 1989. *America's Ailing Cities: Fiscal Health and the Design of Urban Policy*. Baltimore: Johns Hopkins University Press.

Light, Alfred R. 1978. "Intergovernmental Sources of Innovation in State Administration," *American Politics Quarterly* 6:147–165.

Lindblom, Charles E. 1965. *The Intelligence of Democracy: Decision Making Through Mutual Adjustment*. New York: Free Press.

Lowery, David, and Lee Sigelman. 1981. "Understanding the Tax Revolt: Eight Explanations," *American Political Science Review* 75:963–974.

Lutz, James M. 1987. "Regional Leadership Patterns in the Diffusion of Public Policies," *American Politics Quarterly* 15:387–398.

Mahajan, V., and R. A. Peterson. 1985. *Models for Innovation Diffusion.* Beverly Hills, Calif.: Sage.

Mayhew, David. 1974. *Congress: The Electoral Connection.* New Haven: Yale University Press.

Mann, Arthur J. 1980. "Wagner's Law: An Econometric Test for Mexico: 1925–1976," *National Tax Journal* 33:189–201.

Menzel, Donald C., and Irwin Feller. 1977. "Leadership and Interaction Patterns in the Diffusion of Innovations Among the American States," *Western Political Quarterly* 30:528–536.

_____. 1978. "The Adoption of Technological Innovations by Municipal Governments," *Urban Affairs Quarterly* 13:469–490.

Midlarsky, M. I. 1978. "Analyzing Diffusion and Contagion Effects: The Urban Disorders of the 1960s," *American Political Science Review* 72:996–1008.

Mikesell, John L. 1978. "Election Periods and State Tax Policy Cycles," *Public Choice* 33:99–105.

Mintrom, Michael. 1997. "Policy Entrepreneurs and the Diffusion of Innovation," *American Journal of Political Science* 42(July):738–770.

Mintrom, Michael, and Sandra Vergari. 1996. "Advocacy Coalitions, Policy Entrepreneurs, and Policy Change," *Policy Studies Journal* 24:420–434.

Mohr, Lawrence. 1969. "Determinants of Innovation in Organizations," *American Political Science Review* 75:963–974.

Mooney, Christopher Z., and Mei-Hsien Lee. 1995. "Legislating Morality in the American States: The Case of Pre-Roe Abortion Regulation Reform," *American Journal of Political Science* 39:599–627.

Nathan, Richard P. 1989. "The Role of the States in American Federalism." In Carl Van Horn, ed., *The State of the States.* Washington, D.C.: Congressional Quarterly Press

Peterson, Paul E., and Mark C. Rom. 1990. *Welfare Magnets.* Washington, D.C.: Brookings Institution.

Reeves, H. Clyde. 1986. *Measuring Fiscal Capacity.* Boston: Oelgeschlager, Gunn & Hain.

Regens, James L. 1980. "State Policy Responses to the Energy Issue." *Social Science Quarterly* 61:44–57.

Rockefeller, N. A. 1968. *The Future of Federalism.* New York: Atheneum.

Rogers, E. M., and F. F. Shoemaker. 1971. *Communication of Innovations: A Cross-Cultural Approach.* New York: Free Press.

Rogers, Everett M. 1983. *Diffusion of Innovations.* New York: Free Press.

Savage, R. 1978. "Policy Innovativeness as a Trait of American States," *Journal of Politics* 40:212–219.

Schneider, Mark, and Paul Teske with Michael Mintrom. 1995. *Public Entrepreneurs.* Princeton: Princeton University Press.

Sigelman, Lee, and Roland E. Smith. 1980. "Consumer Legislation in the American States: An Attempt at Explanation," *Social Science Quarterly* 61:58–69.

Simon, Herbert. 1947. *Administrative Behavior.* New York: Macmillan.

Wagner, Adolph. 1877. *Finanzwissenshaft*, Part 1. Leipzig: C. F. Winter.

Walker, Jack L. 1969. "The Diffusion of Innovations Among the American States," *American Political Science Review* 63:880–899.

Walker, Jack L. 1973. "Comment." *American Political Science Review* 67:1186–1191.

Welch, Susan, and Kay Thompson. 1980. "The Impact of Federal Incentives on State Policy Innovations," *American Journal of Political Science* 24:715–729.

8

The Policy Process and Large-N Comparative Studies

WILLIAM BLOMQUIST

PURPOSE

The behavioral revolution brought several changes to American political science. One intended change within the field of comparative politics was to supplement or replace the traditional area studies approach of thick descriptions of governments with multiple-unit studies of political systems and their operations and effects (Mayer, 1989, p. 28). A related goal for political science generally was to focus research on public policy, shifting from descriptions of political institutions to analyses of their products.

Beginning in the early 1960s, some political scientists pursued a combination of these aims, developing the subfield of comparative policy studies. Through the study of political systems and their policy products, these colleagues hoped to advance our understanding of comparative politics by examining the similarities and differences in the operation and effects of systems, and to advance our understanding of the public policy process by finding the commonalities and differences among systems that might offer clues about how policies are generated and changed (Mayer, 1989, pp. 43–49). Hopes were highest that such progress would come from studies involving a large number of cases and employing sophisticated data analysis techniques.

Nearly thirty-five years have passed since the beginning of publications in comparative policy studies, conceived of as a disciplinary subfield. This chapter assesses the contribution of some of the work in that subfield to our understanding of the policy process. Specifically, this chapter reviews what we have learned about the policy process from large-N (twenty cases or more) comparative studies.

FOCUS

The amount of published work in the subfield of comparative policy studies is substantial. It includes comparisons of policy outputs at the national, subnational, and local levels. This chapter will consider all of those types of studies, while recognizing that the largest share of the published large-N comparative studies have involved the American states. Accordingly, the comparative state policy studies receive the largest share of attention in the chapter. If the subfield of comparative policy studies has enhanced our understanding of the policy process, that contribution should be evident in the comparative state studies; conversely, if the state studies haven't contributed much to our understanding of the policy process, the smaller body of cross-national and cross-local studies is unlikely to have contributed much more.

The reasons for the prominence of comparative state policy studies in the comparative policy literature are practical and easy to understand, although not driven by theoretical or epistemological considerations. Researchers have found that aggregate data of respectable quality are available for the American states concerning policy outputs, political activity and institutions, and economic, social, and cultural conditions. The same cannot be said with assurance of cross-national data (Leichter, 1979, p. 71), which may be why more of the cross-national studies focus on a small number of countries—for example, Smith (1975; $N = 4$), Hibbs (1976; $N = 10$), Hibbs (1977; $N = 12$), Cameron (1978; $N = 18$), and Leichter (1979; $N = 4$).[1] Even interlocal studies within the United States have data availability problems: Reliable data on some variables are collected and reported for counties, and those on other variables are collected and reported for cities, towns, townships, or metropolitan statistical areas.

In addition, the governmental structures and policy responsibilities of the American states are more similar to one another than are those of countries, or of local governments within the United States.[2] In the words of two pioneers of comparative state policy research, "The fifty states share a common institutional framework and general cultural background, but they differ in certain aspects of economic and social structure, political activity, and public policy. Therefore, they provide a large number of political and social units in which some important variables can be held constant while others are varied" (Dawson and Robinson, 1963, p. 265).

Finally, it is possible to include all of the states in a study, and the size and membership of the set has remained fixed for a generation. Comparative state studies therefore allow one to avoid methodological arguments about which countries or local governments were selected for a study and on what basis.[3]

EMERGENCE OF THE SUBFIELD

Even if it were useful to do so, it probably would be impossible to identify a moment in which political scientists first became interested in the determinants of public policies. Broad inquiries into which types of political systems and social structures are associated with efficient or egalitarian or just public policies has forebears at least as ancient as Plato and Aristotle and would include deTocqueville, Marx, and several others (Dawson and Robinson, 1963).

The Watershed Year

It is possible, however, to identify a watershed year in large-N comparative policy studies. In 1963, Richard Dawson and James Robinson's article "Inter-Party Competition, Economic Variables, and Welfare Policies in the American States" appeared in the *Journal of Politics*. Another cross-state study appeared in book form, Jerry Miner's *Social and Economic Factors in Spending for Public Education*, and an influential interlocal study by Maurice Pinard was published in the *American Journal of Sociology* on the relative influence of political behavior and community characteristics on the passage of fluoridation referenda in 262 communities.

Dawson and Robinson were careful to note their intellectual debt to small-N studies by V. O. Key and Duane Lockard of the relationship between state welfare policies and political variables such as the degree of interparty competition.[4] Dawson and Robinson's study encompassed forty-six states[5] as cases and three measures of state welfare policies as dependent variables, and it used as independent variables some political indicators such as measures of party competition and some indicators of economic development in the states. The results are now well known to most policy scholars: Although measures of party competition correlated weakly with measures of the welfare orientation of state policies, measures of economic development (per capita income, industrialization, and urbanization) correlated much more strongly with the policy measures. Dawson and Robinson concluded by raising the question whether policy differences among the states might be more strongly influenced by "environmental" variables (those outside the political system, such as economic conditions) than by various aspects of politics.

The Politics-Versus-Environment Debate Joined

In a 1965 article in the *Journal of Politics*, Thomas Dye examined the relationships (or lack thereof) between legislative malapportionment and the degree of intrastate party competition, and between party competition and state welfare expenditures. Citing Dawson and Robinson's work, Dye added measures of per capita income and industrialization as controls. Dye measured the effect of malapportionment and party competition on state policies in education, welfare, and taxation. He employed thirty policy indicators, each with data for all fifty states from 1960 and 1961—twelve measures of education policies, ten measures of welfare policies, and eight measures of tax structure and burden (Dye, 1965, pp. 590–591).

The measures of malapportionment failed to show statistically significant correlations with most of the state policy indicators, once the environmental variables of income and industrialization were controlled (Dye, 1965, pp. 595–599). Dye (p. 599) concluded, "On the whole, the policy choices of malapportioned legislatures are not noticeably different from the policy choices of well-apportioned legislatures. Most of the policy differences which do occur turn out to be a product of socio-economic differences among the states rather than a direct product of apportionment practices."

The next year, Dye's book *Politics, Economics, and the Public* appeared, as did two articles by Richard Hofferbert on the relationship between socioeconomic variables and public expenditures in the states. Dye (1966) reported that in welfare and in other policy areas, socioeconomic variables seemed to account for more of the variation among states than political characteristics such as apportionment, party competition, and turnout. Hofferbert (1966b) used the Dawson-Robinson measures of state welfare expenditures, plus some data on state financial aid to cities, and also found that environmental variables such as the extent of industrialization affected these indicators of state policies to a greater extent than the political variables of apportionment, party competitiveness, and divided government. Other studies during the late 1960s confirmed that measures of socioeconomic differences among states or localities or countries showed stronger statistical relationships to policy measures than did differences in their political institutions or behaviors.

The subfield flourished. The early activity in comparative policy studies was so prolific and its emergence so rapid that retrospective assessments of its progress and problems began to appear within just a few years (Wilson, 1966; Froman, 1967). As early as 1970, Ira Sharkansky was able to produce his edited volume, *Policy Analysis in Political Science,* consisting largely of papers presented and articles published from 1966 through 1968, offering and applying models and presenting and testing hypotheses about the determinants of public policies, especially at the state level.

The Dawson-Robinson question—whether environmental or political variables matter more—continued to frame the entries into the subfield for several years. A series of articles concerning redistributive policies of the American states is illustrative: Fry and Winters (1970) found a larger role for political variables, then Booms and Halldorson (1973) weighed in on the side of the socioeconomic environment, and then Uslaner and Weber (1975) and Tompkins (1975) published rejoinders emphasizing interactive effects.

A Shift During the 1970s

The environment-versus-politics tone of the literature diminished during the 1970s. Researchers such as Cnudde and McCrone (1969), Uslaner and Weber (1975), Tompkins (1975), and Lewis-Beck (1977) began to employ path analysis to comparative studies, showing interactive as well as partial effects of independent variables. Those studies not only appeared to rescue the importance of political variables but also suggested that policy outputs were complex products of several factors (Hofferbert, 1990, p. 147). At the end of the decade, Mazmanian and Sabatier (1980) emphasized that throughout the comparative state policy literature, the proportion of explained variance in policies had been less than half, leaving open the possibility (indeed the likelihood) that state policies were also heavily influenced by other factors such as the preferences of policymakers.

Near mid-decade, Hofferbert (1974) made an effort to include some of those other factors, and to portray their relationships to one another and to the political and socioeconomic variables that had been used in previous comparative studies. His reformulation of the basic policy output model presented a sequence of related sets of variables, from the broadest background variables capturing historical and geographic circumstances of the polity, on through socioeconomic attributes of the population, mass political attitudes and behavior, governmental institutions, and elite behavior. Reading it backward, policy outputs were decisions produced by elites operating within governmental institutions but affected by the mass public, the socioeconomic environment, and ultimately by the historic-geographic setting.

These mid-1970s methodological and theoretical reconsiderations within the subfield of comparative policy studies had important impacts upon subsequent studies. Prior to this shift, virtually all of the variables employed were aggregate, system-level characteristics, and all of the data gathered and analyzed were secondary data. Since the 1970s, a greater proportion (though by no means all) of published comparative policy studies have included some variables reflecting elite and/or mass preferences, with data from surveys, referenda, and/or interviews of decisionmakers in multiple organizations.[6] And nearly all post-1970s comparative policy studies reviewed for this chapter employed data analysis techniques designed to show interactive or configurative effects among the variables rather than simple correlation analysis in which the variable(s) with the largest partial coefficient(s) was interpreted as having the greatest explanatory effect.

A SYNOPSIS OF THE DYE-SHARKANSKY-HOFFERBERT APPROACH

We will return to some of these more recent efforts to conduct improved comparative policy studies later in the chapter. At this point, it is time to pause and assess the basic theoretical thrust of the generation of large-N comparative studies that has accumulated since the early 1960s.

After Dawson and Robinson originated the large-N comparative state policy study, Dye, Sharkansky, and Hofferbert (DSH) may be said to have contributed the most to the development and maturation of the subfield. Their work has influenced an extensive and still-growing body of studies exploring cross-system differences in a host of independent variables to see which are and which are not associated with differences in policy indicators.

Figure 8.1 reproduces the models of the public policy process presented by Dawson and Robinson (1963), Dye (1966), Sharkansky (1970), and Hofferbert (1974). Clearly, the models are variants on systems theory: An external environment influences a political system that produces policies that feed back into the environment.

Equally clearly, the models are similar to one another. The differences among them have to do with such subtleties as whether to represent political behavior or activity in addition to the political "system," whether to represent policy outputs separately from outcomes or impacts, and how many potential stops there are along the feedback loop.

Hofferbert's (1974) attempt to produce a more comprehensive and sophisticated model represents the process as a "funneling" of influences toward a formal decisionmaking event. It certainly departs visually from the other three. The amount of visual difference is not matched by a like amount of conceptual difference, however. Although it identifies more direct and indirect effects of a larger number of independent variables upon policy outputs, Hofferbert's model nonetheless resembles the others in its fundamental portrayal of an external environment (historic-geographic circumstances plus socioeconomic conditions) processed through a political system (the public, governmental institutions, and elite policymakers) that yields policy outputs.

These models have been applied in a variety of settings, to policy outputs in cross-national, interstate, and interlocal studies. From the time of the first rush (1966–1970) of large-N comparative policy studies based on the Dye, Sharkansky, or Hofferbert models to the present, the basic approach has been the same. (This statement is not meant to gainsay the creativity of scholars in this literature with respect to variable operationalization, data collection, and statistical analyses, as noted both above and below.)

Typically, the scholar embarking on a DSH-style comparative study (using the American states as units) will specify a set of independent variables that are hypothesized to differentiate the states from one another with respect to some policy. The set of variables will include some elements of the socioeconomic environment of the state. Economic measures (income, industrialization, etc.) are universal in these studies. Demographic indicators are also common (especially urbanization in the early studies). The construction of indices combining economic measures or demographic ones, or both, has been an area of considerable creativity among scholars producing DSH-style studies.

Another set of independent variables will represent purportedly important aspects of the political behavior and institutions of a state. Data on voter registration or turnout, measures of party competition or instances of divided government, and more recent measures of interest group influence are used frequently in these studies. In addition, after Elazar and Sharkansky in the early 1970s emphasized the

Dawson and Robinson's (1963) model:

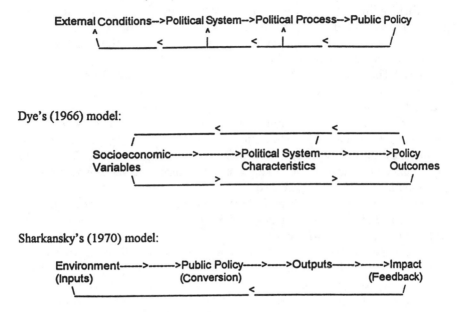

Dye's (1966) model:

Sharkansky's (1970) model:

Hofferbert's (1974) model:

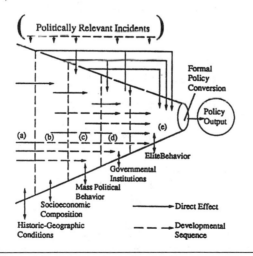

FIGURE 8.1   Models Used in Comparative Policy Studies

importance of political culture and regionalism to an understanding of the states and their political systems, many DSH-style studies have also included constructed variables indicating region and/or the Elazar culture types. Again, scholars have been inventive in constructing indicators of these political variables.

The dependent variables in these studies are what the models depict as policy "outputs." The early studies leaned heavily upon public expenditures in order to obtain interval-level data on the dependent variable. Thus, a state's welfare policy would be measured in terms of, for example, total state expenditures for welfare programs or monthly Aid to Families with Dependent Children (AFDC) benefits per recipient household. Since the late 1970s, many DHS-style studies have employed a categorical dependent variable indicating the presence or absence of a state policy or policy change during a specified time interval, the adoption or nonadoption of a state law, and so on.[7]

The rising frequency of categorical dependent variables was occasioned by the introduction of different statistical techniques into DSH-style studies. In the 1960s and early 1970s, multiple-regression analysis was the standard statistical method employed in DSH-style studies, and ordinary least-squares regression required interval-level data on the dependent variable. From the 1970s through the present, additional techniques have supplemented regression analysis, particularly logistic regression and discriminant analysis. These methods allow scholars to extract and analyze univariate and multivariate statistics indicating the relationships among variables and the explanatory power of models when the dependent variable is simply a (0,1) category (see Chapter 7 by Berry and Berry).

THEORETICAL AND METHODOLOGICAL
DEFICIENCIES OF THE DSH APPROACH

Comparative policy studies using the DHS approach—and comparative state studies in particular—represent a considerable proportion of the body of literature in the field of public policy studies. Perhaps only the stages heuristic has been more influential in shaping the field than the DSH method of analyzing the relative contributions of environmental and political variables to policy differences.

Whether and to what extent the DSH approach has advanced the ability of policy scholars to understand and explain the policy process is another question. On methodological and theoretical grounds, the DSH models of the policy process and the accumulated body of DSH-style empirical studies still leave us well short of a theory of the policy process. The reasons for this deficit are set forth in this section.

Policy Events Versus a Process of Policy Change

The Identification of Policies. Let us dispense with the most obvious methodological problems first. As noted above, the DSH models depict policies as outputs of the political system, and DSH-style empirical studies have tended to operationalize those outputs either as discrete policy adoption events or as levels of public expenditure. These operationalizations are subject to legitimate criticisms.

Levels of public expenditure are not valid indicators of policy choices across political systems. The simple reasons are that (1) costs and prices vary from place to place, so greater or lesser expenditure may not indicate a proportionally greater or lesser degree of governmental activity or commitment, and (2) efficiency and level of corruption also vary from place to place, so that it is still less clear whether level of expenditure translates into a similar degree of activity or commitment. Castles and Mitchell (1993, pp. 96–99) presented a brief but eloquent commentary on the use of expenditure data in comparative policy studies as a sort of unavoidable yet troublesome measure.

To these observations, Smith (1975) and Leichter (1979) have added that the assignment and allocation of policy activity differ from place to place as well, both between levels of government and between the private and public sectors. Comparing public expenditures at one level of government will overlook these differences, obscuring substantial differences between some cases and exaggerating small differences between others.

Of course, these problems of using public expenditures as policy indicators can be overcome in a couple of ways. A researcher can try to correct the problems by investigating policy implementation and funding within every state and then controlling for the differences by combining state and local or public and private sector expenditures and constructing a corruption-and-slack index with which to deflate each state's expenditures. One might expect that the costs of such efforts would be high relative to the benefits attained, and evidently the scholars who produce DSH-style studies have reached that conclusion as well, since such efforts are rarely attempted. An alternative to this kind of heavy lifting is to measure policies as events rather than as levels of expenditure.

As to this alternative, the criticism has been voiced that a policy adoption event is not a policy (Greenberg et al., 1977, p. 1533). The problem here is *not* that the sorts of governmental actions often counted as policy adoption events (the passage of a law, the creation of an agency, etc.) may be symbolic rather than substantial—after all, the DSH models do not exclude symbolic policies as system outputs.

There are three deficiencies involved in employing policy adoption events as dependent variables. First, such counting begs the question of which policy adoption events a researcher should select to represent incidents of policy change produced by the political system in response to environmental conditions and/or political behavior. As early as 1965, Thomas Dye (1965, p. 590) acknowledged this problem in his study of the policy effects of legislative malapportionment: "In the 1960–61 legislative biennium, more than 104,000 bills were introduced in the state legislatures throughout the nation. Each bill rejected or enacted represents a separate policy choice. What policies are to be selected in order to assess the impact of malapportionment?" If one broadens the field of vision to include administrative regulations adopted or rejected and court decisions issued or deferred, the difficulty Dye identified is multiplied.

Second, there is the problem of capturing the context within which a policy adoption event occurs. The context may reveal that apparently similar (even apparently identical) policy adoption events had different (even opposite) intentions as policies. In their study of state occupational safety and health enforcement, for example, Thompson and Scicchitano (1985) found that states had adopted worker safety laws and created worker safety agencies for either of two reasons. Some had created their own laws and agencies in order to promote workplace safety conditions above and beyond the federal standards. Others had created their own laws and agencies in order to satisfy the state-primacy requirements of the federal Occupational Safety and Health Administration (OSHA) law and to "keep the feds out," in order to have their own employees do a more lax job of enforcement. Both groups of states would have been counted as having adopted occupational safety and health laws and agencies, but the two groups were clearly pursuing substantially different occupational safety and health *policies*.

Third, there is the problem of the selection of a time period within which policy adoption events are counted. As we have learned from the policy diffusion literature, adoptions of new policies work their way across jurisdictions over a (sometimes lengthy) period. If a researcher waits until all jurisdictions have displayed a policy adoption event, then a DSH-style study is moot because there is no variation on the dependent variable. But if a researcher chooses a time-stopping moment at which some jurisdictions have completed the policy adoption event and others haven't, two methodological questions arise: First, by what criteria was the time-stopping moment selected (Greenberg et al., 1977, p. 1535), and second, does the DSH model really explain the differences between the adopting and nonadopting jurisdictions (Salisbury, 1968, p. 154)? To elaborate on the second question: If at time t twenty-five states had experienced policy adoption events but at time $t[th]+[th]x$ thirty states had done so, what have we learned about state policymaking from a DSH-style study performed at either point, especially if during the interval x there was no significant change in the values of the environmental or political variables in those five states? These problems do not seem to me to be amenable to correction; they appear to be inherent methodological defects of the DSH approach.

DSH Models and the Concept of a Policy Process.   However carefully done, cross-sectional comparisons of expenditure levels or adoption events do not shed much light on the policy *process*, conceived of in terms of either stages or policy change over time. Regardless of whether one views the stages approach to the study of the policy process as retaining considerable heuristic utility (see Chapter 2, by deLeon) or as an outdated and poor substitute for a policy theory (see

Chapter 1, by Sabatier), it is legitimate to point out, as Hofferbert (1990, p. 146) himself acknowledged, that DSH models focus primarily if not exclusively on policy formation and adoption. Little or no attention is given to implementation, evaluation, or feedback in the empirical studies, despite their appearance in the models.[8]

Although the debate over the value of the stages heuristic may affect one's view of whether the failure of the DSH approach to incorporate these stages is a serious flaw, there is little question that the DSH models and the empirical studies based upon them employ a definition of policy that ignores the prospect that the intention of a policy as formulated and adopted may be undermined or even undone in implementation. To that extent, DSH models are of limited helpfulness in building a theoretical explanation of the policy process.

There are several reasons for the inability of the DSH approach to provide an account of policy change over time. Some of those reasons will be considered in the subsections below, because they result from other deficiencies in the models. But one additional reason merits consideration at this point because it represents a methodological deficiency owing to a data-selection bias in favor of initial policy adoptions and away from policy modification or abandonment.

Initial policy adoptions occur when no state law or regulation or agency (or state authorization or mandate for the creation of local versions of the same) existed at time $t[th]-[th]1$, a policy adoption event occurs at time t, and the state law, regulation, and so on exist from time $t[th]+[th]1$ forward. *Policy modifications* are changes in established state policies—a law or regulation is amended, an agency is reorganized or its resources are changed in ways that affect its operation, or an authorization or mandate for local action is altered. Hogwood and Peters (1983) contended that most policy change falls into this category of policy modification, or what they called "policy replacement." *Policy abandonments* mark the withdrawal of state government activity from an area—repeal, rescission, termination, devolution to local governments, or preemption by the national government.

DSH-style studies published since the mid–1960s ordinarily focus on initial policy adoptions. This focus is probably not coincidence. Operationalizing the DSH approach tends to lead one in the direction of discrete policy adoption events—the passage of a law, the creation of an agency—that unambiguously (or at least less ambiguously) mark an occurrence of policy change.[9] The researcher who thinks about developing and employing indicators of policy modifications may recognize that he or she is likely to spend years fending off methodological quibbles (e.g., which amendments, changes in funding, reorganizations, etc., in which states represented real policy *changes* and should have been coded as a 1 versus those that were insignificant and should have been coded as a 0) and will give up the effort before the paper is written, much less sent out for review.

Moreover, the availability and cost of data tend to direct one toward initial policy adoptions and away from policy modifications and abandonments (perhaps especially the latter). Certainly the cost in time and effort of developing one's own database on some aspect of state government activity has dropped significantly since the arrival of desktop computers with Internet access. Nevertheless, it remains much easier to identify, count, and date the passage of laws and the creation of agencies than it is to find significant amendments or to determine that a state mandate has effectively been abandoned via nonenforcement. Policy abandonments seem particularly likely to be overlooked, since they may resemble the dog that didn't bark, unless signaled by a visible event such as the repeal of a law or the elimination of an agency.

If the DSH approach harbors a methodological bias in favor of initial policy adoptions and against other forms of policy change, how does that bias affect our ability to develop a valid understanding of the public policy process? It may distort our understanding of the role of information and analysis in the process of policy change. Let us acknowledge once again that social and economic conditions, political activity, and ideas and information are all important factors in the policy process, but let us also entertain for the moment the possibility that the relative importance of these factors may differ from one situation to another. With that possibility granted, a logical argument exists that, although information and ideas always matter in initial policy adoptions (especially information about policy innovations as they diffuse among jurisdictions), those adoptions may be affected to a greater degree by environmental and political variables. Policy modifications and abandonments are also affected by changes in political and environmental factors, to be sure, but a logical argument exists that information and analysis play a greater role in the decision to change or end a policy than in the decision to adopt it in the first place.

We do not yet have the body of evidence to support these assertions (indeed, as empirical propositions they beg the very questions we hope to answer with improved political theories of the policy process). But if their logic has merit, the DSH approach may distort our understanding of the policy process by underrepresenting cases of policy change via modification or abandonment. That underrepresentation may diminish our attention to the role of information and analysis in the process of policy change, leaving us with an understanding of the process that artificially inflates the relative importance of socioeconomic conditions and political structure.

The Description of the Political System

Both the DSH models and DSH-style empirical studies leave the political system underdescribed in ways that have inhibited their usefulness for building political theories of the policy process. Among the most important deficiencies that impinge upon our ability to improve understanding and explanation of the policy process are failure to incorporate the existence of multiorganizational governments and multigovernmental systems,[10] failure to incorporate institutionally defined roles, and failure to recognize the requirements or possibilities of either joint or sequential action among multiple actors.

The American states—the very jurisdictions to which the DSH models have been most frequently applied—are both multiorganizational governments and parts of a multigovernmental system. Ironically, the DSH models and DSH-style empirical studies rarely account for either characteristic despite their importance in policymaking. The political "system" modeled in the DSH approach is unitary: Inside Dye's or Sharkansky's box or at the end of Hofferbert's funnel is a single, abstracted decisionmaker, an idealized executive, legislature, or court producing policies.

The point here is not merely that the DSH models fail to fully describe empirical reality; models, of course, never do. The important consideration is whether a particular abstraction or simplification in a model removes a theoretically significant element of the object or process one hopes to explain. If our purpose is to construct a valid explanation of the policy process, models that present governmental organization as unitary and governmental decisionmaking as singular remove from view vital elements of the very process we are trying to represent.

In multigovernmental systems such as that of the United States, policy change occurs not only through innovation, termination, or replacement of policies, programs, or organizations, but also as the result of shifts in intergovernmental responsibilities and relationships (Hogwood and Peters, 1983, pp. 20–21). Furthermore, the existence of multiple governments within a political system creates opportunities for strategic action by policy entrepreneurs, as we shall discuss in connection with human agency below. Yet political scientists who proclaim their interest in the policy *process* usually have excluded intergovernmental interactions and processes from their field of vision (Van Dyke, 1968, pp. 26–27). This criticism is especially valid as it pertains to DSH models.

In a similar vein, the presence of multiple organizations within a government (i.e., separated powers) is a vital element of the policy process that is also underdescribed or ignored in DSH models.[11] Yet policy scholars outside the DSH tradition, from Salisbury (1968) through Baumgartner and Jones (1991), have acknowledged that the existence of multiple decisionmaking entities—not only formal branches of government but also informal arrangements such as policy subgovernments—profoundly affects the course of policy formulation and argumentation, as well as the likelihood of adoption or modification. If they are correct, then a needed dimension of comparative studies of the policy process is including some range of institutional alternatives available to policy entrepreneurs.

Within the multiple organizations of a government and the multiple governments of a nonunitary political system, institutional rules (at what the institutional rational choice framework calls the constitutional and collective-choice levels of action) define essential roles or positions that individuals may fill. Among the vital implications of the existence of institutionally defined roles is that all members of a political community are not equally positioned in the policy process (Gergen, 1968, p. 181). A subset of individuals at a given moment occupy positions that allow or require them to be agenda setters, gatekeepers, and veto holders. Although a strong case can be made that the existence of these roles is vital to understanding the policy process within as well as across jurisdictions, the DSH approach does not recognize them.

Policy change, especially in governmental systems such as those of the American states, often occurs through the interaction of actors in multiple institutionally defined roles. Those interactions may be joint or sequential.

Recognizing the existence of multiple actors does not mean simply that political decisionmaking is usually a joint enterprise, for instance, that legislators and the executive have to agree before policy change occurs. Policy change certainly is often a joint enterprise, but it does not have to be. Policy change can also involve a sequence of actions and reactions taken unilaterally by individual actors in institutionally defined roles.

Knott (1993, pp. 6–7) employed the example of a court altering the substantive meaning or the practical applicability of a state law through the act of interpretation. The interpretation by that court—perhaps even by an individual judge—is itself a policy change, but it is also an event in a sequence. If the legislature or the executive is dissatisfied with the court's modification of the policy, some sort of legislative response is likely to occur to restore the previous meaning and operation of the law. This sort of sequential interaction represents policy change occurring without changes in the values of socioeconomic or political system variable, and is therefore outside the explanatory capacity of DSH models. Yet even casual observation reveals that this sort of process frequently drives policy change.

The Role of Human Agency and Strategic Action

The Unit of Analysis and Explanations of the Policy Process.   The units of analysis in DSH-style studies are the cases, that is, the states. It is the policy behavior of *states* that supposedly is described by a model that incorporates their socioeconomic conditions and political configurations.

Yet the states are typically *not* the focus of *explanations* in DSH-style studies. As Andrew Abbott (1992, p. 57) pointed out, the explanations supplied by researchers who perform DSH-style studies describe the variables rather than the cases as acting or being acted upon: "Most narrative sentences here have variables as subjects; it is when a variable 'does something' narratively that the authors think themselves to be speaking most directly of causality."[12] Thus, malapportionment does (or does not) lead to higher welfare expenditures, or industrialization does (or does not) generate greater state aid to cities. Only when we encounter anomalous results are narratives that focus on the political systems pressed into emergency service. for example, "Oh, yes, of course we all know that Nebraska is an outlier skewing the results, because in Nebraska . . . "

Why is this a problem for policy theory? First, the variable-driven explanations have an automaticity that largely removes human agency from view, never mind a central place in explanation and understanding. As per capita income rises, so do educational expenditures. No one actually *does* anything to raise educational expenditures; it just happens. States with moralistic political cultures adopt groundwater protection laws; states without do not. Although these insights have some utility, as we shall discuss below, they do not contribute much to the enterprise of constructing an explanation of the policy process that is grounded in a model of the individual, describes the policy process as a human-driven process, and can be used comparatively to account for developments over time.

Thus, it is not just the empirical results of DSH-style studies that appear to suggest that "politics doesn't matter" relative to environmental conditions; it is the construction and the interpretation of such studies that yields this conclusion. If the behavior of human beings is not the focus of analysis or explanation, then politics—with its interactions, arguments, quests for power or control, and all of its uncertainties as a form of human social behavior—has been largely eliminated from the scene. As scientists, we might not be worried over its elimination if the remaining explanatory variables performed well in accounting for policy differences across jurisdictions or over time, but they do not. A huge unexplained residual remains, which some political scientists have recognized represents human agency (Mazmanian and Sabatier, 1980), but which DSH-style studies regard simply as error (Abbott, 1992).

The automaticity of the variable-driven explanations provided in DSH-style studies reflects two other problems—one for empirical theories of the policy process, the other for the normative utility of policy theory. The problem for empirical theory is that one cannot build from these types of explanations an account of the policy process that leaves room for contingencies, for failure or collapse. Since people are not at the heart of the explanation, their skill or learning or miscalculations do not—cannot—produce the outcomes. An empirical theory of the policy process that does not center upon human agency is unlikely to be able to explain much of what transpires.

Furthermore, even if DSH-style studies could explain a higher proportion of the variance in policies across jurisdictions, the question remains whether anyone could use that information to alter the likelihood of success in changing policy. Hofferbert (1990, p. 147) recalled the early efforts to build models that would account for the highest possible amount of policy variance by using socioeconomic and political structure variables, and he described it as "'basic research' at its most elegant level of irrelevance. . . . It says that the only way to change policy is to change social, economic, and political structures." In comparative state studies, where region and political culture frequently outperform all other independent variables, this irrelevance has occasionally reached farcical heights. U.S. Senator Daniel P. Moynihan (D–NY) composed a sarcastic op-ed commentary in the *New York Times* commenting on educational policy studies that showed that the independent variable most strongly correlated (negatively) with standardized test scores was distance of the state capital from the Canadian border. Want to raise your students' test scores? asked Moynihan. Move your state capital!

Failure to Include Multiple Levels of Action and the Scope of Conflict. On a more serious note, the DSH models and DSH-style studies leave little or no opportunity for policy scholars to explore or pursue the usefulness of the concept of *levels of action.* In the DSH approach, the political system is not only static it is a given. As we noted above, the political structure simply *is* whatever is at the end of the funnel—an abstracted and idealized decisionmaker. Individuals do not achieve or block policy change by shifting to another level of action and reconfiguring the organizational structure or institutional rules of governmental decisionmaking. Yet, studies employing the institutional rational choice (IRC) framework have concluded that the ability to change levels of action is an important aspect of the process of policy change, as well as a vital strategic tool for policy entrepreneurs and their opponents.

Beyond the IRC framework, many scholars of the policy process have emphasized the importance of "arena shifts" in the process of policy change (e.g., Baumgartner and Jones, 1991; Heintz and Jenkins-Smith, 1988; Montgomery, 1995). The ability to redefine the jurisdiction or authority of a governmental body (what IRC theorists call action at the constitutional or collective-choice level) in order to make it accessible or off-limits to a policy proposal is a critical aspect of strategic political action. The same is true of policy implementation as well as adoption activity (Macey, 1992).

In fairness, DSH-style studies are usually focused on the short term and thus may be defended in the same way that economists defend static analyses of what will happen in an industry if demand or supply shifts suddenly, that is, that in the short term the capacity and structure of the industry are fixed for all practical purposes. One could apply a similar observation to the governmental realm (i.e., states are unlikely to change their governmental structures overnight), and thus holding structure fixed is a reasonable way to approach the design of an empirical study of policymaking in the states. Granting that, the absence of a means of accounting for shifts in the level of action remains a deficiency of the DSH approach for the enterprise of building a valid political theory of the policy process.

Related to the concept of levels of action is the concept of the scope of conflict. Relevant actors are also institutionally defined, though not solely through formal rules. From Key and Schattschneider to the present, policy scholars have proposed and shown that an important element of strategic political action in the policy process is the ability to expand or restrict the scope of conflict (see Bauer, 1968; Baumgartner and Jones, 1991). DSH models and empirical studies implicitly treat the scope of conflict as fixed; the degree of elite or mass public involvement, the configuration of interest groups, and other such measures are taken at a moment in time and not allowed to vary, except across jurisdictions. Cross-jurisdictional variation in these indicators is, almost by definition, not a result or a reflection of strategic behavior.

Recognizing the vital role of human agency in the policy process and the importance of strategic shifts in level of action and in decisionmaking venue, Smith (1982) followed the sociological methodology of Alfred Schutz and the economic methodology of Ludwig Lachmann and advocated a phenomenological approach that focuses on rational individuals as policy entrepreneurs who formulate "plans" and attempt to transform their plans into policies through strategic action. Key elements of that strategic action are (1) the actor's anticipation of conflict or opposition, which affects (2) his or her choice of political institutions through which to work, both of which affect (3) his or her expectations about likely outcomes of the process. During the actual political process of policy change, individuals may (and usually do) alter 2 and 3, depending upon the extent to which conflict or opposition is greater or lesser in intensity or in scope than anticipated.

Information, Ideas, Beliefs, and Interests

The idea of policy entrepreneurs reacting to new information by altering their strategies brings us to the view of the individual that is at work in comparative policy studies, and to the role of information, perception, and interests in guiding individuals' actions. Here we encounter two questions: What view do DSH models and studies take of individuals' political interests, and how do those models and studies treat information and perception as sources of change?

The Identification of Interests. With their systems theory focus on "demands and supports," DSH models of the policy process tend to objectify the political interests of participants and correspondingly to neglect the importance of beliefs, ideas, and information in the policy process. Accordingly, they have not been able to generate useful propositions about the impact of information, and of changes in the beliefs and ideas held by participants, upon the policy process.

The DSH models do not contain or accommodate intermediate steps between the presence of certain socioeconomic conditions (e.g., wealth, industrialization, urbanization) and the demands made upon or supports provided to the political system and to which the system responds. More bluntly, in the DSH models, individuals derive their political interests directly and objectively from their socioeconomic conditions. Accordingly, beliefs and ideas are comparatively unimportant: If socioeconomic conditions change, so will the beliefs and ideas that constitute participants' perceptions of their interests, and such change in interests is unlikely to occur in the absence of changed conditions. Individuals (to the extent that they exist at all in DSH models) are epiphenomena—statistical ciphers whose interest indicators flick on and off in varying configurations as their incomes rise or fall, their residences become urban or rural, their occupations become industrial or agrarian, and so on.[13]

At the time of the first rush of DSH models and studies, Raymond Bauer (1968, p 5)wrote, "Policy formation is a social process in which an intellectual process is embedded." He added (p. 16):

> Of course, there are constraints of reality beyond which a sane man cannot be per-
> suaded his interests lie. But within these limits there is sufficient latitude that self-in-
> terests cannot be taken for granted. We need to determine empirically not only how
> the persons in the policy process define their self-interest, but how the social process
> of communication brings about the definition and redefinition of self-interest over
> the course of time.

Not only have DSH-style studies failed to make this determination, but it also is not clear that the underlying model on which such studies are based is amenable to doing so.

The Role of Information and Perception.   The newer contributions to policy theory, especially the advocacy-coalition, policy-streams, and punctuated-equilibrium approaches, have taken the intellectual or developmental aspect of the policy process more seriously. For instance, instead of treating policy analysis as an objective element in the evaluation stage of the policy process, these newer treatments regard policy analysis as a consciously cultivated tool of persuasion that may be employed throughout the process of policy change in order to try to alter, enhance, or undermine one's position or the positions of one's opponents (Heintz and Jenkins-Smith, 1988). Several studies employing these emerging frameworks indicate that (1) the beliefs and ideas of participants are important elements of the ways in which they attempt to change public policies, (2) participants endeavor to cultivate information with which to counter or alter the beliefs and ideas of others, and (3) information sometimes has these effects upon participants' beliefs and ideas (Knott, 1993).

The effort to change the image or perception of a policy is related to, but not the same as, the effort to expand or contract the scope of conflict. Altering images and perceptions is an important aspect of an attempt to change the scope of conflict. Still, one may engage in efforts to alter images and perceptions even if the scope of conflict remains unchanged and even of one is not trying to change it. Altering images and perceptions through the development and communication of information is part of influencing policy learning, that is, reinforcing the perceptions held by one's allies and weakening those held by one's adversaries. Even when the scope of conflict remains stable, information and perception may play important roles in redefining the balance of power among the set of participants (Sabatier and Jenkins-Smith, 1993).

Because they present a static analysis of policymaking and because they do not encompass a model of the individual that incorporates an intellectual process, DSH models and their associated empirical studies are unlikely to contribute to a political theory of the policy process that gives a central role to information and perception. One might even translate this observation into a choice facing scholars interested in the further development of policy theory: If a central role is to be accorded to information and perception, we will need a model of the policy process that describes or predicts the actions of individuals rather than the aggregate characteristics of systems.

I should add that some scholars have attempted to add information about mass and elite preferences, or about elite beliefs and information, or both, within the confines of a DSH model. Among the most ambitious such efforts (although again in a small-N context) was the work of Mazmanian and Sabatier on the policy decisions of the California Coastal Commissions. In that work, they employed Hofferbert's (1974) model and collected and added information about mass preferences, elite preferences, and elite beliefs and information to the usual data on socioeconomic conditions, in order to try to isolate and identify the relative contribution of these factors. Their efforts succeeded: The revised model explained nearly all of the variance among commissioners in their decisions whether to grant or deny coastal development permits. However, fleshing out the Hofferbert model with these kinds of information took approximately five years and as much as $200,000 and still provided evidence only across an N of four governments within the same state.[14]

To conclude this discussion of methodological and theoretical deficiencies in the DSH approach as a basis for understanding the policy process, we return to Hofferbert's 1990 review and self-critique. In DSH-style comparative policy studies, he acknowledged (p. 147), "Theory was and still is light. Induction . . . has driven the inquiry." Let us now consider what fruits this inductive approach has brought to the development of policy theory.

MERITS OF THE DSH APPROACH
(PERHAPS UNDERAPPRECIATED)

The DSH approach has constituted much of public policy scholarship since the 1960s. The discrepancies between this approach and a political theory of the policy process have been described. But this review does not mean that the approach lacks merit or that it has not made significant contributions to political science generally and policy studies in particular. In this section, we devote some attention to the research activity that has occurred and the insights that have been gained under the guidance of the DSH approach. Furthermore, we need to acknowledge again the efforts in more recent comparative policy studies to address and correct some of the deficiencies identified above.

The DSH models, as well as the early studies that revealed stronger correlations between environmental variables and policy differences than between political variables and policy differences, shifted the field of policy studies even as it was emerging. The DSH-style studies demonstrated that however the new field of policy studies was to be constructed, it would have to involve more than an examination of political actors operating within governmental institutions (Salisbury, 1968, pp. 163–164). The studies also showed that policymakers are constrained by a host of conditions over which they have limited control, at least in the short run (Hofferbert, 1990, p. 145). Both of these findings have informed scholars in the field of policy studies that a valid account of the policy process will have to be more complex than might have otherwise been anticipated.

Although inductive and data-driven, the DSH approach has also provided an accumulation of empirical studies that have identified patterns in policy activity. The many comparative state studies, for example, have established that economic development, region, and culture all aid in distinguishing states from one another with respect to their likelihood of adopting certain forms of policies.[15] Cross-national studies have yielded similar findings for economic development, demography, and culture, and comparative local studies have found that economic development, region, population, and (occasionally) governmental structure matter.

Those patterns, seen again and again in DSH-style studies, have become part of the empirical foundation on which theoretical frameworks are currently being constructed, even if this influence is not always evident to the builders of those frameworks. The IRC framework includes "attributes of the community" among the influences upon a decision situation, which include such elements as cultural and economic characteristics. The advocacy coalition framework's elaboration of coalition members' core and secondary beliefs opens the door to cultural framing of perceptions, and the inclusion of exogenous factors allows changes in social and economic conditions to affect the intercoalition competition. Baumgartner and Jones's punctuated-equilibrium framework acknowledges that an important aspect of manipulating "policy image" entails sensitivity to culture, and that changed economic conditions can lead to changed perceptions of a policy. These emerging approaches to a theory of the policy process were developed primarily during the 1980s and built upon a base of empirical studies showing that culture and economic conditions affect the possibilities in and constraints upon policymaking.

Once empirical patterns are well established within the intellectual framework of a model, then the impetus for additional theory building can arise from the discovery of anomalies (Leichter, 1979, p. 100). When the "iron triangles" model could not explain the flurry of deregulation in the late 1970s, for example, policy scholars began to construct new approaches: issue networks, advocacy coalitions, punctuated equilibria. Similarly, no matter how skillfully scholars performing DSH-style comparative state studies constructed their models, operationalized their variables, and gathered and analyzed their data, they were rarely able to explain as much as half the policy variation among states.

The debate over political versus socioeconomic influences, and the persistence of a large unexplained variance even when both types of variables were included, became grist for a new round of examination of the role of policy elites; the importance of beliefs and information (Sabatier and Jenkins-Smith, 1993); reconsideration of the relationship between public opinion, political parties, and public policy (Erikson, Wright, and McIver, 1989, 1993); and in the comparative state context, a reconsideration of the role of governors and legislatures (Ferguson, 1996). We are still deeply engaged in that new round of examination.

Finally, despite all the criticisms in the previous section to the effect that cross-sectional studies are poorly suited to the task of explaining and understanding a longitudinal process, longitudinal policy studies have limitations of their own that would have weighed down the theory-building enterprise without the insights of the cross-sectional approach. By the late 1960s, policy scholars had both discovered and despaired of incrementalism. Study after study focusing on a policy topic within a government over time tended to find "that nearly all the time policy will vary only marginally from what it has been" (Salisbury, 1968, p. 164). Especially with respect to public expenditures, but also with other implementation-stage measures of governmental activity (arrests made, citations issued, grants awarded, inspections conducted, etc.), the next year's actions could be predicted with great reliability and accuracy by the use of this year's actions, this year's actions from last year's, and so on. Such observations were hardly fertile soil in which to develop a political theory of the policy process, especially if one hoped to advance a theory that could explain change.

And so, as Hofferbert (1990, p. 109) recalled, policy researchers searched for some variance. They found it in comparative studies. Welfare expenditures in Pennsylvania may not have changed much from year to year, but they sure were different from West Virginia's, which were different from North Dakota's, and so on. The pursuit of some accounting for these differences yielded an empirical base, some reliable patterns, and some unexplained puzzles upon which the field of policy studies has been built and upon which it continues to be built today.

ARE LARGE-*N* STUDIES INCOMPATIBLE
WITH A VALID THEORY OF THE POLICY PROCESS?

Large-*N* comparative policy studies have not achieved either of the grandest hopes wished for them in the heyday of the behavioral revolution. In the emerging field of policy studies, scholars hoped that the comparative approach would break the deadlock of incrementalism and vault the field forward toward a theoretical approach that could describe within-system stability and change as well as across-system similarities and differences. In the well-established field of comparative politics, scholars hoped that large-*N* policy studies would finally turn the field away from its tradition of country-by-country description and toward genuinely comparative research that might hold the promise of theory building (Mayer, 1989; Smith, 1975).

It was a lot to hope for. It is probably fair to say that large-N comparative policy studies have had more effect on the policy field than on the comparative politics field, but even so, the impact on the policy field has fallen short of the hope of providing anything like a policy theory.

Two questions remain: Did the DSH models and studies "fail," or was the hope itself vain? And as several policy scholars are currently trying to develop valid theoretical approaches to the public policy process, can large-N comparative studies be of much help to the enterprise?

The most promising contemporary approaches to a political theory of the policy process are building on some of the issues discussed in this chapter and wrestling with others. All are trying to place human agency and strategic action squarely at the center of their explanations.

The institutional rational choice framework places boundedly rational individuals in decision situations shaped by multiple factors, assigns them positions defined by institutional rules, and embeds them in a multilevel analytic space where they are both constrained by rules and equipped with limited opportunities to shift levels and alter rules. The framework has begun to incorporate learning through search and trial-and-error but continues to wrestle with the roles played by beliefs and norms and with change (as distinct from choice) over long periods.

The advocacy coalition framework focuses on the belief structures of individuals engaged in the struggle to make and define policy over time within subgovernments. It incorporates information and learning more explicitly than other approaches but still wrestles with how coalitions form, sustain themselves, and break up, and with the effect of environmental change.

The punctuated-equilibrium framework focuses on policy image and the decisionmaking venue, seeing both as subject to change in response to the strategic action of individuals. It incorporates the multiple possibilities for restraining or expanding the scope of conflict, leaving a role for public opinion as well as elite preferences, but it wrestles with the causal driver that sets off a period of rapid change, and with an explanation of how the different "sides" of a policy issue come together and coordinate their actions (or fail to do so).

The policy streams framework gives a prominent role to policymakers' perceptions of issues, and to the efforts to shape and change those perceptions through the cultivation and use of information, and (like the punctuated-equilibrium approach) to the prospects for rapid change following long periods of stability. It wrestles with governmental complexity and with the occasion that opens the window of change.

But it is obvious what all of these efforts have in common: Whatever theories they produce will be extraordinarily complex. Similarly complex, if less promising, are efforts to build upon the policy stages approach (e.g., Rose's twelve-step policy process research agenda), and upon the DSH-style studies (e.g., Leichter's thirty-nine-item elaboration of a framework incorporating situational, structural, cultural, and intergovernmental factors).

Searching through these efforts, one can extract a set of broad requirements for a valid account of the public policy process. Such an account would be:

- *Multidimensional,* incorporating the influences of the social and economic context of political decisionmaking, the structure and processes of the political system, and the development and evolution of information and ideas;
- *Multi-institutional,* recognizing the diverse forums that may be available for decisionmaking, the roles available to individuals and the terms and conditions of that availability, and the possibility of institutional alteration through shifts among levels of action; and
- *Dynamic* or at least diachronic, capable of accounting for policy change as a process occurring through time and not only as an outcome at a point in time.

It seems, then, that internal complexity is bound to be a feature of valid theories of the policy process. Given the direction in which theory development is currently headed, policy theory will involve multiple actors with complex cognitive processes and diverse motivations interacting in a multiorganizational arena shaped by institutional and environmental factors over which they have varying degrees of control, and their interactions will occur over (sometimes long) periods.

Now back to the question posed earlier: What role can large-N comparative studies play in developing and testing a theory with these features? At present, I am inclined to think that the answer is not much, for two reasons.

First, the complexity of the policy process theories will make the information-gathering and analytic tasks of even individual case studies daunting. A skillful scholar with plenty of time and no institutional pressures to publish results right away may even be able to mount some small-N comparative studies.[16] The variable-operationalization, data-collection, and analytical tasks of a large-N study based on a multidimensional, multi-institutional, dynamic or diachronic policy theory seem to be beyond the pale.

Second and more important, the emerging theoretical approaches to the policy process are by design longitudinal. Their empirical manifestations will be narratives, not cross sections. Even if it were within the realm of feasibility, the large-N comparative study is methodologically inconsistent with a narrative account of policy change over time.

In the end, large-N comparative studies and valid theories of the policy process appear to be like epidemiology and etiology as different aspects of the science of pathology. One who understands the etiology of a disease can describe the course it will take in an individual patient (with varying degrees of precision and accuracy from one disease to another, according to how well the disease has come to be understood). The etiologist can, in other words, provide the narrative account of the disease.

An epidemiologist may be able to provide a scenario for the spread of the same disease across a population. The epidemiologist's account will be probabilistic and will be based on a set of information almost entirely different from that employed by the etiologist (obviously, information about the mode of transmission and the duration of incubation and recovery periods will be relevant to both accounts). The epidemiologist will focus on attributes of the relevant population and its environs, such as density, sanitation, age profile, educational attainment, availability of medical treatment, and ability and willingness to seek and pay for medical treatment. To the extent that the epidemiologist provides a "narrative" at all, it will be a narrative of a likely disease diffusion scenario.

On one superficial level, the epidemiologist and the etiologist are talking about the same disease. But their interests in and their knowledge of that disease diverge substantially beyond that surface. The etiologist is interested in providing a narrative-style explanation of the disease *process*. The epidemiologist is interested in providing a likelihood scenario of the disease's appearance and prevalence in a population of size N. Their subject matter is similar, but they are trying to answer different questions. So, too, are the emerging frameworks of the policy process and the comparative policy studies from the Dye-Sharkansky-Hofferbert tradition.

NOTES

1. For a recent large-N cross-national study, see Burkhart and Lewis-Beck (1994). Their dependent variable, however, is a measure of the extent of democracy in national political systems rather than a public policy measure.

2. Notwithstanding the myriad other forms of local government in the United States, cities alone differ in governmental form to a considerable degree, for example, whether they have a separately elected executive or one appointed by the city council, whether the executive position is primarily ceremonial or administrative, whether the council members are elected at large or individually from districts, and whether elections are formally nonpartisan. These differences have spawned their own research studies, focusing on such questions as whether at-large elections make a difference in minority representation or whether "strong" mayors, "weak" mayors, and city managers allocate their time differently, but those studies are for the most part outside the inquiry of this chapter.

Functions as well as forms vary from city to city in the United States, a variation compounding the difficulties of conducting large-N comparative policy studies. This point was made early in the development of the subfield (Wilson, 1966). In some locations, city governments are responsible for mass transit; in others, they are not. Some cities fund and operate water and sewer systems; others do not. Some cities own and manage public parks and libraries, and in other cities, these are the responsibilities of special districts. Connecting the diverse forms of municipal government organizations in the United States with their diverse responsibilities involves enormous information costs, which many researchers have rationally decided were not likely to be offset or overcome by the marginal yield in additional information about the public policy process.

3. That still leaves plenty of room, of course, for discussions about one's choices of time period and variables.

4. Key's work appeared in *Southern Politics in State and Nation* (1951), Lockard's in *New England State Politics* (1959). Dawson and Robinson (1963, p. 270) wrote, "Our study is an attempt to expand further on the hypotheses of Key and Lockard concerning party competition and welfare policies, testing them in a larger 'laboratory,' and applying slightly more rigorous statistical techniques."

5. Dawson and Robinson excluded Alaska and Hawaii, which were so new to the Union at the time of the 1960 Census from which they drew much of their data, and Minnesota and Nebraska, which had nonpartisan legislative elections that made it difficult to determine certain measures of state party competition.

6. Especially noteworthy in this regard, although in a small-N context, was the effort produced by Mazmanian and Sabatier (1980). Some examples of large-N studies that have incorporated data on elite and/or mass preferences include comparative local studies by Ostrom, Parks, and Whitaker (1977), Schneider and Teske (1992), and Feiock and West (1993); comparative state studies by Erikson, Wright, and McIver (1989, 1993); and the cross-national work reported by Godwin (1992).

7. The literature on innovation and diffusion of policies among the American states, which also grew rapidly during the 1970s and 1980s, relied heavily on these sorts of indicators of state policy adoptions, and there has been a considerable overlap and cross-fertilization of methods and findings between innovation-diffusion studies (see Chapter 7, by Berry and Berry) and the DSH-style studies covered in this chapter.

8. For a couple of noteworthy exceptions, see Thompson and Scicchitano (1985) and Ringquist (1993).

9. This is not to say that the passage of a state law or the creation of a state agency is necessarily a *valid* indicator of what we might call "real" policy change. The creation of an agency, for example, may represent the establishment of an active governmental role in some states while amounting to mere symbolism in others.

10. Paul Sabatier suggested in correspondence that the Hofferbert (1974) model could be adapted to link funnels, for instance, so that a federal policy output would feed into the funnel of a state policy decision at, say, the governmental institutions stage. This might well be a useful adaptation, but it is not currently a property of the model, nor has it been applied, so for now it must be acknowledged merely as a possibility.

11. Of course, some DSH-style state studies have included the presence or absence of divided government as an independent variable, which implicitly recognizes the existence of more than one decisionmaking body within state government.

12. Abbott also criticized the latest methodological trend in comparative policy studies—event history analysis—for merely aggravating the tendency. Citing as an example Pavalko (1989), Abbott (1992, p. 60) pointed out that in her study, the forty-eight states became 369 "cases," as she transformed the states into time-place fragments known as *events:* "(Each state appears once for each year in which it lacks a compensation law as well as once for each year in which it acquires one.) All of these are seen as independent realizations of a stochastic process. . . . [Thus] in the paper 48 complex, chained narratives are made to seem like 369 independent, one-step narratives and the 'causal' steps in those 369 stories all become one-step rational-action stories."

13. Although the language may seem similar, this point is not the same as the one made earlier about the automaticity of the relationship between the independent and dependent

variables in DSH studies. Here we are discussing individuals and the implicit assumptions of DSH models about their political interests.

14. I appreciate Paul Sabatier's willingness to share this reflection with me in correspondence.

15. Again, this empirical base of comparative state studies has been closely linked to, and has influenced and been influenced by, the literature on policy innovation and diffusion. See Chapter 7, by Berry and Berry.

16. See, for example, the excellent collection of comparative policy studies collected in Castles (1993). These studies, rich in context and detail, are nevertheless for the most part confined to three, four, or five countries at a time.

REFERENCES

Abbott, Andrew. 1992. "What Do Cases Do? Some Notes on Activity in Sociological Analysis." In Charles C. Ragin and Howard S. Becker, eds., *What Is a Case? Exploring the Foundations of Social Inquiry,* pp. 53–82. Cambridge, England: Cambridge University Press.

Alt, James E., and Robert C. Lowry. 1994. "Divided Government, Fiscal Institutions, and Budget Deficits: Evidence from the States," *American Political Science Review* 88(4) (December):811–828.

Barilleaux, Charles J., and Mark E. Miller. 1988. "The Political Economy of State Medicaid Policy," *American Political Science Review* 82(4) (December):1089–1107.

Bauer, Raymond A. 1968. "The Study of Policy Formation: An Introduction." In Raymond A. Bauer and Kenneth J. Gergen, eds., *The Study of Policy Formation,* pp. 1–26. New York: Free Press.

Baumgartner, Frank R., and Bryan D. Jones. 1991. "Agenda Dynamics and Policy Subsystems," *Journal of Politics* 53(4) (November):1044–1074.

Berry, Francis Stokes, and William D. Berry. 1990. "State Lottery Adoptions as Policy Innovations: An Event History Analysis," *American Political Science Review* 84(2) (June):395–415.

Blomquist, William. 1991. "Exploring State Differences in Groundwater Policy Adoptions, 1980–1989," *Publius: The Journal of Federalism* 21(2) (Spring):101–115.

Boeckelman, Keith. 1991. "Political Culture and State Development Policy," *Publius: The Journal of Federalism* 21(2) (Spring):49–62.

Booms, Bernard H., and James R. Halldorson. 1973. "The Politics of Redistribution: A Reformulation," *American Political Science Review* 67(2) (June):924–933.

Brown, Robert D. 1995. "Party Cleavages and Welfare Effort in the American States," *American Political Science Review* 89(1) (March):23–33.

Burkhart, Ross E., and Michael S. Lewis-Beck. 1994. "Comparative Democracy: The Economic Development Thesis," *American Political Science Review* 88(4) (December):903–910.

Cameron, David R. 1978. "The Expansion of the Public Economy: A Comparative Analysis," *American Political Science Review* 72(4) (December):1243–1261.

Castles, Francis G., ed. 1993. *Families of Nations: Patterns of Public Policy in Western Democracies.* Aldershot, England: Dartmouth Publishing.

Castles, Francis G., and Deborah Mitchell. 1993. "Worlds of Welfare and Families of Nations." In Francis G. Castles, ed., *Families of Nations: Patterns of Public Policy in Western Democracies,* pp. 93–128. Aldershot, England: Dartmouth Publishing.

Clingermayer, James C., and B. Dan Wood. 1995. "Disentangling Patterns of State Debt Financing," *American Political Science Review* 89(1) (March):108–120.

Cnudde, Charles F., and Donald J. McCrone. 1969. "Party Competition and Welfare Policies in the American States," *American Political Science Review* 63(3) (September):858–866.

Cutright, Phillips. 1965. "Political Structure, Economic Development, and National Social Security Programs," *American Journal of Sociology* 70(5) (March):537–550.

Dawson, Richard E., and James A. Robinson. 1963. "Inter-Party Competition, Economic Variables, and Welfare Policies in the American States," *Journal of Politics* 25(2) (May):265–289.

Dye, Thomas R. 1965. "Malapportionment and Public Policy in the States," *Journal of Politics* 27(3) (August):586–601.

———. 1966. *Politics, Economics, and the Public: Policy Outcomes in the American States.* Chicago: Rand McNally.

———. 1969. "Income Inequality and American State Politics," *American Political Science Review* 63(1) (March):157–162.

Erikson, Robert S., Gerald C. Wright, Jr., and John P. McIver. 1989. "Political Parties, Public Opinion, and State Policy in the United States," *American Political Science Review* 83(3) (September):729–750.

———. 1993. *Statehouse Democracy: Public Opinion and Policy in the American States.* New York: Cambridge University Press.

Feiock, Richard C., and Jonathan P. West. 1993. "Testing Competing Explanations for Policy Adoption: Municipal Solid Waste Recycling Programs," *Political Research Quarterly* 46(2) (June):399–419.

Ferguson, Margaret. 1996. *Gubernatorial Policy Leadership in the Fifty States.* Ph.D. Dissertation, University of North Carolina, Chapel Hill.

Froman, Lewis A. 1967. "An Analysis of Public Policies in Cities," *Journal of Politics* 29(1) (February):94–108.

Fry, Bryan A., and Richard Winters. 1970. "The Politics of Redistribution," *American Political Science Review* 64(2) (June):508–522.

Gergen, Kenneth J. 1968. "Assessing the Leverage Points in the Process of Policy Formation." In Raymond A. Bauer and Kenneth J. Gergen, eds., *The Study of Policy Formation,* pp. 181–203. New York: Free Press.

Glick, Henry R., and Scott P. Hays. 1991. "Innovation and Reinvention in State Policymaking: Theory and the Evolution of Living Will Laws," *Journal of Politics* 53(3) (August):835–850.

Godwin, R. Kenneth. 1992. "Policy Formation and Implementation in Less Industrialized Countries: A Comparative Analysis of Institutional Effects," *Western Political Quarterly* 45(2) (June):419–439.

Greenberg, George D., et al. 1977. "Developing Public Policy Theory: Perspectives from Empirical Research," *American Political Science Review* 71(4) (December):1532–1543.

Hancock, M. Donald. 1983. "Comparative Public Policy: An Assessment." In Ada Finifter, ed., *Political Science: The State of the Discipline,* pp. 283–308. Washington, D.C.: American Political Science Association.

Hanson, Russell L. 1991. "Political Cultural Variations in State Economic Development Policy," *Publius: The Journal of Federalism* 21(2) (Spring):63–81.

Heintz, H. Theodore, Jr., and Hank C. Jenkins-Smith. 1988. "Advocacy Coalitions and the Practice of Policy Analysis," *Policy Sciences* 21(2,3):263–277.

Hibbs, Douglas A., Jr. 1976. "Industrial Conflict in Advanced Industrial Societies," *American Political Science Review* 70(4) (December):1033–1058.

_____. 1977. "Political Parties and Macroeconomic Policy," *American Political Science Review* 71(4) (December):1467–1487.

Hill, Kim Quaile, and Patricia A. Hurley. 1988. "Uniform State Law Adoptions in the American States: An Explanatory Analysis," *Publius: The Journal of Federalism* 18(1) (Winter):117–126.

Hofferbert, Richard I. 1966a. "Ecological Development and Policy Change in the American States," *Midwest Journal of Political Science* 10(4) (November):464–483.

_____. 1966b. "The Relation Between Public Policy and Some Structural and Environmental Variables in the American States," *American Political Science Review* 60(1) (March):73–82.

_____. 1974. *The Study of Public Policy*. Indianapolis, Ind.: Bobbs-Merrill.

_____. 1990. *The Reach and Grasp of Policy Analysis: Comparative Views of the Craft.* Tuscaloosa: University of Alabama Press.

Hogwood, Brian, and B. Guy Peters. 1983. *Policy Dynamics*. New York: St. Martin's Press.

Hwang, Sung-Don, and Virginia Gray. 1991. "External Limits and Internal Determinants of State Public Policy," *Western Political Quarterly* 44(2) (June):277–298.

Jennings, Edward T., Jr. 1979. "Competition, Constituencies, and Welfare Policies in American States," *American Political Science Review* 73(2) (June):414–429.

Jordan, A. Grant. 1981. "Iron Triangles, Woolly Corporatism and Elastic Nets: Images of the Policy Process," *Journal of Public Policy* 1(1):95–123.

Kingdon, John W. 1984. *Agendas, Alternatives, and Public Policies*. Boston: Little, Brown.

Knott, Jack H. 1993. "Policy Change and Deregulation: Explaining Differences in Legislative Outcomes," *Policy Currents* 3(1) (February):1+.

Leichter, Howard M. 1979. *A Comparative Approach to Policy Analysis: Health Care Policy in Four Nations*. Cambridge, England: Cambridge University Press.

Lewis-Beck, Michael. 1977. "The Relative Importance of Socioeconomic and Political Variables for Public Policy," *American Political Science Review* 71(2) (June):559–566.

Macey, Jonathan R. 1992. "Organizational Design and Political Control of Administrative Agencies," *Journal of Law, Economics, and Organization* 8(1) (March):93–110.

Mayer, Lawrence C. 1989. *Redefining Comparative Politics: Promise Versus Performance.* Newbury Park, Calif.: Sage.

Mazmanian, Daniel, and Paul Sabatier. 1980. "A Multi-Variate Model of Public Policy-Making," *American Journal of Political Science* 24(3) (August):439–468.

Miller, David Y. 1991. "The Impact of Political Culture on Patterns of State and Local Government Expenditures," *Publius: The Journal of Federalism* 21(2) (Spring):83–100.

Miner, Jerry. 1963. *Social and Economic Factors in Spending for Public Education*. Syracuse, N.Y.: Syracuse University Press.

Montgomery, John D. 1995. "Beyond Good Policies." In John D. Montgomery and Dennis A Rondinelli, eds., *Great Policies: Strategic Innovations in Asia and the Pacific Basin*, pp. 1–13. Westport, Conn.: Praeger.

Nice, David C. 1986. "State Support for Constitutional Balanced Budget Requirements," *Journal of Politics* 48(1) (February):134–142.

Ostrom, Elinor. 1994. "Self-Organizing Resource Regimes: A Brief Report on a Decade of Policy Analysis," *Policy Currents* 4(3) (August):1+.

Ostrom, Elinor, Roger B. Parks, and Gordon P. Whitaker. 1977. *Policing Metropolitan America*. Report for the National Science Foundation. Washington, D.C.: U.S. Government Printing Office.

Pavalko, Eliza K. 1989. "State Timing of Policy Adoption: Workmen's Compensation in the United States, 1909–1929," *American Journal of Sociology* 95(3) (November):592–615.

Pinard, Maurice. 1963. "Structural Attachments and Political Support in Urban Politics: The Case of Fluoridation Referendums," *American Journal of Sociology* 68(5) (March):513–526.

Ragin, Charles C. 1992. "Introduction: Cases of 'What Is a Case?'" In Charles C. Ragin and Howard S. Becker, eds., *What Is a Case? Exploring the Foundations of Social Inquiry*, pp. 1–17. Cambridge, England: Cambridge University Press.

Ranney, Austin. 1968. "The Study of Policy Content: A Framework for Choice." In Austin Ranney, ed., *Political Science and Public Policy*, pp. 3–21. Chicago, Ill.: Markham.

Regens, James L. 1980. "State Policy Responses to the Energy Issue: An Analysis of Innovation," *Social Science Quarterly* 61 (June):44–57.

Ringquist, Evan J. 1993. "Does Regulation Matter? Evaluating the Effects of State Air Pollution Control Programs," *Journal of Politics* 55(4) (November).

Sabatier, Paul A., and Hank C. Jenkins-Smith, eds. 1993. *Policy Change and Learning: An Advocacy Coalition Approach*. Boulder: Westview Press.

Salisbury, Robert H. 1968. "The Analysis of Public Policy: A Search for Theories and Roles." In Austin Ranney, ed., *Political Science and Public Policy*, pp. 151–175. Chicago: Markham.

Schneider, Mark, and Paul Teske. 1992. "Toward a Theory of the Political Entrepreneur: Evidence from Local Government," *American Political Science Review* 86(3) (September):737–747.

Sharkansky, Ira. 1967. "Government Expenditures and Public Services in the American States," *American Political Science Review* 61(4) (Deceember):1066–1077.

_____. 1968. "Regionalism, Economic Status, and the Public Policies of American States," *Social Science Quarterly* 49 (June):9–26.

_____. 1970a. "Environment, Policy, Output and Impact: Problems of Theory and Method in the Analysis of Public Policy." In Ira Sharkansky, ed., *Policy Analysis in Political Science*, pp. 61–79. Chicago: Markham.

Sharkansky, Ira, ed. 1970b. *Policy Analysis in Political Science*. Chicago: Markham.

Sharkansky, Ira. 1970c. "The Political Scientist and Policy Analysis." In Ira Sharkansky, ed., *Policy Analysis in Political Science*, pp. 1–18. Chicago: Markham.

Sharkansky, Ira, and Richard I. Hofferbert. 1969. "Dimensions of State Politics, Economics, and Public Policy," *American Political Science Review* 63(3) (September):867–879.

Smith, T. Alexander. 1969. "Toward a Comparative Theory of the Policy-Process," *Comparative Politics* 2 (July):498–515.

_____. 1975. *The Comparative Policy Process*. Santa Barbara, Calif.: Clio Press.

_____. 1982. "A Phenomenology of the Policy Process," *International Journal of Comparative Sociology* 23(1,2):1–16.

Thompson, Frank J., and Michael J. Scicchitano. 1985. "State Implementation Effort and Federal Regulatory Policy: The Case of Occupational Safety and Health," *Journal of Politics* 47(2) (May):686–703.

Tompkins, Gary. 1975. "A Causal Model of State Welfare Expenditures," *Journal of Politics* 37(2) (May):392–416.

Treadway, Jack M. 1985. *Public Policymaking in the American States.* New York: Praeger.

Uslaner, Eric, and Ronald E. Weber. 1975. "The Politics of Redistribution: Toward a Model of the Policy-Making Process in the American States," *American Politics Quarterly* 3(2):130–170.

Van Dyke, Vernon. 1968. "Process and Policy as Focal Concepts in Political Research." In Austin Ranney, ed., *Political Science and Public Policy,* pp. 23–39. Chicago: Markham.

Wetstein, Matthew E., and Robert B. Albritton. 1995. "Effects of Public Opinion on Abortion Policies and Use in the American States," *Publius: The Journal of Federalism* 25(4) (Fall):91–105.

Wilson, James Q. 1966. "Problems in the Study of Urban Politics." In Edward H. Buehrig, ed., *Essays in Political Science,* pp. 131–150. Bloomington: Indiana University Press.

Zahariadis, Nikolaos. 1995."Comparing Lenses in Comparative Public Policy," *Policy Studies Journal* 23(4) (Summer):378–382.

PART V

Conclusions

9

A Comparison of Frameworks, Theories, and Models of Policy Processes

EDELLA SCHLAGER

The striking diversity of approaches developed and used by top policy scholars raises questions concerning the meaning of "the policymaking process." The term *process* connotes temporality, an unfolding of actions, events, and decisions that may culminate in an authoritative decision, which, at least temporarily, binds all within the jurisdiction of the governing body. In explaining policymaking processes, the emphasis is much more on the unfolding than it is on the authoritative decision. In examining the unfolding, attention is devoted to structure, to the context and constraints of the process, and to actual decisions and events that occur. All of the contributions, but for one, provide an explanation of policymaking processes and thus fit comfortably with the commonly accepted notion of policymaking processes.[1]

The diversity of approaches found in this volume emerges in part from the generality and in part from the scope of the explanations. The generality of the explanation rests on the distinction that Ostrom makes among frameworks, theories, and models. The scope of the explanation rests on the distinctions made in deLeon's chapter among the different stages of the policy process. Frameworks, theories, and models, not to mention different policy stages, are well represented in this collection of papers. How do we distinguish among frameworks, theories, and models? How do we know when an author has presented a framework rather than a theory, or a theory rather than a model? What constitute meaningful comparative and evaluative criteria that would allow us to make sense of the chapters in relation to each other, and to judge their usefulness in explaining policymaking? Are theories of a more limited scope less useful than theories of a more general scope? What does this collection of papers tell us about the field of policy studies?

FRAMEWORKS

Frameworks bound inquiry and direct the attention of the analyst to critical features of the social and physical landscape. Frameworks provide a foundation for inquiry by specifying classes of variables and general relationships among them, that is, how the general classes of variables loosely fit together into a coherent structure. Thus, frameworks organize inquiry, but they cannot in and of themselves provide explanations for, or predictions of, behavior and outcomes. Explanation and prediction lie in the realm of theories and models. Or as Ostrom (in chapter 3 of this book) states: "Frameworks organize diagnostic and prescriptive inquiry. . . . They attempt to identify the universal elements that any theory relevant to the same kind of phenomena would need to include."

All of the theories and models presented in this volume derive from some sort of framework, although not all frameworks are explicitly identified.[2] This section focuses on comparing explicitly stated frameworks. The criteria used are primarily comparative, and not evaluative.[3] Criteria for comparing frameworks are not well developed. As Ostrom (Chapter 3, this volume) states: "The differences between frameworks, theories, and models are not even generally recognized." The criteria are (1) types of actors, (2) development of general classes of variables and relationships among them, (3) units of analysis, (4) levels of analysis, and (5) scope. I use these criteria because (1) they appear to be reasonable, (2) they interest me, and (3) I have something to say about each. In other words, since well-developed and generally accepted criteria for comparing frameworks do not exist, these criteria are heavily dependent on this analyst.

Types of Actors

The chapters that explicitly present frameworks are Ostrom, Sabatier and Jenkins-Smith, and Berry and Berry.[4] Blomquist (in Chapter 8 of this book) identifies Hofferbert's model for the comparative study of policy formulation as a dominant framework in the comparative state policy literature, and it, too, will be included.

Frameworks must specify who motivates action, or change. They must do so if they are to provide the basis for theory development. Theories, which provide explanations, and not simply descriptions, tell stories of why actors act and to what effect. Numerous candidates could fill the role of actor, but these frameworks have a common type of actor; each framework posits the individual as the motivator of action. Thus, well-developed theories and models derived from the frameworks require that assumptions be made about individual behavior, and about why individuals act as they do. The institutional analysis and development (IAD) framework most clearly specifies the individual as actor and posits a set of general variables that structure the individual. At a minimum, a theory based on the IAD framework must identify the structure of preferences, general types **of** selection criteria, levels and types of information an individual is likely to possess, and so forth.

Although the remaining frameworks do not identify general variables that structure the individual as explicitly as does the IAD framework, the advocacy coalition framework (ACF) certainly comes close. The individual is structured by a hierarchically ordered set of beliefs, the ability to process information, and a set of goals, or preferences. Notice that the ACF does not require a specific model of the individual, just as the IAD framework does not suppose a specific model. The variables are so general that several different models of the individual could be used.

The Berry and Berry and the Hofferbert frameworks imply the individual as actor. The Berry and Berry framework consists of three general classes of variables: motivation to innovate, obstacles to innovation, and resources available to surmount these obstacles (Berry and Berry, Chapter 7, this volume). In their discussion of the framework, Berry and Berry repeatedly refer to individuals as actors. Furthermore, in the models they derive from the framework, the dependent variable is the probability that a state will adopt a policy. In other words, the specific explanations provided by the models focus on the factors that influence the likelihood of an authoritative decision by a state government, that is, the factors that influence the collective choices of individuals that constitute a decisionmaking body of the state. Confusion occurs because the data collected and used to test models derived from the framework are typically at the system level and not the individual level. Thus, in their discussion of motivation to innovate in Chapter 3, Berry and Berry write about the goals of elected officials, which they then operationalize at the system level, that is, interparty competition or the time until the next election.

For Hofferbert (1974), the final stage before policy adoption is elite behavior.[5] However, elite behavior constitutes one of the least-developed aspects of the framework. Hofferbert failed to identify variables that could be used to adequately represent the concept (Hofferbert, 1974; Mazmanian and Sabatier, 1984). As Blomquist (Chapter 8) points out, many models derived from the framework do not attempt to represent individual actions.

Variable Development

In addition to positing actors, frameworks also posit general classes of variables that structure, constrain, guide, and influence the actions taken by actors. Once again, the IAD framework, followed by the ACF, provides the most well-developed classes of variables. The most well-developed classes of variables within the IAD framework are those that constitute the action arena. Theories derived from the framework must attend to participants, the positions they hold, the actions that they take, the information that they possess, the outcomes that are achieved, and the distribution of the costs and benefits of those outcomes. Somewhat less developed are some of the classes of variables that structure the action situation. Although the rules-in-use are clearly well defined and complete, the characteristics of the physical environment and of the community are not. Ostrom pointed to excludability, subtractability, and storage, as important characteristics of the physical environment, although there are no doubt more. As Ostrom (Chapter 3) suggests:

> Analysts diagnosing resource problems need to be sensitive to the very large difference among resource settings and the need to tailor rules to diverse combinations of attributes rather than some assumed uniformity across all resources in a particular sector within a country.

No variables are developed to characterize critical features of a community, although Ostrom (Chapter 3) suggests such things as norms of behavior, common understandings, and homogeneity of preferences.

The ACF consists of well-developed classes of variables as well. And just as in the IAD framework, some classes of variables are better developed than are others. For instance, the variables that characterize a stable, mature policy subsystem are carefully developed, as are the variables that constitute belief systems. On the other hand, many of the variables that need to be incorporated within the framework, and that need further development, thus far appear in the hypotheses. For instance, a critical set of variables for the ACF are forums in which coalitions contest and engage each other and perhaps eventually experience policy learning. Important characteristics of forums could be identified, and forums could be formally incorporated within the framework. Or the concept of forums could be defined as political venues within which contestation and decisionmaking occur.

Variables within each of the policy stages of the Hofferbert framework are relatively well developed, with the exception of two of the stages: governmental institutions and elite behavior. Hofferbert (1974), in his own empirical work, focused on the systemic and macro features of government institutions, such as the division of powers among branches of government. As Mazmanian and Sabatier (1984) pointed out, such gross operationalizations of government structure are rarely significant. They suggested a more careful delineation of institutional arrangements devoted to specific policy decisions. Furthermore, Hofferbert (1974) stated that elite behavior is one of the most interesting, but least understood, stages of the policy process, providing no further direction for incorporating elite behavior into policy analyses.

Hofferbert (1974) carefully explicated the relations among the different policy stages. Each stage directly affects the one proceeding it. For instance, historical-geographic conditions directly affect socioeconomic conditions of the jurisdiction, and socioeconomic conditions directly affect mass political behavior. Stages not directly adjacent to each other indirectly affect each other. For instance, the socioeconomic composition of a jurisdiction indirectly affects elite behavior. Hofferbert's policy stages are cumulative and interactive. The lesson, as Mazmanian and Sabatier (1984, p. 464) pointed out, is "that partial information can be dangerous, or at least misleading." Examining just the interaction between socioeconomic variables and policy outputs at best captures a part of the policy story. Rather, in any analysis, each of the stages must be accounted for.

General variables within the policy innovations framework are not as well specified and probably will have to be if full-blown theories of policy innovation are to be developed. Poorly specified variables cause several problems, the most critical of which is that they lead to ad hoc theorizing and model building. For instance, Berry and Berry (Chapter 7, this volume) state that explaining the adoption of specific policies requires attention to ad hoc variables, such as strong teacher unions or fundamentalist populations. Rather than being regarded as constituting an ad hoc explanation, these groups may be characterized as interest groups, which could be incorporated within the framework. Interest groups may be grouped with variables relating to obstacles to innovation, or with variables relating to resources available to surmount obstacles to innovation. Interest group strength and activity seem to be consistent and critical factors in explaining policy innovations and would constitute a reasonable addition to the framework.

Units of Analysis

Unlike the other frameworks, the IAD and the Hofferbert frameworks maintain their flexibility and generality by leaving it up to the analyst to identify the unit of analysis. The setting that the analyst wants to examine and the questions that the analyst wants to address will determine the unit of analysis. Therefore, the unit of analysis can be almost anything: a family, a church, a city, a coastal fishery, an irrigation project, and so forth. The Hofferbert framework is almost as flexible. It can be applied to any formal public decisionmaking body, whether that is a university board of regents, a city council, or Congress.

The policy innovations and the advocacy coalition frameworks are wedded to specific units of analysis. For policy innovations, it is the United States state, and for the ACF, it is the policy subsystem. It is possible, however, to play with these units of analysis. For the policy innovations framework, as Berry and Berry (Chapter 7) point out, the unit of analysis could be organizations, cities, counties, or countries; it would not have to be the state. The concept of a policy subsystem is sufficiently flexible so that it could encompass a highly specific policy, such as stream riparian protection, or a broad policy area, such as watershed protection. As Sabatier and Jenkins-Smith (Chapter 6, this volume) note, subsystems may be nested. Thus, although each framework is grounded in a particular unit of analysis, there remains substantial flexibility in how the unit of analysis is applied in any particular instance.

Levels of Analysis

The concept of levels of analysis provides a richer, more meaningful, and imminently useful approach to understanding the myriad of activities that occur in relation to policymaking processes. Sometimes actors develop strategies and make choices about their daily activities within a given set of rules. The outcomes that actors achieve, and the benefits and costs they experience, may at some point induce them to attempt to change the rules. They move to a collective-choice level of action to change the rules. Or actors may choose to reconstitute or design new collective-choice decision processes and may move to the constitutional-choice level to do so. All of these activities are part of, or at least feed into, policymaking processes.

Only the IAD framework pays explicit and careful attention to levels of analysis. Although the analyst can choose to keep the analysis focused on a single level, the other two levels are always implicitly included. If the analyst chooses to focus on an action situation exclusively at the operational level, the collective-choice, and perhaps the constitutional-choice, level is nevertheless included because the rules-in-use that structure the operational level originate from the other two levels. Or if an analyst chooses to focus on an action situation at the collective-choice level, the rules that structure the situation are from the collective-choice level, and outcomes from the operational level feedback into and influence collective-choice decisionmaking processes.

The remaining three frameworks implicitly incorporate levels of action. For instance, the dependent variable posited by the policy innovations framework, policy adoptions, is the outcome of a collective-choice process. However, the classes of independent variables used to explain adoptions include operational-level activities and outcomes. The ACF implicitly incorporates levels of action, but like the policy innovations framework, it appears to be designed primarily to account for action at the collective-choice level, however, the other levels of action are not precluded. The ACF emphasizes policy change over a decade or more, the coalitions that attempt to engage and shape policy changes, and the strategies and the information that the coalitions use in their attempts to change policy. Coalitions, the heart of the ACF, are coalitions at the collective-choice level. Thus, a primary focus on collective-choice-level activity is implied. On the other hand, operational-level actions of individual members of coalitions feed into collective-choice activity. Members of advocacy coalitions, through operational-level activities, gain information and knowledge about the nature of the problems or issues that most concern them, and about the nature of other actors who are interested and active around the same issues. Day-to-day experiences provide members of advocacy coalitions with critical information that they in turn use to influence collective-choice processes. Nevertheless, the ACF is predominantly a collective-choice-level framework, just as is the policy innovations framework.

The Hofferbert framework does not pay explicit attention to levels of action either. Although the framework is devoted to structuring analyses of a collective-choice event, a policy adoption, most of the framework's variables occur at the operational level. The categories of variables, or stages, that are best developed, and that dominate the framework, are historical-geographic conditions and socioeconomic composition. Mass political behavior includes some collective-choice activities. Just the two least-developed categories of variables—governmental institutions and elite behavior—constitute collective-choice variables.

Scope

The levels of action that a framework comfortably addresses strongly affect the scope of the framework, that is, the number and types of policy stages the framework embraces. Before the scope of each of the frameworks is examined, however, the basis for defining *scope,* the policy stages, needs to be addressed. As deLeon (Chapter 2 in this book) points out, the concept *policy stages* has had a profound effect on the policy studies field, guiding research and identifying neglected aspects of policymaking processes. Its effect has been substantial because it presents a useful categorization of behavior and action within entire policy processes. The policy stages caution scholars that policy processes are much more complex and rich than simply policy adoption or policy implementation. The stages, however, do not constitute a framework. They fail to constitute a framework because the fundamental essence of a framework—general classes of variables, or "universal elements," and general relationships among them—has not been developed for any of the stages. What, then, are the policy stages? Even deLeon has trouble with this, referring to the policy stages variously as a system, a model, and a heuristic—and that in just a single paragraph. Perhaps the policy stages are best thought of as a typology that completely describes policy decisions and actions that occur around a policy.[6]

The IAD framework easily encompasses each of the stages, in part because of its explicit attention to levels of action. Some of the stages occur at a single level of action; other stages occur at multiple levels of action. Each of the policy stages could be captured in a series of interactive action situations, capturing the different choice levels at which actions and decisions occur. These policy-stages action situations could in turn be linked together. The collective-action situation of the policy adoption stage could feed into the collective-action situation of the policy implementation stage, as a public agency engages in rule making in order to carry out its legislative mandate. This action situation could in turn be linked to the operational-level action situation of the implementation stage, as the public agency applies and implements the rules. Feedback loops could exist between the implementation operational-action situation, and the implementation collective-choice situation, and between the implementation operational-action situation and the policy adoption collective-action situation. Both the legislature and the agency could act to change the operational-level rules if the outcomes produced were undesirable. When the policy stages are represented within the IAD framework, the configural, recursive nature of the stages, as well as their multilevel, multiorganizational nature, becomes abundantly clear. It would certainly be too complex to represent the dozens of action situations that characterize the policy process of a single policy, and therefore, it is not advisable.

The remaining three frameworks cannot rival the IAD framework in scope. The policy innovations and the Hofferbert frameworks focus predominantly on a single stage: policy adoption or selection. The ACF focuses predominantly on initiation, estimation, and selection, the stages that occur primarily at the collective-choice level of action.

Frameworks set the stage for theory development. They establish general classes of variables and relationships among those variables, from which theories may be developed. The explicit frameworks found in this volume are varied, in their breadth of scope, their comprehensiveness, and the variables posited. Although the IAD framework is sufficiently general so that it can encompass numerous situations and settings, not just policymaking processes, the ACF is more particular to policymaking, and the policy innovations and Hofferbert frameworks are specific to policy adoptions. The theories developed from two of these frameworks, the theory of common-pool resources and the advocacy coalition theory, will be examined and contrasted with multiple-streams and punctuated-equilibrium theories in the next section. Models, but not theories, have been developed from the policy innovations and Hofferbert frameworks. A discussion of policy innovations models occurs in the models section. For an excellent comprehensive discussion and critique of comparative state policy models see Chapter 8 by Blomquist.

THEORIES

Theories place values on some of the variables identified as important in a framework, posit relationships among the variables, and make predictions about likely outcomes. For instance, the theory of common-pool resources makes a series of predictions about the ability of resource users to organize themselves and develop self-governing institutions, the robustness of self-governing institutions, the effects of resource user behavior on the sustainability of the resource, and so forth, depending on the values of the variables that define the institutional arrangements, the characteristics of the resource, and the characteristics of the resource users. These variables are derived from the IAD framework, with more specific values placed on them, reflecting the situation to be explained.

In this section, the following theories will be compared and contrasted: common-pool resources, advocacy coalitions, punctuated equilibrium, and multiple streams. The criteria are those set out by Blomquist (Chapter 8, this volume) in his examination of large-*N* comparative policy studies. Those criteria are (1) a model of the individual, (2) collective action, (3) institutions, (4) policy change, and (5) boundaries and scope of inquiry. These criteria represent essential elements of theories of the policymaking process and provide critical points of comparison for the four theories. Criteria 1 and 5, model of the individual and boundaries and scope of inquiry, are methodological and permit an examination of the extent to which the theoretical approaches explain the same phenomena from the same starting point, as well as an examination of the comprehensiveness of the theories (Schlager and Blomquist, 1996, p. 658). Criteria 2, 3, and 4 capture critical aspects of theories of policymaking processes. If theories of policymaking processes "explain how interested political actors interact within political institutions to produce, implement, evaluate, and revise public policies" (Schlager and Blomquist, 1996, p. 653), then the theories must pay careful attention to the collective action of actors, to the institutions that provide the context of that action, and to how policies change over time.

Model of the Individual

Each of the theories uses rationality models. Individuals are assumed to be goal-oriented. They act in ways that they believe make them better off. Furthermore, individuals are assumed to be boundedly rational in each of the theories. The contexts of policymaking drive the assumption of bounded rationality. Uncertainty, complexity, and weak selective pressure (Ostrom, Chapter 3, this volume) characterize those contexts. Or as Zahariadis (Chapter 4) explains:

> The problem under conditions of ambiguity is that we don't know what the problem is; its definition is vague and shifting. Distinguishing between relevant and irrelevant information is problematic and can lead to false and misleading facts. Choice becomes less an exercise in solving problems and more an attempt to make sense of a partially comprehensible world.

Substantial variation exists, however, among the rationality models. In the theory of common-pool resources, complex situations involving unstructured problems strongly affect assumptions concerning selection criteria, preferences, and information-processing capabilities. Individuals are not maximizers. Instead, they are satisficers: "Appropriators in many setting are strongly motivated to find better solutions to their problems if they can" (Ostrom, 1990, p. 34). Searching for better solutions, however, is constrained and guided by norms of behavior: "Norms of behavior therefore affect the way alternatives are perceived and weighed" (Ostrom, 1990, p. 35). Norms of reciprocity, for instance, limit opportunistic behavior. Individuals who are guided by reciprocity will generally not attempt to improve their welfare at the expense of others.

Furthermore, complex situations involving unstructured problems mean that "assuming complete preference functions of any shape is not meaningful" (Ostrom, 1990, p. 38). Thus, preferences may become more complete over time as individuals gain a better understanding of their situation over time. The extent to which individuals gain a better understanding of their situation over time is affected by their information-processing capabilities. Information-processing capabilities are limited by the context of the situation and the information that is available at any point in time. Within a common-pool resource setting, uncertainty, both about the structure and dynamics of a common-pool resource and about the actions of resource users in relation to the resource and to each other, may be quite high. Uncertainty can never be completely eliminated. Not only are certain processes, such as rainfall or disease, unpredictable, but the institutions within which resource users act provide different incentives and opportunities to learn. Thus, "the only reasonable assumption to make about the discovery and calculation processes employed is that appropriators engage in a considerable amount of trial-and-error learning" (Ostrom, 1990, p. 34).

Individuals within the theory of common-pool resources may use information strategically, and they may act opportunistically. However, for the most part, individuals are presumed to search out and gather information to better their understanding of the world and to reduce their mistakes: "Over time, however, they can acquire a greater understanding of their situation and adopt strategies that result in higher returns" (Ostrom, Chapter 3, this volume).

Individuals within the theory of common-pool resources are intendedly rational, but because of the complex situations and poorly defined problems that they confront, their preferences may be poorly structured, the information they possess may be incomplete, and thus, they will learn through experience. As Ostrom (1990, p. 193) pointed out, simply asserting "that individuals will select strategies whose expected benefits will exceed expected costs" does little to promote the predictive capabilities of the theory. That is, "such a prediction is vacuous" (Ostrom, 1990, p. 193). More needs to be known. The theory needs to be more completely specified. How should specificity be accomplished? Ostrom rejected empirically determining individuals' preferences and information-processing capabilities. Instead, she turned to carefully defining the characteristics and structure of the situation in which individuals interact: "This general conception of rational action places most of the explanatory weight on situational variables, rather than on assumptions made about the internal calculation process" (Ostrom, 1990, p. 193).[7]

The model of the individual found in the punctuated-equilibrium theory is similar to that found in the theory of common-pool resources. Preferences are relatively fixed and slow to change. Furthermore, explanation is grounded in characteristics of the decisionmaking process, and not in "internal calculation processes." Characteristics of the decision setting are critical because they frame the problem individuals confront. Individuals, because of their limited information-processing capabilities, do not attend to all characteristics of a situation. Instead, they attend to those that appear to be most salient, and they make their decisions on that basis. According to Jones (1994, p. 8), "preferences get activated by how individuals interpret context, and it is this combination of preferences and context that yields choice."

Individuals confronted with the same situation at two different times may make different decisions each time, not because their preferences changed, and not because they possess better information, but because they attend to different characteristics of the same situation each time. Thus, characteristics of the situation are critical for the individual in punctuated-equilibrium theory because the characteristics that the individual attends to determine her or his choice.

This "twist" on the model of the individual that is used in the theory of common-pool resources not only represents a progressive problem shift but makes possible a more complex use of information. Recall that the use of information in the theory of common-pool resources is relatively narrow and straightforward. Information may occasionally be used opportunistically to advance one's welfare at the expense of others, but more typically, information is used to update the individual's understanding of the world, and thereby to adopt strategies that make the individual better off. Thus, if an individual makes a different choice in an identical situation later in time, that choice is not the result of changing preferences or shifts in attention; it is most likely the result of an improved understanding of the situation.[8]

Information in punctuated-equilibrium theory may be used for these purposes—updating individuals' understanding of the world—but information can also be used so as to reframe a situation; that is, information can be used so as to change the characteristics of a situation that individuals are paying attention to and thereby to change the choices they make. Individuals' frames of reference can be manipulated through the use of information. As Jones (1994, p. 23) argued, "Information is viewed as inherently ambiguous, so that there is a very important role for leadership and policy entrepreneurship in the framing of issues. . . . The manipulation of information plays a key role in forcing governmental attention to problems."

The model of the individual found in the theory of advocacy coalitions is boundedly rational, just as in the previously discussed theories. However, the similarities end there. Instead of focusing on the structure of the situation to explain individual decisionmaking, the theory of advocacy coalitions empirically identifies the inner world of individuals and uses it to explain individual action. The parts of the inner world that are empirically verified are belief systems. Belief systems are a set of basic values, causal assumptions, and problem perceptions (Sabatier, 1988, p. 139). Belief systems, not characteristics of the situation, determine individual choices and actions. Acting on the basis of their beliefs, individuals form coalitions and press to have their beliefs realized in public policy.

Belief systems, as well as limited information-processing abilities, affect how individuals acquire, use, and incorporate information. Belief systems may act as information filters, with individuals resisting or rejecting information that challenges their core beliefs and readily incorporating information that is supportive. Furthermore, information may be used in a variety of ways, from persuading others of the correctness of an individual's position to maintaining solidarity among members of a coalition. Thus, just as in the punctuated-equilibrium theory, information can be used in a variety of ways in the policymaking process. But there is a critical difference between the two theories. In the advocacy coalition theory, an individual in a setting faced with a decision may make different choices at two different times because of policy learning. Belief systems and preferences change gradually over time as individuals are persuaded to accept others' arguments, or as they gather information through experience. Belief systems are subject to incremental change, and policy alternatives, which reflect belief systems, are subject to incremental change as well. In the punctuated-equilibrium theory, change in individual choice and consequently in policy can be rapid and radical.

The individual within the multiple-streams theory is firmly grounded in Simon's boundedly rational individual and the garbage can model of choice (Zahariadis, Chapter 4, this volume). Thus, although each model begins from a similar starting point, several of the models diverge to present interesting and useful twists on the boundedly rational model of the individual. Ostrom's boundedly rational individual is an "updater" in a complex world. The boundedly rational individual for True, Baumgartner, and Jones is a "selective attender." The individual for Sabatier and Jenkins-Smith is a "belief-er." For Zahariadis, as for Simon, the individual is a "satisficer."

Collective Action

Policy change occurs as a result of collective action. Because each theory is grounded in a model of the individual, how individuals come together, organize themselves, and promote policy change is important. The theories differ substantially in their explanations of collective action. The multiple-streams theory pays the least attention to collective action as a process of individuals coming together to achieve a shared end. Instead, the theory focuses on the critical roles played by certain individuals, or policy entrepreneurs, and the conditions that support broad-based collective action that leads to major policy change. As Kingdon (1994, pp. 220–221) stated, "One nice property of this picture of agenda change involving entrepreneurial activity is that it makes some sense of 'great man' theories of history. . . . Policy entrepreneurs do not control events, but they can anticipate them and bend events to their purposes to some degree." The conditions that support the emergence of broad-based collective action are those that support the coupling of events and that support the activities of policy entrepreneurs.

Like the multiple-streams theory, the punctuated-equilibrium theory pays attention to policy entrepreneurs. The actions and strategies of policymakers play a critical role in explaining policy change. Change, however, does not occur just through the actions of well-situated individuals. Change results as well from collective action, whether that action involves mass mobilizations, a collection of interest groups, or groups of policymakers. Instead of examining the emergence of groups and the coordinating mechanisms used to promote collective action, however, the punctuated-equilibrium theory examines the "residue" of collective action, such as changes in policy images and changes of venues. In other words, punctuated-equilibrium theory does not pay attention to how interests organize themselves. Rather, it pays attention to the consequences of such organization and activity.

The advocacy coalition theory pays close attention to collective-action issues. This attention is driven by the theory's definition of a coalition. Furthermore, coalitions are not assumed to exist; rather, their existence must be empirically verified through the identification of a coalition's belief system, and through a demonstration of coordinated action among the coalition's members. The initial version of the theory did not attend to collective-action processes and instead assumed that individuals who held shared beliefs would act collectively to realize those beliefs. Only more recently have the theory's creators incorporated concepts and hypotheses designed to capture the emergence and continuation of collective action. Substantial refinements remain to be made.[9]

First, appropriate empirical measures of action need to be developed and tested. The two survey measures used thus far—having respondents identify those they discuss policy issues with and those they regard as their allies and/or opponents on policy issues—do not clearly address action. They are just as likely to measure political awareness on the part of respondents. A respondent who identifies discussion partners and allies and opponents demonstrates that he or she is politically aware and perhaps active in some way, that is, in talking policy and taking policy positions.[10] More appropriate survey measures of action would identify specific actions(e.g., letter writing, testifying, lobbying, holding strategy sessions), the extent to which those actions are coordinated with others, and who those others are.[11]

The collective-action issue within the advocacy coalition theory needs to be resolved because the theory makes strong claims that imply that coalitions engage in a high degree of coordinated behavior. Yet the evidence of this coordinated behavior presented by Sabatier and Jenkins-Smith can be accounted for by competing explanations. For instance, Sabatier and Jenkins-Smith (Chapter 6, this volume) state that "the ACF assumes that coalitions will seek to utilize their resources in the most efficient manner possible." This statement implies a very high degree of coordinated behavior. Sabatier and Jenkins-Smith go on to claim that "the bottom-line conclusion is that coalitions should (and do) spend an enormous amount of time 'venue shopping'"—again, a strong claim about highly structured coordinated behavior.

The evidence that Sabatier and Jenkins-Smith presented, however, supports two competing explanations. They listed fifteen strategies that members of the environmental coalition have pursued since 1984 in response to the decline of the San Francisco Bay/Delta fisheries. Sabatier and Jenkins-Smith state (Chapter 6) that they believe that "this is probably typical of the number of strategies involving multiple venues that most coalitions pursue." However, these strategies do not speak to the underlying collective-action processes that occurred. The strategies could be the result of members of a coalition's regularly meeting and engaging in joint decisionmaking about which strategies to pursue and when, and about who will bear the costs and benefits of such action. The strategies could also be the result of a very loosely linked set of organizations that occasionally have an interest in Bay/Delta fisheries, depending on the issue. Some organizations may be more interested in water quality issues and thus may become active when they see an opportunity to realize stricter requirements. Other organizations may be more interested in protecting wildlife and may thus become active around the endangered-species laws. These organizations need not have engaged in any joint action to realize the outcomes that Sabatier and Jenkins-Smith have listed. These outcomes may be the result of the activity of a series of organizations, generally interested in the same area, that are periodically active; from the results, it may appear that they are a long-term coalition. The problem of collective action needs to be resolved, given the critical role it plays in the advocacy coalition theory.

The centerpiece of the theory of common-pool resources is an explanation of collective action that challenges those found in three different but dominant models: the tragedy of the commons, the prisoner's dilemma, and the logic of collective action (Ostrom, 1990). These three models make strong assumptions about the inability of individuals to cooperate to achieve outcomes superior to those achieved by individuals acting alone. The theory of common-pool resources challenges such strong assumptions. However, it does not presume that individuals will act in concert, particularly if they share a common set of beliefs. Instead, it posits a set of conditions and relations among those conditions that supports collective action and inhibits free-riding behavior. For instance, according to Ostrom (1990, p. 211), appropriators of a common-pool resource are much more likely to cooperate to address a shared dilemma if they (1) "share a common judgment that they will be harmed if they do not adopt an alternative rule"; (2) "will be affected in similar ways by the proposed rule changes"; (3) "have low discount rates"; (4) "face relatively low information, transformation, and enforcement costs"; and (5) "share generalized norms of reciprocity and trust"; and if (6) their numbers are relatively small and stable. Finally, the theory of common-pool resources does not place as much weight on political entrepreneurs as the spark for collective action. Although entrepreneurs easily fit within the theory, greater attention is given to other factors, factors that most likely support the emergence of entrepreneurship as well as collective action. Thus, instead of assuming that individuals rarely cooperate, or that individuals typically cooperate, or that collective action depends on the actions of an entrepreneur, the theory of common-pool resources focuses on the characteristics of the physical world, the community, and the rules-in-use to explain collective action.

Institutions

Not only do the theories provide different treatments of collective action, but they also provide different treatments of the context within which individuals act: the institutional setting. The multiple-streams theory pays the least attention to institutional arrangements and is more firmly grounded in the behavioral tradition of political science.[12] The focus remains on individual behavior and the behavioral factors that affect individual choice, and little attention is paid to the institutional context of decisionmaking. This focus is most clear in relation to the political stream. The political stream is the most amenable to and the most likely to encompass institutional arrangements as part of the explanation. This stream consists, however, of "the national mood, pressure-group campaigns, and administrative or legislative turnover" (Zahariadis, Chapter 4, this volume).[13] Even the refinement of Zahariadis, combining the three variables into one ideology of governing parties, does not capture institutional arrangements, although the refinement was prompted by his extension of multiple-streams theory to encompass more than just the governments of the United States.

Also, the focus on policy entrepreneurs very indirectly brings in institutional arrangements. The institutional positions of entrepreneurs affect their ability to successfully couple the streams: "Higher administrative or partisan rank increases access and potential influence over decision makers" (Zahariadis, Chapter 4, this volume). And institutional position affects an entrepreneur's access to and choice of strategies for joining streams.

Paying attention to institutional arrangements would provide greater structure and consistency to the multiple-streams theory. Zahariadis (1997:21–22) states that the structure of policy communities within the proposal stream affects the trajectory of policies, that is, whether they are rapidly developed and swiftly moved to prominence. Teasing out the institutional structure of policy communities, something that the advocacy coalition theory is beginning to do, would allow a consistent comparison across policy communities and would permit an examination of the influence of the policy alternatives offered by the different communities.

Incorporating institutional structure within the politics stream would allow the theory to capture critical traits of specific governing structures and would further the work of Zahariadis in generalizing the theory across different governing systems. As the advocacy coalition, common-pool resources, and punctuated-equilibrium theories demonstrate, different venues (i.e., different institutional arrangements) even within a single governing system powerfully affect the policy decisionmaking process. Clarifying the institutional structures of different venues would allow the multiple-streams theory to better identify what are the varying processes of the politics stream and how different processes affect the coupling of the streams. Finally, defining the institutional structure within which streams are coupled and through which major policy changes occur would permit consistent and controlled comparisons across a range of policies. The multiple-streams theory, as it currently stands, only implicitly takes account of institutional arrangements, and such arrangements play only a very minor role in explaining major policy change.

Institutional arrangements play a significant role in major policy change within the punctuated-equilibrium theory. Institutional arrangements appear at a number of different junctures. First, the structure of governing systems sets the general context that affects political decisionmaking. The U.S. political system of "separated institutions, overlapping jurisdictions, and relatively open access to mobilizations" supports policy stasis (True, Jones, and Baumgartner, Chapter 5, this volume). Policy challengers must overcome a number of veto points in order to realize the adoption of their preferred policies. On the other hand, "once a mobilization is underway the diffuse jurisdictional boundaries that separate the various overlapping institutions of government can allow many governmental actors to become involved in a new policy area"(True et al., Chapter 5, this volume). Thus, much of the time, policy activity occurs within policy subsystems that allow for adjustment, but not major policy change. When policy subsystem processing breaks down, policy problems are addressed by macropolitical institutions: Congress and the president. It is in these institutions that major changes tend to occur.

Second, within a governing system, there are often multiple venues that control or have the potential to engage in decisionmaking around a policy issue. One means of controlling a policy is to control the venue that oversees the policy. Conversely, a critical strategy for instigating policy change is to try to change venues, or to have participants from other venues become involved in the policy issue. As Baumgartner and Jones (1991, p. 1047) stated: "Each venue carries with it a decisional bias, because both participants and decision-making routines differ. When the venue of a public policy changes, as often occurs over time, those who previously dominated the policy process may find themselves in the minority, and erstwhile losers may be transformed into winners."

Institutions not only establish the general framework within which decisions are made but also play a critical role in defining the strategies of individuals and groups as those political actors search for receptive decisionmakers and decision-making venues.

Even though institutions play a central role in the punctuated-equilibrium theory, they are conceptualized at a relatively gross level. Further refinement and development of the institutional arrangements hold the potential of sorting out the dynamics between microlevel processes and macrolevel outcomes and suggest additional avenues of research. For instance, Baumgartner and Jones (1991) argued that in a system of positive feedback, relatively small events can produce relatively large, systemwide changes. Being able to pinpoint those events, especially institutional changes, would substantially enhance the explanatory power of the theory. One approach would be to identify the configuration of rules, using the IAD framework, in place in the venue controlling the policy, and to explore whether and which rules changed, and how those rule changes precipitated, or participated in, the cascade of changes. The IAD framework could also be useful in the development of careful cross-policy comparisons, and in a search for general patterns in major policy changes. Do particular rules, or particular venues, appear to be pivotal in punctuated policy changes? How are venues interconnected? Furthermore, the IAD framework could be used to incorporate a more federal flavor into the punctuated-equilibrium theory. Although federalism is a part of the theory (some policy areas examined include state activity), the role that state venues play in inhibiting or promoting major policy change could be further spelled out. An examination of punctuated change prior to the New Deal, when federalism was, more or less, still firmly in place, versus punctuated change after the New Deal may shed significant light on the relations between policy change and federalism.

Much as in punctuated-equilibrium theory, institutional arrangements play a significant role in explaining changes in beliefs and policy in the advocacy coalition theory. Institutional arrangements clearly appear in the framework, both as system-level variables, such as constitutional structure, and as policy subsystem variables, in which subsystems encompass several levels of government. Institutional variables appear as part of the theory. They appear as part of the strategy set of coalitions, as coalitions decide which policymaking venues would be most sympathetic to their goals. Implicitly, institutional arrangements appear in Hypotheses 9 and 10 in Chapter 6, by Sabatier and Jenkins-Smith, in terms of the structure and characteristics of policy forums and the institutional structure and setting of public agencies.

Much as in the punctuated-equilibrium theory, institutions appear at a relatively gross level. The roles and structures of institutional arrangements need to be more carefully spelled out, both to clarify parts of the theory, and to boost its explanatory power. One particularly critical area that needs clarification is the relationships between the structure and content of a public policy and the structure and content of belief systems. It constitutes a major premise of the theory: "Public policies/programs incorporate implicit theories about how to achieve their objectives and thus can be conceptualized in much the same way as belief systems" (Sabatier and Jenkins-Smith, Chapter 6, this volume).[14] Furthermore, this premise is used to justify the dominant focus on belief systems and policy learning. As Sabatier and Jenkins-Smith (Chapter 6) argue, "This ability to map beliefs and policies on the same 'canvas' provides a vehicle for assessing the influence of various actors over time, particularly the role of technical information in policy change."

This premise, however, poses an interesting empirical question, once careful attention is paid to institutions. The relationship between policies and belief systems is mediated by institutions. How close the relationship is between policy and belief systems of dominant coalitions depends on the institutional structure that defines and constrains collective decisionmaking. For instance, in the United States, federalism and separation of powers create many openings for decision-making, making it unlikely that a dominant coalition can push through its policy relatively unscathed (Moe, 1990). Most major U.S. policies reflect multiple and conflicting belief systems, which may be combined in unusual ways, so that it is difficult to map policies and beliefs onto the same canvas in order to assess the influence of various actors at different times.[15]

The task becomes even more complex when one attempts to identify a dominant coalition, and/or to trace specific policy changes to specific actors. Sabatier and Jenkins-Smith have never defined the concept *dominant coalition* or provided a basis for such a definition. At the very least, a definition of *dominant coalition* must include the institutional positions of members of coalitions and the institutional resources individuals can bring to bear on behalf of coalitions. Institutional position and resources can give a coalition substantial influence beyond its numbers. If we are to adequately explore the connections between coalitions, belief systems, and policy, the institutional setting and the institutional resources that coalition members control must be more carefully specified by the advocacy coalition framework and theory.

Institutional arrangements critically affect individuals' choices of strategies and venues in at least two ways. First, the institutional context within which coalitions decide their strategies and choose venues in which to pursue their policies affects their actions. A policy subsystem dominated by an independent commission versus an executive agency headed by a political appointee presents many fewer political points of access through which to influence the agency and therefore affects a coalition's choice of strategies. In addition, institutional structure affects the ease by which coalitions may move among different levels of action in pursuit of policy change. From the rules governing the placement of initiatives on the ballot, to the rules governing how public agencies conduct public hearings, to the rules governing the standing required to bring a lawsuit, institutional arrangements affect the attractiveness of various strategies. Second, the institutional positions of members of a coalition affect the choices of strategies and venues and the collective-action capabilities of coalitions. Although Sabatier and Jenkins-Smith (Chapter 6, this volume) are correct in asserting that the advocacy coalition theory does not simply reduce individuals to their institutional positions, as greater attention is given to developing the parts of the theory devoted to action as opposed to beliefs, institutional arrangements will become increasingly important.

The theory of common-pool resources, more than any of the other theories, lavishes attention on institutional arrangements. Ostrom (Chapter 3, this volume) defines institutions as "the shared concepts used by humans in repetitive situations organized by rules, norms, and strategies." Institutions play two critical roles in the theory of common-pool resources. First, institutions provide the structure within which individuals interact and the incentives that individuals have in making choices about actions. Second, when individuals attempt to achieve better outcomes, they turn to collective-choice and/or constitutional-choice institutions to change operational-level institutions. In other words, individuals use institutions to attempt to change the rules of the game in order to achieve improved outcomes. The theory of common-pool resources rests the weight of explanation primarily on institutions.

Institutions are treated at a microlevel within the theory of common-pool resources. Individual rules, classified by means of the IAD framework, are painstakingly identified, for it is through the configuration of rules, characteristics of the physical system, and culture that explanations are developed and predictions are derived. As Ostrom (Chapter 3) demonstrates, this approach has been remarkably productive and successful in explaining the emergence and maintenance of self-governing institutions for the management of common-pool resources.

A microlevel approach to institutions does, however, make the theory of common-pool resources unusually complex. First, in any given action situation, except for the simplest, hundreds of rules are in operation and can potentially be called upon by the participants. Certainly the participants, let alone the analyst, cannot attend to all of the rules all at once. However, although the participants may have an idea of the rules that they attend to at any given time, and of the rules they may call upon if circumstances change, the outside analyst does not. Thus, the analyst is left with little guidance, trying to identify and interpret rules.

Second, the difficult position of the analyst is further compounded by the configural nature of rules. As Ostrom (Chapter 3, this volume) points out, "The impact on incentives and behavior of one type of rule is not independent of the configuration of other rules. . . . One needs to know the value of other variables rather than simply asserting that they are held constant." For an analyst to make sense of a situation, she or he not only must identify the numerous rules that structure an action situation but must also come to understand the configural relationships among those rules, particularly if she or he intends to make meaningful policy recommendations.

Unfortunately the IAD framework, from which all of this complexity emerges, and the theory of common-pool resources fail to provide any guideposts to direct the analyst to particular rules and not others. That is, there are no metarules for guiding the analyst through this complexity. Good judgment and perseverance are the analyst's best friends.

Policy Change

Frameworks, theories, and models of the policy process, by definition, must account for policy change. Each of the theories comes to grips with policy change slightly differently, and together they raise some difficult questions regarding how to measure change.[1617] Three of the theories—multiple streams, punctuated equilibrium and advocacy coalitions—share a focus on major policy change. The theory of common-pool resources treats institutional change incrementally.

The theories that attend to major policy change point to similar types of events and factors that set the stage for major policy change. These factors include dramatic events or crises, changes in governing coalitions, and administrative and legislative turnover. "Macro-political forces intervene" (True et al., Chapter 5, this volume) to push an issue onto a government agenda. Once it is on an agenda, whether an issue catches fire depends. In the advocacy-coalition and the punctuated-equilibrium theories, it depends on what has occurred around the issue over a long period of time. Although major change may appear to occur overnight, it is preceded by a series of events, activities, and occurrences that may extend to several decades. Appearance on a government agenda is the outcome of a longer process of change, as policy images change and belief systems coalesce.

Even if this buildup has occurred, it does not guarantee major change. A large part of the explanation rests, at least for now, on serendipity. In the multiple-streams theory, serendipity revolves around the ability of political entrepreneurs to identify windows of opportunity that would permit them to successfully couple the streams. The advocacy coalition theory makes a similar argument. Proponents of policy change must recognize and exploit opportunities for change. In the punctuated-equilibrium theory, opportunities for change depend on a policy system's experiencing positive feedback: "Like earthquakes and avalanches, these policy punctuations can be precipitated by a mighty blow or by relatively minor events" (True et al., Chapter 5, this volume). Is it possible to predict which blow or minor event will promote rapid change? Not according to True et al., "Punctuated equilibrium, as a theory, can lead us to expect that these punctuations will happen and that the magnitude of change will be related to its frequency of occurrence, but it will not help us to make specific predictions for particular policy issues."

A related issue is how to determine whether a policy change is major or minor. Multiple-streams and punctuated-equilibrium theories do not address this issue explicitly (at least in the chapters in this volume). The answer given by the advocacy coalition theory appears simple: "Major change is change in the policy core aspects of a governmental program, whereas minor change is change in the secondary aspects" (Sabatier and Jenkins-Smith, Chapter 6, this volume). This is an unsatisfactory answer because it is difficult to test empirically, and because it calls into question the definition of belief systems and policy subsystems. First, as discussed earlier, given the push and pull of politics, many policies do not easily reflect the belief systems of the dominant coalition. A major policy most likely consists of an uncomfortable mix of policy cores and secondary aspects. Because policies are not so neatly structured around a single policy core and secondary aspects, determining what constitutes change in the core may be difficult. Second, Sabatier and Jenkins-Smith make a troubling statement that potentially undermines the advocacy coalition theory: "The same change may be 'minor' for one subsystem and 'major' for a subsystem nested within it." This statement implies that the definition of a subsystem is rather loose. Changes in policy cores are a matter of perspective. If a policy change occurs and in a subsystem it appears minor, then the secondary aspects must have changed. But if that same policy change appears major from the perspective of a subsystem nested within the subsystem, then the policy core of the subsubsystem must have changed. Just what, then, is a subsystem, and what is a subsubsystem? Are there different definitions for each? Furthermore, the statement challenges the structure of belief systems. Apparently, the secondary aspects of the belief system of a subsystem make up the policy core of the belief system of a subsubsystem nested within the subsystem. But don't all belief systems possess the same structure? If that is the case, then how can the secondary aspects of one belief system constitute the policy core of another belief system? Are belief systems nested within belief systems? If all of this seems hopelessly confusing, that is because it is. The advocacy coalition theory has not, contrary to the claims of its creators, provided a relatively clear-cut distinction between major and minor policy change. Rather, in attempting to provide a relatively clear-cut distinction, it has called into question critical aspects of the theory: subsystems and belief systems.

The theory of common-pool resources mostly treats policy change, or institutional change, as an incremental process. The supply of institutions is an iterative process. Appropriators invest in and build on small changes. Ostrom (1990) argued that even though the action situation may change substantially over a period of time, substantial change is likely to be the cumulation of a number of incremental steps.

Boundaries and Scope of Inquiry

What do the theories seek to explain, and what do they hold constant? And how sweeping are their explanations? Do they seek to explain a single stage of the policymaking process, or multiple stages? Given the complexity of the theories, the first question is difficult to answer. Each of the theories seeks to explain many things; that is, each has multiple dependent variables, and depending on the dependent variable, different things are held constant.

The primary dependent variables of the multiple-streams theory are agenda setting and the specification of policy alternatives (Zahariadis, Chapter 4, this volume). These dependent variables also delimit the scope of the inquiry. Thus, the multiple-streams theory addresses and attempts to explain the predecision processes of the larger policymaking process. Numerous exogenous variables are relied on to explain the dependent variables. These variables are used to build an explanation of the dependent variables; however, they are not themselves subject to explanation. In explaining agenda setting and why a particular problem is on a government agenda, the weight of explanation rests on the three streams of problems, policies, and politics. The structure and content of the three streams are taken as given, and the analyst uses them to account for how issues arise on an agenda.

On the other hand, the specification of policy alternatives requires the analyst to explain the policy stream. The policy stream becomes a dependent variable, which can no longer be taken as a given but must be explained. Why do we see the types of policies, or ideas, that we do in the policy stream? According to Kingdon (1994), analysts are better off answering that question by focusing not on where policies come from, but on the environment in which they emerge and survive.

The punctuated-equilibrium theory focuses on the same part of the policy-making process as does the multiple-streams theory: the predecision activities. The punctuated-equilibrium theory explains agenda setting by focusing on the interaction between ideas and actions of citizens and public officials, as attention and institutions mediate these things. The dependent variable of agenda setting is explained by the independent variables: interest group activity, mass mobilizations, media images, and so forth.

The advocacy coalition theory is modestly more expansive than either the multiple-streams or the punctuated-equilibrium theories. It focuses not only on predecision activities, but on the decision itself. The dependent variable, policy decisions emerging from a subsystem, is explained by advocacy coalition activity and exogenous events. The use of the advocacy coalition theory to explain policy decisions has occurred primarily through the careful development of case studies in which the existence and structure of advocacy coalitions are accepted, and the push and pull of politics, as well as the occurrence of systemwide events, are used to explain the decision. The creators of the theory of advocacy coalitions have typically not engaged in such case study development. Rather, they have been patiently and painstakingly examining the structure and development of belief systems and the emergence of advocacy coalitions. Sabatier and Jenkins-Smith have taken belief systems and advocacy coalitions as dependent variables, as things to be explained, and have used public positions of policy actors, measures of coordination, policy actor types, and policy venues as the independent variables.

The theory of common-pool resources encompasses all of the stages of the policymaking process, from the supply of policy (i.e., the predecision and decision processes), to the implementation and evaluation of policy. The theory's ability to be so encompassing emerges from its firm grounding in the IAD framework. The theory can explain a specific action situation in which a given set of rules, or policies, is implemented and evaluated. In this case, the dependent variables are the outcomes of the action situation, and the independent variables are the rules-in-use, the characteristics of the resource, community characteristics, and the resources and characteristics of individuals. The theory, however, can just as easily explain the origins of operational level, rules-in-use, or policies. In this case, what were independent variables, particularly operational-level rules, become dependent variables. The independent variables remain substantially the same, except for the rules, which are the collective and constitutional choice rules that structure operational-level rule-making activities.

The theories presented in this volume vary substantially in the content and scope of the explanations they provide. Although each focuses on the policymaking process, each emphasizes different characteristics and different actors. For instance, although the bulk of the work around the advocacy coalition theory centers on belief systems, the bulk of the work around the theory of common-pool resources centers on rules. Furthermore, most of the theories, with the exception of the common-pool resource theory, are relatively narrow in scope. They focus primarily on predecision and decision processes. Although their scope is rather narrow, each of them could be expanded to include more stages of the policymaking process. In fact, some of the most interesting extensions of the theories will occur as they are expanded to include implementation and evaluation processes.

MODELS

According to Ostrom (Chapter 3, this volume), "Models make precise assumptions about a limited set of parameters and variables." Analysts use models to fix variables at specific settings and to explore the outcomes produced. Models allow analysts to test specific parts of theories. In other words, there should be a one-too-many progression from frameworks, to theories, to models. A framework sets the foundation from which more than one theory may be developed, and from a theory, multiple models may be developed. Situating models within theories and theories within frameworks keeps analysts honest, supports the scientific enterprise, and encourages the cumulation of knowledge (Ostrom, Chapter 3). This ideal, however, is rarely met. As we have seen in this collection of papers, theory development may proceed independently of any attempt to consciously situate the theory within a particular framework. Occasionally, models may be developed from frameworks, with little theory development occurring in between. This is the case with the policy innovations framework. Through a careful reading of the critique of the policy innovations literature by Berry and Berry (Chapter 7, this volume) and their suggestions for improvement, one could reasonably conclude that for the most part, theory development has lagged far behind model development and testing.

One model that Berry and Berry examine and critique is the national interaction model. The model is structured around a limited set of variables: "The probability that a state will adopt a program is proportional to the number of interactions its officials have had with officials of already-adopting states." Berry and Berry are uncomfortable with some of the model's assumptions. The model does not differentiate among states. All states are equally likely to adopt a policy. If an analyst chooses not to make such an extreme assumption about states, then, as the Berrys point out, that analyst will have to engage in theory development. The analyst must "introduce a priori predictions about which states will never adopt (and for what reasons these states are 'immune')." The Berrys reach the same conclusion for regional diffusion models. More realistic assumptions about states' interactions need to be adopted—analysts must engage in theory development.

Berry and Berry make a powerful and convincing argument for developing a more complex model of policy innovation among the states, a model that includes both internal and external determinants of adoption. Their methodological and data collection claims are equally convincing. However, their answer to the question that will inevitably arise among researchers who follow their lead is less convincing. The question: What happens when the data are critically incomplete? Their answer: Use appropriate methods for the data. Certainly their answer is correct as far as it goes, but it should go further. In some sense, that answer suggests that data should drive the development of policy innovation models. However, as Berry and Berry suggest, the field of policy innovations suffers not just from methodological shortcomings, but from a failure of theory development. The problems encountered in the policy innovations literature cannot be solved through more sophisticated methodologies and richer, more complete data sets. Basic theory development and testing must occur.

In order to understand how problematic the failure of theory development is for the policy innovations literature, a discussion of models within the theory of common-pool resources is necessary. The theory of common-pool resources explains the ability of resource users to organize themselves and develop and sustain self-governing institutions, the robustness of self-governing institutions, and the effects of resource user behavior on the sustainability of resources, by exploring the relationships between characteristics of natural resources, cultures, and rules-in-use. From this theory, models have been derived and tested to determine whether the theory is sensible in its explanations. For instance, a model of a simple, open-access common-pool resource has been developed and extensively tested (Ostrom, Gardner, and Walker, 1994). The theory predicts that a common-pool resource in which there are no restrictions on entry or use will be overutilized and possibly destroyed. In fact, tests of the model support the theory's prediction. Under open-access conditions, rent from the common-pool resource is dissipated. However, the theory also predicts that communication will not affect outcomes. Allowing resource users to communicate does not change the payoffs that they obtain; therefore, communication neither supports not detracts from the incentives users face concerning the common-pool resource. When the model is changed to allow for communication among resource users, users typically determine the optimal level of harvesting from the resource, agree upon a set of rules that will guide their harvesting behavior, and capture, rather than dissipate, most of the rent from the resource. The outcomes produced by a model of an open-access common-pool resource that permits communication among resource users presents an anomaly in the theory. Ostrom and others have then returned to the theory to change it and further develop it. In the case of the theory of common-pool resources, theory supports model development, and models support theory development. Theory helps make sense of models and vice versa.

Policy innovations models do not have the benefit of interactions with theories. The give and take between theories and models cannot occur. The outcomes generated by the models, then, do not feed into a larger story. There is no structure within which cumulation of the outcomes of the models can occur. Given the extensive model development and testing that has taken place around policy innovations, however, theory development appears to be a reasonable next step.

CONCLUSION

The contributions that constitute this volume should dispel many of the misunderstandings that surround the field of public policy. First, these contributions demonstrate that multiple and rigorous methods are used to explain public policymaking processes. Case studies are simply one tool among many that are used to develop explanations. The best of the theories creatively combine qualitative and quantitative approaches in developing rich and powerful explanations. Second, these contributions demonstrate that careful and sound theory development is a central part of the enterprise of explaining policy processes. Explanations of policymaking processes are not ad hoc. Third, several active research programs are in existence through which cumulation of knowledge is occurring. Far from being a backwater that harbors more than its share of ne'er-do-well scholars and scholarly work, the field of policymaking is home to a number of top political scientists who have had a substantial impact on the discipline.

Finally, there are two contributions to this volume that have received little attention in this review: the pieces by Blomquist and deLeon. These contributions received little direct attention because they do not fit easily within the structure of this chapter. Neither chapter consists of a framework, theory, or model of the policymaking process. However, although they received little direct attention, both pieces permeate this chapter. I have drawn heavily on each to develop the criteria I have used in comparing frameworks, theories, and models. Both chapters consist of reasoned, thoughtful assessments and critiques of literatures that have strongly impacted and influenced the development of the field of policy studies and, in particular, policymaking processes. Both scholars have made their own critical contributions by pulling together such a wide range of work into such easily accessible chapters.

NOTES

1. The exception is the comparative state policy adoption literature, as presented by Berry and Berry, and critically examined by Blomquist. The comparative state policy adoption literature focuses on policy adoptions and their timing, and not on decision-making processes per se.

2. The punctuated-equilibrium theory and the multiple-streams theory are not explicitly derived from frameworks. That is certainly not a weakness, and the authors should not rush out and explicitly identify frameworks. That work has already been done for them. Each theory could easily fit within either the institutional analysis and development (IAD)framework, or the advocacy coalition framework (ACF).

3. Ostrom (Chapter 3, this volume) layed out "key questions" that would need to be answered in the assessment of a framework. These questions are evaluative and well beyond the scope of my competency to address for each framework presented in this volume; therefore, although they are valuable, I will not use them.

4. The ACF is a framework, even though its creators are backing away from calling it one (Chapter 6, this volume). A brief examination of Figure 6.1 in the ACF chapter confirms its framework status. The ACF posits a series of variables (with no values assigned to them) and relationships among them. The variables capture both system-level characteristics and external events, actors, institutional arrangements, policy outputs, and impacts. Don't be fooled by the claims of the authors that all they have done in their chapter is further develop the theory of advocacy coalitions; they have also further developed the framework of advocacy coalitions. For instance, "The subsystem is much more clearly defined" refers to the framework, not to the theory, as the authors claim. The necessary and sufficient criteria for the existence of a mature policy subsystem define a framework variable. The authors then go on to suggest interesting theoretical avenues that could be explored, now that they have better defined a framework variable, such as the emergence of new policy subsystems.

5. Although Hofferbert (1974) defined a series of stages that affect policy choices, these stages do not describe a decisionmaking process. Rather, the stages are a hierarchical ordering of related variables that influence the adoption of public policies.

6. Failure to further develop the policy stages typology into a full-blown framework, or series of frameworks, has been a source of both weakness and strength. Because scholars have had difficulty in knowing exactly how to treat the typology, it has been misused and abused: misused in the sense of being applied too literally (i.e., when the stages are treated as if they proceed in a linear fashion), and abused by being damned for not being a theory, or at lest sufficiently theory-like so that hypotheses can be derived from it. On the other hand, the policy stages typology has had a significant impact on the policy studies field because of its generality. Scholars from diverse theoretical approaches and disciplinary backgrounds can embrace it and work within its context. Perhaps because it has not been tied to a particular framework, the typology has promoted and sustained a myriad of research agendas, making the policy studies field that much more vibrant.

7. Ostrom (1990, p. 38) explained why she takes this stance: It accepts Popper's methodological advice to emphasize the way we describe the situations in which individuals find themselves so that we can use observable variables to reject our theories, rather than internal, in-the-mind, subjective variables, which are far more difficult to measure.

8. Or as Jones (1994, p. 23) stated in discussing rational choice models, "Information is viewed as neutral and costly, and hence subject to the laws of declining marginal returns."

9. See Zafonte and Sabatier (1997) for an attempt to further develop collective action within the theory. However, their definition of coordination is so broad that it encompasses all policy action, and their empirical measures of collective action are inadequate, as discussed in the following paragraphs.

10. Sabatier and Jenkins-Smith appear to have recognized the limitations of their measures of collective action without quite owning up to those limitations. They have suggested imagination as an explanation. They state (Chapter 6 in this book), "Although neither of Jenkins-Smith's surveys contains items dealing with coordinated behavior, it certainly doesn't require much imagination to see many national lab and UCS scientists as active members of opposing coalitions."

11. A rigorous test for the existence of a coalition, from the perspective of the advocacy coalition theory, would be to first identify a coalition just on the basis of regular interaction, and then to examine whether members share a set of beliefs.

12. The multiple-streams theory is not the only contribution in this volume that provides an explanation of policy adoption, without a consideration of institutional arrangements. As Blomquist argues, comparative state policy fails to account for political institutions. Such studies fail to recognize that states are both multiorganizational and part of a multigovernmental system. The political system is modeled as unitary, "a single, abstracted decisionmaker, an idealized executive, legislature, or court producing policies" (Chapter 8, this volume). In addition, multiorganizational systems and multiple decision-making entities strongly affect policy adoption, change, and termination, an effect that is not captured by the studies. Finally, institutionally defined roles are neglected that powerfully affect policy, such as gatekeeper, veto holder, and agenda setter. What this neglect generally means is that some sorts of very important policymaking are simply outside the purview of comparative state policy studies, such as sequential decisionmaking (e.g., a judge hands down a major decision, and a legislature reacts). "This sort of sequential interaction represents policy change occurring without changes in the values of socioeconomic or political system variables and is therefore outside the explanatory capacity of DSH models" (Blomquist, Chapter 8, this volume).

13. Kingdon's explanation of the proposal stream focuses not on where policies come from, but the environment in which they emerge and survive; however, little of that environment is ascribed to institutions. Kingdon focused on what make policies catch on in certain communities at certain times, paying attention to how policies evolve, and how they get combined and recombined (Kingdon, 1995).

14. Kingdon (1995) does claim that the theory contains substantial structure.

15. Note that in Chapter 6 of this book, Sabatier and Jenkins-Smith do not distinguish between public policies as adopted and public policies as implemented. The "implicit theories" within a policy are likely to vary depending on the stage at which the policy is examined.

16. A different governing system may support greater congruence between belief systems and policies. For instance, the belief systems of Britain's ruling party and its supporters are more likely to be clearly expressed in the policies adopted. "

17. Blomquist (Chapter 8, this volume) argues that comparative state policy studies cannot account for policy change over time because of a "data selection bias in favor of initial policy adoptions and away from policy modification or abandonment."

REFERENCES

Baumgartner, Frank, and Bryan Jones. 1991. "Agenda Dynamics and Policy Subsystems," *Journal of Politics* 53:1044–1074.
Hofferbert, Richard. 1974. *The Study of Public Policy.* Indianapolis, Ind.: Bobbs-Merrill.
Jones, Bryan. 1994. *Reconceiving Decision-Making in Democratic Politics: Attention, Choice, and Public Policy.* Chicago: University of Chicago Press.
Kingdon, John. 1994. "Agendas, Ideas, and Policy Change." In Lawrence Dodd and Calvin Jillson, eds., *New Perspectives on American Politics*, pp. 215–229. Washington, D.C.: Congressional Quarterly Press.
Mazmanian, Daniel, and Paul Sabatier. 1984. "A Multivariate Model of Public Policy-Making," *American Journal of Political Science* 24(3):439–468.
Moe, Terry. 1990. "Political Institutions: The Neglected Side of the Story," *Journal of Law, Economics, and Organization* 6:213–253.
Ostrom, Elinor. 1990. *Governing the Commons.* Cambridge, England: Cambridge University Press.
Ostrom, Elinor, Roy Gardner, and James Walker. 1994. *Rules, Games and Common-Pool Resources.* Ann Arbor: University of Michigan Press.
Sabatier, Paul. 1988. "An Advocacy Coalition Framework of Policy Change and the Role of Policy-Oriented Learning Therein," *Policy Sciences* 21:129–168.
Schlager, Edella, and William Blomquist. 1996. "A Comparison of Three Emerging Theories of the Policy Process," *Political Research Quarterly* 49(3):651–672.
Zahariadis, Nikolaos. 1997. "Ambiguity, Time, and Multiple Streams." In Paul Sabatier, ed., *Theories of the Policy Process.* Boulder: Westview Press.

10

Fostering the Development of Policy Theory

PAUL A. SABATIER

The first chapter of this book argued that in a field as complex as public policy, simplifying theories are an absolute necessity. Furthermore, those "lenses" through which the world is viewed should be explicit rather than implicit. Each of the next chapters presented one such theory: (1) the stages heuristic, (2) the IAD variant of institutional rational choice, (3) the multiple-streams framework, (4) the punctuated-equilibrium framework, (5) the advocacy coalition framework, (6) the policy diffusion framework, and (7) a related set of frameworks used in large-N comparative studies. In Chapter 9, Edella Schlager compared and evaluated the frameworks using a variety of criteria.

In this chapter, I would first like to briefly review the current status of policy theory and then suggest several guidelines for improving it. In my view, most of the frameworks discussed in this book are relatively promising general frameworks, but they need to be developed into more logically coherent and "denser" theoretical frameworks and, eventually, into fully developed theories. The basic strategy in this chapter is to use the two frameworks that have developed the most since the mid–1980s—IAD and ACF—in an effort to discern fruitful guidelines for theoretical development.

THEORIES, FRAMEWORKS, AND MODELS

A theory is a logically related set of propositions that seeks to explain a fairly general set of phenomena. The criteria by which a scientific theory should be judged

---

A previous version of this paper was published in *Policy Currents* 7(December):1–10.

are reasonably clear (Lave and March, 1975, pp. 59–73; King, Keohane, and Verba, 1994, pp. 99–113):

1. It should be logically coherent. The major terms should be clearly defined and the major relationships should be logically consistent. Without coherence, falsifiability is problematic and the implications of a set of propositions are unclear.
2. It should have clear causal drivers and a sense of causal process. Scientific theories are causal theories that seek to explain how certain patterns of phenomena have come about. They should identify the critical causal drivers—what is assumed to be fundamentally moving events within the system—and then the processes or mechanisms by which those drivers affect other variables. One of the fundamental shortcomings of many frameworks in policy studies—including Lowi's arenas of power and the stages heuristics of Jones (1970)—is that they fail to specify causal drivers and processes.
3. Some of the major propositions should be empirically falsifiable. Falsifiability is what distinguishes science from other fields of human knowledge. To the extent that those propositions are logically related to others, the validity of untested aspects of the theory can also be assessed.
4. The intended scope of the theory should be clear and relatively broad, although it can clearly change over time.
5. The theory should be "fertile"; that is, it should (1) give rise to nonobvious implications, preferably beyond its original scope, and (2) produce a relatively large number of interesting predictions per assumption.

Note that the third and fifth—and even the fourth—criteria are heavily dependent upon the first. To the extent that Propositions 1, 2, and 3 are logically related, invalidating Proposition 1 has serious implications for Propositions 2 and 3. In addition, a logically coherent set of propositions is much more likely to give rise to nonobvious implications.[1] And in the process, the scope of the theory is likely to be expanded or contracted. I stress logical coherence as a critical aspect of scientific theories because it is a point that some authors (e.g., Hill, 1997) miss completely.

Both the introductory chapter of this volume and Edella Schlager's chapter rely upon the distinctions made by Elinor Ostrom among frameworks, theories, and models. A conceptual framework identifies a set of variables and relationships that should be examined in order to explain a set of phenomena. A framework can provide anything from a skeletal set of variables (or variable sets) to something as extensive as a paradigm. It need not specify the direction of relationships or identify critical hypotheses, although it may do so. A theory provides a denser and more logically coherent set of relationships, including direction and hypotheses, that self-consciously seek to explain a set of phenomena. It applies values to some of the variables and usually specifies how relationships may vary, depending upon the values of critical variables. Numerous theories may be consistent with a general conceptual framework. A model is a representation of a specific situation. It is usually much narrower in scope than the relevant conceptual framework and theory, and it should contain quite specific assumptions about the values of critical variables and the nature of specific relationships. Ideally, it is mathematical. In my view, frameworks, theories, and models can be conceptualized as operating along a continuum of increasing logical interconnectedness and specificity of values and relationships, but decreasing scope.[2]

For example, the principal-agent literature in political science can be seen as a rather minimal conceptual framework identifying the relationships between principals and agents in institutional settings as its scope. There are also a number of models of the effects of specific interventions by principals on the behavior of specific sets of agents (e.g., Wood and Waterman, 1991, 1994; Jenkins-Smith et al., 1991). But despite the early efforts of Moe (1984), there is nothing yet resembling a theory—at least in political science. Such a theory would have to identify the goal structure, the information assumptions, and the other resources available to both principals and agents, as well as to identify the relevant institutional and other contextual variables, and to provide hypotheses about what strategies by principals are likely to be effective, null, and counterproductive.[3]

Most theoretical constructions in policy studies would qualify as frameworks. There are also numerous models. This chapter seeks to identify a set of guidelines for turning minimal frameworks into more extensive ones and eventually into theories.

PRESENT STATUS OF POLICY THEORY

With respect to the present status of positive theories of the policy process, I agree with Schlager's (1997, p. 14) contention that the field is not a wasteland but characterized by "mountain islands of theoretical structure, intermingled with, and occasionally attached together by foothills of shared methods and concepts, and empirical work, all of which is surrounded by oceans of descriptive work not attached to any mountain of theory."

The most impressive mountain is, of course, institutional rational choice or "actor-centered institutionalism" (Shepsle, 1989; Scharpf, 1997). The critical arguments are that (1) humans are intendedly rational, (2) their behavior is strongly influenced by institutional rules, and (3) they seek to influence institutional rules in order to alter others' behavior. Adherents include Chubb and Moe (1990) and Schneider et al. (1997) on school choice, Kagan (1978) and Scholz (1984) on regulatory compliance, Scharpf (1997) on European macroeconomic policy, Shepsle and Weingast (1987) and McCubbins and Sullivan (1987) on Congressional policymaking, and a host of scholars on administrative decisionmaking (Bendor, Taylor, and Van Gaalen, 1987; Knott and Miller, 1987; Miller, 1992). At a minimum, these authors share a conceptual framework. In most cases, they have been developing theories of behavior in different institutional settings and several models within each of those theories and have been testing them over a number of years.

Within the institutional rational-choice tradition, probably the most impressive body of work relevant to policy studies is that of Elinor Ostrom and her colleagues (see Chapter 3 in this volume for a summary). Her institutional analysis and development (IAD) framework is probably as close to a "covering theory" as we have in the social sciences. Her theory applying the IAD framework to the management of common property resources (Ostrom, 1990; Ostrom, Schroeder, and Wynne, 1993; Ostrom, Gardner, and Walker, 1994; Crawford and Ostrom, 1995) is clearly one of the most important theoretical developments in political science since the early 1980s. It has attracted a half million dollars in funding annually from the National Science Foundation (NSF) and other agencies, resulting in an impressive series of empirical tests in both field and laboratory settings.

I also agree with Schlager (1997) that the advocacy coalition framework (ACF) developed by Hank Jenkins-Smith and myself—and critically applied in at least thirty-four settings by different scholars—is a viable and coherent research program. In fact, I would contend the ACF has evolved from a fairly complex theoretical framework in 1988 to a much denser and more logically coherent framework and/or theory, in which several of the major holes are in the process of being filled (see Chapter 6 in this volume).

Both of these research programs would fit Lakatos's (1978) characterization of "progressive"; that is, they are being used by a variety of scholars and seem to be developing increasing coherence and scope. Therefore, they should provide clues about how to move from relatively simple frameworks to much more developed frameworks and theories.

THE ORIGINS AND DEVELOPMENT OF THEORIES

The development (or elaboration) of a theory needs to be distinguished from its verification. The first deals with the generation of a set of logically interrelated set of propositions—whatever the source—whereas the second deals with the empirical testing of the validity of some of those propositions. This discussion is concerned primarily with theory development, although one of the critical arguments is that development and verification should, of course, be linked.

Scenarios of Theory Development

Traditionally, scholars have distinguished two processes of theory development: inductive and deductive (see, for example, Reynolds, 1971). Both of these pure types strike me as being of limited value.

According to the inductive conception of theory development, theories arise out of the accumulation of "facts" from a variety of empirical studies; these facts are then synthesized into a set of coherent, more abstract propositions. The central problem with this conception is that it starts from a positivist view of perception that assumes we can observe facts unmediated by prior beliefs or presuppositions. This view has been subjected to some devastating critiques since the 1970s (Kuhn, 1970; Brown, 1977; Hawkesworth, 1992). At any rate, I shall assume that when seeking to understand any reasonably complex set of phenomena—and public policy processes are clearly complex—the observer must begin with a set of presuppositions concerning the entities worthy of notice, their characteristics that are worth remembering, and the types of relationships among entities that are worth observing. In other words, I assume that perception of complex phenomena is mediated by a set of presuppositions constituting at least a simple conceptual framework. The problem with much of policy research is that these conceptual frameworks are often implicit rather than explicit and are thus not subjected to any serious scrutiny by the author or by many readers. In sum, a purely inductive approach to theory development in public policy strikes me as illusory.

In contrast, in a deductive (or axiomatic) conception of theory development the author begins with a set of fundamental axioms and definitions and logically derives from them a more elaborate set of propositions, some of which are falsifiable. This conception is certainly consistent with a presuppositionist philosophy of science. And it may occasionally happen—game theory being a possible example (von Neumann and Morgenstern, 1944). But the pure form of axiomatic theory development assumes that theories are developed in a vacuum, unconstrained by perceived regularities in portions of the phenomena of interest. That assumption strikes me as unlikely to be correct, since anyone proposing a theory typically has twenty to fifty years of experience in a given field, and therefore, some of the propositions are likely to be inductively derived.

More likely than either a pure inductivist or a pure deductivist process is a third scenario: A scholar becomes dissatisfied with an existing conceptual framework or body of theory, develops an alternative framework (or initial theory) to address its shortcomings, and then progressively elaborates that framework until it becomes a more fully developed theory over time. This is, I think, the case for both Elinor Ostrom and myself.

Ostrom began with a general appreciation of the theoretical elegance and potential explanatory power of microeconomic theories applied to political behavior, but she was profoundly disturbed by proponents' general neglect of the role of institutions (Ostrom, 1986). Public-choice theorists tended to implicitly assume a set of institutional arrangements without recognizing that those arrangements were subject to manipulation and that the same individual would behave differently in different institutional settings. With respect to the more limited case of the management of common property resources, Ostrom was disturbed by Hardin's (1968) analysis of the "tragedy of the commons." It implicitly assumed a given set of institutional rules—particularly, that local herders could not communicate with each other and themselves reach a set of agreements to regulate access to the common property resource—and thus that intervention by external agents was necessary to regulate and enforce access restrictions (Ostrom, 1990). The basic IAD framework was initially elaborated in Kiser and Ostrom (1982) and was applied shortly thereafter to the management of common property resources in Bill Blomquist's dissertation research on groundwater basins in Southern California (see Ostrom, 1990, preface).

Likewise, the advocacy coalition framework grew directly out of my dissatisfaction with (1) the bifurcation of implementation studies in the early 1980s into top-down and bottom-up perspectives, (2) most policy scholars' neglect of the role of technical information in the policy process, and (3) the overly simplistic model of the individual in most rational-choice approaches to policy (Sabatier, 1986). The ACF was an effort to develop a new synthesis combining the best features of both implementation perspectives, together with Carol Weiss's (1977) insights on the long-term "enlightenment function of policy research" and a model of perception drawn largely from social psychology. It was strengthened when my intuitions concerning the factors affecting the role of scientific information were independently confirmed by the experience of Hank Jenkins-Smith (1988) as a policy analyst in Washington. The ACF was initially presented at a Rotterdam conference in 1983, was revised for several years, and was then published for the first time in the late 1980s (Sabatier, 1987, 1988).

Both the IAD and the ACF have, however, undergone considerable revision since their original publication. Both started out as fairly extensive conceptual frameworks (Kiser and Ostrom, 1982; Sabatier, 1988). The IAD has evolved into both a more elaborate *framework* for understanding virtually all of social behavior and a much more elaborate *theory* of the management of common property resources (see Chapter 3). The ACF has become a much more integrated framework and/or theory for understanding long-term policy change in modern societies with a significant division of labor and some capability for organized dissent (see Chapter 6).

From Modest Frameworks to More Extensive Frameworks and/or Theories

What are some of the reasons why the IAD and ACF have evolved from fairly modest frameworks in the early/mid–1980s to much more extensive frameworks and/or theories today? Conversely, why has Kingdon's multiple-streams framework—initially published at about the same time (1984)—attracted much less empirical testing and undergone much less elaboration?[4] Following are some preliminary conclusions crafted in the form of guidelines for theory development.

Be Clear Enough to Be Proven Wrong.   This guideline applies both to concepts and to proposed relationships (hypotheses). The basic argument is that we learn from our mistakes. Vague concepts and propositions are never proven wrong, and thus, little learning occurs. Without learning, there is little incentive to correct inconsistencies, to revise falsified relationships, or to elaborate the framework to fill serious voids.

Since its inception, for example, the ACF has defined an *advocacy coalition* as "a set of people from a variety of positions (elected and agency officials, interest group leaders, researchers) who share a particular belief system . . . and who show a non-trivial degree of coordinated activity over time" (Sabatier, 1988, p. 139). In a 1995 article, Edella Schlager observed that all the empirical tests of the existence of coalitions by Jenkins-Smith and myself had focused simply on shared beliefs and thus had implicitly assumed that shared beliefs are a sufficient condition for coordinated behavior. Anyone remotely familiar with the literature on collective action (Olson, 1965) realizes this assumption is patently false. As a result, my students and I have spent a lot of time seeking to define and operationalize different levels of coordination (Zafonte and Sabatier, 1998), as well as addressing Schlager's suggestions concerning the conditions conducive to greater coordination. Thus, the clear definition of an advocacy coalition plus its clear—and invalid—operationalization have led to a major effort to specify the problematic nature of coordinated behavior within the framework.

Clear, explicit hypotheses attract serious scrutiny by other scholars. Several people who regularly use the ACF in their graduate courses have indicated that the major reasons are that the ACF has always identified a number of explicit hypotheses and that the authors of the ACF seem willing to revise those hypotheses on the basis of solid empirical research. Along the same lines, in a review of Ostrom et al. (1994), Jonathan Bendor (1995, p. 189) remarked that he found the evidence from testing game-theoretic hypotheses in laboratory settings to be more persuasive than the field studies precisely because the former involved quantitative predictions that could be more easily falsified (or supported) by the evidence.

Conversely, the multiple-streams framework has no explicit hypotheses and is so fluid in its structure and operationalization that falsification is difficult.[5] Given the paucity of tests by other scholars, it is not surprising that Kingdon (1996, postscript) has found no need to make revisions.

Make the Concepts of the Framework/Theory as Abstract as Possible. The more abstract the concepts, the broader the scope of the framework or theory. Broader propositions are more likely to be falsified in some situations and confirmed in others. That, in turn, should lead to the identification of intervening variables and/or conditional relationships, that is, to an elaboration of the theory. Ambition plus clarity lead to error, which, in turn, produces revision and elaboration (Lave and March, 1975, p. 42; King et al., 1994).

Think Causal Process. What exactly are the mechanisms by which A affects B, which, in turn, affects C, and so on (Lave and March, 1975, p. 40)? Thinking carefully about the steps in a causal process is one of the principal steps in going from general frameworks to denser, more logically interconnected theories. The failure to develop clear chains of causal relationships is probably one of the reasons that several policy frameworks that were popular in the 1970s—including Lowi's arenas of power and the large-N comparative studies of Hofferbert, Dye, et al.—no longer attract much attention.

Develop a Coherent Model of the Individual. One of the major reasons that neither Lowi nor Hofferbert et al. ever developed clear chains of causal processes is that neither framework ever really developed a model of the individual actor (see Chapter 8 by Bill Blomquist). Such a model should include the goals or rules fundamentally driving actors' behavior, actors' capacity to acquire and process information, their decision rules, and their politically relevant resources. Since policymaking is fundamentally done by human beings, it is extraordinarily difficult to develop much of a sense of process if the linchpin of the entire process—the individual (or corporate) human actor—is a "black box."

One of the fundamental tasks confronting several frameworks of the policy process—including Kingdon's multiple-streams framework (see Chapter 4) and the diffusion framework of Berry and Berry (see Chapter 7)—is to develop a much more explicit and coherent model (or models) of the individual. Conversely, some of the most interesting differences between the initial versions of the IAD theory of common property management, more recent versions, the ACF, and the punctuated-equilibrium framework of Jones et al. concern differences in their models of the individual (see Chapter 9 of this volume; also Jones, 1994; Ostrom, 1998).

Work on Internal Inconsistencies and Interconnections. This guideline is another of the fundamental tasks in going from minimal frameworks to much denser, internally consistent frameworks and theories. It usually involves both empirical work that identifies inconsistencies and anomalies and then logical thinking about how to resolve them.

In the advocacy coalition framework, for example, the delineation of policy core beliefs—as opposed to deep core and secondary aspects—is critical because (1) policy core beliefs are one of the essential means of defining a coalition, (2) they are critical to distinguishing major (policy core) from minor (secondary aspects) policy change, and (3) most of the original ACF hypotheses hinged on the distinction between policy core and secondary aspects. Yet the original versions of the ACF were unclear about whether the critical component of a policy core belief was (1) degree of abstraction or (2) scope. This ambiguity became critical when some of the research by Jenkins-Smith et al. (1991) on Outer Continental Shelf (OCS) leasing identified very concrete beliefs—material self-interest operationalized as expanded leasing—to be the fundamental glue holding the proleasing coalition together. This finding led us to select subsystemwide scope dealing as being a defining characteristic of a policy core belief.[6]

Clarification of the policy core, in turn, led to the query: What are the defining characteristics of a subsystem? Again, this question was precipitated when several empirical research projects sought to apply the ACF to "subsystems" that were narrower in scope than traditional ones: landsat within science and technology, eutrophication within water pollution, and automotive pollution control within air pollution control (Thomas, 1996; Loeber and Grin, 1999; Sabatier, Zafonte, and Gjerde, 1999). These led to a series of discussions resulting in a relatively clear set of necessary and sufficient conditions for the existence of a subsystem (see Chapter 6 of this volume, as well as Zafonte and Sabatier, 1998). These conditions, in turn, helped guide empirical research concerning the relative importance of shared beliefs and organizational interdependencies in determining coalition behavior within a set of partially overlapping subsystems related to San Francisco Bay water policy (Zafonte and Sabatier, 1998). The end result is that the relationships among policy core beliefs, subsystems, advocacy coalitions, and policy change are much more extensive and much clearer today than they were in either the 1988 or the 1993 version of the ACF.

Develop a Long-Term Research Program Involving Both Theoretical Elaboration and Empirical Testing Among a Network of Scholars. Of all the guidelines, this one is probably the most important. As we saw above, theoretical elaboration and empirical testing go hand in hand: Empirical studies identify inconsistencies, areas in need of elaboration, and propositions that are probably invalid (at least for a set of cases). These should stimulate revision and elaboration of the theory. All of this takes time—at least a decade. For example, probably 80–90 percent of Lin Ostrom's scholarship since the mid–1980s has been related to the IAD. The same can be said of my focus on the ACF. It helps enormously if a group of scholars working in a variety of field settings become involved in the empirical applications and contribute to the theoretical revisions. But it is probably also desirable if the original proponents of the framework continue to guide the overall research program so that the internal coherence of the theoretical framework is maintained over time.

Both Elinor Ostrom and I have been self-consciously pursuing such a strategy since the early 1980s. My perception is that John Kingdon has not. In both the IAD and the ACF cases, the strategy has involved (1) the initial publication of the framework; (2) empirical research by the authors to critically apply the framework in a variety of settings; (3) explicit encouragement to other scholars to do the same in settings where they are expert; (4) a clear willingness to revise the framework on the basis of empirical research and logical analysis; and (5) the fostering of a network of scholars involved in a shared research program. Specific techniques for fostering such a network include (1) explicitly encouraging other scholars to critically apply the framework; (2) reviewing dissertations and conference papers of young scholars interested in the framework; (3) providing incentives (e.g., grant funds or publication outlets) to stimulate such interest; and (4) establishing newsletters, conferences, and other mechanisms as communication outlets for scholars interested in the framework.[7]

Use Multiple Theories If Possible.   This is pretty standard advice (Platt, 1964; Stinchcombe, 1968). It involves both being knowledgeable about multiple theories and, when possible, applying several theories in empirical research. The advantages are, first, that this guideline provides some guarantee against assuming that a particular theory is *the* valid one. Second, it leads to an appreciation that different theories may have comparative advantages in different settings. Third, knowing other theories should make one much more sensitive to some of the implicit assumptions in one's favored theory. For example, much of the elaboration of the theory of the individual in the ACF has been the result of Edella Schlager's explicit comparisons of the IAD and the ACF.

CONCLUSIONS

This chapter has suggested a number of guidelines for encouraging the development of denser and more coherent frameworks of the policy process. But I would like to second Schlager's (1997, p. 15) contention that advice and exhortation, although helpful, are not sufficient to improve the status of theory. We need to work on the institutional incentives affecting behavior. When it comes to research, there are at least two major types of incentives: funding and publication.

Funding

I'm not sure funding is a major problem—at least in the United States.[8] Although the NSF does not have a policy studies program per se, a number of its programs—including Political Science, Decision and Risk Management, and Law and Society—fund policy research, and the NSF usually requires funded proposals to pay serious attention to theoretical development. Many federal (and even some state) agencies—including Justice, Environmental Protection, Energy, International Development, Defense, Agriculture, Transportation, Education, and Social Security—fund policy research. My experience with the Environmental Protection Agency's exploratory grants program has been that the peer review process is directly modeled on NSF's and thus strongly encourages funded proposals to have a significant theoretical component. To the extent this is not the case with research programs in other agencies, attempts should be made to alter the review process and funding criteria.

Publication

With respect to books, the series I edit for Westview Press on "Theoretical Lenses on Public Policy" is explicitly devoted to the improvement of theory. In addition, the series edited by James Alt and Doug North for Cambridge University Press on "The Political Economy of Institutions" is a centerpiece for work on institutional rational choice. I would simply encourage the editors of other policy series (Joe Stewart and Anne Schneider at the State University of New York and Bert Rockman at Pittsburgh) to perhaps accord a little higher priority to the quality of theory in their publications.

The problem is probably more serious with respect to journals. Although most of the general policy journals—the *Journal of Public Policy,* the *Journal of Policy Analysis and Management, Policy Sciences,* the *Journal of European Public Policy,* and the (PSO) journals—sometimes publish theoretical articles, many of their articles are not explicitly grounded in any body of theory. Given institutional inertia, I doubt that situation will change. There is a strong argument for someone—perhaps the Public Policy Section of the American Political Science Association—to develop a new journal explicitly devoted to encouraging theoretically relevant and methodologically sophisticated scholarship on the policy process by both American and European scholars. This is an argument I have made before (Sabatier, 1991, pp. 153–155). Hopefully, persistence will pay. If it does, such a journal should provide the sort of institutional incentive necessary to accelerate the development of policy theory.

The fundamental change required is, however, attitudinal. This volume assumes that (1) understanding something as complex as the policy process requires simplifying lenses that tell us what to look for and what to ignore and (2) those lenses should be explicit rather than implicit.[9] Once those premises become accepted, the frameworks provided in this volume should represent a preliminary set of lenses from which to choose. Hopefully, there will be sufficient progress in those (and other) frameworks so that, in five years or so, a second edition of this book will be warranted.

NOTES

1. For example, scholars like Popkin (1979) and Becker (1976) have taken the basic principles of microeconomic theory and derived implications far beyond the original scope of the theory. Some of those implications have been empirically verified, and others have not. It was the logical coherence of the theory, however, that allowed creative minds to wonder: If it applies to market transactions in Western countries, why not other aspects of human behavior?

2. This conclusion grew out of an E-mail exchange that I had with Lin Ostrom in the winter of 1996–1997, but I'm not sure that she would entirely agree. For informative, and reasonably consistent, discussions of the distinctions among frameworks, theories, and models, see Ostrom (1998), Ostrom et al. (1994), Schlager (Chapter 9 of this book), and Scharpf (1997).

3. One of the most serious limitations of the principal-agent literature is its models of the agent. Much of this literature (e.g., Wood and Waterman, 1994) has essentially no model of the agent. The agent is simply a passive receptor responding to stimuli from principals. Another strain follows Niskanen's (1971) overly simplistic view that agents are simply budget maximizers; for critiques, see Downs (1967), Miller (1992), and Worsham,

Eisner, and Ringquist (1997). At a minimum, any principal-agent analysis needs to start with clear and reasonably valid models of (1) the principal(s) and (2) the agents.

4. Although Kingdon (1984) is cited by many people, I am aware of only one scholar—Nikolaos Zahariadis (1992, 1996)—who has actually critically applied the multiple-streams framework seriously (confirmed by Chapter 4 in this volume). The framework itself has undergone only minor revision. Kingdon's postscript in the 1996 edition contains no serious revisions. Zahariadis's work (1) provides evidence that the framework can be extended outside the United States and to situations that are less "ambiguous" and (2) suggests a couple of related hypotheses: Crises in the problem stream are conducive to searches for solutions specific to the problem, whereas electoral mandates produce a search for doctrinal (general) solutions.

In contrast, the ACF has been seriously applied by scholars other than Sabatier and Jenkins-Smith in at least twenty-six cases in ten countries and has undergone at least a dozen significant revisions since 1988 (see Chapter 6 in this volume). The IAD theory of common property management has also been seriously applied by several dozen scholars in numerous countries (see Schlager, 1997, for a partial list) and has undergone quite substantial revision and elaboration (see Ostrom et al., 1994; Ostrom, 1998). As for citations, in 1996 multiple streams received about 58 citations in the Social Science Citation Index (SSCI), the ACF about 40, and the IAD well over 100.

5. In my view, the fundamental problems with the multiple-streams framework are that (1) it's unclear whether the dependent variable is the set of viable policy alternatives or the selection of an alternative; (2) the critical assumption of the independence of streams cannot be falsified because Kingdon has never told us how to identify which actors are in which streams; and (3) the causal drivers are underspecified, in part because there are no clear models of the individual (except perhaps for legislators).

6. Unfortunately, this definitional issue was still ambiguous in the concluding chapter of the 1993 book and was not really clarified until Sabatier (1998).

7. In virtually all of these areas, Lin Ostrom is the master and I'm the apprentice.

8. I just don't know the situation in European countries well enough to comment. I realize, of course, that arguing that research funding is not a major problem is considered a capital crime by most scholars.

9. This is, however, contingent upon a logically prior commitment to social science, that is, to developing general understandings of the policy process that are clear enough to be proven wrong. I have no problem with policy analysts who wish to provide advice to practitioners in specific situations or who wish to develop "intuitive" understandings of such situations. I would simply urge them to make those "intuitions" clear enough and general enough so that they become falsifiable.

REFERENCES

Baumgartner, Frank, and Bryan Jones. 1993. *Agendas and Instability in American Politics.* Chicago: University of Chicago Press.

Becker, Gary. 1976. *The Economic Approach to Human Behavior.* Chicago: University of Chicago Press.

Bendor, Jonathan. 1995. "Review of Ostrom et al., Rules, Games, and Common-Pool Resources," *American Political Science Review* 89 (March):188–189.

Bendor, Jonathan, Serge Taylor, and Roland Van Gaalen. 1987. "Politicians, Bureaucrats, and Asymmetric Information," *American Political Science Review* 81 (November): 796–828.

Berry, Frances Stokes, and William Berry. 1990. "State Lottery Adoptions and Policy Innovations: An Event History Analysis," *American Political Science Review* 84 (June):395–415.

Brown, Harold. 1977. *Perception, Theory, and Commitment: The New Philosophy of Science.* Chicago: University of Chicago Press.

Chubb, John, and Terry Moe. 1990. *Politics, Markets, and America's Schools.* Washington, D.C.: Brookings Institution.

Crawford, Sue, and Elinor Ostrom. 1995. "A Grammar of Institutions," *American Political Science Review* 89 (September):582–600.

Downs, Anthony. 1967. *Inside Bureaucracy.* Boston: Little, Brown.

Hardin, Garrett. 1968. "The Tragedy of the Commons," *Science* 162:1243–1248.

Hawkesworth, Mary. 1992. "Epistemology and Policy Analysis." In W. Dunn and R. M. Kelly, eds., *Advances in Policy Studies,* pp. 295–329. New Brunswick, N.J.: Transaction Books.

Hill, Kim Quaile. 1997. "In Search of Policy Theory," *Policy Currents* 7 (April):1–9.

Jenkins-Smith, Hank. 1988. "Analytical Debates and Policy Learning: Analysis and Change in the Federal Bureaucracy," *Policy Sciences* 21:169–212.

Jenkins-Smith, Hank, et al. 1991. "Explaining Change in Policy Subsystems: Analysis of Coalition Stability and Defection Over Time," *American Journal of Political Science* 35:851–872.

Jones, Bryan. 1994. *Reconceiving Decision-Making in Democratic Politics.* Chicago: University of Chicago Press.

Kagan, Robert. 1978. *Regulatory Justice: Implementing a Wage-Price Freeze.* New York: Russell Sage Foundation.

King, Gary, Robert Keohane, and Sidney Verba. (994. *Designing Social Inquiry.* Princeton: Princeton University Press.

Kingdon, John. 1996. *Agendas, Alternatives, and Public Policies.* New York: HarperCollins. (Originally published in 1984.)

Kiser, Larry, and Elinor Ostrom. 1982. "The Three Worlds of Action: A Metatheoretical Synthesis of Institutional Approaches." In E. Ostrom, ed., *Strategies of Political Inquiry,* pp. 179–222. Beverly Hills, Calif.: Sage.

Knott, Jack, and Gary Miller. 1987. *Reforming Bureaucracy: The Politics of Institutional Choice.* Englewood Cliffs, N.J.: Prentice-Hall.

Kuhn, Thomas. 1970. *The Structure of Scientific Revolutions,* 2d ed. Chicago: University of Chicago Press.

Lakatos, Imre. 1978. *The Methodology of Scientific Research Programmes,* ed. by John Worrall and Gregory Currie. Cambridge, England: Cambridge University Press.

Lave, Charles, and James March. 1975. *An Introduction to Models in the Social Sciences.* New York: Harper & Row.

Loeber, Anne, and John Grin. 1999. "From Green Waters to 'Green' Detergents: Processes of Learning Between Policy Actors and Target Groups in Eutrophication Policy in the Netherlands, 1970–1987." In P. Sabatier, ed., *An Advocacy Coalition Lens on Environmental Policy.* Cambridge, Mass.: MIT Press.

McCubbins, Mathew, and Terry Sullivan, eds. 1987). *Congress: Structure and Policy.* Cambridge, England: Cambridge University Press.

Miller, Gary. 1992. *Managerial Dilemmas.* Cambridge, England: Cambridge University Press.

Moe, Terry. 1984. "The New Economics of Organization," *American Journal of Political Science* 28 (November):739–777.

Niskanen, William. 1971. *Bureaucracy and Representative Government.* Chicago: Rand Mc-Nally.

Olson, Mancur. 1965. *The Logic of Collective Action.* New York: Schocken.

Ostrom, Elinor. 1986. "An Agenda for the Study of Institutions," *Public Choice* 48:3–25.

_____. 1990. *Governing the Commons.* Cambridge, England: Cambridge University Press.

_____. 1998. "A Behavioral Approach to the Rational Choice Theory of Collective Action," *American Political Science Review* 92 (March):1–22.

Ostrom, Elinor, Roy Gardner, and James Walker. 1994. *Rules, Games, and Common-Pool Resources.* Ann Arbor: University of Michigan Press.

Ostrom, Elinor, Larry Schroeder, and Susan Wynne. 1993. *Institutional Incentives and Sustainable Development: Infrastructure Policies in Perspective.* Boulder: Westview Press.

Platt, John. 1964. "Strong Inference," *Science* 146 (October):347–353.

Popkin, Samuel. 1979. *The Rational Peasant.* Berkeley: University of California Press.

Reynolds, Paul. 1971. *A Primer in Theory Construction.* Indianapolis, Ind.: Bobbs-Merrill.

Sabatier, Paul. 1986. "Top-Down and Bottom-Up Approaches to Implementation Research: A Critical Analysis and Suggested Synthesis," *Journal of Public Policy* 6:21–28.

_____. 1987. "Knowledge, Policy-Oriented Learning, and Policy Change," *Knowledge* 8 (June):649–692.

_____. 1988. "An Advocacy Coalition Framework of Policy Change and the Role of Policy-Oriented Learning Therein," *Policy Sciences* 21:129–168.

_____. 1991. "Toward Better Theories of the Policy Process," *PS: Political Science and Politics* 24 (June):147–156.

_____. 1998. "The Advocacy Coalition Framework: Revisions and Relevance for Europe," *Journal of European Public Policy* 5 (March):98–130.

Sabatier, Paul, and Hank Jenkins-Smith, eds. 1988. "Policy Change and Policy-Oriented Learning: Exploring an Advocacy Coalition Framework" (Symposium Issue), *Policy Sciences* 21:123–277.

_____. 1993. *Policy Change and Learning: An Advocacy Coalition Approach.* Boulder: Westview Press.

Sabatier, Paul, Matthew Zafonte, and Michael Gjerde. 1999. "Coalition Stability in U.S. Automotive Pollution Control Policy, 1963–1990." In Paul Sabatier, ed., *An Advocacy Coalition Lens on Environmental Policy.* Cambridge, Mass.: MIT University Press.

Scharpf, Fritz. 1997). *Games Real Actors Play: Actor-Centered Institutionalism in Policy Research.* Boulder: Westview Press.

Schlager, Edella. 1995. "Policy Making and Collective Action: Defining Coalitions Within the Advocacy Coalition Framework," *Policy Sciences* 28:243–270.

_____. 1997. "A Response to Kim Quaile Hill's *In Search of Policy Theory*," *Policy Currents* 7 (June):14–15.

Schneider, Mark, Paul Teske, Melissa Marschall, Michael Mintrom, and Christine Roch. 1997. "Institutional Arrangements and the Creation of Social Capital: The Effects of Public School Choice," *American Political Science Review* 91:82–93.

Scholz, John. 1984. "Cooperation, Deterrence, and the Ecology of Regulatory Enforcement," *Law and Society Review* 18:179–224.

Shepsle, Kenneth. 1989. "Studying Institutions: Some Lessons from the Rational Choice Approach," *Journal of Theoretical Politics* 1:131–147.

Shepsle, Kenneth, and Barry Weingast. 1987. "The Institutional Foundations of Committee Power," *American Political Science Review* 81:85–104.

Stinchcombe, Arthur. 1968. *Constructing Social Theories*. Chicago: University of Chicago Press.

Thomas, Gerald. 1996. "Policy Subsystems, the Advocacy Coalition Framework, and U.S. Civilian land Remote Sensing (Landsat) Policy." Paper presented at the Annual Meeting of the Western Political Science Association, San Francisco, March 14–16.

von Neumann, J., and O. Morgenstern. 1944. *Theory of Games and Economic Behavior*. Princeton: Princeton University Press.

Weiss, Carol. 1977. "Research for Policy's Sake: The Enlightenment Function of Social Research," *Policy Analysis* 3 (Fall):531–545.

Wood, B. Dan, and Richard Waterman. 1991. "The Dynamics of Political Control of the Bureaucracy," *American Political Science Review* 85:801–828.

_____. 1994. *Bureaucratic Dynamics*. Boulder: Westview Press.

Worsham, Jeff, Marc Allen Eisner, and Evan Ringquist. 1997. "Assessing the Assumptions: A Critical Analysis of Agency Theory," *Administration and Society* 28 (February):419–440.

Zafonte, Matthew, and Paul Sabatier. 1998. "Shared Beliefs and Functional Interdependence as Determinants of Ally Networks in Overlapping Subsystems," *Journal of Theoretical Politics* 10(4):473–505.

Zahariadis, Nikolaos. 1992. "To Sell or Not to Sell? Telecommunications Policy in Britain and France," *Journal of Public Policy* 12:355–376.

_____. 1996. "Selling British Rail: An Idea Whose Time Has Come," *Comparative Political Studies* 29 (August):400–422.

About the Editor and Contributors

Editor

Paul A. Sabatier is a professor in the Department of Environmental Science and Policy and chair of the Environmental Policy Area of Emphasis of the Graduate Group in Ecology at the University of California–Davis. He has coauthored (with Dan Mazmanian) several books on policy implementation, as well as several books and articles on the advocacy coalition framework (most notably, *Policy Change and Learning*, with Hank Jenkins-Smith). His goals include improving the theoretical literacy of political scientists interested in public policy, most notably, Peter deLeon and Ken Meier.

Contributors

Frank R. Baumgartner is a professor of political science at Pennsylvania State University. His published work has focused on questions of agenda setting and the roles of interest groups in national politics. Recent publications include *Basic Interests: The Importance of Groups in Politics and in Political Science* (with Beth L. Leech; Princeton University Press, 1998) and *Agendas and Instability in American Politics* (with Bryan D. Jones; University of Chicago Press, 1993).

Frances Stokes Berry is a professor in the Askew School of Public Administration and Policy at Florida State University, where she serves as MPA director. Her research interests include policy and management innovation, state public policy, and public management. She has published in the *American Political Science Review*, the *Public Administration Review*, the *American Journal of Political Science*, and the *Public Productivity and Management Review* and serves on the editorial boards of the *Journal of Public Administration Research and Theory* and the *State and Local Government Review*.

William D. Berry is a professor of political science at Florida State University. He has been a frequent contributor to journals such as *American Political Science Review, American Journal of Political Science*, and *Journal of Politics*—and has served on the editorial board of the latter two. Among his books are *Understanding U.S. Government Growth* (Praeger) and three volumes in the Sage Publications Quantitative Applications in the Social Sciences series. Berry is winner of the Policy Studies Organization's 1997 Harold Lasswell Award for career contributions to the study of the policymaking process.

William Blomquist is an associate professor and chair of the Department of Political Science at Indiana University-Purdue University in Indianapolis. He has been a member of the faculty there since completing his Ph.D. at Indiana University-Bloomington in

1987. In addition to working on political theories of the public policy process, he performs applied policy work in the field of western water resource management.

Peter deLeon is a professor of public policy at the Graduate School of Public Affairs at the University of Colorado–Denver. He has recently become noted as the "Don Quixote" of policy studies for his steadfast support of long-abandoned concepts (witness his chapter in this volume). His most recent book is *Democracy and the Policy Sciences*.

Hank Jenkins-Smith is professor of political science and director of the Institute of Public Policy at the University of New Mexico. He is the author of *Democratic Politics and Policy Analysis*, as well as numerous articles on risk perception and the role of science in public policy.

Bryan D. Jones is professor of political science and director of the Center for American Politics and Public Policy at the University of Washington. Formerly at Texas A&M and Wayne State Universities, he is author of *Reconceiving Decision-Making in Democratic Politics* as well as coauthor of *Agendas and Instability in American Politics*.

Elinor Ostrom is Arthur F. Bentley Professor of Political Science and codirector of the Workshop in Political Theory and Policy Analysis and of the Center for the Study of Institutions, Population, and Environmental Change (CIPEC), Indiana University–Bloomington. She is the author of *Crafting Institutions for Self-Governing Irrigation Systems* (1992) and *Governing the Commons* (1990); coauthor with Robert Keohane of *Local Commons and Global Interdependence* (1995), with Roy Gardner and James Walker of *Rules, Games, and Common-Pool Resources* (1994), and with Larry Schroeder and Susan Wynne of *Institutional Incentives and Sustainable Development* (1993).

Edella Schlager is an associate professor in the School of Public Administration and Policy at the University of Arizona. Her research focuses on the emergence and evolution of local level institutional arrangements for governing common-pool resources. Currently, she is studying how local organizations in the western United States acquire and coordinate their ground and surface water supplies to meet a variety of goals, from environmental protection to drought protection.

James L. True is the founding holder of the Jack Brooks Chair in Government and Public Service and an assistant professor of political science at Lamar University, Beaumont, Texas. He retired as a colonel from the U.S. Air Force after serving in a variety of assignments in air operations, financial management, and education. He was a distinguished graduate from the Air War College and has a Ph.D. in political science from Texas A&M. He has authored or coauthored articles appearing in the *Air University Review, Public Budgeting and Finance*, the *Journal of Politics*, and the *American Journal of Political Science*.

Nikolaos Zahariadis is assistant professor in the Department of Government and Public Service at the University of Alabama–Birmingham. His research interests focus on comparative public policy and European political economy. He is the author or editor of *Markets, States and Public Policy: Privatization in Britain and France* (1995), *Theory, Case and Method in Comparative Politics* (1997), and *Contending Perspectives in International Political Economy* (1999). His work has appeared in *International Studies Quarterly, Comparative Politics, Comparative Political Studies, Journal of Public Policy, Policy Studies Journal, Policy Studies Review*, and elsewhere.

Index